CW00543151

The
LONDON
&
NORTH WESTERN
RAILWAY

A History

TRANSPORT

Atlantic
PUBLISHERS

The
LONDON
&
NORTH WESTERN
RAILWAY

A History

M. C. Reed

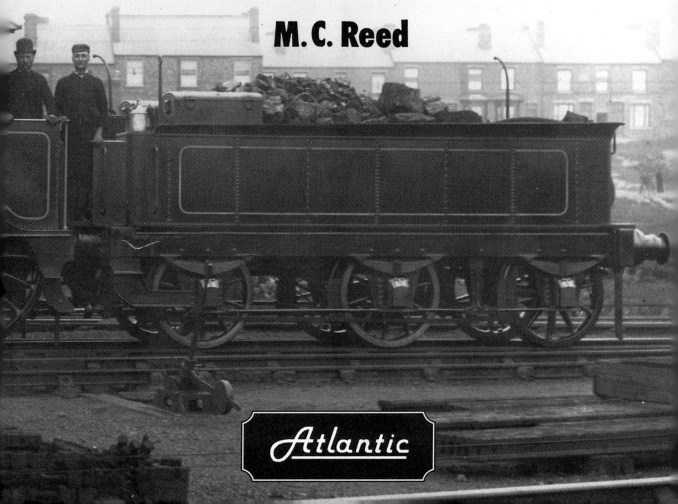

Atlantic

Published by Atlantic Transport Publishers,
Trevithick House, West End, Penryn, Cornwall TR10 8HE

© M.C. Reed 1996

ISBN 0 906899 66 4

Typeset by Posthouse Printing and Publishing, Findhorn, Scotland
Printed in Great Britain by Redwood Books, Trowbridge, Wiltshire

All uncredited illustrations are from the author's collection

*All rights reserved. No part of this publication may be
reproduced, stored in a retrieval system, or transmitted, in any form or by any means, electronic,
mechanical, photocopying, recording or otherwise,
without prior permission in writing from the
publishers.*

British Cataloguing in Publication Data
A catalogue record for this book is available from the British Library

Preface and Acknowledgements

Writing a book is a personal journey, and this particular excursion began more than thirty years ago. The stimulus for my attempt to sketch the history of the London & North Western Railway was the realisation that, although the company played so central a part in the development of the railway system in Britain, there was no single modern study which gave an account of its emergence and of it subsequent evolution over the period of its independent life. This gap is all the more obvious because so much British railway history has been written from the perspective of undertakings which were in competition with the LNWR, a factor which has inevitably coloured its treatment in the literature.

But while the LNWR may not have been well served in terms of the exposition of its general history since the publication of W L Steel's book in 1914, any researcher starts with four advantages. Firstly, it is difficult to think of any other British pre-grouping railway which is better represented in the quality and diversity of the published works by members of its own staff, starting with Henry Booth and ending with J M Dunn. This corpus also encompasses the classic accounts by George Findlay and G P Neele, as well as the writings of a number of other senior officers. Secondly, most technical aspects of the LNWR's operations – including its locomotives, rolling stock, signalling, and marine activities – have been covered in recent authoritative monographs, and there is in addition Terry Gourvish's pioneering analysis of its management during the 1840s and 1850s. Thirdly, there are modern studies of many of the LNWR's individual lines, some of its major stations and workshops, and several of the railway towns associated with it. Lastly, the company's own surviving archives, now held by the Public Record Office at Kew, represent a rich and probably inexhaustible quarry for the student.

With such a wealth of material, selectivity is unavoidable. My primary aim in putting together this book was to provide a broad description of the LNWR's origins and progress as a railway undertaking, and to relate this both to the company's place within the wider network and to some of the economic and political factors which affected railway development in Britain. I have attempted to give a reasonably full account of the physical growth of the company's system and to outline some of the influences on the level and composition of the traffic which it carried. But while I have tried to place changes in the LNWR's operating methods and equipment in their context, this does not purport to be a locomotive or technical history of the company – others far better qualified than I have covered such elements in ample detail. Nor was it possible, in a work of this nature, to discuss specific routes and constituents at the level which could be achieved in a more extensive treatment. The history of the LNWR is a subject which deserves far more detailed examination, and within the scope of a single volume one cannot hope to provide anything other than an introductory overview.

Even within this limited framework, however, shortcomings are inevitable. In particular, the usual warnings about railway chronology apply – although I have attempted wherever possible to verify dates from company records or reliable contemporary publications, some gaps and ambiguities remain. I am all too aware of the scope for misinterpretation in this and in other aspects of the research, while the extent of the available sources is such that, no matter where the line is drawn in the process of gathering and checking information, other relevant material will almost certainly have been overlooked.

Such errors and omissions are, of course, my responsibility as author. However, it is pleasing to be able to acknowledge also the assistance that has been received in the course of this book's preparation. In particular, I am indebted to the various institutions whose collections I have consulted during my research, and to the staff of these bodies for their unfailing helpfulness and courtesy despite the pressures placed upon them by government expenditure constraints. My primary obligation in this connection is naturally to the Public Record Office at Kew, but my research extends back to the days of the former British Transport Historical Records Office at Porchester Road, whose material was inherited by the PRO. In addition, my thanks are due to several other repositories and libraries for access to their holdings, including the House of Lords Record Office; the Scottish Record Office; the Cumbria, Lancashire, Staffordshire, Gwynedd, and Warwickshire record offices; the National Library of Scotland; the University of Glasgow archives; the British Library newspaper collection at Colindale; and the Mitchell Library in Glasgow.

I am also grateful to James Wood and to my daughter Fiona for investigating local sources on my behalf in Carlisle and Manchester respectively, and to John Gough and Peter Braine, who kindly gave me the benefit of their own research in discussion and in responding to a number of queries. In addition, they both read the manuscript in draft and contributed materially to its final form, as did Mike Blakemore, to whom my thanks are also due for help with picture research. Many other individuals and institutions have assisted by locating and providing illustrations, and besides the indebtedness which is acknowledged in the captions I should like to thank Beverley Cole at the National Railway Museum; my former colleague Andrew Jackson, who alerted me to the late Graham Langmuir's bequest of photographs to the Mitchell Library; and Dr W P Honeyman, for access to his own collection. I am also grateful to Colin McAlpine, who drew the maps, and to Eve Boyle and Ron Cowan for technical assistance with some of the illustrations.

Lastly, particular thanks are due to my publisher David Joy, who rashly took on this project after a chance discussion in the spring of 1995. Without his encouragement it would probably still be incomplete, and in addition to being obliged to him for his forbearance and flexibility I am also grateful to him for his vision of how the finished work should appear and for the illustrations which he has supplied from his own collection. I have enjoyed collaborating with him and the many others who have helped to make this book possible.

Malcolm Reed
Glasgow, July 1996

CONVENTIONS AND ABBREVIATIONS

Imperial measurements and old currency have been employed throughout in this book, together with their usual symbols or contractions: viz ' for foot, " for inch, lb for pound avoirdupois, s for shilling, and d for [old] pence. For some calculations in the text £ sterling have been expressed to three decimal places to avoid the use of fractional parts of a penny, which, although often adopted in nineteenth-century railway statistics, would needlessly have complicated conversion and manipulation of the data. The symbol % has been preferred for percentages, and million has generally been abbreviated to m.

Modern spellings have been followed for Welsh place-names – for example, Caernarfon or Porthmadog – but the contemporary form has been retained when the place-name is part of a company title, such as Bangor & Carnarvon Railway. The English version has been retained for names with Welsh or Irish alternatives when the English version was generally employed at the time – thus Holyhead and Kingstown have been used rather than Caergybi and Dun Laoghaire. 'Junction' has been given an initial capital only when it forms part of a station (or company) name, as in Llandudno Junction; otherwise lower case has been employed, even when the word appears as part of a signal box's designation, such as Acton Wells junction. Ships' names have been italicised, while those of locomotive classes and specific trains have been placed within single inverted commas.

The ampersand – & – has been used in company (and ducal) titles and railway company names have been contracted to their initials wherever possible. The ampersand has been omitted if it is the second element of such a contraction – thus LNWR, not L&NWR – but retained for two-initial titles and where the ampersand falls after the second element: L&Y; LB&SC. However, in the case of references to the London Midland & Scottish Railway I have followed that company's practice in using only the initials LMS (and also in leaving the full title unpunctuated). Besides its omission in this instance, the final 'R' (for Railway) has not been included when an ampersand appears in an abbreviated title. While it is hoped that any unfamiliar contraction will be recognisable from its context, each initialised company title appears in the index with an explanatory cross-reference.

Contents

List of maps, other figures, and tables

Statistical and financial appendix

The Premier Line

Before the 1923 grouping that swept away the identities of all but one of Britain's major railway companies, the London & North Western Railway's entitlement to style itself as the Premier Line was generally undisputed. Yet many of the constituents of the four new groups, as defined in Schedule 1 of the Railways Act, 1921, could boast a longer continuous corporate existence: even among those undertakings that, like the LNWR, had been formed by amalgamation, it was not the oldest – its partner in the new London Midland & Scottish Railway, the Midland Railway, could claim two years' priority. Indeed, a purist could argue that the LNWR was one of the youngest of all of Britain's railways, for the company of that name which became part of the LMS had been formally reincorporated as recently as the beginning of 1922 through a preliminary amalgamation with the Lancashire & Yorkshire Railway. In these terms its only junior was the North Eastern Railway, which was likewise reconstituted when it amalgamated with the Hull & Barnsley on 1 April 1922.

Nor could a case be argued solely on route mileage. Although for much of its early life the LNWR was undoubtedly the most extensive British railway system, the Great Western Railway's acquisition in 1876 of the lines beyond Bristol gave it a larger network. If Irish subsidiaries are included the Midland, too, could claim a greater mileage than the LNWR after taking over the Belfast & Northern Counties in 1903. Similarly, the LNWR's earlier lead in traffic volume also began to be challenged: the GWR surpassed it in passenger receipts and numbers by 1908, and from the 1890s both the Midland and NER could vie with it in terms of total freight tonnage. While the NER's average hauls were shorter, and its earnings were therefore less, the Midland could point both to a higher total freight train mileage and to greater mineral receipts than the LNWR.

When passenger and freight traffic were taken together, however, the LNWR remained the busiest carrier right up to the grouping, earning the highest net revenue of all the railway companies in Britain. Its paid-up capital, too, was greater than that of any of its contemporaries: indeed, its position as the largest joint-stock undertaking in the country remained unchallenged and was inherited by the LMS. This leading position among British railways was reflected in other key indicators, such as total staff complement, number of locomotives, and quadruple track mileage.

In terms of the overall extent of its business, therefore, the LNWR could amply justify a claim to pre-eminence throughout its independent life. The underlying basis for its identification as the Premier Line, however, lay in its pre-amalgamation antecedents, for the LNWR included within its system the Liverpool & Manchester Railway, the company which above all others laid the foundation for the railway age. Other lines could rightly claim seniority: in particular, the Stockton & Darlington Railway marked the first application of steam locomotive technology, developed largely by George Stephenson and his contemporaries on the private mineral wagonways of the north-east of England, to a public railway authorised by Act of Parliament. The latter was a form of undertaking which had hitherto been typified mainly by horse-worked feeders to canals and many of the earliest public steam railways were at first simply an extension of this concept: the LNWR itself included at its formation one such line, the Bolton & Leigh, which pre-dated the L&M both in its authorisation and in its opening.

But although several other steam railways were built during the 1820s, the L&M was differentiated from the outset by the scale on which it was planned and undertaken, while the successful Rainhill trials of 1829 demonstrated for the first time the potential of the locomotive for passenger and merchandise transport as well as for heavy mineral haulage. It was on the line between Liverpool and Manchester that railway technology, previously a specialised solution to particular local requirements, underwent the transformation which made the creation of a new national transport system a practical prospect, and the other eventual components of the LNWR included the first companies to take this process to the next stage of development.

The thread of George Stephenson's involvement likewise runs forward from the L&M through much of the early history of the LNWR's constituents: though he was a wayward genius and a difficult associate, the statue of him which dominated the Great Hall of Euston station was a direct reminder of a continuity which the company was proud to acknowledge. Its post-amalgamation history blended this continuity with adaptation, and in making its own distinctive contribution to the development of the British railway system the LNWR remained the most significant component of that system throughout its independent life.

CHAPTER ONE

The Origins of the System

The Act of Parliament incorporating the London & North Western Railway received the Royal Assent on 16 July 1846. It was therefore a product of the parliamentary session which saw the greatest volume of railway legislation ever brought forward in the United Kingdom, resulting in the approval of over 4,500 miles of route and more than £131m in new capital. But whereas the majority of the railway companies which gained statutory authorisation in 1846 were new undertakings, floated in the enthusiasm of the railway mania, the LNWR Act sanctioned the amalgamation of three existing railways, two of them the earliest trunk lines in Britain. The company thus created had almost 400 miles of route already in operation and a share capital of over £17m, dwarfing even the Midland Railway, which had been formed by a similar tripartite merger two years earlier.

The largest partner in the amalgamation was the London & Birmingham Railway, which up to the end of 1845 had spent almost £12m on its main line and branches. A railway between Birmingham and the capital had first been proposed in the 1820s, but parliamentary approval was not obtained until 1833, after failure in the previous session. This promotional activity followed agreement in 1830 by two separate companies to unite their interests, and the resultant combined project inherited initial surveys by Francis Giles. However, the firm of George Stephenson & Son was engaged as engineers on 18 September 1830 and with Robert Stephenson as the more active partner parliamentary surveys were undertaken for a revised route between Camden in London and Nova Scotia Gardens in Birmingham which included several deviations from Giles's original line. After obtaining its initial Act, the company appointed Robert Stephenson as chief engineer in his own right, and he surveyed further modifications to the route, including the extension from Camden to Euston.

Although the bulk of the funding for the L&B was obtained in Liverpool, the company's management was at the outset shared between committees in Birmingham and London; after authorisation, however, effective control passed to London. The first chairman was Isaac Solly, a City merchant, but after his bankruptcy in 1837 he was succeeded by George Carr Glyn, a partner in the London banking firm of Glyn, Mills & Co. The London committee appointed an army agent, Richard Creed, as its secretary; the equivalent Birmingham post was held by Captain Constantine Richard Moorsom, a member of a family with a distinguished naval tradition. Despite the decreased importance of the Birmingham committee, Moorsom remained as joint secretary until 1839 and took on much of the 'outdoor' supervision of the railway's affairs. His contribution was recognised by his appointment as a director soon after he ceased to be a salaried officer of the company.

As with many other early railways, construction of the 112½-mile line between London and Birmingham proved to be a more difficult undertaking than had originally been expected: the initial estimate was £2·5m, but by the end of 1838 almost £5m had been invested. Although additional borrowing was authorised in 1835 and 1837, the company had to admit to a House of Commons committee in 1839 that it had exceeded its financial powers. Some of the excess was attributable to the Euston extension, which had not been included in the original estimates; part was because land and compensation cost more than twice the expected amount. Much of the overspend, however, arose from extra outlays in constructing and equipping the line: one major source of difficulty was the 1⅓-mile Kilsby tunnel, which eventually cost £280,000, more than double the initial estimate of £120,000.

Because of delays in completing various engineering works, the line was opened in stages. The first portion, from Euston to Boxmoor, was brought into operation on 20 July 1837 and on 16 October that year

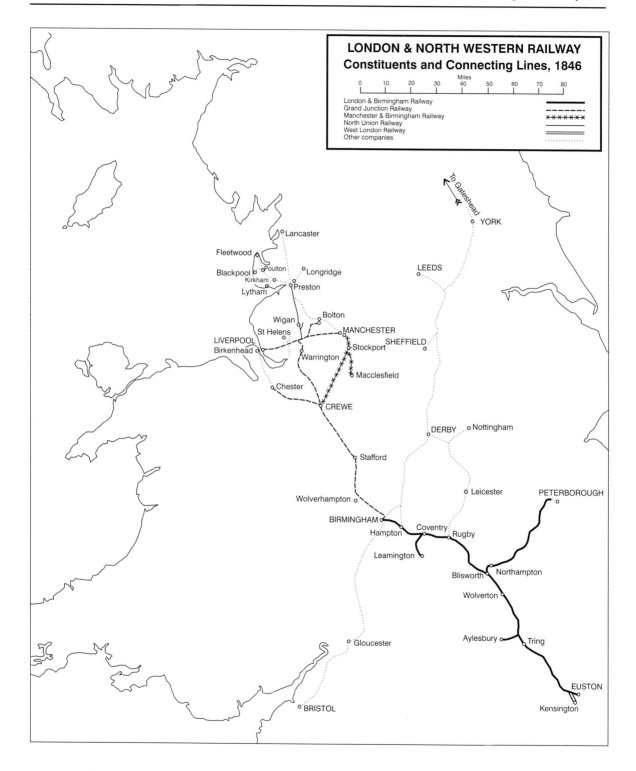

Figure 1.1 – London & North Western Railway: constituents and connecting lines, 1846.

services were extended to Tring. The next northward extension came on 9 April 1838, when the line was opened between Tring and Denbigh Hall, north of Bletchley; on the same day the section between Rugby and the Curzon Street terminus at Birmingham was brought into service. While work continued in Kilsby tunnel, and also at Blisworth cutting, coach connections were provided between Denbigh Hall and Rugby to link the two parts of the railway route. However, the completion of a single track through the tunnel allowed the introduction of one regular working in each direction between Euston and Curzon Street on Sundays from 24 June 1838, supplemented on occasion by special trips: on 20 August 1838, the day before the company's general meeting, a train ran between London and Birmingham in 5 hours. The full through passenger service commenced on 17 September 1838, when the temporary station at Denbigh Hall was closed.

Goods trains were not operated on a regular basis until 1839, although when the Grand Junction Canal ran short of water at its Tring summit in September 1838 Pickfords arranged for its canal traffic to be transhipped at Wolverton and worked by rail between there and Camden. From the start of 1839 freight was hauled between London and Birmingham for Pickfords and two other carriers, and from 15 April that year similar services were offered to other firms. In relying on carriers, rather than handling goods traffic on its own account, the L&B gained the approval of those who argued that railways should be operated like canals and that their lines should be available to any users on payment of tolls. However, the directors' principal objective appears to have been to limit the railway's direct operational responsibilities, and initially they considered contracting the entire freight business to Pickfords, which had built a warehouse at Camden with direct rail and canal access. When doubts emerged about the appropriateness of such an arrangement, the board opted instead to make the L&B's facilities available to all carriers, but the closeness of the link with Pickfords was emphasised by the appointment of a partner in that firm, Joseph Baxendale, as the railway's superintendent in February 1839. This arrangement ceased after a few months and Captain H P Bruyeres was appointed to succeed Baxendale as superintendent, but Pickfords continued to handle the collection and delivery of all goods not consigned by other carriers.

The L&B likewise entrusted the collection and delivery of parcels in London to the coaching firm of Chaplin & Horne, which had provided the temporary Denbigh Hall–Rugby link.

A similar approach was at first planned for the provision of motive power. Wolverton, which was approximately half-way between the two termini, was selected as the company's main locomotive depot, and in 1836 the company drew up a contract with Edward Bury, a partner in a Liverpool engine-building firm, under which he would operate and maintain the L&B's fleet for a fixed mileage rate. Bury's firm supplied many of the locomotives, but his operating contract was not implemented because traffic proved insufficient to generate an adequate income on the agreed terms; however, Bury remained as locomotive superintendent on a salaried basis. His responsibilities also included the stationary engines at Camden that were provided to haul passenger trains up the 1¼-mile

Working shaft in Kilsby tunnel, from J C Bourne's *Drawings of the London & Birmingham Railway...* (1839). The drawing is dated 8 July 1838, and shows the single track through the tunnel which was brought into public service on 24 June 1838.

incline from Euston. Rope haulage was abandoned in July 1844 because of the board's concern to eliminate the delays caused by attaching or detaching engines at Camden. Instead, trains were locomotive powered throughout, with assistance up Camden bank. This procedure was not however a novelty – it was required during the early months of operation, before the commissioning of the stationary engines in October 1837. Moreover, because it was at first expected that the Great Western Railway would share the L&B's London terminus, the section between Euston and Camden had been built with quadruple track: since only two of these tracks were cable-equipped, loco-motives remained necessary when another track was used for departure.

Initially, the 'first class trains', calling only at the more important stations, were timed to cover the Euston–Birmingham journey in around 6 hours, with stopping services taking about 30 minutes longer. Once earthworks had consolidated the schedules were progressively improved, and by 1845 the 10 am down

Bourne's drawing of Camden, showing the locomotive shed on the down side of the sub-surface engine house at the head of the Euston incline. The main line passed between the stationary engines' twin 132' chimneys, which Whishaw described as 'a fair sample of the approach to perfection which has in our own times been made in this, as in many other of the useful arts'. Note the points mechanism in the foreground.

morning mail was reaching Birmingham at 1.55 pm local time (which was 7 minutes slow of London). Third-class passengers were less fortunate: they were not conveyed until 5 October 1840, when they were provided with one daily train in each direction. This took slightly more than 8 hours for the down journey and about 7½ hours up. The principal expresses were accelerated further in May 1845, when one train was given a 3-hour timing between London and Birmingham. These improvements were all the more remarkable because the company's passenger services were worked entirely by light inside-framed four-wheeled engines, a reflection of Bury's views on locomotive design. His 'luggage engines', though slightly heavier and with coupled wheels, were also carried on two axles, and it was not until 1845 that larger locomotives were ordered in response to the growing volume of goods traffic.

By then the L&B was handling passenger and freight traffic to and from a wide range of destinations. Its possibilities as a route into London from the north and west were appreciated at an early stage: as noted above, the Great Western Railway's initial Act of 1835 envisaged using Euston as the London terminus for the line from Bristol, by means of a junction with the L&B at Kensal Green. This plan was soon abandoned, ostensibly because of disagreements about the terms on which accommodation would be made available at Euston, but with the complications resulting from Brunel's adoption of the broad gauge as an underlying factor. However, further proposals for connecting lines emerged during the promotional boom of the mid-1830s. One of the earliest was the Aylesbury Railway, a short single-track branch from the main line at Cheddington, which was authorised in 1836 and opened for passengers on 10 June 1839; goods traffic commenced during November that year. Although the Aylesbury Railway was a separate undertaking, it was built under Robert Stephenson's supervision and was worked from the outset by the L&B under a rental agreement. The L&B was also closely involved with a proposed railway from Tring to Oxford and Cheltenham, which would have carried its influence deep into GWR territory; this scheme foundered in Parliament in 1837, but was later to reappear in various guises. Further south, two planned feeder lines in London successfully passed the parliamentary hurdle in 1836, but subsequently encountered difficulties. One, the London Grand Junction Railway, would have provided a link from Camden to Skinner Street, in the City, but its powers were allowed to lapse. In contrast, the Birmingham, Bristol & Thames Junction Railway, which changed its name in 1840 to the West London Railway, eventually opened its 3-mile line between Willesden and the Kensington Canal on 27 May 1844. However, the financial difficulties that had delayed the line's completion soon reappeared and services were withdrawn on 1 December 1844. From 11 March 1845 the WLR was jointly leased by the L&B and GWR and a limited goods service was reinstated by the Birmingham company.

Connecting schemes further north proved more substantial. In 1836 two routes were authorised into the east midlands: the Midland Counties Railway, from Rugby to Derby and Nottingham via Leicester; and the Birmingham & Derby Junction Railway, which justified its title by its intended termination in a junction with the L&B at Stechford, three miles east of Curzon Street. However, the B&DJ also obtained powers for a southward connection from Whitacre to Hampton-in-Arden, which offered the possibility of an alternative through route between Euston and Derby in competition with the Midland Counties line via Leicester. Derby itself was the starting point for the North Midland Railway to Leeds, and other companies authorised in 1836 and 1837 carried the projected system onwards from Yorkshire to the north-east. In addition to its initial purpose of linking London with the west midlands and Lancashire, the

Engraving of a Bury-engined L&B train at Coventry, from Osborne's *London & Birmingham Railway Guide*. This was the first station at Coventry, which by 1840 had been replaced by a more substantial structure to the east of the original site.

L&B thus became part of the planned trunk route to York, Leeds, and Newcastle.

The B&DJ deferred construction of the Whitacre–Stechford section, so when the remainder of its line opened on 12 August 1839 the junction at Hampton was used to provide through services between Derby and both Euston and Birmingham. The L&B's Birmingham station was also subsequently shared with the Birmingham & Gloucester Railway, which was opened from Gloucester to a temporary terminus at Camp Hill in Birmingham on 17 December 1840. It was extended to a junction just outside Curzon Street on 17 August 1841 and in November 1842 through

carriages were introduced between Euston and Gloucester. There were several personal links between the B&G and L&B: a number of directors served on both boards, while the Gloucester line's engineer until 1841 was Captain William Scarth Moorsom, brother of Captain C R Moorsom. The latter became a B&G director shortly before his brother's appointment as engineer ceased, and he was almost immediately elected as the company's chairman to fill the vacancy left by the resignation of Joseph Walker, who was also a member of the L&B board.

Because of its various connections with the companies which ultimately became part of the Midland Railway, the L&B could not escape being affected by the events which led up to that company's formation. The North Midland Railway – which until 1842 was chaired by George Carr Glyn – was opened between Derby and Rotherham on 11 May 1840 and extended to Leeds on 1 July, the date on which the York & North Midland Railway was also completed. For statutory reasons the Midland Counties Railway had built the northern parts of its system first, opening between Nottingham and the joint station in Derby on 4 June 1839 and reaching Leicester on 5 May 1840. A few weeks later, on 30 June, its main line south was opened to a temporary terminus at Rugby. On 17 August the junction with the L&B and a new Rugby station were brought into use, allowing the MCR to challenge the B&DJ's previous monopoly of the through route southward from Derby. The strong competition which developed between these two companies for traffic between London and the east midlands and Yorkshire weakened them both financially, and gave George Hudson the opportunity to use his effective control of the NMR from 1842 onwards to secure the amalgamation of all three railways radiating from Derby under his chairmanship in 1844.

By then the B&DJ, concerned at the L&B's toll charges for access to Curzon Street, had promoted an alternative route from Whitacre to an independent

The two termini of the London & Birmingham Railway, as depicted by Bourne. His drawing of Euston (*above*) shows the main station buildings beyond the famous arch, with the original train shed just visible between the two lodges to the right of the picture. Philip Hardwick, the architect of Euston, also designed Curzon Street station in Birmingham (*below*): unlike its London equivalent, his Curzon Street portico still survives.

Birmingham terminus at Lawley Street. This was brought into use on 9 February 1842, marking the first stage in the relegation of the Hampton branch. By March 1843 this had been singled, and its importance declined even more after the Midland amalgamation left Rugby as the main junction for traffic between the L&B and the east midlands. A further significant stage in the redrawing of railway relationships in the west midlands came in 1845, when the Birmingham & Gloucester Railway, which had reached agreement at the beginning of that year to amalgamate with the broad-gauge Bristol & Gloucester, passed with its southern partner into the control of the Midland Railway. Although this seems to have been an opportunistic coup by the latter, the objective of preventing the two Gloucester companies from falling into the hands of the GWR was shared by the L&B, which agreed to meet half the Midland's losses on the arrangement over a ten-year period.

While Euston's initial sphere of influence through these early connecting railways was affected by the emergence of the Midland Railway, by the mid-1840s the L&B was already expanding in other directions, bolstered by the financial success of its main line. By 1842 the company was carrying 780,000 passengers annually, and the volume of goods and passenger traffic interchanged with other railways led Glyn to draw on his banking experience to propose the establishment of the Railway Clearing House as a means of settling transactions between the various undertakings. This was set up that year in L&B premises near Euston, and proved invaluable as a means of simplifying through traffic arrangements and promoting inter-company co-operation.

Despite the size of the L&B's capital account and the depth of the contemporary economic depression, revenue in 1842 was sufficient to pay a dividend of 10% to the ordinary shareholders, a level which the company maintained for the rest of its independent life. With its shares at a premium of 100% or more, the L&B could readily obtain money to build new lines or subscribe to other railways, especially since it structured its new share issues in ways which offered substantial financial returns to existing shareholders. The first extension of the system financed by an addition to the L&B's capital was the Warwick & Leamington Union Railway, incorporated in 1842 to build a line from Coventry to Leamington. The L&B was empowered to lease or purchase the new undertaking, and in the following year the WLUR was vested entirely in the larger company. The 9-mile branch was built at close to its estimated cost and was opened to its terminus at Milverton on 9 December 1844.

The next extension, authorised from the outset as part of the L&B, was a 47-mile railway from Blisworth to Northampton and Peterborough, which received parliamentary approval on 4 July 1843 and was opened for passengers between Blisworth and Northampton on 13 May 1845; services were extended to Peterborough on 2 June that year. Like the Leamington branch, the Peterborough line was built with single track, but it was consciously planned on the 'cheap principle', avoiding heavy earthworks and using level crossings instead of road bridges wherever possible. As a result, capital expenditure up to June 1845 was under £10,000 per mile, less than a fifth of the cost of the main line, but by the time the branch had opened for goods traffic, on 15 December 1845, preparations were in hand for doubling the track. This was a reflection of the line's new strategic importance: it struck into the territory that would be served by the proposed direct route between London and York, and its potential was further enhanced in 1844 when the Eastern Counties Railway was authorised to extend from Ely to an end-on junction at Peterborough. Though the ECR line was not completed until the end of 1846, its Peterborough station was brought into service on 2 June 1845 to handle L&B trains.

To complement the introduction of passenger services between Northampton and Peterborough Chaplin & Horne, the company's agents, established a network of connecting coach routes. This reached as far as Lincoln and Boston, and was clearly an attempt to extend and protect the L&B's hinterland in the face of mounting competition. As part of the growing wave of railway promotion the L&B also obtained authorisation for several further branches in 1845 and 1846. None of these, however, was completed before the creation of the LNWR, so in terms of operational mileage the southern portion of the new company comprised the Euston–Birmingham main line, its Leamington and Peterborough branches, a joint interest in the West London Railway, and the Aylesbury Railway, which the L&B absorbed on the day that it was itself incorporated within the larger grouping.

* * *

The second-largest constituent of the LNWR was the Grand Junction Railway, which formed the northern continuation of the trunk route to Lancashire. The GJR obtained its Act on 6 May 1833, the same day as its southern partner, but could similarly trace its origins back to proposals mooted in the mid-1820s. Like the L&B, the GJR was an amalgam of separate proposals: Bills were promoted in 1831 by two companies, one based in Liverpool and the other in Birmingham, with the intention of creating a through Liverpool-Birmingham route from the two sections. The parliamentary progress of these schemes was cut short by the Reform crisis, but when new Bills were submitted later in 1831 the Birmingham company restricted its plans to the Birmingham–Wolverhampton section, causing the loss of the entire project. In the light of this experience the Liverpool promoters – who were mostly Liverpool & Manchester directors – assumed the lead, and the 1833 Act provided for a single undertaking to make a line between the Warrington & Newton Railway and the northern outskirts of Birmingham. The origins of the scheme were however reflected in its deposited plans: the northern portion, as far as the boundary between Cheshire and Staffordshire, was the responsibility of George Stephenson, the engineer employed by the Liverpool promoters, while the southern section was surveyed by James Urpeth Rastrick, who had been appointed by their Birmingham counterparts. Rastrick undertook several early railway schemes, and is probably best known as the engineer of the London & Brighton line.

The ascendancy of Lancashire in the control of the GJR was reinforced by the fact that the bulk of its finance came from Liverpool. The new undertaking was chaired by John Moss, the deputy chairman of the Liverpool & Manchester Railway: like Glyn, he was a banker. Liverpool interests took up most of the other directorships, but three Birmingham representatives remained, all also members of the L&B board. As in the case of the southern company, the Birmingham directors made up a local committee, but the main GJR board left this committee with extremely limited powers. As a result, all three Birmingham directors resigned by the end of 1834 and were replaced by further Liverpool members.

The management of the railway was similarly

concentrated in Liverpool. The company employed the same firm of solicitors as the L&M, and the GJR's secretary and treasurer, J R Chorley, was based in Liverpool, where the board meetings were held. Rastrick's appointment was terminated after the Act of Incorporation was obtained and George Stephenson was confirmed as engineer of the entire undertaking on 25 September 1833. Joseph Locke and William Allcard were later appointed as assistant engineers for the northern and southern sections respectively. The new team adjusted Rastrick's original route at several points, while surveys were also undertaken for a mile-long tunnel under Birmingham, to link the GJR with the L&B's intended terminus in Nova Scotia Gardens, and for a branch to Wolverhampton. Powers for the alterations and extensions in Staffordshire and Warwickshire, together with a deviation at Warrington, were obtained in 1834, and these changes contributed to the slow start to work on the line: only thirteen miles were under construction by August of that year.

More fundamentally, however, there were difficulties between the directors and their engineer. These seem to have arisen from the board's insistence on close specification and supervision of contracts and from Stephenson's unwillingness to devote sufficient time to the GJR. Increasingly, the board was forced to rely on Locke, who was promoted on 24 November 1834 to become joint engineer for the entire line. The problems with Stephenson continued, but after his role had been reduced in August 1835 to that of consulting engineer matters were finally resolved on 16 September 1835 when the board accepted his resignation. This left Locke as engineer, with Allcard as his assistant, and work was pressed ahead under their supervision.

Further alterations had become necessary at the Birmingham end, where the opposition of James Watt's son to the route through Aston Park prompted a further Act in 1835 to authorise an alternative entry into Birmingham, parallel to the final stretch of the L&B; the same Act included powers for a branch to Walsall. This further change in the approach to Birmingham, and negotiations with the London company over terminal arrangements, led to delays in

Newton Road, a local station on the Grand Junction Railway about seven miles from Birmingham.

completion of the final section, so a temporary station was built at Vauxhall, about a mile from the intended terminus. A fortnight into Victoria's reign, on 4 July 1837, the GJR route was opened between Vauxhall and its junction with the Warrington & Newton line. Although this was Britain's first trunk railway, the opening took place with little ceremony.

Through passenger trains were thus established between the midlands and Lancashire, with principal services initially allowed about 4½ hours between Birmingham and Liverpool or Manchester; those calling at all stations required almost an hour longer. Goods services commenced on 1 February 1838, though some merchandise and livestock traffic was being carried by passenger train before the end of 1837. Goods agents had been appointed at Birmingham, Manchester, and Liverpool in 1837, and in the following year, as the pressures of managing the line increased, the secretary's post was separated from that of the treasurer in order to provide more executive support to the chairman. Out of a field of seventy-one applicants Captain J E Cleather was appointed as secretary and outdoor superintendent at a salary of £800 per annum; however, he later lost the confidence of his employers, and was replaced in 1841 by Captain Mark Huish, the 33-year-old secretary of the Glasgow, Paisley & Greenock Railway.

An engraving of the Grand Junction Railway's temporary Birmingham terminus at Vauxhall, from Drake's *Road book of the Grand Junction Railway*

Discussions with the L&B about joint station arrangements at Birmingham had begun as early as 1835, but mutually satisfactory terms could not be agreed. In 1837 the GJR suggested an alternative scheme for a direct connection between the two routes east of the proposed terminus, to allow through running between London and Lancashire without

reversal, but this proved unacceptable to the L&B. The GJR therefore went ahead with plans for its own station adjacent to the London line's Curzon Street site and this was brought into use on 19 November 1838, replacing the previous terminus – on 2 January 1839 the board ordered the removal of Vauxhall's passenger shed to Warrington. However, Vauxhall retained its functions as the GJR's principal goods depot in Birmingham and as the main locomotive shed for the southern end of the line.

While the GJR's new passenger terminus at Curzon Street was under construction, temporary arrangements were made to exchange through traffic via the L&B station: this was under discussion within a few days of the opening of the line to Rugby on 9 April 1838, and definite agreement to work GJR carriages into the L&B terminus had been reached by 6 June. Since the L&B management committee was told on 11 April 1838 that Pickfords was seeking the extension of a Manchester–Birmingham goods train to Rugby, the completion of a junction between the two lines cannot have been regarded as a major problem.

In 1838 the GJR gave serious consideration to establishing a joint goods service with the L&B under Baxendale's management, but the London's company's eventual decision to leave goods traffic to the carrying firms gave its northern partner problems, especially as the L&B refused to handle goods despatched on the GJR's own account. Though the GJR provided services between Lancashire and Birmingham for some of the carriers (and also allowed colliery proprietors to work their locomotives over parts of its line), it operated its own freight traffic, and its inability to consign goods beyond Birmingham restricted the development of this business. After negotiations with a number of carriers, the company appointed Chaplin & Horne at the beginning of 1840 to act as its agents for goods traffic over the L&B, apparently at the instigation of Locke. By that stage Locke was engineer of the London & South Western Railway and was therefore closely associated with W J Chaplin, who had diversified his coaching interests by becoming chairman of that undertaking. Despite this arrangement, the need to rely on carriers for its London traffic continued to irk the GJR, which more than once considered seeking powers to work its own goods trains south of Birmingham.

Relations with the carriers were also not helped by

disputes over their bulking of parcels traffic. The railways contended that such items should be consigned and charged separately and that carriers who took advantage of bulk freight rates to undercut the railways' own parcels charges were depriving them of revenue. The carriers argued in return that their delivery networks enabled them to provide a better public service and that by bearing the risks of conveyance they were entitled to take advantage of lower rates. In 1841 Pickfords went to court on this matter, but although judgment was eventually given in the carrier's favour the decision had little influence on the slow attrition of the independent carrying trade.

Despite the obstacles to the development of through traffic to the south, the GJR was from the outset an outstanding financial success. Its cost per mile was less than half that of the L&B, and revenue was sufficient for a dividend of 10% to be paid in the first year of operation; it reached 14% in the financial year ending in June 1841. The company then began to reduce its gearing by issuing further shares to pay off part of its borrowings, but it was nevertheless able to maintain dividends of 10% or more for the rest of its independent existence, despite a downturn in revenue during the depression of the early 1840s.

* * *

Although the GJR gave access to the other routes radiating from Birmingham, it failed to exercise its own powers for branches in the west midlands, to Walsall and to Wolverhampton. In contrast with the L&B, which became the basis for an entirely new network, it was essentially an extension of an existing system based in Lancashire, and this system was already well developed by the time the trunk line southwards was opened for traffic. The core of this network, and the stimulus of much subsequent promotion, was of course the Liverpool & Manchester Railway, first projected in 1821 and opened on 15 September 1830 after gaining parliamentary approval in 1826. Its 30-mile route ran between Crown Street passenger station in Liverpool and the Liverpool Road terminus in Manchester; in addition a 1½-mile goods branch, mostly in tunnel, served the Liverpool docks at Wapping. Both the Crown Street and Wapping tunnels were worked by stationary engines, but on the main line the L&M kept abreast of locomotive practice by adopting first Stephenson's improved 'Planet' class

design and then the new 2-2-2 'Patentees' when the latter were introduced in 1833. By 1836 a summer service of twelve passenger trains daily in each direction between Liverpool and Manchester was in operation, with first-class trains booked to take 75–90 minutes between Edge Hill and Manchester.

The close ties between the boards of the L&M and GJR have already been mentioned. While relations were not always harmonious – the GJR looked more than once at the possibility of a less indirect approach to Liverpool and sometimes chafed at having to rely on its partner's facilities – the interdependence of the two concerns was demonstrated by the 25% increase in the net profits of the L&M when the GJR began carrying goods over its system in 1838. The extension to Lime Street, authorised in 1832, had been justified primarily because of the need to provide a more central passenger station for the projected line to Birmingham; its opening on 15 August 1836 – also with cable haulage – relegated the former Crown Street station to use as repair shops and for mineral traffic. However, while the L&M undertook this and several other improvements to meet GJR requirements, problems in reconciling the latter's interests with those of other parties led to inaction on proposals for lines across Manchester to link with either the Manchester & Leeds Railway at Hunt's Bank or with the Manchester & Birmingham Railway at Store Street. It was only in 1842 that a revised scheme was authorised for a northern junction line to the M&L: this extension, slightly more than a mile in length, was opened to the Leeds company's new Victoria station on 4 May 1844, allowing the Liverpool Road station in Manchester to be closed for passenger traffic.

The L&M was restricted by a section in its authorising Act which effectively limited its dividend payments to an annual maximum of 10%. Although this ceiling was not reached until 1835, lower dividends were paid on only three occasions after the GJR was opened: even then, the shortfall was only ½%. While the L&M had its own dense local traffic as well as the long-distance traffic brought on to its line by the GJR, the strong links between the two companies made amalgamation an obvious step, and the growing threat from competing lines provided the eventual stimulus for the negotiations between the GJR and L&M in 1844 which culminated in parliamentary approval for a merger on 8 August 1845. John Moss retired as chairman of the GJR at its general meeting on 1 August 1845; his place was taken by Charles Lawrence, the chairman of the L&M and Moss's previous deputy. It was under Lawrence, therefore, that the enlarged company's identity was subsequently merged into the LNWR, and a further direct connection with L&M antecedents was provided by a provision in the 1846 Act establishing the LNWR which entitled the Duke of Sutherland to appoint a director to its board. This could be traced back via the 1845 amalgamation between the GJR and L&M to the latter's Act of incorporation, which had given the then Marquis of Stafford the right to appoint three directors to reflect his financial interest in the undertaking. The Marquis was created Duke of Sutherland in 1833, the year of his death, and the entitlement passed to his successors.

As authorised in 1833, however, the GJR's route had not connected directly with the L&M: north of the Mersey it relied on the metals of the Warrington & Newton Railway. While the latter included L&M proprietors among its promoters, it was originally an independent undertaking, with Robert Stephenson as its engineer. The company's Act was obtained on 14 May 1829, and provided for a 4½-mile line from a triangular junction with the L&M west of Newton-le-Willows to Dallam Lane in Warrington, together with two short branches, one terminating close to the Mersey at Bank Quay and the other to Cockhedge, east of Warrington. When the railway was opened on 25 July 1831 neither the Cockhedge branch nor the eastern spur of the triangular junction had been built, and it is not clear exactly when the Bank Quay line was completed. However, by the time of its opening the little company had wider ambitions: it obtained powers in 1830 for a branch northwards as far as the Newton viaduct, which, although ultimately abortive, was clearly intended as the first stage in a through connection to Wigan. In addition, in November 1829 the W&N had deposited plans for a line southwards from Bank Quay to the Trent & Mersey Canal at Sandbach. Although there was a good local traffic case for a railway linking the Lancashire coal measures with the canal and with the Cheshire saltfield, the extension was seen by Robert Stephenson as the first step in a route towards Birmingham.

The Liverpool–Birmingham projects then under discussion involved either a more westerly crossing of the Mersey at Runcorn or a line via the Wirral, and the

emergence of a Warrington route as a possible contender was significant enough for John Moss to bring pressure to bear on the W&N to withdraw its proposal. Accordingly, no Bill was introduced in 1830 for the Sandbach project, but in the two parliamentary sessions of 1831 a further W&N scheme for a line across the Mersey to join the projected Liverpool–Birmingham route near Preston Brook made some progress before failing on a technicality after the Bill for the Liverpool line was withdrawn. The merits of the Warrington route were however quickly appreciated by the promoters of the larger scheme – besides avoiding the more costly direct approach to Liverpool it would also serve Manchester – so by November 1831 it had been adopted in preference to the earlier proposal for a line via Runcorn. In its 1833 Act, therefore, the GJR took Bank Quay as its northern starting point. Although powers were obtained in 1834 for an alternative route through Warrington, which would link with the W&N at the junction of its Dallam Lane and Bank Quay lines, it was eventually decided to revert to the original plan.

Despite the fact that the GJR had taken over its proposal for a southern extension, the W&N remained separate. Perhaps confident in their line's new strategic significance, its directors offered in November 1833 to transfer it to the larger company at a price of 1¼ Grand Junction £100 shares for each £100 W&N share, with an entitlement either to the profits from the existing undertaking or payment of 5% interest if possession was taken immediately. These terms were rejected, and further negotiations during 1834 failed to result in agreement. The GJR thereupon deposited plans for an alternative line direct to the L&M, crossing the Mersey at Fiddler's Ferry, west of Warrington. To prove that this was no idle threat, work was suspended on the authorised route north of Preston Brook and a general meeting of shareholders on 29 January 1835 empowered the board to proceed with a Bill for the Fiddler's Ferry line. At this stage the W&N directors realised that they

Isaac Shaw's etching of the scene looking east at Edge Hill on the opening day of the Liverpool & Manchester Railway, 15 September 1830. The celebrated Moorish arch, designed by John Foster, spanned the line between the two engine houses which provided the haulage for the Wapping and Crown Street tunnel inclines.

Lime Street station in Liverpool, opened in 1836.

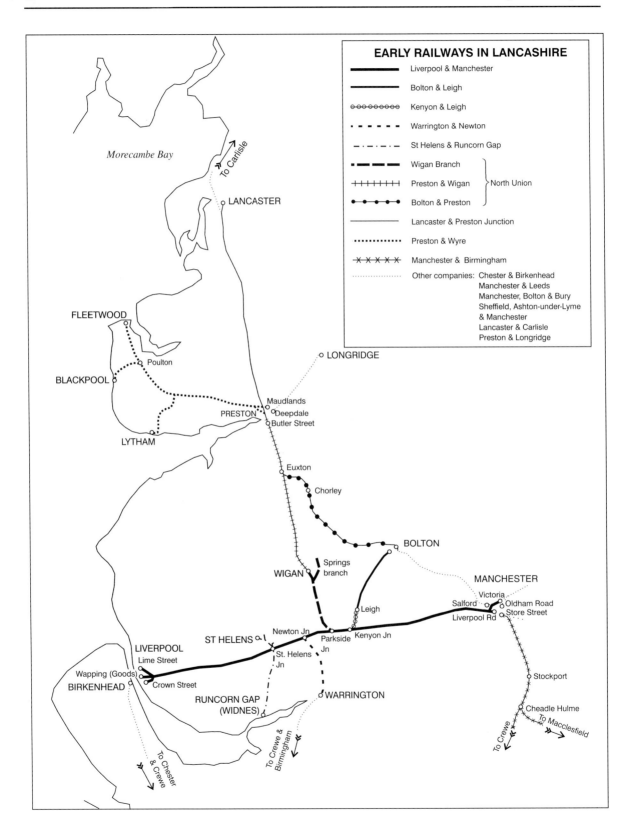

had overreached themselves, and on 4 February the GJR board agreed to absorb the smaller company and assume its debts on the basis of a one-for-one share conversion and a guarantee of 4% annually until dividends were declared. Parliamentary approval for the purchase and for the issue of the necessary 518 extra shares was obtained on 12 June 1835, but the GJR took effective control immediately. Pending the opening of the main line, arrangements were made for the former treasurer and general agent of the W&N, Peter Stubbs, to lease the line on terms which would meet the annual guarantee payments and yield a small profit to its new owners.

While the GJR was under construction the Warrington branch continued to function as a local line, and the west-facing connection at Newton Junction appears to have been adequate for traffic both to Liverpool and Manchester: though Locke surveyed a branch for Manchester traffic in November 1835 no further action was taken at that stage. However, the approaching completion of the main line made the question of a direct eastward connection more urgent, and on 27 February 1837 the company's solicitor was instructed to purchase the necessary land. The constraints of the layout required the spur to be constructed with an extremely tight radius, and a week after the opening of the GJR to through traffic difficulty was being reported with six-wheeled locomotives on this curve. The board's immediate response was to recommission the three original W&N locomotives to work the Manchester portions of trains to and from Birmingham; in the longer term, however, the junction had a direct influence on GJR locomotive practice, since it encouraged the adoption of outside cylinders and motion in place of vulnerable crank axles.

The Warrington line, although a key link in the route south, was just part of the network of railways connecting with the Liverpool & Manchester Railway. In fact, a section of this network actually antedated the L&M. This was the Bolton & Leigh Railway, authorised in 1825 to build a line from Bolton to the Leeds & Liverpool Canal at Leigh. The plans were prepared by George Stephenson and reflected current railway engineering practice in the north-east of England by including inclined planes which would require cable haulage by stationary

engines. Work on the line was started by a local engineer, Robert Daglish, but by 1827 Stephenson's association with the line had been renewed, and on 1 August 1828 the northern section of the line was ceremonially opened between Chequerbent and the Deansgate terminus in Bolton. The occasion was distinguished by the use of the 'Lancashire Witch', the first steam locomotive in Lancashire, which had been constructed that year for the L&M at the Stephensons' works in Newcastle but transferred to the B&L because of the latter's advanced stage of construction. At the opening the locomotive hauled a passenger train of adapted goods wagons and a single carriage lent by the L&M, but although a carriage was similarly borrowed in December 1829 for 'an experiment in passenger carrying', regular traffic on the line was confined to coal. The 'Lancashire Witch' was returned in July 1829 for construction work on the L&M, but after the Rainhill trials Timothy Hackworth's 'Sans Pareil' found employment on the Bolton line and further locomotives were obtained soon afterwards.

The B&L was completed to its intended terminus at the canal at Leigh by the end of March 1830, but by then construction of a connection with the L&M was already well advanced. The initiative for this seems to have come from the latter's board, which ordered the preparation of plans for a junction line as early as 9 July 1827. This presaged a Liverpool take-over of the Bolton company, and in 1829 powers were obtained for a 2½-mile connection between the B&L and the L&M, diverging from the Bolton line north of the Leeds & Liverpool Canal and terminating in a triangular junction at Kenyon. Although the Kenyon & Leigh Railway was nominally an independent company, eleven out of its twenty-one subscribers were L&M directors. Two of its officers also subscribed, together with George Stephenson. Work was pressed ahead vigorously and through freight working between the L&M and Bolton began on 3 January 1831. An excursion train to Newton races ran on 2 June that year and on 11 June regular passenger services were inaugurated between Liverpool and Great Moor Street station in Bolton, which was reached by a short spur south of the Deansgate goods terminus. By that stage the B&L had contracted with John Hargreaves junior, a local carrier, coal owner, and engineer, to work its line. He operated throughout between Bolton and Liverpool, and also worked goods services to Manchester; as the east-facing spur

Figure 1.2 – Early railways in Lancashire.

at Kenyon was not built, passengers for Manchester had to change at the junction. The K&L was thus never an independent operational entity and remained closely linked with the Bolton company.

Another railway which was similar to the Bolton line in its initial concept was the St Helens & Runcorn Gap Railway, which was authorised on 29 May 1830 with the object of providing a link to the Mersey from the collieries and industries of St Helens, in this case to supplement an existing waterway connection. The railway was surveyed by Charles Vignoles, who had worked with the Rennie brothers on the successful second parliamentary submission for the Liverpool & Manchester line. The 8½-mile route between Cowley Hill colliery and Runcorn Gap crossed the L&M by an overbridge about four miles west of Newton Junction, and the Act authorised a connecting spur in each quadrant of the intersection. Powers were also obtained for a branch north-west from Bold towards the Liverpool line at Elton Head colliery, a dock at the Mersey, and no less than eight branches to collieries and glass-works in the St Helens area. Only the north-to-east connection with the L&M was built, and the section between this junction and St Helens was opened for goods traffic on 2 January 1832, using stock hired from the larger company. Though some coal traffic was worked between Broad Oak colliery and the Mersey on 28 November 1832, formal opening of the entire line did not take place until 21 February 1833; even then the dock at Runcorn Gap was incomplete. A horse-drawn passenger carriage was put into operation between St Helens Junction and the town in September 1832 and a year later a limited passenger service was inaugurated to Runcorn Gap, which soon became more generally known as Widnes. Through coaches between St Helens and both Liverpool and Manchester were later provided, but the railway remained independent of its larger neighbour and eventually amalgamated in 1845 with the competing Sankey Brook Navigation to become the St Helens Canal & Railway.

The St Helens & Runcorn Gap Railway was one of two Vignoles lines authorised on the same day in 1830. The other was the Wigan Branch Railway, which connected with the L&M at Parkside, east of Newton-le-Willows. The deposited plan shows connecting spurs towards both Liverpool and Manchester, and a branch to New Springs leaving the main line about a mile south of the terminus at Wallgate Street in Wigan. When the line opened on 3 September 1832 only the connection towards Manchester had been installed, and work on the Springs branch had been deferred. The company evidently experienced financial difficulties and from its opening relied on the L&M to work its traffic.

The Wigan company's prospects improved in 1831 when the Preston & Wigan Railway was authorised to build a line northwards. In addition to its main line from an end-on junction with the WBR, the Preston & Wigan was empowered to build three branches, one to replace the Lancaster Canal tramway between Penwortham and Walton-le-Dale. Again, Vignoles was chosen as engineer, and several of the new company's Liverpool directors also served on the board of the WBR. However, the directors were reluctant to make a start in the unsettled conditions of the early 1830s and indeed met only twice in 1832. The first chairman, Samuel Hope, resigned on 5 August 1833 and at the same meeting the board decided to seek amalgamation with the Wigan Branch Railway. On 22 May 1834 an Act was obtained to amalgamate the two companies under the title of the North Union Railway and to authorise deviations in the Preston line; in the same year the new undertaking made an arrangement for Hargreaves to work the goods traffic on the Wigan section, leaving passenger services with the L&M. Construction of the northern section eventually started in 1835, and on 31 October 1838 the main line to Preston was opened. On the same day goods services began on the Springs branch, which the amalgamated company had been required to construct at the same time as the Preston line. However, powers for the three branches authorised in 1831 were allowed to lapse

The opening of the North Union made it possible to travel entirely by rail between Euston and Preston, and although through passenger services and bookings did not begin until 19 August 1839 the influence of the new route quickly extended far beyond Lancashire. When Joseph Pease went from County Durham to London to give evidence to a parliamentary committee in June 1839 he travelled by coach to Preston and thence by train, the railway portion requiring three separate bookings. To ease through journeys a new station was provided in 1839 at the junction at Parkside, east of the existing L&M station. The latter company agreed to meet 25% of the cost, and the balance was shared between the North Union and Grand Junction companies. As an alternative, the GJR had in 1837 considered reviving the Warrington & Newton's 1831 scheme for a direct connection between the Warrington and Wigan lines, which would have anticipated the eventual cut-off between Winwick and Golborne. This was rejected because of its cost, so Preston traffic accordingly had to be worked via the east curve at Newton Junction, with a reversal at Parkside. The Wigan company's powers for a west-facing connection at Parkside, which would have permitted through running, were not revived until 1845.

The 1845 Act for the Parkside connection was promoted by the L&M, though not passed until after its amalgamation with the GJR, and to establish the background to this it is necessary to trace the development of the network in north and east Lancashire. Before the North Union had opened its line to Preston, the wave of further promotion in the mid-1830s had made that town the hub of a number of newly-authorised projects. One was purely local: the Preston & Longridge Railway, authorised in 1836, was planned with no physical connection with other lines, and relied on horse-haulage when it opened on 1 May

1840 for freight traffic between its Preston terminus at Deepdale and the quarries at Longridge; a limited passenger service began the following day.

In contrast with the P&L, the two other lines from Preston fitted into the evolving trunk system. The first to be authorised was the Preston & Wyre Railway: its 1835 Act provided for a rail link to the new port which the local landowner and MP, Peter Hesketh Fleetwood, was promoting at the mouth of the River Wyre, and in 1839 the railway and harbour undertakings were merged into one company. The single-track line opened for regular traffic on 16 July 1840, after formal inauguration the previous day, and in May 1841 a steamship service was introduced between the new harbour (which took the name of Fleetwood) and the rail-served port of Ardrossan. This completed a rail and sea route to Glasgow, and shipping services

The St Helens & Runcorn Gap Railway's bridge over the Liverpool & Manchester Railway, portrayed in an 1832 Ackermann print. The mineral train is hauled by a vertical-boilered Braithwaite & Ericsson locomotive; the L&M engine in the left foreground is of the 'Northumbrian' type, a development of the 'Rocket' design which preceded the inside-cylindered 'Planet' class.

were also established to Whitehaven, Belfast, and the Isle of Man. However, the P&W did not neglect the potential for local development: excursion trains to Fleetwood began in 1844 and in the following year branches were authorised from Poulton to Blackpool and from Kirkham to Lytham, with a spur to Lytham dock. The Lytham branch opened on 17 February 1846 and the Blackpool line followed on 29 April.

The Preston & Wyre was planned with a separate station at Maudlands, on the north side of Preston. However, another line was authorised in 1837 which cut across the approach to Maudlands. This was the Lancaster & Preston Junction Railway, a Locke-engineered line which was seen as the first step in plans for an overland route to Scotland. Its starting place at Dock Street in Preston was close to the Lancaster Canal's basin; the North Union's parliamentary line also extended to this point, but the latter company had selected a site for its terminus on the south side of Fishergate at Butler Street, about a furlong south of Dock Street. Although the L&PJ's Act authorised it to effect a junction at Butler Street, these powers were left in abeyance for three years to allow the North Union to extend its own line, and this was the course that was adopted, although the Lancaster undertaking contributed to the cost. The Lancaster company's Act also empowered the P&W to make a connection into its line. The L&PJ was opened for public traffic on 26 June 1840, so when the P&W was completed three weeks later it was able to work through carriages over the two junction lines into the North Union station. However, at first all P&W passenger trains crossed the L&PJ to serve the Maudlands terminus – a manœuvre which was apparently undertaken twice by through Butler Street workings – and the hazards of the layout were demonstrated by a fatal collision on 18 December 1840.

The P&W and L&PJ initially relied on the North Union to work their services, though the Lancaster company purchased locomotives of its own which were operated on its behalf. Lancaster became the northern terminus of the route from London, with two through trains daily in each direction, and a further connectional service via Parkside. In addition, through carriages were provided between Lancaster and both Liverpool and Manchester. Similar through services were available at Fleetwood, where the establishment of the North Euston Hotel reminded the traveller of the rail link with London, 238 miles and about

11½ hours away.

The apparently logical northwards progression of the trunk route was however disturbed by two local influences. The first was the competition provided by the Lancaster Canal for local goods and passenger traffic beyond Preston, which left the L&PJ in an exposed financial position. The second was the intervention of another company for traffic southwards from Preston. This was the Bolton & Preston Railway, which had been authorised in 1837 as a continuation of the Manchester, Bolton & Bury Canal Navigation & Railway. The form of the latter undertaking was partly due to a flirtation in 1830 between canal interests and the promoters of a railway from Liverpool to Leeds, who saw that they could also create an alternative line between Liverpool and Manchester by adopting the Manchester, Bolton & Bury Canal's route for a connecting railway. Though the larger scheme collapsed, the canal company obtained railway powers in 1831 and opened its line between Salford and Bolton on 29 May 1838.

As authorised, the B&P would have run from the MB&B to the Lancaster Canal's tramway near Chorley, and from there it would have superseded the tramway in order to gain access to its terminus at the canal's Preston basin, north of Fishergate. However, in order to protect the North Union, the B&P's Act prohibited it from undertaking work north of Chorley for three years, and in 1838 it was authorised instead to join the former's line at Euxton, though it retained powers for its own Preston station at the Lancaster Canal basin. Progress was slow because of engineering problems: after opening between Bolton and Rawlinson Bridge on 4 February 1841, the line was extended to Chorley on 22 December the same year, but the connection to Euxton was not opened until 22 June 1843.

Locomotive working for the B&P was undertaken by John Hargreaves junior, who also supplied power for the MB&B's trains; in February 1841, Hargreaves, who, as noted, already operated on the North Union, began in addition to work goods trains over the L&PJ. When the North Union gave notice later that year that it would cease to operate on behalf of the Lancaster company, the Bolton lines provided the nearest alternative, and from 1 January 1842 Hargreaves took over responsibility for L&PJ motive power. Locomotive provision became part of a wider dispute over access to the North Union's Butler Street station, so the

L&PJ also turned to the B&P for assistance in accommodating its traffic. As mentioned above, the Bolton company retained rights to Lancaster Canal land north of Fishergate; since the L&PJ could achieve direct access to this property from its own route, it established a small station there early in 1842 as an alternative to terminating its trains on the running lines north of the disputed section. Passengers prepared to pay the 6d toll demanded by the North Union for passage over the 200 yards of track which linked the L&PJ with Butler Street were conveyed through, but many preferred to walk. However, faced with this obstruction from the North Union for its onward connections, with delays before its Bolton ally would be in a position to run services into Preston from the south, and with continuing canal competition, the L&PJ remained in a difficult situation, so when the Lancaster Canal offered to lease the line from 21 September 1842 the railway's hard-pressed directors seized this opportunity to resolve their company's problems. Responsibility for the L&PJ's operations accordingly passed to the canal undertaking and in 1843 an Act was obtained to authorise the lease.

With the completion of the B&P line to Euxton it became the North Union's turn to find itself exposed to competition, although as the Bolton company relied on the other's metals to gain access to Preston from Euxton it made no overt move to provoke hostility. However, its position was helped by the fact that its route to Manchester was considerably shorter than that via Parkside, and the extension of Lancaster trains to Manchester was a practical indication that through traffic might be attracted to the Bolton route. The North Union accordingly began to reduce its fares to offset this competition and also resorted to delaying Bolton trains, prompting the B&P to reintroduce coach connections between Chorley and Preston and to consider reviving plans for a separate line. But although the North Union's shares went to a discount, its control of the shared route north of Euxton remained a vital tactical advantage, since the Bolton company was not in a position to sustain a long rate-cutting war until it gained independent access to Preston. In the autumn of 1843 the rival companies agreed to amalgamate with effect from 1 January 1844 and this received parliamentary approval on 10 May 1844. The share capitals of the North Union and B&P, respectively £477,326 and £262,000, were merged as 'A' and 'B' stock of the enlarged company,

with the former Bolton stock entitled to half the dividend received by the 'A' stock. The North Union's name was perpetuated by the combined undertaking and its chairman, Theodore Woolman Rathbone, was appointed to the same office by the amalgamated board. Rathbone had been a director of both the L&M and L&B since 1833 and was chairman of the Wigan Branch Railway when it amalgamated with the Preston & Wigan Railway in 1834.

The enlarged company survived until 1888, but its independent existence was short. While this amalgamation was another early demonstration that competition tended to resolve itself in combination, the North Union's strategic position astride the routes from Euston and Manchester to the north was too important for its southern neighbours to ignore in the competitive atmosphere of the mid-1840s. The L&M directors were already considering absorbing the Bolton & Leigh Railway into their undertaking and amalgamation with the North Union was an obvious further step. By November 1844 terms had been agreed for the consolidation of capital at the rate of £75 L&M stock for each £100 'A' share, and £45 for each 'B' share. The L&M therefore included the west curve at Parkside in the plans deposited for its forthcoming Bill in expectation that the two companies amalgamate during 1845.

By then a further factor had entered into the equation. The GJR, conscious that its indirect approach to Liverpool left it vulnerable to competing lines, had previously considered reverting to a more direct route across the Mersey and in August 1844 began discussions with the L&M about the terms on which the portion of the latter's line between Huyton and Liverpool might either be transferred to the GJR or made joint property. These discussions quickly turned instead to whether the GJR should become a partner in the amalgamation that the L&M was already negotiating with its Lancashire feeders and agreement was soon reached on the basis of an equal ranking of GJR and L&M £100 shares, with a further issue of £25 shares to Grand Junction proprietors to reflect the slightly higher dividend and better stock market price of their company. A Bill was therefore prepared for the amalgamation of the GJR, L&M, North Union, and the two Leigh companies. The B&L directors had previously agreed that their company's £100 shares would be consolidated at £46, and they and the K&L directors then obligingly simplified subsequent arrangements by agreeing an outright purchase of the Kenyon line by the B&L.

However, some North Union shareholders had reservations about the enlarged amalgamation proposals, since other routes to the south were by then in prospect and they saw no advantage in tying their line's future solely to that of the GJR. There was also a feeling that the scheme was now dominated by arrangements between the two largest partners and that insufficient attention had been paid to North Union interests. Accordingly, when the latter company held a general meeting on 4 June 1845, its shareholders overwhelmingly rejected the terms of the amalgamation, so the North Union was not included in the Act of 1 July 1845 which created a larger Grand Junction Railway. The meeting did however endorse the Bill for a short branch to the Ribble at Preston, to be made jointly with Preston Corporation; this was duly authorised and the line was opened on 16 July 1846.

This reluctance to amalgamate quickly paid off: the Manchester & Leeds Railway was already looking north and west of Manchester and had begun negotiations with the MB&B in 1844. The prospect of a connection at Bolton with so substantial an undertaking as the M&L gave the North Union a strong bargaining position, and in August 1845 its directors made approaches to both the GJR and M&L, offering to lease their line to either or both companies. Since neither could afford to allow the other to gain undisputed control of access to Preston, on 16 September the GJR and M&L jointly agreed to lease the North Union with effect from 1 January 1846; parliamentary authorisation was obtained on 27 July 1846, after the LNWR had been formed. Under the terms of the lease North Union 'A' shareholders were guaranteed a dividend of 10% in perpetuity, and 'B' shareholders 7½%, with the costs being divided 60:34 between the GJR and M&L. The line between Parkside and Euxton was to be worked by the GJR, with the M&L taking the Bolton-Euxton portion; beyond Euxton the line was to be worked jointly. A joint committee was established to deal with the financial arrangements and to manage the section between Euxton and Preston: its costs were also to be shared 60:34 and the rolling stock was divided between the lessees in the same proportion. With the exception of the section north of Euxton, this effectively separated the North Union into its component portions, but the company's shareholders had

been able to secure a guarantee on far better terms than had been available either under independent ownership or through the proposed amalgamation. It is not surprising, therefore, that the agreement left both lessees with a deficit in its early years.

* * *

The 1845 amalgamation with the L&M and the B&L, and the joint lease of the North Union, defined the final extent of the GJR's network as it passed into the LNWR. Parts of the Lancashire system, of course, remained outwith its control: the St Helens Railway and L&PJ had both chosen to unite with rival canals, while besides the M&L and its dependencies (soon to be consolidated as the Lancashire & Yorkshire Railway) the Preston & Wyre and Preston & Longridge remained independent, although the M&L had taken advantage of its secure access to Preston to obtain powers in 1846 to absorb the P&W. Further developments were, however, to affect the status of the lines beyond the Ribble, and in fact the L&PJ was already disentangling itself from its ties with the Lancaster Canal.

The Liverpool-Manchester line had given an early stimulus to railway expansion and competition in its area, and thus shaped the eventual GJR system. By the mid-1830s similar influences were already at work to the south of Manchester and the Mersey, where they resulted in another extension of GJR mileage and were responsible for the emergence of the third constituent company of the LNWR, the Manchester & Birmingham Railway. In addition, these pressures played an important part in establishing the inter-company dynamics that were to lead eventually to the 1846 amalgamation.

Ironically, it was one of the GJR's initial strengths that encouraged the development of competition within its territory. The decision to aim for Warrington and thence to a junction at the virtual mid-point of the L&M line not only saved the expense of the more direct approach to Liverpool that had originally been planned, but also entitled Moss and his colleagues to claim, quite legitimately, that their company would serve Manchester equally well. Since other schemes were already being proposed in the early 1830s for links south from Manchester these were material arguments. They enabled the GJR to offer a prospectus for a single route which would consolidate the trunk traffic of the two great Lancashire cities and yet would require the minimum amount of new construction, important considerations at a stage when railways were relatively untried and when political and financial uncertainty made it difficult to raise funds for major new projects. However, within less than three years of the company's authorisation in 1833 circumstances had changed significantly: a developing economic boom and the growing technical and promotional confidence of railway projectors made the GJR's indirect routes to both Liverpool and Manchester obvious competitive targets. Even before its completion, therefore, the GJR was having to fight defensive battles on two fronts.

On the west, the Wirral peninsula provided an alternative approach to the Mersey estuary which had previously been of interest to railway promoters. By 1836 two rival schemes were in the field for lines between Chester and Birkenhead, one engineered by James Walker and the other by George Stephenson. After a parliamentary contest in 1837 the Chester & Birkenhead Railway was authorised on the basis of Stephenson's plans, but with the addition of branches to safeguard the interests of various ferries which would have been served by the defeated project. Under the supervision of John Dixon, Stephenson's resident engineer, contracts were let in 1838, but progress was slow in the more difficult financial circumstances of the late 1830s and it was not until 23 September 1840 that the line was opened between Chester and Grange Lane, Birkenhead. A short extension to Monk's Ferry was opened on 23 October 1844.

The Chester & Birkenhead was planned and initially built in close co-operation with the Chester & Crewe Railway, which was authorised on 30 June 1837 to build a 20½-mile line from Brook Street in Chester to the GJR at Crewe. This too was a Stephenson line, with Dixon in immediate charge. In 1838 Dixon transferred his assistant on the Birkenhead scheme, Murray Gladstone, to the Crewe line, and the connections between the two companies were further demonstrated by their adoption of joint specifications and orders for locomotives and rolling stock. However, although the GJR opposed the Birkenhead Bills, depositing plans for a line via Fiddler's Ferry to Huyton early in 1837 to establish its parliamentary *locus standi*, it did not seek to hinder the progress of the Chester & Crewe. In a shrewd move the GJR board opened negotiations with the

Chester company in 1839 and terms for its absorption were agreed in September of that year. These were ratified by an Act of 19 May 1840, which incorporated the Chester & Crewe within the larger undertaking from 1 July 1840. C&C shareholders received one £25 GJR share for each of their £50 shares – an indication of the financial difficulties faced by their company – and their chairman, John Uniacke, joined the GJR board, although he resigned in 1841. Murray Gladstone continued as resident engineer, but after some friction Locke was put in overall charge. He discovered to his alarm that the Chester line, in common with several other contemporary railways, was being laid out to a 4' 9" gauge, and on 16 June 1841 the board instructed him to ensure that any sections not yet built, and all points and crossings, conformed to the 4' 8½" standard.

The line between Chester and Crewe was opened on 1 October 1840, thus completing the through connection with Birkenhead. By obtaining ownership of a portion of the route the GJR had thus succeeded in minimising the threat to its Liverpool traffic, and also secured an approach to north Wales. While the company's directors and their successors later had cause to regret that the section beyond Chester had not also been brought under their control, it appears that the L&M board – always concerned about potential rival routes to the Mersey – was opposed to the GJR's taking a direct interest in a line serving Birkenhead.

In addition to providing a tactical solution to the threat posed by the Birkenhead line, purchase of the C&C gave the GJR an opportunity to resolve another pressing problem. The curves at Newton Junction were just one of the difficulties facing the locomotive department – many of the early engines delivered to the company proved unsatisfactory; the space available at Edge Hill in Liverpool, where the GJR had built its main locomotive shops alongside the L&M establishment, was limited; and Thomas Melling, the company's locomotive foreman, had caused problems because of his abrasive personality. This last problem was the first to be solved: Melling, who also acted in a similar capacity for the L&M, was replaced as GJR locomotive superintendent by William Barber Buddicom on 1 January 1840. Buddicom was appointed on Locke's recommendation, and although his stay with the company was short – he left for the Paris & Rouen Railway at the end of August 1841 – he immediately put in hand a series of modifications and experiments in order to try to improve the reliability of the company's fleet of 'Patentee' type 2-2-2 locomotives. Two outside-cylinder 2-2-2s were purchased from Buddicom's former employer, the Liverpool firm of Forrester & Co, in the summer of 1840 and some existing engines were rebuilt, the start of a gradual process of development which was carried forward by Buddicom's successor, Francis Trevithick, and which enhanced the GJR's design and engineering capabilities to the point where it could confidently undertake its own locomotive production.

Before that stage was reached the decision had been taken to move the workshops from Liverpool, since opportunities for expansion there were limited and the L&M given notice in March 1840 that any additional capital expenditure which it undertook for the GJR would attract interest equivalent to the L&M dividend, rather than the 6% previously charged. The Chester company had purchased some land adjacent to its line at Crewe as early as 1838, and in June 1840, shortly after the passage of the Act authorising its absorption into the GJR, the latter's board had instructed Locke to prepare plans for the removal of the locomotive works from Liverpool to Crewe. The GJR also began to add to the landholding it had acquired with the C&C and proposals for providing carriage and wagon shops on the Crewe site soon followed, together with plans for cottages for the workforce. As building progressed, Crewe, hitherto a scattered country community, quickly developed into one of the earliest railway towns, along with Wolverton and its GWR contemporary, New Swindon. By the autumn of 1843 the first Crewe-built locomotives had been turned out, and the directors celebrated the establishment of the company's new works and town by holding a banquet and ball in the main shops on 2 December.

Although Crewe was created in a rural setting, the development opportunity there arose because it was the point of junction for the Chester line, so the location already had operational advantages. Its convenience was also enhanced by the fact that it was roughly half-way between Birmingham and Liverpool or Manchester, and it certainly offered a more satisfactory location for the railway's main repair shops than the cramped facilities at Liverpool, reached over another company's metals. But when Crewe was selected as the site of the company's principal works it was already potentially more important

as a junction, since another undertaking intended to feed into the GJR there. This was the Manchester & Birmingham Railway, which was the eventual outcome of attempts to outflank the GJR on the east and provide a more direct route to Manchester. However, the M&B's line to Crewe was only part of a complex series of proposals, which were also shaped by the desire of the Potteries for railway communications and by the possibility of shorter routes to London, avoiding Birmingham. Such prospects posed a more substantial threat to GJR interests during their development than the limited local abstraction that might have resulted from the Birkenhead line, and the question of alternative routes between Manchester and the south was one which occupied considerable attention for more than a decade.

The revival of interest in schemes in the area south of Manchester seems to have started in the autumn of 1835. The GJR was itself then assessing the possibility of a branch into the Potteries, while George Stephenson, who had only just ceased to be the company's consulting engineer, was involved in independent surveys for a line from Manchester to Stockport and for a loop line into the Potteries from the Grand Junction main line. Another of the company's former engineers, James Rastrick, was engaged by the Manchester & Cheshire Junction Railway to prepare plans for a line from Manchester to Crewe, with branches to Heaton Mersey, Poynton, Congleton, and Macclesfield. On 11 November 1835 the GJR board agreed not to oppose the M&CJ scheme, perhaps in deference to the views of the chairman, John Moss, who generally sought to avoid parliamentary confrontation, but probably also in the knowledge that George Stephenson's Potteries survey had now been developed into a much more ambitious scheme, the Manchester South Union Railway. This company's prospectus proposed a line from Manchester via Stockport, Macclesfield, and the Harecastle valley to join the GJR near Stafford. By the time the M&CJ Bill had been introduced into Parliament in 1836 the MSU had altered its intentions, and instead proposed a route via Macclesfield, the Churnet valley, and Leek to join the Birmingham & Derby Junction Railway at Burton-on-Trent, leaving the Potteries to be served by a branch from Leek to the GJR. Although the MSU had been too late on the scene to introduce a Bill in 1836, it opposed the M&CJ scheme in Parliament, and despite the active support of the GJR the Cheshire Junction scheme was defeated in the House of Lords.

Preparations were immediately begun by all the interested parties for the following session of Parliament. The M&CJ, conscious of the need for support from the Potteries and also anxious to reach agreement with the MSU, expanded its scheme to include a line from Alderley Edge via Stoke to join the GJR close to the junction previously proposed by the MSU. Though there were some negotiations between the two groups of promoters in the autumn of 1836, the MSU publicly retained its commitment to the Churnet valley route while secretly turning its attention back to a line via the Potteries. In addition, Moss and his colleagues instructed Locke to draw up plans for a direct line from Stafford to Rugby via the Trent valley in an attempt to protect the GJR's position.

When plans were deposited in November the extent of the forthcoming contest was revealed. The former M&CJ, which had changed its name to become the Manchester, Cheshire & Staffordshire, had supplemented its planned new route via the Potteries with a direct line from Stone to join the GJR's Trent valley scheme at Rugeley. The Crewe line was retained as a branch, while a further branch from Shelton to the GJR at Madeley would provide a connection northwards from the Potteries to Liverpool. The MSU, for its part, was proposing to retain its earlier route as far as Macclesfield, but the Churnet valley section was relegated to a branch to Leek. Stephenson's intended main line beyond Macclesfield was a reversion to his earlier proposals and was similar to Rastrick's route, running via Harecastle and Stone. Stephenson was also engineer of the newly-authorised Birmingham & Derby Junction Railway, which had decided to enter the fray with a line from Tamworth to Rugby. The MSU therefore proposed to complete an alternative Trent valley line by extending beyond Stone to connect with this scheme at Tamworth; in addition a branch from Armitage to Wichnor was intended to provide a further link with the B&DJ. The GJR was not however to be completely by-passed: its line was about four miles west of the intended MSU route near Stone and Stephenson proposed to throw out spurs to allow through running both northwards and southwards between the two lines.

The GJR board decided not to proceed with a Bill because of irregularities in Locke's plans for a Trent valley line, and while seeking to persuade the MC&S not to carry its line beyond Stone it also supported attempts to encourage the two competing Manchester companies to reach an agreement. However, the MSU promoters were apparently unwilling to compromise, so the two schemes were brought before Parliament in 1837, together with the B&DJ's Tamworth–Rugby proposal. The B&DJ Bill was opposed by the Midland Counties and L&B as well as by the GJR and was quickly rejected on a technicality. As a consequence, the committee on the Bills for the two Manchester schemes agreed on 18 April to restrict consideration to the portions north of Stone, and strongly recommended an agreement between the two companies. The MC&S and MSU accordingly decided to merge their schemes and to leave the ultimate selection of the route to the committee. A military surveyor, Captain Alderson, was already examining the two routes, and he recommended adoption of the MC&S line north of Harecastle and the MSU thence to the GJR at Chebsey (close to the present Norton Bridge junction). He further recommended that part of the northern section of Stephenson's line should be adapted to provide a branch to Macclesfield. The combined scheme was authorised on 30 June 1837 as the Manchester & Birmingham Railway, with a main line from Store Street, Manchester, to Chebsey, with branches to Macclesfield and Crewe.

Initially MC&S interests were in the ascendant in the new company and Rastrick was appointed engineer, with George Buck as resident engineer; he had previously worked on the London & Birmingham line. However, at the beginning of 1838, before construction had started, the M&B approached the GJR about the terms on which it would exchange traffic, clearly intending to use the availability of two authorised junctions as a bargaining counter. Negotiations quickly broke down and the M&B instructed George Stephenson to deposit plans for a Stone–Rugby line; the GJR, concerned that the Manchester company intended to abandon its Crewe branch, countered by preparing plans for a line of its own from Crewe to Alderley. In the meantime Rastrick, affronted by the renewed involvement of George Stephenson, resigned; George Buck was offered the post of engineer, but Robert Stephenson was also engaged as consulting engineer. Plans for the Stone–Rugby line were pushed ahead by the Manchester & Birmingham Extension Railway, a

The 22-arch viaduct at Stockport, designed for the Manchester & Birmingham Railway by John Lowe and George Buck, the company's engineer, and opened in 1842. This view by A F Tait, engraved *circa* 1848, shows how the structure dominated the townscape. (*National Railway Museum/Science & Society Picture Library*)

nominally independent company. However, new parliamentary standing orders had the effect of preventing the introduction of a Bill before 1839, so there was an opportunity for further negotiations. In October 1838 agreement was reached between the M&B and the GJR that the latter would be allowed an equal share in the line to Rugby, but when the M&B directors made it clear that they would not concede an equivalent share in the management of the project the agreement broke down.

Both the GJR and L&B opposed the Stone–Rugby scheme when it was brought before Parliament in 1839, and though the Bill passed the committee stage it eventually ran out of time. Thus chastened, the M&B responded to further overtures from Moss and Lawrence, and an agreement was reached in October 1839 which guaranteed the GJR use of the Trent valley line if it was built. However, the agreement did not commit the GJR to supporting the scheme, while the M&B undertook not to make the extension line

without also building the Crewe branch. In return, the M&B's right to make junctions at Chebsey and Crewe was confirmed, but since it was promised more favourable charges for traffic via Crewe the inference was clear. Within a few days the Manchester company had decided to concentrate on the completion of its line to Crewe.

The loss of the extension Bill was not the only factor which induced the M&B board to reach this compromise. The revival of a competing Churnet valley line was also a possibility, since in one clause of the agreement the GJR undertook not to support such a scheme. More immediately, however, the Manchester company was in financial difficulty: its shares were at a discount of almost 50%; many shareholders were in arrears; there were problems with contractors; and a number of directors had resigned. Although the settlement left the M&B free to pursue its Trent valley ambitions, the priority after 1839 was to generate revenue as quickly as possible and completion of the Crewe section was the only feasible way of doing this. The section between Heaton Norris and a temporary station at Travis Street in Manchester was brought into use on 4 June 1840, generating a heavy short-distance traffic which averaged 1,920 passengers daily in the first 20 weeks of operation.

However, beyond Heaton Norris lay the 22-arch viaduct over the Mersey at Stockport, a major undertaking; this had been let in 1838, but a number of contracts on the Crewe section were not advertised until 1840. The terminal station at Store Street in Manchester was to be shared with the Sheffield, Ashton-under-Lyne & Manchester Railway, but construction did not begin until 1841, so when the Sheffield company commenced a service between Manchester and Godley in November 1841 it too used the temporary accommodation at Travis Street.

On 10 May 1842 Store Street station – later generally known as London Road – was opened, and services were also extended to Sandbach. Completion to Crewe was expected later that year, but negotiations for access to the GJR proved difficult, despite the earlier agreement: they were perhaps not helped by the fact that Captain Cleather had moved to the M&B in September 1841 after his replacement by Huish. At one point the Manchester company was driven to seek the use of the L&B's facilities at Birmingham, with the intention of operating its own services over the GJR. However, after the intervention of the Board of Trade, terms were agreed with the GJR under which the latter would work M&B traffic south of Crewe. On this basis the GJR ceased to operate Manchester portions via Newton Junction from 10 August 1842, when services between Manchester and Birmingham commenced over the direct route via Stockport. The M&B's locomotive stock, mostly 2-2-2s from Robert Stephenson & Co and Sharp Roberts, had been ordered in the expectation that the company would work its own trains to and from Birmingham; the curtailment at Crewe enabled the M&B's newly-appointed locomotive superintendent, John Ramsbottom, to dispose of four engines to the South Eastern Railway. This, however, did little to assist the company's overall financial position, which remained relatively weak: its capital cost was over £60,000 per mile and its revenue in its last full year of operation was less than £170,000. The company managed to pay a dividend of 5% in 1844, rising to 6½% the following year, but it had built less than half of its originally authorised mileage. Part of that, the Macclesfield branch, was only completed on 24 November 1845 after powers had been renewed the previous year, although the section between the junction with the Crewe line and Poynton opened for goods traffic on 9 June 1845, together with a mineral spur to Poynton Colliery.

In 1845 the M&B was authorised to build a branch from Heaton Norris to Guide Bridge, on the Sheffield line, and was also empowered, jointly with the SA&M, to subscribe to a revived proposal for a junction line with the L&M. By then, however, the railway mania was in full swing, and the earlier projects for more direct routes south from Manchester through the Trent and Churnet valleys were being actively canvassed once more. These schemes were to play a significant part in the shifting relationships between the partners in the existing route between Lancashire and Euston; while the M&B was very much the weakest of the three companies, its renewed importance in relation to potential alternative trunk routes ensured that it became an essential component of the 1846 amalgamation. Its short independent life therefore ended much as it had begun, in an atmosphere of competition and rivalry.

CHAPTER TWO

Competition and Amalgamation

The creation of the LNWR was the culmination of a complex series of events, played out against the background of the promotional boom of the mid-1840s. The railway mania itself was of course a powerful influence, encouraging the emergence of competitive main line projects in addition to a plethora of local schemes. However, some elements in this more expansionary framework were evident well before the mania got under way: among the earliest were proposals to extend the trunk network to serve Scotland and Ireland, which had direct implications for the companies which eventually made up the LNWR.

A trigger for this activity was the publication during 1840 and 1841 of four reports by Lieutenant-Colonel Sir Frederick Smith and Professor Peter Barlow, who had been commissioned by the government in 1839 to examine the best means of completing railway communication between London and Dublin, Edinburgh, and Glasgow. So far as the route to Scotland was concerned, it was generally accepted that traffic would be sufficient only for one trunk line, and Smith and Barlow ultimately found in favour of the west coast route, in terms which also effectively supported the renewal of the Trent valley scheme. Nevertheless, they did not rule out an east coast route if early progress could not be made with the recommended line via Carlisle: this had the effect of stimulating George Hudson to press ahead with his coalition of existing and projected railways to complete the route to Newcastle, with Edinburgh as the eventual objective.

West coast proposals, however, were well developed and could be traced back to 1835. The GJR board had given early encouragement to the extension of the trunk line beyond Preston, and Locke undertook a number of surveys for a route into Scotland. One practical consequence, already mentioned, was the authorisation of the Lancaster & Preston Junction Railway in 1837. North of Lancaster, Locke planned to follow the Lune valley, although an alternative line via Kendal enjoyed strong local support. Both of these routes would then climb to a summit in the Westmorland hills before descending to Penrith and Carlisle. Another proposal, first surveyed by George Stephenson in 1837, was to avoid the barrier of the fells by building a railway across Morecambe bay and along the Cumberland coast. This would connect with the Maryport & Carlisle Railway, which was sanctioned in 1837 and opened in stages from 1841 onwards; the final section was completed on 10 February 1845. For the continuation of the trunk line beyond Carlisle, Locke initially favoured the Nithsdale route through Dumfries and Kilmarnock, but in 1837 he adopted the Annandale alternative via Beattock, which offered a direct approach to Edinburgh as well as Glasgow. The competing claims of the Nithsdale and Annandale schemes were to remain a major factor in Scottish railway politics.

The depression of the late 1830s and the establishment of the government inquiry delayed further steps to seek authorisation for a line north from Lancaster, but promoters continued to refine their proposals in the hope of obtaining official endorsement: several variations of the route between Lancaster and Carlisle were suggested to improve the line or to meet local wishes. Smith and Barlow reported first on the London–Dublin part of their remit, but then turned their attention to Anglo-Scottish communications and in their second report decisively rejected the Cumberland coast scheme. They also suggested that there might be potential in combining portions of the two main alternative inland routes north of Lancaster. This was confirmed in a short third report, which recommended a line via Grayrigg, and publication of their final report on 15 March 1841 provided a firm basis for taking forward proposals to link Carlisle with Lancaster via the Kent valley, Tebay, and Penrith. Progress was slow at first because of the financial climate, which also made it important to secure the cheapest possible alignment; however, as Hudson pressed on towards Newcastle, speed of construction became a significant consideration. To avoid the cost and delay of building the summit tunnel that had previously been considered necessary Locke surveyed a route over Shap which required gradients of 1 in 75. As an additional economy he proposed that initially only a single track should be laid.

On this basis, and with subscriptions of £250,000 from the GJR, £100,000 from the L&B, and lesser sums from the North Union, L&PJ, and L&M, preparations were made to bring the Bill for the Lancaster & Carlisle Railway before Parliament in 1844. This received the Royal Assent on 6 June, authorising the building of the 70¼-mile line from the L&PJ to Carlisle. Despite the difficulty of the terrain, the Act provided for a share capital of only £900,000, although it also permitted the raising of an extra £300,000 if double track was adopted. Work started quickly: a single contract for the construction of the entire length had been let jointly to the firms of John Stephenson and Brassey & Mackenzie on a conditional basis before the Act was obtained and the first sod was cut on 18 July 1844. Since Locke himself was heavily engaged in work on the connecting Caledonian Railway, which was authorised in the same session, the building of the L&C was overseen by two resident engineers. One, George Larmer, had carried out the detailed surveys that were the basis of much of the eventual line; he supervised construction north of Shap, while his colleague S B Worthington was responsible for the southern section. In 1845 the company decided to avail itself of its extra financial powers in order to lay double track and in the same year several deviations were authorised. A further Act in 1846 gave powers to issue another £100,000 in shares. Although some loans were raised, these were largely to cushion the demands on shareholders, since the revised share capital of £1·3m proved almost sufficient to meet the costs of building the line.

Initial hopes that construction could be completed in two years were also nearly realised. The first portion was brought into service on 21 September 1846, extending from the L&PJ line south of its Penny Street terminus via a new through station at Lancaster to Kendal Junction, the present Oxenholme. Here the main line was joined by the Kendal & Windermere Railway, authorised in 1845, and the two miles to Kendal were opened at the same time as the L&C's

southern section. The opening ceremony for the remainder of the line to Carlisle took place on 15 December 1846 and public services began two days later, using the Newcastle & Carlisle Railway's London Road station; freight traffic commenced on 21 December. While the L&C was under construction its board had entered into a contract with the GJR for the supply of motive power and rolling stock; the amalgamation had taken place by the time of the

Lowther viaduct on the Lancaster & Carlisle Railway, drawn for the *Illustrated London News* of 19 December 1846. *(David Joy collection)*

opening, so the LNWR took on this responsibility and also worked the Kendal & Windermere line, which was completed to its western terminus on 20 April 1847. However, the L&C operated some coal trains between Carlisle and Shap with its own stock. Passenger services north of Kendal Junction were at first limited to two up and down trains daily, and only one working in each direction conveyed through London carriages. Services were improved once the earthworks were consolidated, but during the early months of operation the through Euston–Carlisle journey took more than 14 hours – slower than the best east coast connection via Gateshead – and entailed overnight travel in either direction.

One complication in the direct route from Euston was the link between Lancaster and Preston. Although, as has been seen, a lease of the L&PJ by the Lancaster Canal had been agreed in 1842, the formal documentation remained incomplete. Accordingly, the railway's directors felt themselves free to negotiate with the L&C, and on December 1844 the L&PJ shareholders approved an agreement to lease their line in perpetuity to the Carlisle under-

The terminus of the Kendal & Windermere Railway soon after its opening in 1847, with Lake Windermere in the background. Apart from the adjacent hotel, the station was at first relatively isolated. *(David Joy collection)*

taking in return for a guaranteed annual rental and a share of surplus profits. However, the L&C's decision in 1845 to enlarge its capital disturbed the basis of the proposed profit-sharing arrangement between the two companies, and there were also concerns that the L&PJ's proportion of future returns might be jeopardised by a projected extension of the Leeds & Bradford Railway's newly-authorised Skipton branch, which would offer an alternative outlet to the south, by-passing Lancaster. The L&PJ directors recommended immediate amalgamation with the L&C in order to secure the position, but a general meeting on 18 February 1846 rejected the proposed agreement in the hope that better terms could be obtained. Most of the directors thereupon resigned, leaving the L&PJ without a legally-constituted board. Although the Lancaster Canal continued to work the local train services, the L&C took the view that the canal company's lease was invalid and gave notice that with effect from 1 July 1846 the line

between Preston and Lancaster should be handed over to it in terms of the 1844 agreement. The canal refused to surrender its interest, so when train services to and from Kendal commenced in September 1846 these were simply worked over L&PJ metals between Preston and Lancaster regardless of formal entitlement and without payment of toll. Although the canal company and the L&PJ shareholders made various attempts to resolve this anomalous situation, decisive steps to put the railway back on to a proper legal footing were only taken after a fatal collision in 1848 between a west coast express and a local train operated under Lancaster Canal auspices. After further skirmishing, during which the L&PJ sought an alliance with the East Lancashire Railway and the L&C threatened to build a separate route from Lancaster to Preston, the line between Preston and Lancaster was vested in the Carlisle company in 1849 in return for an agreed division of profits between the two railways, out of which the L&PJ was to pay £4,875 annually to the Lancaster Canal. The question of back-payment by the L&C for its trains' use of the line from 1846 was eventually settled through arbitration by Robert Stephenson, who awarded £55,551 to the canal company.

* * *

The implementation of proposals for continuing the west coast route northwards was otherwise relatively straightforward. Although the GJR took the lead, the project enjoyed the co-operation of its partners in the existing trunk line, and was a logical extension of their existing interests. Developing a rail and sea link between London and Dublin was inevitably more complex, since the selection of a railway route also hinged upon the choice of harbour. In addition, the union of the parliaments of Great Britain and Ireland in 1801 had invested all matters relating to transport connections between the two countries with considerable political sensitivity.

As with routes to Scotland, several proposals for improving communications with Ireland were afoot in the mid-1830s. Holyhead had already been equipped at public expense as the packet station for the Irish mails, but the Menai strait had to be crossed to reach Anglesey. While the opening of Telford's suspension bridge in 1826 had completed the last major stage in the upgrading of the Holyhead road, the strait remained as a formidable obstacle to any railway to Holyhead. Rival schemes therefore emerged for lines to potential alternative harbours on the Welsh mainland: Porth Dinllaen, on the Lleyn peninsula; New Quay in Cardiganshire; and St George's Bay, where the resort of Llandudno was later to develop.

Commissioners had been appointed at the end of 1836 to consider the provision of railways in Ireland, and they extended their remit across the Irish Sea by engaging Charles Vignoles to report on the various proposals for Welsh harbours and for railway access to them. Although the St George's Bay scheme was vigorously canvassed by its promoters, the Commission's report in 1838 effectively narrowed the choice to Holyhead or Porth Dinllaen. However, the completion that year of the trunk line between Euston and Lancashire resulted in the transfer of the main London–Dublin mails to the route via Liverpool, leaving Holyhead with a reduced role. The postal contract was further modified in June 1841, when Birkenhead replaced Liverpool as the railhead for the Irish packet service.

Despite renewed lobbying by the promoters of rival schemes and extensive official investigation of the alternatives, Holyhead was eventually preferred to Porth Dinllaen both by Smith and Barlow in their 1840 report and by a parliamentary inquiry in 1842 into postal communication with Ireland. Although the difficulties of the terrain were recognised, the railway route along the north coast of Wales was also found to be preferable to the various inland options. These recommendations were supported by further reports to the Admiralty in 1843; one of these reports, by James Walker, was to prove influential in determining the ultimate alignment of the crossing to Anglesey.

Firm proposals for a line to Holyhead had first been made in 1838, when Francis Giles had suggested laying a single track over the Menai suspension bridge, leaving space for road traffic. Since locomotives would have imposed too much stress on Telford's structure, Giles proposed that railway vehicles should be drawn over the bridge by means of a stationary engine. George Stephenson, who was commissioned by the Chester & Crewe Railway to examine the route, similarly recommended making use of the suspension bridge; he suggested that horse haulage should be employed for the crossing. A prospectus for the line was published in 1839 and an abortive attempt was made in 1840 to seek a waiver of parliamentary standing orders to allow the early introduction of a Bill, but there was little subsequent progress. This was hardly surprising in the prevailing financial circumstances; moreover, the GJR's absorption of the C&C deprived the Holyhead project of one source of immediate support. Nevertheless, the company formed to promote the line was kept alive and became closely linked with another scheme surveyed by George Stephenson, the North Wales Mineral Railway, which was intended to link Chester with the Denbighshire coalfield. By 1843 both companies felt confident enough to prepare Bills for the following parliamentary session; however, while the NWMR was a small undertaking which could be viably promoted in its own right, the Chester & Holyhead scheme needed support from connecting lines and assurances that a satisfactory mail contract would be forthcoming. Unfortunately, both of these requirements were to lead to dissension between the project's obvious sponsors, the GJR and L&B.

The GJR board undoubtedly felt that a line to Holyhead lay within its natural territory: it would be reached via the Chester branch and any diversion of Irish traffic from Birkenhead or Liverpool would affect its existing revenue. However, the Chester & Holyhead Railway, despite its title, had its offices in

London and the first company it approached appears to have been the L&B. Glyn broached the subject of a line to Holyhead in a letter to the GJR board at the beginning of September 1843, and after some initial hesitation the latter agreed to share the expense of preliminary notices to allow the introduction of a Bill in 1844. In response to repeated pressure from Glyn, Moss travelled to London in November to discuss the project with his counterpart, where he discovered not only that L&B directors were already deeply involved in negotiations with the C&H company but also that they were insistent that it should share in joint arrangements to take the project forward. The GJR directors had envisaged that participation would be restricted to the two existing trunk undertakings, so when Moss reported back to his colleagues they minuted their disappointment and argued strongly that the L&B should reconsider the involvement of the C&H promoters. In the face of the Euston board's refusal to change its attitude, a GJR delegation reluctantly agreed on 14 December 1843 that their company should take a one-third share in the Holyhead scheme, with the proviso that the engineers of the L&B and GJR should jointly examine the projected route.

One reason why the GJR board was prevailed upon to accept the inclusion of C&H interests was that the latter were already in touch with the government about the terms of a mail contract. While the question of the engineers' report was still outstanding, the chairmen of the three railway companies met the prime minister, Sir Robert Peel, and some of his cabinet colleagues on 10 January 1844. The C&H promoters had previously argued that a Post Office contract worth £80,000 per annum would be necessary to justify building a line to Holyhead, but prior to the meeting the railway representatives agreed to reduce their requirement to £60,000. However, when this proposal was put to Peel, he demurred, stating that a cheaper offer had been received and suggesting that the line could be built as an atmospheric railway. In the light of Walker's November 1843 report, the prime minister also effectively ruled out use of the Menai suspension bridge. Next day the railway representatives, with Moss apparently dissenting, wrote to offer a reduced contract price of £40,000 provided that a separate bridge was not required; however, they expressed concern that this amount would not provide an adequate return.

No firm response was received to this proposition and there matters rested on 31 January 1844 when the GJR directors were asked by the C&H secretary to confirm that their company would subscribe a third of the new undertaking's £2·1m capital. The GJR board minuted its refusal to do this on the existing basis but indicated a willingness to co-operate in a cheaper inland route, apparently via Mold. The C&H's reply extended the time allowed to the GJR to take up shares although reducing the proportion available; by the same post, however, Moss received a separate letter informing him that the C&H intended to purchase the Chester & Birkenhead Railway for £500,000. This development was the last straw for the GJR board, which resolved on 8 February to take no part in the Holyhead undertaking, and explained the reasons in a special circular to shareholders.

The C&H project went ahead without the participation of the GJR, the L&B instead taking £1m of the capital, and was successful in gaining its Act on 4 July 1844, after the deletion of the contentious Menai bridge section. Robert Stephenson had become chief engineer after the L&B increased its interest in the company and his plan for an alternative crossing of the Menai strait at the Britannia rock was approved the following year. In the same session of Parliament two competing schemes to serve Irish traffic were also authorised: one was the North Wales Railway, which proposed to revive the Porth Dinllaen project by building a line from that point to the C&H near Bangor; the other was the GWR-backed South Wales Railway, which was authorised to build a line to Fishguard. Neither company attained its objective: although the SWR eventually got as far as Milford Haven, its northern counterpart was abandoned altogether. The latter's near namesake, the North Wales Mineral Railway, was more successful: its line from Saltney to Wrexham was authorised in 1844 and in the following year powers were obtained for an extension to Ruabon. The entire route between Ruabon and the junction with the C&H at Saltney was opened on 4 November 1846 by the Shrewsbury & Chester Railway, which had been formed when the NWMR amalgamated with the Shrewsbury, Oswestry & Chester Junction Railway earlier that year. The section of the C&H as far as Saltney junction was opened at the same time as the line from Ruabon in order to give S&C trains access to Chester; however, completion of the remainder of the route to Holyhead was to prove a protracted process, which perhaps justified some of the GJR board's early reservations.

* * *

The dispute over the C&H marked the first real crisis in relations between the GJR and L&B, and although the episode was concluded with outward expressions of goodwill it reflected a growing divergence in the attitudes of the two companies. Some differences of approach had always been evident and were reflected, for example, in the difficulties about reaching agreement over station facilities at Birmingham or in relatively trivial disputes about connecting services or through bookings. More fundamentally, the L&B's freight policy created major problems for the GJR, which contended that its southern partner's reliance on carriers made charges unnecessarily high and prevented the development of through traffic. One result was that the Manchester & Leeds Railway was able to undercut railway rates between Lancashire and London via Birmingham by conveying goods across the Pennines and making use of shipping services between Hull and London.

Such disputes over operational matters were a manifestation of a deeper tension between the interests of the two undertakings. While the GJR had a valuable domestic traffic between Lancashire and the midlands, and was developing the trunk route northwards, it was entirely dependent on the L&B for access to London. By contrast, although the GJR remained the most important of the L&B's connections, from 1839 it was just one of several feeders to the Euston line. In particular, the lines northwards through Derby offered considerable potential, and Glyn gave early support to George Hudson in his efforts to extend his railway empire. Hudson (whose York Union Bank used Glyn's banking firm as its London agent) also joined the board of the Manchester & Birmingham Railway in 1842, shortly after David Waddington, with whom he became closely associated. While Hudson does not appear to have taken an active part in the M&B's affairs, Waddington, who was elected deputy chairman in December 1842 and was subsequently chairman for a while, played an important role as events developed in 1844 and 1845.

In addition to the existing contacts between Glyn and Hudson, their railways shared a common interest in opposing a direct London–York line, for which proposals began to emerge in 1844, while the Midland's acquisition of the Birmingham–Bristol route in 1845 extended it into territory west of the L&B main line which was already disputed with the GWR. The L&B thus became involved in a complex pattern of inter-company relationships which had little positive bearing on the GJR and indeed might work against it.

Despite the emerging strains in its dealings with the L&B, the GJR seems to have made every effort to compromise, a point which deserves emphasis. John Moss in particular always sought to avoid confrontation, and his hand was probably behind a paragraph in the circular to the company's shareholders in February 1844 about the Chester & Holyhead situation. Endorsing a recent statement by Glyn that the interests of the GJR and L&B were closely identified, it gave reciprocal assurances that the GJR would not impede the C&H but would offer it every assistance. Within a matter of weeks, however, such mutual expressions of good intent were found to have been misplaced.

The starting point for the renewed difficulties was the question of the Trent Valley Railway, which had been revived for the 1844 session. Late in February 1844 Moss suggested that the GJR and M&B should join in making this line and then wrote to Glyn proposing that the L&B should also participate. In this case it was the London company which expressed initial reluctance, but in April Glyn indicated that the L&B had changed its position and now felt that a line through the Trent valley should be made. However, when Moss and his deputy began negotiations, they discovered that once again the L&B had already entered into arrangements with the other parties involved. Although the GJR was prepared to accept the suggested terms – a third of the shares in the new undertaking for the TVR proprietors, with the balance divided equally between the GJR, L&B and M&B – relations between the Liverpool and Euston boardrooms clearly had not been helped.

The issue that brought matters to a head, however, was the question of rail access to Shrewsbury. Locke had surveyed a branch to the town as early as 1838 on behalf of the GJR, but no progress was made, and when local promoters sought assistance in November 1843 they were told that the company was not then in a position to help. Nevertheless, possibly as a consequence of their experience with the Holyhead scheme, the GJR directors decided to take the initiative early in 1844 by instructing Locke to prepare surveys for a line from Shrewsbury to Stafford, with an extension from Stafford to the Birmingham & Derby line at Alrewas. He was in addition asked to survey a branch from the existing main line at Madeley to serve the Potteries. A line from Shrewsbury to Penkridge was also considered, but it was felt that Stafford would be a preferable junction because of the potentially shorter route to London via the Trent valley. This may, in the event, have been a tactical error, though shares in the Shrewsbury–Stafford project, which was floated as a separate company, were soon fully subscribed.

The GJR board next discovered, through a newspaper advertisement on 13 May 1844, that the L&B was offering to guarantee a rival Birmingham–Shrewsbury line. Glyn claimed later that this had been necessary to prevent the scheme's promoters looking to the GWR for support, but, as the contemporary railway press pointed out, that company was then remote from Birmingham. The GJR directors, after adjourning for a day to consider the position, decided that the L&B action could only be interpreted as hostile, and appointed a committee with full powers to take any action necessary to protect their company's interests, including seeking a new outlet to London. They were already aware of one possible alternative route south, since the promoters of an Oxford–Wolverhampton line had approached the GJR in April. There is no direct record of the activities of this special committee, but secondary sources suggest that it gave Locke approval to act as engineer for the London & York Railway, which would of course be inimical to L&B and Midland interests.

At this stage the L&B board had second thoughts, and in a letter dated 23 May 1844 Glyn proposed that the two companies should pool their interests by means of a profit-sharing agreement. Moss replied that if the L&B would withdraw from its commitment to the Shrewsbury & Birmingham Railway the GJR would be ready to enter into an alliance. Discussions and correspondence continued, and on 3 July deputations from the two boards reached a satisfactory agreement. Birmingham was defined as the boundary of each company's territory, though the L&B was to be free to pursue its interests in the Birkenhead and Holyhead lines and the GJR undertook not to compete against the Holyhead line for Irish traffic. The L&B

agreed to cease its support for the Shrewsbury & Birmingham Railway; instead, the GJR undertook to promote a line from Shrewsbury to Wolverhampton, offering half the capital to S&B shareholders. It was further agreed that the Trent Valley Railway – which had failed to secure authorisation in 1844 – should be taken forward jointly on the previous terms. The two boards also decided to establish a joint subcommittee to deal with charges for through traffic.

Matters therefore appeared to have reached a satisfactory conclusion, leaving the GJR board free to concentrate on its discussions with its Lancashire partners. Although there was difficulty with the S&B promoters, who refused to accept the loss of the Birmingham–Wolverhampton section, they were given no overt backing by the L&B and were left to float their scheme independently. However, other promotional activity for the 1845 parliamentary session was to pose a more substantial threat to the agreement, for in addition to the London & York project – from which Locke withdrew in September 1844 – there were two GWR-supported proposals for broad-gauge lines into the midlands, the Oxford, Worcester & Wolverhampton Railway and the Oxford & Rugby Railway. Moreover, besides the revived Trent valley scheme, plans for a line through the Churnet valley emerged once again, offering a direct route south from Manchester via Leek and Uttoxeter. The situation in the Manchester area was further complicated by proposals in the autumn of 1844 for the M&B to lease the Sheffield, Ashton-under-Lyne & Manchester company jointly with the new Midland Railway. This in turn led the GJR, already concerned that the Midland might become a competitor for its Lancashire traffic, to be cautious about including the M&B in discussions with the L&B about through charges.

In response to renewed interest in railways to serve the Potteries, the GJR replaced its scheme for a branch from Madeley with a line from Basford to Stoke, where it would join a projected TVR branch from Stafford and thus form a loop. In answer to broad-gauge schemes in the west midlands, the L&B developed plans for a line from Tring to Worcester and Wolverhampton, with branches from Bicester to Oxford and from near Banbury to Rugby. This staked its claim to the areas the GWR was seeking to enter and also revived its earlier ambitions to strike westwards from Tring. But while the intended extension beyond Worcester to Wolverhampton may have been a marginal breach of the L&B's earlier agreement with the GJR, its further dealings with the Churnet Valley Railway and M&B became a much more serious matter. Once again the L&B ignored previous understandings in order to pursue policies closely associated with other interests, and on this occasion its disregard of the GJR was so blatant that it is difficult to avoid the conclusion that Euston was seeking to free itself of any dependence on its northern partner.

The full extent of the breakdown of the July 1844 agreement only became apparent at the L&B's general meeting on 12 February 1845, when Glyn announced that terms had been concluded for amalgamation with the M&B, Trent Valley, and Churnet Valley companies. It was proposed that the M&B should amalgamate with the L&B in 1848, on the basis of the two companies' share prices on 6 February 1845, giving M&B proprietors the equivalent of £25 10s of L&B stock for each £40 share. In the interim the Manchester company's shareholders would receive a guaranteed dividend of 5%, together with a half share in any surplus profits. The TVR would be leased in perpetuity from its completion, at a rental that would provide a dividend equal to that paid on L&B shares, while the CVR shareholders were offered amalgamation five years after their line's opening, or earlier if wished, on 'fair and equitable terms'. This arrangement effectively gave the L&B the prospect of its own route to Manchester, while the revival of the Shrewsbury & Birmingham scheme would bring it within striking distance of Chester and the connections to Birkenhead and Holyhead. Further evidence that the L&B was positioning itself for competition was provided by the report to the same meeting that more powerful locomotives would be ordered to enable mineral traffic to be carried at low rates. The amalgamation proposals were endorsed at the M&B meeting on 28 February, and though some shareholders argued that better terms could have been obtained it was pointed out that without such an agreement their line would be exposed to competition from the Churnet Valley Railway.

Not unexpectedly, the GJR reacted immediately and strongly, protesting formally to the L&B and serving notice on the M&B that the existing terms for exchanging traffic at Crewe would be replaced by strict mileage rates from 1 May. Coincidentally, the three companies jointly inaugurated improved through express services on the latter date, offering journey times of around $6\frac{1}{4}$ hours between Euston and Liverpool and about $5\frac{3}{4}$ hours on the Manchester route, together with reduced fares. This working co-operation did not, however, deflect the GJR from mounting a vigorous campaign which ultimately carried the day.

The circumstances in which railway legislation was handled in 1845 also affected events. Besides having to deal with an extraordinary weight of business as a result of the promotional boom, Parliament was also adjusting to an extension in the powers of the Railway Department of the Board of Trade and to changes in its own procedures. In addition, the gauge issue was becoming a major concern. Under the new arrangements the Department carried out a prior appraisal of projects and made recommendations upon them, while railway Bills were grouped on an area basis in Parliament so that competing schemes could be assessed together at the committee stage.

Initially the prospects for the new L&B confederation looked promising. The Railway Department had reported favourably on the Trent and Churnet Valley Bills, though proposing that consideration of the TVR's Potteries branch should be deferred, a recommendation which also affected the GJR's proposed link from Basford. The Tring schemes were also preferred to the Oxford & Rugby and Oxford, Worcester & Wolverhampton proposals, the Department expressing particular concern at the implications of extending the broad gauge northwards. However, Parliament was not always disposed to agree with the recommendations that were offered to it and as the session progressed the L&B strategy ran into increasing difficulties. First, the CVR Bill was rejected for non-compliance with standing orders, then, after a vigorous campaign by the GJR (which had failed to receive the support of the Railway Department for its own Shrewsbury–Wolverhampton line or the Stafford alternative) the Shrewsbury & Birmingham scheme was also lost on standing orders.

When the proposals for lines to Wolverhampton and Rugby reached committee the GJR showed its hand even more clearly by supporting the GWR-sponsored schemes against those of the L&B. Despite the Railway Department's recommendations, the broad-gauge lines were eventually approved, and indeed the committee report on the OW&W Bill specifically referred to the need to give the GJR an alternative route to the south. Even before the outcome of the parliamentary contest was known, however, the GJR's directors had given a further demonstration of their determination to fight back against the L&B – when the prospectus of the Birmingham & Oxford Junction Railway was issued on 28 April 1845 Moss was listed in the provisional committee, together with three of his colleagues. This was another broad-gauge scheme, and the final stage in the GJR campaign was the issue of a circular dated 11 June which indicated that the company was prepared to consider adding the broad gauge to its own lines.

The seriousness of this proposal has always been debated. Use of standard-gauge stock on the proposed route southwards from Rugby would have been possible at least as far as Oxford, since a clause empowering the Board of Trade to require the provision of mixed gauge had been inserted by the House of Commons. Furthermore, in 1846 the GWR confirmed its willingness to extend such facilities from Oxford to Basingstoke via Reading, so it seems unlikely that it would have refused to continue mixed gauge to Paddington if this had been the price of securing GJR traffic over its line. It should also be noted that the latter company's circular suggested no more than *adding* the broad gauge, specifically in relation to its potential for higher-speed services. While this may have been feasible, continued standard-gauge operation would have been essential and was clearly part of the GJR's wider strategy – it successfully sought statutory running powers over the Trent Valley Railway, in which it remained a major shareholder. But while it is probable that the announcement about the broad gauge was primarily a further ploy in a highly-charged political contest, it added to the cumulative case for the broad-gauge lines at a critical stage in the parliamentary process. Charles Russell, the GWR chairman, later made suggestions of bad faith, but his company was also playing for high stakes, with the Midland having gained access to Bristol and the future of the broad gauge itself under serious threat. Despite the ultimate outcome, the support of the GJR in 1845 enabled the GWR to obtain two routes into the west midlands: though Paddington subsequently implied that the Birmingham & Oxford Junction (which was authorised in 1846) owed its origins entirely to the GJR, Russell himself served on its initial provisional committee alongside Moss and

the GWR made great efforts to secure this line. In contrast, the Oxford & Rugby was cut short once circumstances had changed, so the vital role that was claimed for this scheme was limited to its contribution to the parliamentary events of 1845.

The O&R and OW&W Acts received the Royal Assent on 4 August 1845, enabling the GJR, rather than the L&B, to emerge from the parliamentary session with its strategy largely intact. Furthermore, other elements within the Euston coalition were already beginning to waver. The Chester & Birkenhead's shareholders had repudiated the agreement with the Holyhead company on 29 April and this was followed by overtures to the GJR. Even the M&B proprietors, who probably had most to gain from the existing alliance, began to grow restive: a stormy general meeting on 5 September forced the directors to seek better terms from the L&B. Meanwhile, the latter had acknowledged the realities of the situation by resuming discussions with the GJR (which by then included the Liverpool & Manchester and Bolton & Leigh) and special meetings of the two trunk companies on 7 November 1845 confirmed terms for amalgamation which had previously been agreed by their boards. The L&B meeting also approved a revised agreement with the M&B which came into effect on 1 February 1846 and so formed part of the wider amalgamation scheme. With these agreements in place, earlier disputes were quickly forgotten: joint meetings of the GJR and L&B boards were held from 13 December onwards, and consolidated accounts were prepared for the second half of 1845 and the first half of 1846 even though the amalgamation Act was not obtained until 16 July that year.

Once the amalgamation had been negotiated it was widely acknowledged as logical and appropriate; the difficulty in finally taking this step probably owed much to the existing financial success of the two principal protagonists. On the one hand the L&B was reluctant to accept agreements which curtailed its opportunities for developing traffic and expanding its territory; on the other the GJR, already affected by the intrusion of the M&B, was unwilling to admit other parties to what it regarded as a natural sharing of interests with the L&B. While causes and motives were complex and probably can never be established retrospectively in sufficient detail, some of the events leading up to the amalgamation seem to confirm the underlying strength of the GJR's position – which was recognised by many contemporary commentators – and also to suggest that a major factor in the intensity of the dispute in 1845 was the L&B directors' repeated undermining of the compromises that their GJR colleagues had been prepared to accept. Equally, however, Moss's retiral in August 1845 removed one of the individuals most directly involved in the disagreements between the two companies.

Because of the subsequent impact of decisions that were taken at the height of the dispute, the ultimate price of resolving these difficulties was heavy. However, the outcome was a combined system whose alignment along an axis between London and Lancashire gave it an underlying strength and coherence and provided an effective basis for subsequent expansion. The union of the interests of the L&B, GJR, and M&B was the essential first step towards this later development, creating a geographical focus and identity for the amalgamated company which its chosen name aptly defined. While the LNWR's hold on its main territory was never as complete as that of some other railways, the complementarity both of its network and of the areas which it served provided a firm base that amply justified the case for the amalgamation and demonstrated over time that, despite the importance of its individual constituents, the united undertaking was very much more than the sum of its parts.

* * *

The Act incorporating the LNWR provided that the new company should have a combined share capital of £17,242,310, with borrowing powers of £5,747,000. Of the equity, £8,653,750 was allotted to former L&B proprietors, £2,800,000 to the M&B, and £5,788,560 to the GJR. This last allocation included a nominal addition of £964,702 10s, effectively valuing GJR stock at 25% more than the L&B equivalent. Special provisions were made for share issues that were not fully called, and the Act also stipulated that ex-M&B shareholders should at first receive a guaranteed dividend of 8% on the paid-up portion of their capital, rising to 9% in 1847. Thereafter this capital was to rank with the rest of the stock.

The Act specified that there should be a central board of directors, with eighteen members at first. One place was allocated to the Duke of Sutherland's

George Carr Glyn, the first chairman of the London & North Western Railway.

nominee – at this stage George Loch MP – and the remainder of the directorate was drawn from the constituent undertakings: eight from the L&B, six from the GJR, and three from the M&B. This board appointed George Carr Glyn, then aged 49, as its first chairman, with Charles Lawrence as his deputy. The Act also required the LNWR to maintain three local committees until 1851, made up of the directors of the former companies. With the exception of Mark Huish, who was appointed as general manager in October 1846 with an 'all-line' responsibility and a salary of £2,000 per annum, the management structure was similarly built up on a divisional basis, although the two northern constituents were combined for some functions. Richard Creed and Henry Booth served as joint secretaries, based respectively at Euston and at Liverpool; Creed retired in September 1848, and was appointed to the London committee before holding office for a short period in the 1850s as a full director alongside his former colleague, Moorsom. His replacement as secretary was Charles Stewart, who had commenced a somewhat unorthodox career by running away to sea; however, he joined the company on the recommendation of Sir Charles Trevelyan, the founder of the modern civil service.

There were also two superintendents, whose responsibilities were divided on a geographical basis. Captain Bruyeres continued at Euston, while Huish's former assistant, Richard S Norris, was given the oversight of the northern divisions. Four goods managers were appointed: Samuel Salt at Manchester, Samuel Eborall at Birmingham, T C Mills at Camden, and Braithwaite Poole at Liverpool. The latter acted as senior manager and represented the company's goods interests at the Railway Clearing House. The three locomotive establishments, at Wolverton, Crewe, and Longsight, were maintained under their respective superintendents, Edward Bury, Francis Trevithick, and John Ramsbottom. Bury stood down in 1847 and was replaced by James McConnell, who had been the locomotive superintendent of the Birmingham & Gloucester Railway. As a consequence the various sections of the LNWR retained distinctive locomotive policies, although engines were transferred between divisions to meet particular needs: the L&B had borrowed a goods locomotive from the M&B even before the amalgamation.

The consulting engineers inherited from the two main constituents, Robert Stephenson and Joseph Locke, retained their respective responsibilities for new works. Though most of these were in Stephenson's division, Locke maintained an active involvement with the LNWR and was a frequent and sometimes critical contributor at general meetings until his death in 1860, less than a year after his colleague and fellow MP Robert Stephenson. Three resident engineers supervised ways and works on the existing lines, one of them Norris, who combined these duties with his northern divisional superintendency and later also took on responsibility for the North Union Railway. Robert B Dockray supervised the southern division, while Henry Woodhouse was responsible for the north-eastern division.

The LNWR's initial structure accordingly owed much to its constituents, and in view of the size of the new organisation such a transitional arrangement was inevitable. The task of creating an effective administration for the combined system therefore fell mainly to the central board and to the general manager, who had already demonstrated outstanding ability in his handling of the GJR's affairs. Despite the scale of the undertaking and the difficulties the LNWR soon had to face, the new company quickly established a clear identity under the leadership of Glyn and Huish and began the process of consolidating its separate elements into a more homogeneous structure.

CHAPTER THREE

Testing Times

The LNWR was born into a difficult world. The railway mania had begun to falter as early as the autumn of 1845, when the scale of the total financial demands from new lines that were being proposed at home and abroad began to be appreciated. More ominously, the first signs of the potato famine had already appeared in Ireland, and as the extent of the Irish disaster became clear in 1846 it was to have both political and financial consequences. Peel, who had cut the first sod of the Trent Valley Railway in his Tamworth constituency on 13 November 1845, was forced out of office at the end of the following June after losing the support of most of his own party over the repeal of the corn laws, while the failure of commercial confidence during the autumn of 1846 marked the start of an economic crisis that was to lead to the suspension of the Bank Charter Act in October 1847. Although the collapse of Chartism in 1848 demonstrated that unrest in Britain was only a pale shadow of the revolutionary fervour that was sweeping much of continental Europe, conditions during these years contrasted sharply with the optimism of the railway mania.

The economy began to recover in 1849 and this resurgence was given a visible symbol by the Great Exhibition of 1851, but the renewed prosperity of the early 1850s was overtaken by the Crimean war of 1854–6. Although wartime demand provided a stimulus for some industries, its adverse financial effects were felt in a number of sectors, including railways. The post-war boom proved short-lived and ended in 1857 when a crisis in the American economy triggered a number of bank failures in Britain; the effects of these and the loss of export trade to the USA pushed unemployment briefly back towards the levels of the late 1840s. Recovery up to the end of the decade was slow and uneven and was hardly into its stride when it was further disturbed by the outbreak of the American civil war in 1861.

While there was underlying expansion in the economy – to which the railways themselves contributed – these generally unsettled conditions provided part of the background to the LNWR's early years. The increased role of the government in railway affairs was another element in this background, and was a new phenomenon for those schooled during the pioneering years of railway development. Although the LNWR's core network predated Gladstone's 1844 Act and was therefore exempt from its more sweeping provisions, subsequent additions to its system did not enjoy this privilege. In addition, to secure the passage of the amalgamation Act it had been necessary to include clauses which reduced some of the maximum rates previously available to the LNWR's constituents and which extended the obligation to carry third-class passengers at the 'parliamentary' rate of 1d per mile throughout the undertaking. The LNWR also found itself increasingly subject to general regulation, first through the new Railway Commission, established in 1846, and then by the Board of Trade, which resumed responsibility for railways in 1851. While the main focus at first was on public safety, the growing tendency of both the legislature and the executive to intervene more widely in railway matters was a matter of concern to successive LNWR chairmen and was to have a decisive effect on the company's future in 1854.

Ironically, however, the most serious challenge facing the LNWR sprang from the *laissez-faire* policies that had ultimately prevailed during the railway mania. Perhaps glossing over the part which the London & Birmingham and its partners had themselves played in the activities of these years, Glyn repeatedly warned shareholders of the impact that competing lines and the extension of the system would have on the company's prosperity, and the basis of the problem was already apparent when the LNWR was formed. In 1846 it accounted for almost 13% of the 2,960 miles of railway then open in Great Britain and about 26% of gross railway receipts; in that year

Figure 3.1 – DIVIDENDS OF SOME LEADING RAILWAY COMPANIES, 1846–60
Source: *Bradshaw's Railway Manual*

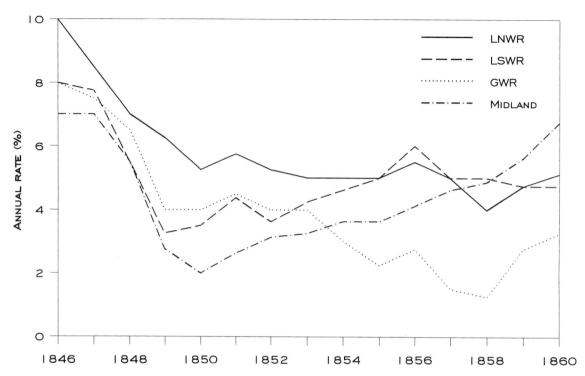

alone, however, a further 3,970 miles were authorised, so the LNWR's predominance clearly could not be sustained. But despite Glyn's foresight, few could have predicted the scale of the impact, or that dividends would reach a nadir of 4% within twelve years of the company's formation. As Figure 3.1 shows, the LNWR was not alone in such difficulties, but this change in its situation was to pose major problems for a company which boasted such an impressive financial pedigree.

* * *

The rapid deterioration of shareholders' returns on their investment in the LNWR was not due to a reduction in the company's revenue: gross receipts held up remarkably well despite the depression, although passenger income did not recover to its 1846 level until 1851, the year of the Great Exhibition. But this decline in passenger earnings was not due to a loss of traffic: apart from a short-term drop in 1848–9, the upward trend in the total number of journeys was sustained. However, the increase was proportionately

less than the growth in route mileage; moreover, because of the lower fares imposed by the amalgamation Act, there was no immediate revenue benefit from the overall expansion in passenger business, though Huish showed his grasp of traffic management by his efforts to pitch special fares at levels which maximised net income. Fortunately, while the level of passenger earnings remained disappointing until 1851, total revenue was sustained by rising goods traffic. Freight charges had also been reduced by the 1846 Act, but the effects of this were outweighed by the vigorous steps that were taken to promote traffic. The most striking of these was the decision to take over from the private carriers on the L&B section in 1847: Chaplin & Horne and Pickfords were instead given contracts for terminal work and cartage, but control of all merchandise traffic rested firmly with the company from then onwards. By 1850 freight was contributing about 39% of total receipts, compared with around 31% in the year of the company's formation.

Some of the additional goods revenue was offset by the costs of the agency agreements with the carriers and an increase in the company's own direct outlays, but Huish and the other officers made strenuous efforts to reduce expenditure, with the encouragement of the board. Locomotive costs per train mile fell significantly between 1847 and 1850, partly as a result of lower fuel costs and partly because of the introduction of more efficient engines. On the southern division, where fuel costs were higher because of remoteness from supplies of coking coal, there was a move towards more powerful 0-6-0 locomotives, which appears to have been reflected in the proportionately greater improvement in fuel efficiency and reduction in goods train running costs in that division. Labour costs were also cut in the drive for savings, and the reduction in footplatemen's wages and prospects in the southern division was sufficient to provoke one of the earliest railway strikes, in August 1848. However, McConnell – who was described by his colleague David Stevenson as 'a strong and determined man of the rough sort' – dismissed the strikers, and kept trains running by importing enginemen from the north and by using his fitters and men borrowed from the Thames steamboats: guards rode on the footplate to assist crews who were unfamiliar with the route. As a result of these measures the strike was defeated after a fortnight, although the men were reinstated through the intervention of George Carr Glyn, who, as MP for Kendal, had found himself drawn into parliamentary discussion of the dispute.

But despite the achievement of a greater net revenue through a combination of higher gross earnings and reduced operating costs, the growth in income was dwarfed by the increase in the company's capital account. In 1846, when the LNWR was formed, the inherited capital account stood at £16·3m. Five years later, at the end of June 1851, total capital expenditure had reached £29·2m, an increase of almost 80%. Though the company had found £9·6m of this through borrowing and was taking advantage of more favourable rates to reduce its interest charges, the available revenue balance for the first half of 1851, £652,392, was some £60,000 less than the total dividends paid for the equivalent period of 1846, when the share capital was much smaller. In addition to the increase in its own capital account, the LNWR was also servicing expenditure by several nominally-separate undertakings through lease payments and guarantees which constituted a prior charge on its own earnings.

Part of the increased burden falling on the company resulted from pre-amalgamation commitments. The first new line opened by the company was the branch from Bletchley to Bedford, authorisation

Crewe in early LNWR days: a drawing of the station by Tait, looking south.

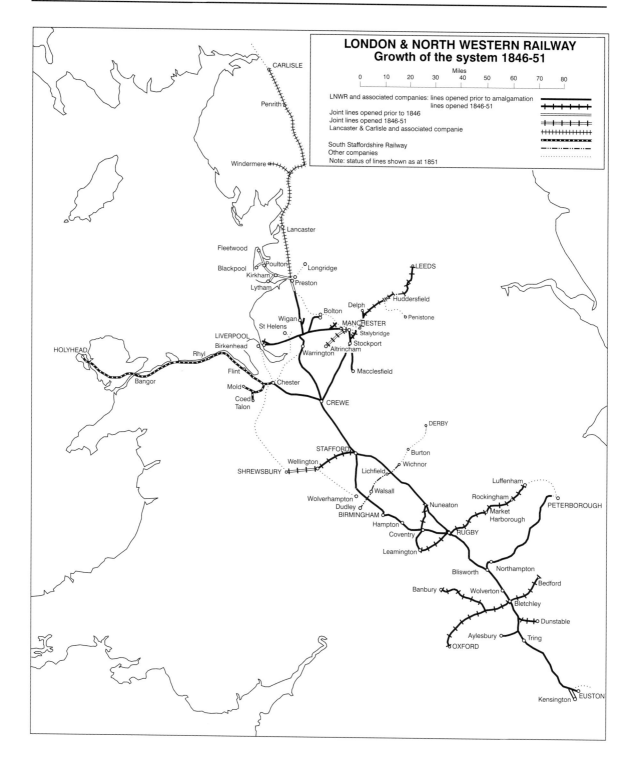

Figure 3.2 – Growth of the LNWR system 1846–51.

for which had been obtained by the Bedfordshire Railway in 1844. However, under the terms of a lease negotiated by the L&B, it was operated from its opening on 17 November 1846 by the LNWR. The west curve at Parkside, built under Liverpool & Manchester powers, was opened on 1 January 1847, and the same year saw the completion of the Trent Valley Railway, which had been acquired outright in 1846. Its opening was delayed by the decision to strengthen the cast-iron bridges on the route after the collapse of the Dee bridge at Chester, but on 15 September goods trains and a limited local passenger service began using the line between Rugby and Stafford. Through expresses took this route from 1 December, reducing the previous distance via Birmingham by 9¼ miles. To coincide with the necessary timetable changes the LNWR adopted Greenwich time throughout its system.

Another undertaking authorised separately in 1845 and absorbed in 1846, a short branch from Leighton Buzzard to Dunstable, was opened on 29 May 1848. The next addition came in 1849, with the opening of the 29-mile line between Stafford and Shrewsbury on 1 June. This particular scheme, though similar to earlier GJR plans, had emerged during the summer of 1845, when an alliance of canal interests in the north-west midlands, with support from the Chester & Holyhead, Manchester & Birmingham, and Trent Valley railways, proposed to adapt canal routes and provide a network of lines linking Crewe with Newtown, Shrewsbury with Stafford and Stone, Wolverhampton with Calveley, and Shrewsbury with Worcester. The Worcester section was omitted when the undertaking was incorporated in 1846 as the Shropshire Union Railways & Canal company, while the Act provided for the last 10½ miles of the line from Stafford to Shrewsbury to be shared with the Shrewsbury & Birmingham Railway, with which its route merged just east of Wellington. The Shropshire Union's wider ambitions soon proved unsustainable, so in 1847 it leased its undertaking to the LNWR and in 1854 obtained powers to abandon its other authorised railway schemes. The financial arrangements between the two companies were complex and were modified by several subsequent Acts, but as a result of the lease the LNWR became responsible for the Shropshire Union's extensive system of canals and connecting tramways as well as for its line between Stafford and Shrewsbury.

The LNWR already had canal interests in the west midlands through an agreement authorised in an 1846 Act. This gave it control of the Birmingham Canal Navigation company's system in return for a guaranteed 6% annual payment and was part of a series of arrangements involving the canal undertaking, the L&B, and the promoters of other railway projects in the area. The Birmingham Canal company and the L&B each subscribed a quarter of the capital for the Birmingham, Wolverhampton & Stour Valley Railway, which was promoted to build a line from Birmingham through Wolverhampton to join the Grand Junction route at Bushbury. In addition, the L&B submitted a Bill of its own for a 1½-mile link from its main line near Curzon Street to connect with the Stour Valley line and planned to locate a new central station for Birmingham on this connecting line. These schemes received the Royal Assent on 3 August, after the amalgamation Act, so the LNWR succeeded to the L&B's powers. A further Act in 1847 authorised it to lease the Stour Valley company.

The LNWR extended its canal responsibilities still further in 1847 through its absorption of the Huddersfield & Manchester Railway. When that company was authorised in 1845 its Act provided for the purchase of the Huddersfield & Manchester Canal and Sir John Ramsden's Canal, both of which were included when the undertaking was leased to the LNWR in 1847. The Leeds, Dewsbury & Manchester Railway, another project authorised in 1845, was leased at the same time, and the two companies were added to the former Manchester & Birmingham section to create an enlarged north-eastern division. These railways, still under construction, made up a shorter route between Manchester and Leeds than the existing line via Rochdale and were therefore an important strategic acquisition. Although running powers over other railways were necessary to complete the LNWR's access to Yorkshire, work had already started on a branch to Guide Bridge which would complement this new cross-Pennine route by giving access from the south.

Construction of the Guide Bridge line had begun in 1846 under the powers obtained by the M&B in 1845. The branch started from a south-facing junction at Heaton Norris, just north of the Stockport viaduct, and ran north-eastwards to Guide Bridge to join the Sheffield, Ashton-under-Lyne & Manchester Railway, which became part of the Manchester,

The joint station at Huddersfield, on the LNWR route from Manchester to Leeds. This photograph was taken after the addition of an island platform and all-over roof in the 1880s, but the classical facade, 416' long, remained substantially unchanged from the line's opening in 1847. *(David Joy collection)*

Sheffield & Lincolnshire Railway in 1847. To reach the Huddersfield line from Guide Bridge it was necessary to rely on the Sheffield company's branch to Stalybridge, completed in 1845, but an alternative connection from Manchester was provided by the Manchester & Leeds's line from Ashton to Stalybridge, opened in 1846. The M&L changed its title to the Lancashire & Yorkshire Railway in 1847, and jointly-owned connections between the L&Y and MS&L lines at Stalybridge were brought into service on 1 July 1849; new joint passenger and goods stations were also opened to replace the two companies' former termini.

The Huddersfield & Manchester line commenced immediately to the east of the MS&L and L&Y passenger station at Stalybridge, striking north-eastwards towards the summit tunnel at Standedge. On the

eastern side of the Pennines, about seven miles beyond the tunnel, the route merged with that of the Huddersfield & Sheffield Junction Railway, authorised in 1845 and absorbed by the then M&L in 1846. Under the H&M Act of 1845 provision was made for the short section between the junction and Huddersfield station to be shared; sole LNWR ownership then resumed as far as the original M&L main line, where connections were made in both directions. L&Y metals were used for $2^{1}/_{2}$ miles from the eastern junction at Heaton Lodge to reach the commencement of the Leeds, Dewsbury & Manchester section at Ravensthorpe.

The M&L had undertaken not to oppose the LNWR's takeover of the LD&M and H&M in return for running powers beyond Huddersfield, and the L&Y inaugurated a passenger service between there and Leeds via Dewsbury on 18 September 1848, terminating at a temporary station at Wellington Street in Leeds. The LNWR opened the Heaton Norris–Guide Bridge and Stalybridge–Huddersfield sections on 1 August 1849 and began working through to Leeds on the same day; its trains to and from

Manchester used the L&Y route between Victoria station and Stalybridge. At the eastern end of the line, a connection from Copley Hill junction to the Midland Railway at Whitehall junction was opened on 1 October 1850, enabling services to use the Midland's Wellington station in Leeds. The connection into the west-facing junction with the L&Y main line at Bradley Wood, north of Huddersfield, was brought into service for goods traffic on 26 November 1850, but passenger trains did not commence until 1 January 1852. These were operated by the L&Y, and though the LNWR used this connection for freight traffic it employed its running powers beyond Bradley Wood only sporadically for passenger services. A further addition was made to the company's Yorkshire mileage with the opening on 1 September 1850 of a short branch from Greenfield to Delph, south-west of Standedge.

The single-track Standedge tunnel, just over three miles long, was slightly longer than Woodhead tunnel on the MS&L, which had previously supplanted Kilsby as the longest railway tunnel in Britain. Morley tunnel, on the Ravensthorpe–Leeds section, which was almost two miles in length, was also longer than Kilsby; from September 1848 until the following August it was thus the longest tunnel open for traffic on the LNWR, although it was then used only by L&Y trains. When Standedge was brought into use on 1 August 1849 Kilsby was further relegated by the opening on the same day of the Victoria tunnel in Liverpool, between Edge Hill and Waterloo goods station. Cable haulage was employed from the outset through this steeply-graded tunnel, which was more than $1\frac{1}{2}$ miles long and had been authorised in 1845 as part of a Liverpool & Manchester scheme to give access to the northern docks. Near the eastern end of the L&M route a $3\frac{1}{2}$-mile line was opened on 2 February 1850 from Patricroft north-eastwards to Molyneaux junction on the East Lancashire Railway, just north of Clifton. This branch had been intended as a counter to the M&L's push westwards to Liverpool from Bury, but after the withdrawal of a short-lived connectional service of ELR passenger trains between Patricroft and Bury in 1850 it was used only for goods traffic.

Apart from a short extension of the M&B's Macclesfield line from its Beech Road terminus to a new station at Hibel Road, which was probably opened on 13 June 1849 when the North Staffordshire

Railway reached that point from the south, the remainder of the new mileage opened between 1846 and 1851 under LNWR ownership or lease was in the southern division. In 1846 the L&B had obtained authorisation in 1846 for a long cross-country branch from Rugby to the Midland Railway's Syston–Peterborough branch. Construction began in 1847, but progress was slow and the single-track line was only opened as far as Market Harborough on 29 April 1850. The section thence to Rockingham was opened on 1 June the same year and the branch was completed to its junction with the Midland at Luffenham on 2 June 1851. A more substantial undertaking was the Coventry & Nuneaton Railway, opened on 2 September 1850. This had been authorised as an L&B branch in 1846, but was reconstituted the following year to allow the scheme to be financed by a local company in return for a 5% guarantee by the LNWR. Besides its potential as a link into the Warwickshire coalfield and with the Trent Valley line, the Nuneaton branch was intended to form part of a through route from Coventry to Leicester and 1848 the LNWR and Midland agreed that the latter should take on responsibility for the connecting Coventry, Nuneaton, Birmingham & Leicester Railway. However, the Midland's shareholders rejected their board's recommendation to purchase this company, which despite its title possessed powers only for the section east of Nuneaton, and after an unsuccessful approach to the LNWR in 1851 the CNB&L's directors allowed the scheme to lapse.

A short extension of the existing branch from Coventry to Leamington was authorised on 27 July 1846 and on 12 August parliamentary approval was received for a further scheme initiated by the L&B, a line from Rugby to connect with the Coventry branch extension at Leamington. The two sections, both single track, were opened together on 1 March 1851, shortly before the completion of another single-track system, the Buckinghamshire Railway. After the unsuccessful attempt to extend westwards from Tring in 1845, a partial substitute was provided by two L&B-inspired companies which were authorised in 1846: the Oxford & Bletchley Junction, and the Buckingham & Brackley Junction. These combined in 1847 to form the Buckinghamshire Railway, and their amalgamation Act also provided for provided for extensions of the Brackley branch northwards to an intended junction with the Oxford & Rugby Railway at Banbury and southwards from Verney Junction to the existing Aylesbury branch. The first section, between Bletchley and Banbury, opened for passengers on 1 May 1850; goods traffic began a fortnight later. The Oxford line was opened as far as Islip on 1 October the same year and extended to Banbury Road, 3½ miles short of the terminus, on 2 December. The junction with the O&R at Banbury was not installed and the Aylesbury extension was abandoned, so completion to Oxford on 20 May 1851 marked the end of construction. Though the Buckinghamshire was a separate company, more than half of its capital was provided by the LNWR, which worked the undertaking from the outset and leased it with effect from 1 July 1851, guaranteeing a 4% dividend to the other shareholders.

There were also additions to the joint interests inherited by the LNWR. The Manchester & Leeds Railway had been authorised in 1846 to absorb the Preston & Wyre Railway, but following the precedent established with the North Union Railway it was agreed to substitute a joint lease, with the L&Y taking a two-thirds share and the LNWR the balance. This took effect in 1847 but did not receive parliamentary approval until 1849, when the LNWR arranged to make retrospective payments to the L&Y. Although the LNWR was the minority partner, it was thus able to secure access to the Fylde coast resorts and to the port of Fleetwood; as with the North Union, however, the lease entailed an initial loss.

A small but important joint undertaking authorised in 1845 was the Manchester South Junction & Altrincham Railway, promoted by the Manchester & Birmingham and Sheffield, Ashton-under-Lyne & Manchester companies, together with Bridgewater Canal interests. This railway's title was self-explanatory: it revived earlier proposals for a southern connection across Manchester by means of a link from the Liverpool line at Ordsall Lane to the M&B just south of the latter's terminus, and also included a branch to Altrincham. The LNWR and MS&L bought out the Bridgewater interest in the MSJ&A in 1847 and thus it was under the two railways' ownership that a service was inaugurated between Oxford Road station in Manchester and Altrincham on 20 July 1849. On 1 August the remainder of the cross-Manchester line was opened, followed on 22 September by a short extension from Altrincham to Bowdon. The LNWR used the link for goods traffic,

but apart from some connectional services the local passenger trains were worked entirely by the MS&L until the 1890s.

Another M&B joint venture had a less promising outcome. This was the Manchester, Buxton, Matlock & Midlands Junction Railway, authorised in 1846 with both M&B and Midland participation. The company ran into difficulties in the post-mania years and built only its southern section, between Rowsley and the Midland main line at Ambergate. This opened on 4 June 1849 and was worked from the outset by the Midland, which in 1852 leased the MBM&MJ jointly with the LNWR. However, the Midland continued as sole operator, so this line remained a somewhat remote outpost of the LNWR's interests.

* * *

The lines described above added over 300 miles, 61 miles of which were joint, to the LNWR's system by the end of 1851. They were, however, only part of the mileage that had been authorised: a parliamentary return in 1854 showed that almost 140 miles for which the LNWR or its constituents had obtained powers between 1845 and 1848 had not been constructed. These included further branches in the southern division, such as the Weedon–Northampton line, authorised in 1846, or the following year's St Albans, Luton, and Dunstable scheme. Several projects in Lancashire and the midlands were also allowed to lapse, including a Huyton–Warrington line authorised in 1846 which would have provided the more direct approach to Liverpool which the GJR had so often considered.

The reason for these abandonments was, of course, the changed financial environment. Even at this early stage of the LNWR's life there were pressures from shareholders for the capital account to be closed altogether, and strong efforts were made to limit further capital expenditure. While the need to provide carriages and wagons for new lines and traffic provided justification for some additional outlays on rolling stock, the construction or purchase of locomotives on capital account was effectively suspended in 1849, since more than forty engines were then in store waiting for lines to open. The extension of the system also provided opportunities for stock to be used more intensively – Glyn was able to tell the general meeting in August 1850 that although the mileage worked had increased by 42% since the company was formed, the locomotive fleet had grown by only 12% and the carriage and wagon stock by 17%.

However, some capital expenditure remained necessary. Powers to enlarge Euston had been obtained in 1846, and this enabled separate platforms to be provided for Midland line traffic. In addition, the scheme included extra headquarters accommodation to meet the needs of the amalgamated company, including a room for general meetings, reached from Hardwick's magnificent Great Hall. Improvements were also carried out at several other stations, including Liverpool Lime Street, but only slow progress was made with the ambitious scheme to create the new central station in Birmingham. Facilities for freight traffic were improved in response to the growth in demand, and relief sidings were provided at various locations – those at the London end of the line enabled the company to postpone quadrupling the track between Watford and Primrose Hill, which had been considered essential in 1847 because of the congestion on the approaches to Camden and Euston.

While the board was able to keep a tight rein on expenditure which was incurred either on the company's own account or through directly-controlled subsidiaries, it was less able to influence some of the other undertakings to which the LNWR or its constituents had committed funds in the mid-1840s. Some of these provided useful feeder lines: the South Staffordshire Railway, for example, to which the LNWR subscribed £131,000, and in which the Midland was also interested, was established in 1847 as an amalgamation of two earlier schemes and built up a valuable local network in and around the black country. The first section, from Walsall to Bescot on the Grand Junction line, was opened on 1 November 1847 for passenger and goods traffic and on 9 April 1849 services were extended beyond Walsall via Lichfield to Wichnor junction on the Midland. The South Staffordshire was to prove to be of more than local significance in LNWR history, for George Potter Neele, who was later to become superintendent of the line at Euston, moved from the Eastern Counties Railway in 1849 to take up the position of chief clerk with the company. When Neele was appointed the southern section of the system, from Pleck junction on the Bescot–Walsall line to Dudley, had not been completed, but he records in his *Reminiscences* that a goods train was worked to Dudley on 1 November 1849 to comply with a provision in the authorising Act that would otherwise have enabled the GWR-sponsored Birmingham, Wolverhampton & Dudley Railway to complete the Dudley end of the route. The southern section, which included an east-to-south curve from the GJR which permitted through working between Birmingham and Dudley, was not however ready for regular goods traffic until 1 March the following year, while passenger services commenced on 1 May. The South Staffordshire initially worked its own trains, but in 1850, after both the LNWR and the Midland had declined to lease the line, a local engineer and entrepreneur, John Robinson McClean, took over responsibility for its operation. In 1852 he in turn subcontracted the LNWR to supply motive power for the line.

Another separate undertaking which was to prove an important adjunct to the LNWR was the East & West India Docks & Birmingham Junction Railway, authorised in 1846 to provide a line from Camden to the West India Docks at Blackwall. The first portion, between Islington and Bow junction on the London & Blackwall Railway, was brought into use on 26 September 1850 for through passenger services between Fenchurch Street and Islington. These were extended from Islington to Camden Town on 7 December, and from 9 June 1851 the junction with the LNWR at Hampstead Road, which had been completed on 15 February, was brought into regular use. The section from Bow to Poplar was opened for coal traffic on 20 October 1851 and the system handled general merchandise from 1 January 1852. The LNWR was always the largest shareholder in this company – which in 1853 changed its name to the North London Railway – and its route across London was to play an important role in the development of freight and local passenger services.

The LNWR's other main investments were in the Scottish trunk line and in the Chester & Holyhead Railway. The Lancaster & Carlisle was the earliest of these ventures, and the LNWR inherited an initial stake of £326,838 in the L&C from its constituents; it subscribed or lent further amounts after 1846, but in 1851 some advances were repaid, leaving the LNWR with a total holding of £350,000. As noted in Chapter Two, the L&C was completed to Carlisle in December 1846; through services between England and Scotland began on 10 September 1847 when the

Carlisle Citadel station. This engraving from the late 1840s, which was based on the architect William Tite's original plan, anticipated the completion of the clock tower, which was subsequently finished to a modified design: the clock was not ordered until 1853. *(David Joy collection)*

Caledonian Railway was opened from Beattock to the new Citadel station in Carlisle, which it owned jointly with the L&C. The latter's trains are believed to have been diverted from their temporary terminus at the Newcastle & Carlisle Railway's London Road station earlier in September 1847, reaching Citadel over a direct approach line from Upperby which had been authorised in 1846 and which crossed the N&C's branch to the Carlisle Canal basin on the level a few chains west of the existing junction between the Lancaster and Newcastle routes.

Proposals for a joint passenger station in Carlisle had first been discussed in 1844 and initially it was hoped that the N&C and the Maryport & Carlisle would also participate in the project. However, mutually acceptable terms could not be agreed with these companies, and when Citadel opened in 1847 parts of the works were still incomplete as a consequence of the delays caused by negotiations and uncertainties over funding. A particular difficulty arose with the M&C, which in December 1844 had built a temporary terminus at Crown Street, near the site proposed for

the joint station. This was reached from an east-facing junction on the N&C's canal branch close to the flat crossing of the L&C's Citadel approach line, which also intersected the Crown Street spur: M&C movements to and from this terminus therefore fouled the main line twice. As the L&C needed land in the area for a goods station it was clearly in its interests to acquire the Crown Street site. However, in 1848 George Hudson briefly extended his control to the N&C and M&C and sought to take advantage of the local situation by demanding a high price for the land. Although the Lancaster company obtained a legal determination in its favour, the M&C refused to give possession, so on 17 March 1849 the L&C simply demolished Crown Street station. Maryport services were then diverted to London Road station, but this still necessitated crossing the main line on the level. Even after the M&C gained access to Citadel in 1851 under a tenancy agreement its trains entered or left the station by setting back over an N&C chord created in 1849 by adapting the foreshortened Crown Street spur. It was not until 8 August 1852 that a connection was opened which gave M&C passenger workings a direct route into Citadel station; however, the flat crossing remained in use for other traffic, and was later to be the scene of a major accident.

The Caledonian Railway was completed to Glasgow and Edinburgh on 15 February 1848 and on

10 March the Post Office transferred the London–Edinburgh mails from the east coast line – which still relied on road connections across the Tyne and the Tweed – to the route via Preston and Carlisle. With the opening north of Beattock, west coast through services were extended to the Scottish cities, with a schedule of about 13 hours from or to Euston. Timings were reduced progressively to 12 hours 10 minutes by July 1848, but were subsequently eased to 12½ hours. Thus the concept fostered initially by the GJR board and Locke in 1835 became a reality, and the LNWR took its place in the first continuous Anglo-Scottish railway route.

However, realisation of this goal was tinged with disquiet at the financial performance of the Caledonian Railway. The Scottish company had burdened itself with expensive land purchases and guarantees to complete its line, and its inability to meet its obligations on its guaranteed and preferred capital quickly became apparent. In October 1849, shortly after the shareholders had appointed a committee of investigation, the possibility that the LNWR might take over the working of its west coast partner was discussed between Glyn and the Caledonian chairman, John James Hope Johnstone, a fellow MP. In addition to any potential operating economies, such an arrangement would have relieved the Caledonian's financial position by releasing the capital tied up in locomotives and rolling stock, since these would have been transferred to the LNWR. The proposal was taken seriously enough to be discussed by deputations from the two boards, but Euston quickly discovered that such a solution would draw it into the Caledonian's internal disputes. Accordingly, while recording that it had been satisfied that the funds made available as a result of such a transaction would be properly applied, and emphasising its desire to assist, the LNWR board concluded with regret on 10 November 1849 that it would not be warranted in entering into the proposed arrangements.

With the closure of this option, and with the failure of a subsequent attempt by the contractor Thomas Brassey to establish a separate company to work the railway, the Caledonian directors were left exposed to the criticisms of the committee of investigation. In February 1850 Hope Johnstone was replaced, along with most of the board, but the new chairman, Captain J E Plunkett, was no more successful in resolving the company's financial disputes and by that autumn

other interested parties were pressing Euston to intervene. Until late in the previous year there had been a contact with the Caledonian board in the person of Robert Fox Maule, MP for Perth, who was both a Caledonian director and a member of the LNWR's London committee; to complete the overlap, he was also a director of the L&C. However, Fox Maule held the office of secretary at war in Lord John Russell's government and at the end of November 1849 he resigned all three railway appointments because of his ministerial duties.

Although the Caledonian declined an offer of LNWR mediation in September 1850, the refusal of the guaranteed and preference shareholders to accept a proposed compromise left the Scottish company in a critical financial situation, so on 1 November its directors seized on the opportunity to renew mutual representation by appointing a member of the LNWR board, the Hon Captain S T Carnegie MP, to fill a vacancy among their numbers. Carnegie's appointment was followed by a letter from Euston offering his services and those of Henry Booth and another LNWR director, William Rotheram, as temporary members of the Caledonian board in order to assist in achieving a settlement of the company's difficulties. The LNWR also undertook to support any arrangements agreed by its nominees, a worthwhile offer in view of the fact that the company held about 7% of the Caledonian's ordinary share capital. The two additional directors were elected on 26 November; while there was some concern in the Scottish press about the extension of English influence over the Caledonian, the LNWR's initiative was welcomed by the *Railway Times* as a means of breaking the impasse. Unfortunately, although the LNWR representatives took an active part in the negotiations with the disaffected shareholders, agreement remained impossible and after reporting back to their parent board the three resigned their temporary directorships at the end of 1850, despite pressure from their Caledonian colleagues to remain. The company's financial problems were eventually resolved in 1851 by the passage of an Act of Parliament which authorised the restructuring of its capital and the adjustment of existing obligations, and the Caledonian paid its first ordinary dividend, the equivalent of an annual rate of ½%, for the second half of that year. The LNWR received £629; its total investment then stood at over £140,000, and although dividends subsequently improved this

hardly represented a good return after such a long gestation.

Nor was this the total of Euston's Scottish commitments: the Caledonian managed to embroil both the LNWR and the L&C in its attempts to secure the route northwards to Perth and Aberdeen, so the LNWR also found itself the owner of more than £90,000 of unproductive Scottish Midland Junction Railway shares and a co-guarantor, together with the Caledonian and L&C, of a 7% annual payment to the Scottish Central Railway. Efforts to resolve the position with the latter company led to legal action which established that the guarantee was unenforceable, but in 1849 the LNWR made provision of almost £5,000 to meet possible obligations to the SCR.

The Scottish imbroglio could perhaps be put down to the LNWR's limited direct participation in the Caledonian's affairs and Euston's consequent over-reliance on the judgement of that company's board, which besides promoting the interests of the west coast route also had internal Scottish objectives. However, the financial difficulties experienced with the other main tributary, the Chester & Holyhead Railway, could not be ascribed to a lack of LNWR involvement. Several of the company's senior directors served on the C&H board in succession to the L&B interest, and one of their number, Captain Moorsom, had been appointed as resident director in 1844, chairing a works committee based at Chester to supervise the construction of the line. Under Robert Stephenson and his assistant, Alexander Ross, who had been the company's engineer before the L&B involvement, contracts for almost all the line were let by the summer of 1845. The exceptions were the crossings of the Conwy estuary and to Anglesey: in order to meet Admiralty requirements for passage through the Menai strait Stephenson was developing his innovatory proposal for a tubular span, and he decided to apply this concept at Conwy as well as to the Britannia bridge.

As noted earlier, the section between Chester and Saltney was completed in 1846, when the Shrewsbury & Chester Railway opened. There was a major setback on 24 May 1847 when the Dee bridge at Chester collapsed under a Ruabon train, with the loss of five lives. The bridge had been built with cast-iron girders, and though it was reopened with temporary supports on 26 July the failure led to a government inquiry into the use of iron for railway structures; as mentioned, it also caused delays in the opening of the Trent Valley line. The report of the inquiry was published in 1849 and recommended the strengthening of similar cast-iron bridges. Although the findings were damaging to Stephenson's professional reputation, the successful installation of the first Conwy tube in April 1848 had in the meantime demonstrated the feasibility and soundness of his proposal for a wrought-iron tubular span. With the Conwy crossing accomplished, the C&H line between Saltney and Bangor was opened on 1 May 1848, followed by the Anglesey section from Llanfair to Holyhead on 1 August; on the latter date the new joint station at Chester, shared by the C&H, LNWR, S&C, and Birkenhead companies, was also brought into service.

The nominally independent Mold Railway, authorised in 1847 to link that town with the Holyhead line, was opened from its junction just west of the Welsh border on 14 August 1849 and by November that year a mineral branch from the Mold line had been completed as far as Coed Talon. The intended terminus of this branch was Ffrith, about a mile further south, but the final section was abandoned because of financial difficulties; powers for a short line to the Dee near the junction with the C&H were also allowed to lapse. The entire Mold undertaking was wound up in 1853 and absorbed by the Holyhead company, which had managed its traffic from the opening. However, motive power for both lines was provided by the LNWR, as was passenger stock: although the C&H had initially planned to work its own services and had placed orders for locomotives in 1845 and 1846, these were transferred by agreement to the southern division of the LNWR to assist in McConnell's programme of replacing Bury four-wheelers. Instead, terms were agreed in 1847 for engines and carriages to be supplied on a mileage basis to the C&H; the latter was to provide its own

Opposite top: Conwy bridge: floating of the second tube on 12 October 1848. *(LNWR Society collection, 739)*

Opposite below: The Britannia bridge under construction in 1849, before completion of the central tower in June of that year: this view from the Anglesey shore shows work well advanced on assembly of the western landward tube for the up line. One of the central tubes can be seen under construction on the mainland shore prior to being floated into position. *(National Railway Museum, 527/1/65)* goods wagons. Rather than recall locomotives from Wolverton, Trevithick drew on the northern division stock to work the Holyhead line.

The main Admiralty packet service was transferred back to Holyhead from the Mersey to coincide with the opening of the Anglesey section, and on the same day, 1 August 1848, the first Irish mail trains operated over the C&H, linked by road connection between Bangor and Llanfair. The railway company obtained parliamentary powers to operate its own vessels on 22 July 1848, but four paddle steamers, the *Anglia, Cambria, Hibernia,* and *Scotia*, had already been ordered in 1847 in the names of the C&H's chairman and vice-chairman. The first of these steamers, the *Cambria*, took up station on the same day as the Admiralty vessels, offering a fast daytime passenger and goods service to Kingstown to supplement the nightly mail crossing. In the following year the government announced that an additional mail service would operate through Holyhead from 1850, replacing the packet boats from Liverpool, Milford, and Portpatrick. Since directors of both the LNWR and C&H had built up close links with Irish railways, there appeared to be good prospects that the Holyhead company would become the key element in an integrated rail and sea network linking Britain and Ireland.

However, problems were already emerging. The route along the coast had proved more costly than had been expected; there were technical difficulties in raising the Britannia tubes; and the C&H had rashly entered into a commitment to contribute to improvements to Holyhead harbour. Initial hopes that the C&H would also be offered the sea portion of the mail route were dashed in April 1850, when the City of Dublin Steam Packet Company (which was then operating from Liverpool under Post Office contract) successfully tendered for an expanded Holyhead service. This was to include the work previously handled by the Admiralty mail steamers, two of which were taken into the City of Dublin fleet. By that stage the LNWR had been forced to lend money to the C&H to keep it from defaulting on its debenture payments and the C&H vessels had been mortgaged to provide further funds for the work on the Britannia bridge. Although a single line was completed across the bridge on 5 March 1850 and the first through train between Euston and Holyhead ran on 18 March, the second tube was not opened until 21 October.

In 1849 Moorsom had been appointed chairman of the C&H in order to protect the LNWR's financial interests in the company, which were approaching £1·5m rather than the £1m that had initially been subscribed. When Euston refused to increase its liabilities the C&H brought forward a Bill in 1850 to empower the LNWR to lease the line in return for further cash advances, but in the face of parliamentary moves to insert additional clauses – including provisions which would have granted running powers to the GWR – the Bill was withdrawn. The C&H directors, who were seeking resources to compete more effectively with the Steam Packet company, next tried to obtain financial assistance from the government, but no help was forthcoming other than a waiving of contributions to the Holyhead harbour improvements. In desperation they turned to the wealthy contractor Samuel Morton Peto, who was elected to the board in August 1850. He personally underwrote interest payments which became due in December 1850 and in February 1851 he was appointed chairman in place of Moorsom, who had previously offered to resign because of the difficulties between the C&H and LNWR. Under Peto's chairmanship a traffic agreement was concluded with the City of Dublin company and a short extension to the mail berth at the Admiralty pier at Holyhead was opened on 20 May 1851. In addition new arrangements were made with the LNWR, which undertook to supply motive power at cost plus an allowance for capital, and also agreed to subscribe further amounts to the C&H. These steps restored a measure of stability to the Holyhead undertaking, but once again LNWR shareholders had been given a practical demonstration of how their own company's position could be affected by external obligations.

* * *

Besides the problems arising from those companies in which the LNWR had a direct interest, the loss of revenue to competing lines posed a further financial threat. This danger was, of course, already familiar from the events which led up to the amalgamation, and the battles with the GWR which had been initiated during that time were at first actively continued, both in Parliament and outside. Despite the loss of the previous GJR backing, the GWR-supported Birmingham & Oxford Junction Railway was sanctioned in 1846, together with an extension to Wolverhampton which paralleled the Euston-sponsored Birmingham, Wolverhampton & Stour Valley Railway. However, because of that session's legislation on the gauge question, these were authorised as standard-gauge lines. After vigorous but unsuccessful attempts by the LNWR to turn the tables by gaining control of the B&OJ for itself, the GWR brought forward a Bill in 1848 to confirm its own purchase of the company and the connecting Birmingham, Wolverhampton & Dudley and to allow the addition of the broad gauge. On this occasion the LNWR was more successful, obtaining clauses which gave it running powers over these lines and part of the Oxford & Rugby and required the GWR to provide a junction between the two systems at Birmingham. The Buckinghamshire Railway's extension to Banbury was also envisaged as a means of gaining more direct access to the B&OJ route to Birmingham than was available from Paddington via Oxford and of thus negating much of its potential competitive value to the GWR.

Nevertheless, neither company could afford a prolonged dispute during the difficulties of the post-mania years. By 1848 the LNWR had already decided to abandon some of its authorised schemes, while the GWR, which was beginning to feel the financial effects of its push into the west midlands, was also under pressure on its southern flank from the London & South Western Railway. Faced with economic depression and falling share prices, representatives of the three 'Western' companies – the GWR, LNWR and LSWR – began discussions in the autumn of 1848. The outcome was a proposal to amalgamate all three undertakings, which progressed far enough for preparations to begin for an application to Parliament the following year. It is doubtful whether such a scheme would have been approved, except perhaps under the most stringent of conditions, and negotiations eventually broke down when the LNWR insisted, not unreasonably, that as the largest company it should have more seats on the united board. But despite the failure of this proposal, which would have significantly changed the future course of railway development in Britain, it marked a break in the open hostility between Paddington and Euston. There was also tacit acceptance that the LNWR and GWR would not set competitive fares and charges where their systems came into contact.

Another result was the start of negotiations between the two companies with a view to rationalising their commitments in Warwickshire and Staffordshire. The GWR proposed sharing the LNWR formation through Leamington to reduce the costs of constructing the B&OJ; it was also suggested that the planned central station in Birmingham should be provided jointly and that the GWR should use the Stour Valley and Leamington–Rugby lines. Pending the outcome of these discussions, final plans for the new Birmingham station were left in abeyance and the GWR postponed construction of its separate line to Wolverhampton. It also abandoned the Oxford & Rugby line north of Fenny Compton, where the B&OJ diverged, and reduced activity on the latter, while the LNWR delayed some work on its Rugby and Leamington branch.

These developments reduced the potential for conflict with one of the LNWR's largest neighbours; of the others, the Midland remained a friendly ally, and was driven into a closer dependency on Euston by the failure of Hudson's stratagems to block the progress of the London & York scheme. Since the Midland was in any case weakened by the financial legacy of these policies, its new chairman, John Ellis, who succeeded Hudson when the latter was exposed in 1849, could only seek to consolidate the company's position as an important feeder to the LNWR. Ellis had been a London & Birmingham director before the amalgamation and continued as a member of the LNWR's London committee, so the ties between the two companies remained close. Similarly, although both the L&Y and MS&L flirted with the Great Northern Railway – as the London & York scheme became known after its authorisation in 1846 – the value of their existing traffic and connections with the LNWR proved more immediately persuasive than possible future benefits from alternative alliances.

But the Great Northern, too, was hampered by the economic conditions of the late 1840s. Although promoted as a direct line between London and York, it deferred the Peterborough–Retford section in favour of the easier but circuitous route via Boston and Lincoln. It also readily acceded to Hudson's proposal that it should substitute a connection with the York & North Midland Railway at Knottingley for its planned direct entry to York. Much of the intended advantage over the LNWR and Midland in terms of distance to York was therefore sacrificed, while the west coast retained its clear superiority as the shortest route to Scotland. Already stretched financially, the GNR was in no position to risk its revenue in a competitive battle with the established companies, so when it began through services from its temporary London station on 7 August 1850 it charged the same fares as the existing routes. This was followed by a traffic pooling agreement, effective from 1 January 1851, which started from the basis of an equal division of London–Edinburgh traffic between the west and east coast partnerships, and then further subdivided the east coast portion, allocating two-thirds of passenger revenue to the established route from Euston via Derby and a third to the Kings Cross alternative. These terms were not, however, as unequal as has sometimes been claimed: there was provision for the virtual reversal of the latter proportions when the direct line to Doncaster was completed, and the GNR route was also guaranteed 50% of east coast goods receipts from the outset. This 'octuple agreement' – so named because eight companies were parties to it – was to run for five years; it was paralleled by the 'sextuple agreement' which governed the division of most other Anglo-Scottish traffic flows. Another proposed agreement, covering traffic between London and Lincoln and the principal towns of south and west Yorkshire was ultimately referred to W E Gladstone for arbitration: though his award on 26 August 1851 came too late to prevent fierce competition for excursion traffic to the Great Exhibition, the exceptional passenger demand allowed the companies involved to reap some financial benefit despite the low fares provoked by competition. Gladstone's eventual ruling, while closer to the GNR's position than that of the LNWR and its allies, followed the same principles of pooling and dividing revenue that had already been accepted for Anglo-Scottish traffic, principles that depended for their application on the accounting systems established through the Railway Clearing House.

Even when there was scope for rivalry, therefore, relations between the trunk railways were normally conducted on a pragmatic basis that reflected the financial difficulties which they all then faced, and dealings with smaller companies usually fell within a similar framework: though there were occasional outbreaks of competition, in most cases equilibrium was re-established relatively quickly. While the LNWR has often been portrayed as abusing its superior power in such situations, reality was much more complex: the preoccupation of independent railways – and canals – with obtaining favourable leases or traffic agreements suggests that in general their prime motive was to extract the best possible terms from a larger company, rather than a disinterested concern to maintain their independence and meet the needs of the local communities which they served. One such example was provided by the North Staffordshire Railway, which opened between Crewe and Burton-on-Trent in 1848, and in the following year extended southwards to Colwich on the Trent Valley line and northwards to Macclesfield via both Harecastle and Leek. As the successor to the Churnet Valley Railway, the NSR contended that agreements which the L&B made with its predecessor in 1845 should bind the LNWR, and in particular claimed that it should share in all Manchester–Euston traffic. Though a traffic agreement was negotiated in 1850, the NSR then questioned the terms of its application, and a reference to arbitration proved to be the prelude to further friction between the two companies which persisted for much of the decade.

The best-known of such disputes, however, was that with the Shrewsbury railways, which also had its origins in the mania years. After the parliamentary impasse of 1845, two competing Bills for railways between Shrewsbury and the west midlands were again brought forward in 1846, with origins which reflected the previous session's contest between L&B and GJR interests. Despite the *rapprochement* which led to the creation of the LNWR, the promoters of these two projects, the Shrewsbury, Wolverhampton, Dudley & Birmingham and the Shrewsbury, Wolverhampton & South Staffordshire Junction, maintained their rivalry, and it was only after authorisation that the schemes were combined under the title of the Shrewsbury & Birmingham Railway. However, the amalgamated company's powers did not extend continuously between the two points named in its title. Because the eastern part of its intended line would have duplicated the Birmingham, Wolverhampton & Stour Valley Railway, it was agreed that the S&B should follow the example of the L&B and Birmingham Canal in subscribing a quarter of that company's capital and that its own metals should commence at Wolverhampton, where a junction would be formed. Furthermore, as already described, the S&B and Shropshire Union routes merged near

Wellington, so joint ownership was authorised between there and Shrewsbury.

At Shrewsbury the S&B linked with the Shrewsbury & Chester Railway, and although this gave the two companies natural affinities both also had early links with the LNWR and its allies. At first the S&C's sole outlet to the rest of the system was over the C&H to Chester, and it was a partner in the joint station there. The S&B's ties were apparently even closer: besides its antecedents, it had a common interest with the LNWR through its stake in the BW&SV, and indeed it shared the same engineer with that company and with the Shropshire Union. However, when the LNWR sought powers to lease those undertakings in 1847, the S&B realised its potential exposure and objected until it was offered arrangements for pooling of traffic and for joint facilities at Wolverhampton. In addition, its right to use the BW&SV was confirmed, although with the stipulation that this would lapse if the Shrewsbury company amalgamated with the GWR or any of its west midland satellites. This last condition probably reflected the fact that as a precautionary move the S&B board had instructed its engineer to build the only tunnel on the line, at Oakengates, to broad-gauge dimensions.

After the opening of the Ruabon–Chester section in 1846, the S&C was completed to Shrewsbury on 14 October 1848; the S&B was opened to a temporary station at Wolverhampton on 12 November 1849. Even before this opening the Shrewsbury companies had let it be known that they would undercut the LNWR; almost immediately, therefore, fierce competition broke out for traffic between the west midlands and the Mersey, with the S&C using the Birkenhead line beyond Chester and the S&B employing coach and canal connections for Birmingham traffic. However, in addition to greatly superior resources the LNWR had other advantages on its side: it controlled the still-incomplete Stour Valley line and because of the shared ownership at Wolverhampton it could obstruct the S&B's access there both to the joint station and to the Birmingham Canal; while at the northern end of the route the S&C had no running powers beyond Chester.

The line to Birkenhead by then formed part of the Birkenhead, Lancashire & Cheshire Junction Railway, which had been authorised in 1846 to provide a line between Manchester and Birkenhead but had limited itself to building the portion between Chester and a junction with the LNWR at Walton, south of Warrington. The Chester & Birkenhead amalgamated with the BL&CJ in 1847 and on 1 August 1848 the latter opened a west curve at the junction of the Birkenhead and Holyhead lines at Chester, thus permitting through running between Shrewsbury and Birkenhead, where a direct link to the docks had been completed on 5 April the previous year. When the competition broke out, the BL&CJ's line to Walton junction was still under construction, opening eventually on 18 December 1850, and as that company would be dependent on the LNWR for access to Manchester it was soon persuaded to cease its co-operation with the Shrewsbury companies. However, the loss of traffic which this entailed and the S&C's threat of parliamentary action were sufficient to produce a change of policy by the BL&CJ, which restored facilities for Shrewsbury traffic in June 1850.

By then both sides were using every tactic open to them, and the Riot Act had to be read on 13 July 1850 when the S&B's navvies tried to force a passage against LNWR opposition to the canal basin beside the uncompleted junction line at Wolverhampton. The episode therefore justifies its reputation as one of the most notorious railway battles of the period, and sympathies have generally lain with the smaller parties to the conflict. But on 30 July 1850 William Ormsby Gore MP, the chairman of the S&B and of the two Shrewsbury companies' joint traffic committee, made a new approach to the LNWR, and the course of these negotiations perhaps suggests a different interpretation. Ormsby Gore offered a traffic pool, with the division of revenue determined by arbitration; the LNWR instead proposed equal fares to all competitive destinations, terms which the official historian of the GWR described as 'eminently reasonable' and which were, apparently, initially acceptable to the S&B. However, they were rejected by its northern partner, for reasons which demonstrate the underlying weakness of the Shrewsbury companies' case: the S&C contended that it needed to charge lower passenger fares than the LNWR in order to offset the disadvantage of the ferry crossing between Birkenhead and Liverpool. This contemporary acknowledgement that the Shrewsbury route was intrinsically inferior is substantiated by consideration of the distances involved: though the mileage between the west midlands and Birkenhead via Shrewsbury was roughly equivalent to that via Crewe to Liverpool, the LNWR line to Chester (and therefore to Birkenhead) was about twelve miles shorter. While Huish was never slow to use pooling arrangements or rate reductions to maintain his company's position in competitive situations, the Shrewsbury case was correctly viewed by the LNWR board as an attempt by two small local companies to extort unjustifiable terms from their natural partner, and the subsequent financial history of these lines confirms that their competition, based solely on undercutting the established route, was artificial and unsustainable.

CHAPTER FOUR

Dropping the Pilot

Despite the difficulties experienced during the late 1840s – of which the unresolved dispute with the Shrewsbury railways was just one example – the LNWR escaped the extreme financial problems which afflicted some of its contemporaries. Consequently, although not immune to attacks by journalists or speculators, it was able to avoid the committees of investigation and internal upheavals encountered elsewhere. However, the amalgamation Act required the LNWR to review its corporate structure by 1851, and while Huish had built up an effective officer organisation which overcame some of the problems caused by the diffusion of responsibility between the central board and the local committees, the approaching expiry of the interim arrangements established in 1846 gave the proprietors an opportunity to review the company's organisation and policies. A committee of shareholders was accordingly appointed at the general meeting in August 1850 to bring forward proposals for the future administration of the undertaking, and these were published in January 1851.

Some shareholders had already voiced concern at aspects of existing policies, particularly the continuing expenditure on extensions and subsidiary lines, and in February 1850 the directors had bowed to earlier criticisms by closing parts of the capital account. In contrast with some other railways, though, there was no attempt to impose change by seeking radical restructuring. Instead, the shareholders' committee recognised the need to strengthen the central board and proposed that, with the abandonment of the local committees, the directorate should be increased to thirty. However, the committee recommended that, to offset the enhanced power of the board, six of its members should retire in rotation each year and that no more than four of these should be eligible for re-election. It also recommended the establishment of an independent audit committee to scrutinise the company's financial management.

While the directors were unhappy with the proposition that two of their number should automatically be replaced each year, and subsequently departed from this recommendation, the proposals were otherwise accepted and laid the general basis for the regulation of the LNWR's affairs from then onwards. An expanded board was accordingly elected in February 1851; among the new members was Richard Moon, who had already made a significant contribution from the floor at several general meetings and who had been a member of the shareholders' committee. The retiring directors included Charles Lawrence, whose departure severed another link with the earliest days of the Liverpool & Manchester Railway. Lawrence was replaced as deputy-chairman by Thomas Smith, a former L&B director.

Although Glyn continued as chairman, his health was giving cause for concern; it is also clear that managing the new, larger board was a more demanding task, since it brought together within a single body the local interests that had previously expressed themselves through the area committees. In addition, he was increasingly of the view that running the affairs of the LNWR demanded a salaried chairman who could devote most of his time to the company and thus more effectively supervise the officers. He therefore stood down as chairman in September 1852, and after unsuccessful approaches to Robert Fox Maule – who had become Lord Panmure in April 1852 – Glyn was succeeded on 18 November by one of his board colleagues, Major-General the Hon George Anson MP. Anson, who was born in 1797, saw service at Waterloo, and was elected as MP for South Staffordshire in 1818. He joined the L&B board shortly before the amalgamation, and was one of the original directors of the LNWR. However, Anson's tenure of the chairmanship proved to be brief: he had remained on the army list and in 1853 was appointed to command a division in Bengal. He accordingly resigned at the general meeting in August that year, and left for India. By the time the Mutiny broke out Anson had become commander-in-chief in India, and he died of cholera in 1857 on the march to relieve Delhi.

To replace Anson the directors turned to another MP, but this time they went outside their own numbers in appointing the Marquis of Chandos, who sat for Buckingham. He was born in 1823, a year after his grandfather had become the first Duke of Buckingham & Chandos. His father, the second duke, had faced near-bankruptcy in 1847, with debts said to be in excess of £1m; the Marquis dealt with the creditors after wresting control of the family estate from his father, who fled abroad. Chandos briefly attained

A Trevithick 2-2-2 locomotive at Broad Green station in Lancashire, probably during the 1860s. (David Joy collection: L&GRP 18341)

ministerial office in 1852 in Lord Derby's government, and appears to have been chosen by the LNWR in deference to Glyn's view that the company needed a chairman who could devote most of his time to the post. In any event, his selection at the age of 30 by the experienced businessmen and politicians who made up the directorate of the LNWR suggests that he had considerable abilities. In August 1855 Chandos was allocated £2,000 per annum in addition to his existing board fees, and from then onwards it was the company's usual practice to make a substantial annual payment to its chairman. Robert Benson, another former L&B director, became deputy-chairman in 1853 in succession to Smith, who remained a member of the board; when Benson stood down in 1858 he was replaced by Constantine Richard Moorsom. Glyn, though no longer an office-bearer, remained an active and influential director and commemorated his

connection with the company by adopting the title of Baron Wolverton when he was elevated to the peerage in 1869. He retired from the board in the following year, and died in 1873 at the age of 76. His son George Grenfell Glyn, the second Lord Wolverton, was appointed to the audit committee in 1874 and served the LNWR in that capacity until his death in 1887.

The strengthening of the board was paralleled by changes in the divisional structure. In 1852 William Baker succeeded R B Dockray as resident engineer for the southern division, and in the same year, following the expiry of earlier maintenance contracts, Henry Woodhouse was appointed permanent way engineer for the whole system, based at Stafford. The central goods division was reduced to a sub-division following the death of Samuel Eborall in 1853, while in 1856 T C Mills, the former London goods manager, was replaced at Camden by David Stevenson and promoted to become chief goods manager, based at Euston. An earlier all-line appointment was that of Fisher Ormandy, who at the end of 1850 had been given the task of developing livestock traffic.

Changes also took place in the locomotive department. In the northern division, Trevithick continued to produce the basic Crewe 2-2-2 and 2-4-0 designs, but some shareholders began to ask whether costs might be reduced if the company ceased to manufacture its own locomotives. Trevithick's capabilities as a manager also came under question, particularly after gross insubordination by his assistant Allen led to the latter's enforced resignation in 1853. In the same year, to give more space for locomotive repairs both at Crewe and at Edge Hill, northern division wagon building and repairs were centralised at the former Jones & Potts works at Newton Junction, under the superintendence of Owen Owens, previously wagon foreman. In 1855 the new establishment was named Earlestown in honour of the LNWR's then senior director, Hardman Earle.

A further change at Crewe in 1853 was the installation of a rail mill; at first this was managed separately, but when it was added to the locomotive department in 1856 it was put not under Trevithick but under Ramsbottom, who was still based at Longsight. This was a reflection of a growing feeling within the board against Trevithick and in favour of amalgamating the locomotive divisions: such a step had been recommended in 1855 by a board committee, and when the LNWR ceased to work Lancaster & Carlisle trains in

1857 the opportunity was taken to merge the two northern divisions. Ramsbottom was appointed to the new divisional post, with headquarters at Crewe, and the superseded Trevithick returned to his native Cornwall with an honorarium of £3,000. The southern division remained separate for the time being, but the higher locomotive expenditure incurred in this division continued to attract criticism, despite McConnell's engineering ability and his pioneering work to equip engines to burn coal rather than coke. Meanwhile, however, Ramsbottom's vigorous pursuit of modernisation and standardisation at Crewe, and his introduction as early as 1858 of the 'DX' 0-6-0 class in place of the previous 2-4-0 Crewe goods design, showed that he was fully alive to the need to respond to the pressures on the department.

* * *

Such pressures were primarily a reflection of the renewed financial difficulties faced by the company. Dividends recovered in 1851, partly as a result of Exhibition traffic, but this was not sustained and in 1858 shareholders received their lowest-ever annual return, 4%. However, apart from a drop in traffic with the onset of depression in 1858, the underlying revenue trend remained upwards, reflecting the continued growth in freight business. Although working expenses also rose, initially in response to the abnormal traffic conditions of 1851 and then as prices increased during the Crimean war, operating profits remained reasonably buoyant. The problem once again was the increase in the company's capital and the growth in the calls on revenue from guarantees and interest payments. Capital expanded by almost a quarter between 1851 and 1861, while the level of prior charges more than doubled.

Shareholders were naturally alarmed by this worsening of their position. In 1855 a committee of consultation was set up by the proprietors to examine the company's affairs, but although its members included one persistent critic of the board, George Hadfield MP, the resultant report recognised the external factors affecting the LNWR. Whilst calling attention to the losses incurred as a result of extending the system and questioning the existing locomotive policy, the committee concluded that the undertaking was fundamentally sound and that it was well administered. Indeed, as the report acknowledged, the directors themselves had not been idle in the face of the decline in the company's fortunes: they had established their own committee of investigation under Moon, which carried out a detailed examination of several aspects of management and policy. In addition, a standing executive committee was set up in 1855 to advise the chairman and deal with matters of urgent business. As a result, the board's immediate supervision of the management of the company was strengthened and officers came under increasing scrutiny. Besides the search for economy and efficiency, a series of scandals gave the directors of the LNWR, in common with those of several other companies, added reasons for looking more deeply into officers' performance of their duties. The first of these was the discovery in 1854 of embezzlement involving the company's chief auditor, Thomas Goalen. This was followed in 1856 by the dismissal of two of the goods managers, Braithwaite Poole and Samuel Salt, Poole for failing to deal with frauds by his staff and Salt for wrongful use of company property. Other respected officers also came under investigation, and though Huish's integrity was not questioned the board's confidence in its senior staff was undoubtedly affected.

There is ample evidence, however, that executive management responded effectively to the changing financial and organisational environment. A renegotiated contract with the company's agents in 1852 enabled goods handling costs to be reduced, and other economies were made as opportunities permitted – train mileage was carefully controlled and working expenses were closely monitored. A statistical section was created in 1854 to assist in this work and in the following year Huish established officers' conferences, which provided a valuable forum for communicating and developing policy and for scrutinising performance. However, some increased expenditure proved unavoidable: extra provision was made for rail replacement as the growing weight and volume of traffic forced the re-examination of earlier assumptions about rail life, while in 1855 the LNWR introduced a rudimentary block signalling system, made possible by the extension of the electric telegraph.

In general terms, therefore, the LNWR's traffic and engineering management was able to react positively to the need to contain and justify costs, while the board scrupulously avoided the false economies or lax accounting practices that might have assisted them to present more favourable financial results. Though the committee of consultation questioned some details of internal policy – as noted, it expressed doubts about locomotive practice – and it also reiterated, again without permanent effect, the 1851 recommendation that not all retiring directors should be eligible for re-election, its main emphasis was on the need to minimise future capital expenditure. The earlier attempt to close part of the capital account had been quickly abandoned as impracticable, but the committee of consultation successfully insisted that any additions to capital or proposals for financial guarantees to other railways should be expressly authorised by a general meeting. This measure was clearly intended to increase the proprietors' control over their liabilities, and while the recommendation did not prevent the board from bringing forward plans for further expenditure it was a reminder of the strength of shareholders' feelings on this issue.

* * *

The renewed expansion that ultimately led to this reaction began as a response to more favourable economic conditions and to growing traffic; indeed, several of the schemes undertaken during the 1850s were projects that had previously been abandoned or postponed. Two further branches were added to the Leeds line: the first, from Batley to Birstall, opened on 9 September 1852 and the Greenfield–Oldham branch followed on 5 July 1856. In the London area, a line from Watford to St Albans, authorised in 1853 to replace a more ambitious 1847 scheme, was opened on 5 May 1858, while a nominally independent company, the Hampstead Junction Railway, was authorised in 1853 with the support of the LNWR and North London Railway to provide an alternative connection between their systems by linking Willesden with Kentish Town. With the continuing growth in freight traffic, additional main line capacity at the London end of the route could no longer be deferred, so goods relief lines, down from the western portal of Primrose Hill tunnel to Willesden and up from Bletchley to Primrose Hill, were brought into service during 1858 and 1859. To minimise construction costs the up tracks were gauntleted through Watford tunnel.

The Hampstead Junction route, opened on 2 January 1860, enabled the Primrose Hill bottleneck to

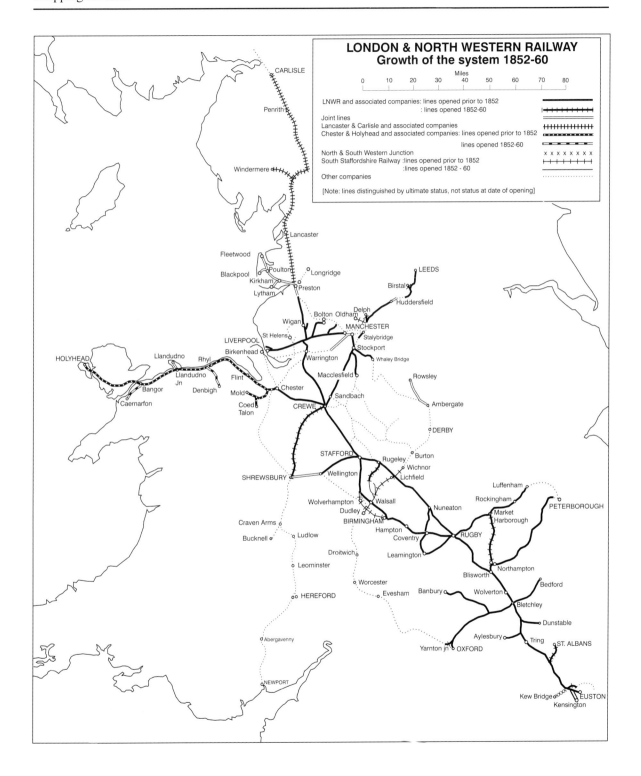

Figure 4.1 – Growth of the LNWR system 1852–60.

be avoided by trains to and from the NLR line, and it was principally used by through passenger workings over the North & South Western Junction Railway, with which it was connected by a direct high-level spur at Willesden. The N&SWJR was authorised in 1851, and although separately promoted it was jointly guaranteed by the LNWR and LSWR. Goods trains began running between Willesden and Kew on 15 February 1853 and passenger services, operated by the NLR, commenced on 1 August that year; a branch from Acton to Hammersmith was opened on 1 May 1857 for goods traffic and on 8 April 1858 for passengers. There were fitful attempts to provide a through passenger service to LSWR stations, but these were short-lived until the introduction of trains between Camden Town and Twickenham via Richmond on 20 May 1858. This involved reversals at Kew and Barnes, both of which were eliminated when the LSWR opened triangular junctions at each location on 1 February 1862. From that date the NLR through trains, most of which had been diverted in 1860 to run via the Hampstead Junction line, used a new station at Kew Bridge, in the east fork of the junction with the LSWR. Until 1866, however, a vestigial passenger service was maintained to the original N&SWJ station at Kew, on the west-facing curve.

On the other side of London the London & Blackwall Railway obtained powers in 1852 to build a short branch just east of Fenchurch Street station to a site at Haydon Square which the LNWR had acquired for a City goods station. The branch and depot were opened on 13 March 1853 and were reached over the North London line via Poplar junction. This new terminus was the first several of depots established in the London area which lay on 'foreign' metals: Haydon Square's particular value was in giving direct rail access to the City, thus allowing a significant reduction in cartage to and from Camden, and by the end of 1854 traffic had grown so much that an enlargement of the depot became necessary. In 1863 the LNWR purchased the connecting spur outright, replacing the previous arrangement under which it met the interest charges on the Blackwall company's outlay in building the branch on its behalf.

While such local extensions and improvements accounted for some of the additions to capital during the 1850s, the completion of projects delayed by the depression of the late 1840s provoked a further round of competition, with hopes of economic recovery

providing extra stimulus to new ventures. This affected both established and recent companies and soon began to influence not only the LNWR's proposals for new construction but also its attitude to some of the separate undertakings with which it connected. Despite the experience of the 1840s, the promotion of extensions and alliances to gain and consolidate territory once more became a major factor in the growth of the system after 1850, and the unconcluded struggle with the Shrewsbury companies proved to be the first element that disturbed the temporary balance which had been achieved between the LNWR and its main competitors.

After the failure of the overtures for a settlement in the autumn of 1850, the S&B and S&C turned to the GWR, which thereupon broke off negotiations with the LNWR for joint arrangements in the west midlands. Instead, it gave notice of a Bill in 1851 to seek powers for a revised junction with the extension from Curzon Street and for access to the planned new station at Birmingham. In the same session the S&B sought confirmation of its right to use the Stour Valley line, while the S&C applied for running powers between Saltney and Chester and over the Birkenhead system. This completely transformed the position, since it introduced the threat of competitive services between Paddington and Birkenhead via Shrewsbury, using the LNWR's own metals and taking advantage of its heavy investment to serve central Birmingham. Euston adopted vigorous counter-measures and attempted to gain control of the boards of the Shrewsbury companies in order to establish alternative traffic agreements; however, these efforts failed, so the GWR was able to conclude terms for the ultimate absorption of the S&B and S&C, meanwhile guaranteeing their dividends. The GWR and its Shrewsbury partners also reached agreement for a perpetual lease of the Birkenhead, Lancashire & Cheshire Junction and for its optional inclusion in an larger amalgamation.

Although both the GWR and S&B were unsuccessful in their parliamentary applications for compulsory use of LNWR assets, the S&C succeeded in gaining running powers to Chester and over the Birkenhead undertaking. As the latter extended to Warrington, the GWR thus secured a potential route to Manchester as well as to the Mersey. In 1851 it also began the construction of its long-deferred line from Birmingham to Wolverhampton and in 1852 obtained

powers for a short junction line to give a through connection with the S&B at Wolverhampton. However, in the latter year the BL&CJ defected from the GWR alliance, after the LNWR promoted a precautionary Bill for an alternative line from Chester to Birkenhead. Subsequent attempts to incorporate the BL&CJ within the LNWR in 1853 and 1854 were frustrated by the parliamentary events discussed below, so for the time being it remained independent.

The GWR suffered a further setback in 1853, when a Bill seeking powers to extend the broad gauge northwards to Birkenhead was rejected by Parliament, thus limiting any future through working to the standard gauge. Until the GWR route to Wolverhampton was complete, the only potential link between S&B metals and Birmingham was over the Stour Valley line, and the LNWR was able to hinder access first by delaying its opening until 1 July 1852 and then through the formalities of Board of Trade approval for the junction at Wolverhampton. Moreover, the protracted negotiations with the GWR and the pressure to reduce capital expenditure had also delayed progress with the new central station at Birmingham and the extension from Curzon Street, so to allow the opening of the line

New Street, Birmingham – 'the new grand central railway station' – as depicted in the *Illustrated London News* of 3 June 1854.

from Wolverhampton for local traffic the LNWR provided a temporary platform at Navigation Street, at the western end of the site of the permanent station. Since the S&B's running powers were restricted to the Stour Valley section proper and did not extend over LNWR metals into the temporary platform, this also provided a basis for postponing access to Birmingham by Shrewsbury trains; legal proceedings about the tolls for use of the line had the same effect. However, while competition continued unabated, further attempts were also made to reach a comprehensive agreement with the GWR. In August 1852 Glyn wrote to Charles Russell, his opposite number at Paddington, with another proposal of amalgamation; this was rejected, and the counter-offer of equal charges and a joint committee was unacceptable to the LNWR board because it was made conditional upon recognition of the GWR's arrangements with the Shrewsbury companies. A renewed approach by the LNWR in 1853 similarly broke down over

The former L&B station at Curzon Street, Birmingham after its relegation to goods traffic. The locomotive, southern division no 18, is a Jones & Potts long-boiler 4-2-0 goods engine, ordered originally for the Chester & Holyhead Railway but delivered to the LNWR in 1848. It was withdrawn in 1859. *(LNWR Society collection, 574)*

Paddington's insistence that the S&B and S&C should be parties to any negotiations.

On 4 February 1854, after the legal skirmishing was concluded, the S&B was at last able to run beyond Wolverhampton to Birmingham; its trains were extended to the permanent station, by then known as New Street, when it opened on 1 June. On the same day the LNWR diverted its main line trains to New Street, leaving Curzon Street to goods trains and the Midland Railway until the latter's junction lines were completed a month later – Midland access to New Street on nominal terms had been secured as long ago as 1847 by an agreement which in return released the LNWR from its obligation to assist in meeting the deficit on the Birmingham & Bristol guarantee. Shrewsbury trains were transferred to Birmingham Snow Hill with the opening of the GWR's Wolverhampton line on 14 November 1854, six weeks after the amalgamation of the S&B and

S&C took effect. Snow Hill itself had opened when broad-gauge services were extended from Banbury on 1 October 1852, leaving only the unfinished Duddeston viaduct as a reminder of former intentions to connect the two systems at Birmingham and of the breakdown of the previous co-operation. The proposed junction with the Buckinghamshire line at Banbury was also a victim of the renewed hostilities between the LNWR and GWR: although mixed gauge was installed between Oxford and Birmingham to coincide with the opening of the line north of Banbury in 1852, the lapse of the plans to form connections at Leamington and Birmingham eliminated any remaining value in the LNWR's statutory running powers over this route and thus removed the requirement for a junction at Banbury.

The ultimate cost to the LNWR of the widening of its dispute with the Shrewsbury companies was heavy and extended beyond the lost possibilities of sharing capital expenditure: Huish calculated in 1855 that GWR competition to Birmingham and beyond was losing the LNWR £70,000 annually. But the extension to Chester also cost Paddington dear: besides the financial burden of completing lines that had been left in abeyance since the late 1840s and of providing generous guarantees to the Shrewsbury companies' proprietors, the GWR was compelled to reduce its charges to comply with parliamentary requirements and to become a standard-gauge operator for the first time.

Moreover, just as the independence of the Shrewsbury lines proved to be an Achilles' heel for the LNWR, so too the competition which they provoked exposed a weak flank in the GWR defences. In this case it was the Oxford, Worcester & Wolverhampton Railway, which by October 1850 had completed only four miles of its intended route. This section, between Abbott's Wood and Worcester, was being worked by the Midland as a branch from its Birmingham–Bristol line. Samuel Morton Peto then took an interest in the company's affairs and at about the same time that he was negotiating with the LNWR on the Chester & Holyhead's behalf he also arranged that the OW&W should be completed to the standard gauge and worked by the Midland and LNWR. This carried the competition into intended broad-gauge territory: although the GWR had this agreement overturned, its own attempts to agree terms with the OW&W broke down in the autumn of 1851. The latter, with still only a fraction of its authorised mileage complete, then demonstrated its independence by promoting a line from north of Oxford to a junction with the London & South Western Railway at Brentford. This was unsuccessful in Parliament in 1852, as was an LNWR Bill for a direct spur from the Buckinghamshire Railway to the OW&W at Yarnton. The Brentford scheme – the Mid Western Railway – was resubmitted the following year and was again unsuccessful, but the LNWR obtained powers for the Yarnton connection in that session. The tactical advantage gained in 1853 came very close to being converted into a strategic victory, for earlier LNWR ambitions were revived in the shape of a Bill for a direct line from Tring to Oxford which progressed as far as the House of Lords before being defeated. In addition, a company supported by the LNWR and Midland was authorised to build a line between Worcester and Hereford.

This last scheme was also of more than local significance: in response to the GWR's alliance with the Shrewsbury companies the LNWR had reached an agreement in 1851 with the Newport, Abergavenny & Hereford Railway, a company which although authorised in 1846 had done nothing to implement its

powers. Since however the independent Shrewsbury & Hereford Railway, authorised in the same year, was by then under construction and the LNWR was also contemplating a line from Crewe to Shrewsbury, there was a prospect of balancing the GWR's invasion of north Wales and the Wirral with LNWR routes into south Wales. Here the proposed Worcester & Hereford Railway became important, since by using existing or improved links with the OW&W the LNWR could create a through route from London which would offer a reasonable alternative to the GWR's line via Gloucester and the connecting South Wales Railway. South Wales and its coal measures had always been the ultimate objective of the Tring–Cheltenham project; while it was further from London to Cardiff via Worcester than via Cheltenham and Gloucester, the Hereford route offered opportunities to strike directly into the coalfield from Abergavenny, thus reducing this disadvantage. It also gave good access from the midlands and north.

A Bill for the Worcester & Hereford line was unsuccessful in 1852; it was renewed the following year, together with NA&H Bills seeking powers to extend to Swansea and Brecon and also to allow the sale or lease of that undertaking to the LNWR. This last Bill was lost, for reasons which will be described below, so the extension Bills were accordingly withdrawn. The Worcester & Hereford obtained its Act, but without the clauses enabling the LNWR and Midland to subscribe. Deprived of this support, the company languished, and when its powers were revived in 1858 it was without LNWR participation. The latter's agreement with the Newport company had been conditional upon the opening of the Worcester line, although when the NA&H was partially opened on 2 January 1854, between Pontypool and Hereford, the LNWR worked this section under a temporary agreement. A renewed application was also made for powers to purchase the company. However, as the LNWR refused to route traffic over the S&B or S&C the agreement was terminated by mutual consent and the transfer Bill abandoned. With the encouragement of the LNWR, the NA&H instead made arrangements for Thomas Brassey to work its line. Brassey was already working the Shrewsbury & Hereford, which had opened from Shrewsbury to Ludlow on 21 April 1852 and was completed to Barr's Court station in Hereford on 6 December 1853. After the handover to Brassey the

An interior view of Rewley Road station in Oxford, the terminus of the Buckinghamshire Railway's line from Bletchley, which was also used by Oxford Worcester & Wolverhampton Railway local passenger services in the autumn of 1857 before the resolution of that company's disputes with the GWR. *(LNWR Society collection, 203)*

LNWR temporarily withdrew from direct interest in the southern marches, although the authorisation of the Crewe–Shrewsbury line in 1853 gave it an alternative approach via Shrewsbury. This branch, initially promoted to connect with proposed lines into mid-Wales, opened on 1 September 1858.

While these proposals were developing the LNWR's relations with the OW&W also flourished. The latter had reached Wolvercot on 4 June 1853, where at first it exchanged traffic with the GWR; however, with the opening of the Yarnton spur on 1 April 1854 through services were inaugurated between Euston and Wolverhampton via the OW&W. These were worked by the LNWR as far as Handborough and also between Dudley and Wolverhampton, making use of the South Staffordshire curve at Tipton to run into Wolverhampton High Level station on the Stour

Valley line. North of Oxford, a west-to-south junction was installed between the Yarnton spur and the main Buckinghamshire line, allowing OW&W goods trains to use the LNWR facilities at Oxford; this curve also carried local passenger services during the autumn of 1857 when, because of the continuing difficulties between the Worcester company and the GWR, these were diverted for a time from the latter's Oxford station and handled at the LNWR's Rewley Road terminus. In addition, a chord was brought into use at Bletchley in October 1854 to permit direct running between Euston and the Buckinghamshire line, and during the same month a connection was completed between the LNWR at Bushbury junction and the northern extremity of the OW&W at Wolverhampton Low Level station. Although the Bushbury link was mainly used by goods traffic, it became a frequent handover point for royal train workings.

By the end of 1854, however, the conflict between the LNWR and GWR had largely ceased; despite the failure of earlier attempts to reach formal agreement, in practice the two companies continued to charge equally to points where they were in competition and refrained from promoting new lines which invaded each other's territory. Once the future of the Shrewsbury lines had been determined, prolongation of this particular contest served no purpose for the LNWR, while the GWR's disastrous dividends after 1853 provide sufficient explanation for that company's renewed pacifism. And although financial stringency also affected the LNWR, a more compelling reason for seeking settled relations with Paddington was provided by the emerging pressures from other quarters, which threatened to disturb still further an equilibrium that had already been shifted by the conflict with the Shrewsbury companies.

These new pressures arose primarily from the completion of the direct route from Kings Cross to Doncaster: although the LNWR had initially succeeded in containing the threat posed by the Great Northern, the traffic agreements by which this had been achieved were due to expire at the end of 1855. The rival parties naturally sought to protect their positions before the forthcoming revision, and in this situation the Midland was probably the most exposed of all the LNWR's partners. The GNR main line provided a shorter route to York and Leeds and besides intercepting the Midland's straggling branch to Lincoln it also provided a potential starting-point for thrusts into the east and north midlands. Although the Midland was able to compensate for its diminished role as a through trunk passenger route by successfully developing its bulk coal traffic to London, the GNR began to encroach on this traffic too once its facilities in London were properly established and it had gained a foothold in the south Yorkshire coalfield.

As has been seen, the Midland enjoyed the close support of the LNWR, and their joint lease of the Manchester, Buxton, Matlock & Midlands Junction Railway in 1852 has to be viewed not only in the context of their contemporary collaboration in the west midlands but more particularly in the light of their parallel attempt to gain control of a proposed continuation, the Ambergate, Nottingham & Boston & Eastern Junction. Though the latter scheme was reduced to a line between Colwick and Grantham, it would have secured a route between Manchester and London or the eastern counties via Derby and the MBM&MJ. In the event the Midland and LNWR were unsuccessful and the GNR reached a traffic agreement with the Ambergate company in 1852 which gave it access to Nottingham.

The first hint that the interests of the Midland and the LNWR might ultimately diverge came in the same year. A year after his election to the full board of the LNWR, John Ellis, the chairman of the Midland Railway, told his own shareholders of the need to consider 'permanent identification' with a company capable of providing access to London, and negotiations for amalgamation with the LNWR were opened soon afterwards. However, the two companies failed to reach agreement by a narrow financial margin, and in August 1852 Edmund Denison, the GNR chairman, seized the opportunity to make an alternative offer of amalgamation to the Midland.

In proposing this Denison was motivated not simply by a desire to gain access to the territory west of his company's main line: the Midland also offered a way out of the constraints imposed on the GNR's Anglo-Scottish traffic by the agreements of 1851. One of Hudson's bequests to the Midland had been the Leeds & Bradford Railway, which extended to Skipton, and in 1846 a separate company – the 'little' North Western Railway – had been authorised to build a continuation to Lancaster and Morecambe, with a branch northwards from Clapham to the L&C near Low Gill. However, while the southern section of this branch was built as far as Ingleton and opened in 1849, construction was abandoned beyond that point and services to Ingleton were withdrawn on 1 June 1850 when the line to Lancaster was opened. Although some traffic was exchanged with the L&C via a link between Green Ayre and Castle stations at Lancaster, the NWR was regarded as a purely local route and so did not figure in the Anglo-Scottish traffic pools. The company made several attempts to revive interest in its proposed direct line northwards through the Lune valley and obtained an extension of the time allowed for construction, but no financial backing was forthcoming, even from the Midland, which took over the working of the undertaking from the beginning of 1852.

Nevertheless, the GNR was well aware of the scope for a third approach to Scotland via north-west Yorkshire and was already in contact with some of the companies authorised in the mania years to build lines through the northern Pennines. While its own interest in the NWR had been forestalled by the Midland's working agreement, this existing outlet to the L&C – still an independent company – provided additional justification for seeking amalgamation with the

Midland, although by the time Denison's offer was received the LNWR and Midland had resumed negotiations. One outcome, however, was the GNR's agreement not to oppose the Midland's application to Parliament in 1853 for a line between Leicester and Hitchin. This had first been authorised in 1847, but powers had been allowed to lapse. The revival of this scheme caused some concern to the LNWR, which protected its own interests in the south midlands by promoting a branch from Northampton to Market Harborough. Construction of this single-track branch proceeded slowly in the more difficult financial circumstances of the later 1850s, but it was eventually opened to passengers on 16 February 1859; goods traffic was probably handled before the end of 1858.

Despite the hesitation caused by the promotion of the Hitchin and Northampton lines, the Midland and LNWR boards were not deflected from their intended merger, and a Bill for this purpose was introduced in 1853, reserving the financial terms of the amalgamation for subsequent settlement by three referees. The proposed union with the Midland was not however the only such application affecting the LNWR before Parliament that session: a separate Bill was brought forward for an amalgamation with the North Staffordshire Railway. This was the eventual outcome of the earlier disputes with that company over the 1850 traffic agreement; after twice rejecting the findings of arbitration, the NSR tried to force the issue by promoting three Bills in 1852. While one was for amalgamation with the LNWR, the others were hostile, seeking powers for a new line from Colwich to Wolverhampton and to extend the company's authorised Harecastle–Sandbach branch to Warrington, where it would have connected with proposed lines to Manchester and towards Liverpool. This prompted the LNWR to agree to further arbitration by James Hope QC and Robert Stephenson, who recommended absorption of the NSR on the basis of an initial guarantee of 3% on its ordinary shares, rising progressively to $3\frac{1}{2}$%. The proposal was approved by the two companies in December 1852 and the apparent restoration of friendly relations was marked by the co-option of the North Staffordshire chairman, John Lewis Ricardo, to the LNWR board. Earlier that year it had also been agreed that the L&Y and LNWR should each appoint a director to the other's board.

Several other companies brought forward amalga-mation Bills in the session of 1853, and the government and Parliament were sufficiently concerned at the extent of these proposals to establish a select committee – the Cardwell Committee – to investigate the wider implications. As a result, all proposals for amalgamations, leases, and working or financial arrangements were deferred, affecting not only the LNWR's Bills for amalgamation with the Midland and the NSR, but also those proposing arrangements with the BL&CJ and the two Hereford companies. The select committee eventually recommended against further amalgamations, preferring instead properly-regulated traffic agreements, and some of its recommendations were given effect by the Railway & Canal Traffic Act of 1854. This compelled railway companies to provide facilities for forwarding through traffic over lines or canals which they controlled and forbade undue preference in charges, thus striking at some of the tactics which Huish and other railway managers had used in the battles to secure traffic and territory. However, some of the more sweeping recommendations – including an extension of the powers of the Board of Trade over railway schemes and agreements – were rejected, while Parliament, ever zealous to demonstrate its independence in railway matters, showed in 1854 that it was not opposed in principle to amalgamation by approving the creation of the North Eastern Railway and the absorption of the Shrewsbury companies by the GWR. The LNWR was less successful: though the Midland and North Staffordshire amalgamation proposals were reintroduced in 1854, the latter with amended financial terms, these failed once more, together with renewed Bills for arrangements with the NA&H and the BL&CJ.

After this second setback to their amalgamation proposals, the LNWR and Midland negotiated a 'common purse' agreement later in 1854, effective for ten years from 1 July. This also included the 'little' North Western Railway, under the aegis of the Midland, and two of the LNWR's associated companies: the Manchester, Sheffield & Lincolnshire and the North Staffordshire; indeed, for financial purposes the latter had effectively merged with the LNWR from the beginning of 1853 under the terms of the arbitration award. The agreement provided for a pooling of revenue and its distribution between the companies on an agreed basis, and was clearly designed to unite the partners' interests in preparation for the renewal of the traffic agreements with the GNR. Huish was thus in a strong position when formal negotiations with Seymour Clarke, the GNR general manager, began in 1855. Although a revised Anglo-Scottish agreement was brought into effect from 1 January 1856 which gave the east coast route a share in passenger and goods traffic to Glasgow for the first time as well as an improved proportion of Edinburgh revenue, the GNR board overruled its general manager on the question of terms for pooling traffic to competitive points in England. For a short period in 1856 there was intense competition for traffic between London and these towns, which was finally resolved by a renewed reference to Mr Gladstone.

Meanwhile, the 'little' North Western, dissatisfied with the limited recognition it had received in the revised Anglo-Scottish agreement, had once more renewed its ambitions to be part of an alternative route to Scotland, and introduced a Bill in 1856 to revive its powers for a line through the Lune valley, which would be coupled with running powers over the L&C and Midland railways. The GNR gave its support, but the Bill met vigorous parliamentary opposition and was eventually withdrawn, though not before details of the 'common purse' agreement had been disclosed in evidence. Since parts of the agreement were, in strict terms, *ultra vires*, the participant companies were open to legal challenge, so on the advice of their solicitors the Midland and LNWR cancelled the agreement in May 1857 when a GNR director commenced such an action after having qualified himself by the purchase of £200 of LNWR stock. With the exception of the Anglo-Scottish agreement, most of the traffic pooling arrangements with the GNR were also abandoned soon afterwards.

* * *

While the termination of these agreements marked the formal ending of the LNWR's system of alliances, the so-called 'Euston Square confederacy', the break-up had started much sooner. Following the failure of another NSR amalgamation Bill in 1855, the LNWR considered that it had met the terms of the arbitration award, which required three attempts to be made to obtain parliamentary approval. The NSR felt otherwise and repeated its earlier tactics by introducing a series of Bills in 1856 which would have given it independent access to Wolverhampton and to Liverpool

via Warrington and Garston. These measures all failed, as did an 1857 Bill to gain control of the Cannock Mineral Railway, which had obtained powers in 1855 to build a line from Rugeley to connect with the South Staffordshire's Cannock branch, authorised the previous year. The Cannock Mineral's Act also contained provisions to allow its undertaking to be leased or purchased by the LNWR, and in 1857 the NSR sought unsuccessfully to modify these powers in its favour and to promote an extension to its own system. Unable either to force amalgamation with the LNWR or to gain independent outlets for its traffic, and having also failed in an attempt to gain control of the Bridgewater Canal in order to improve its competitive position, the NSR finally came to terms with its larger neighbour and in 1858 settled for a comprehensive exchange of running powers and a favourable traffic agreement. Although temptations were to recur, the company thereafter generally accepted its role as a feeder line and as the LNWR's partner in designated traffic flows, such as the service between Manchester and Euston via Stoke.

No such accommodation proved possible with the MS&L, despite that company's acquisition of the services of the LNWR's former assistant secretary, Edward Watkin, as its general manager at the end of 1853. While the agreement which he negotiated with the LNWR in 1854 gave the MS&L more favourable financial results than it had managed to achieve by its own efforts, difficulties began to emerge on two counts. Firstly, the MS&L was concerned at the LNWR's financial support for the Stockport, Disley & Whaley Bridge Railway, which was authorised in 1854. This overlapped with an earlier scheme for a branch to Whaley Bridge from the Sheffield main line; though this branch had been abandoned south of Hyde, the MS&L retained a stake in the area through its ownership of the Peak Forest Canal. Secondly, the LNWR for its part was suspicious of MS&L interest in a route to Liverpool via Warrington, which, as noted, had also attracted the attention of the NSR. In 1855 the latter unsuccessfully proposed amalgamation with the St Helens Canal & Railway, which had been authorised in 1846 to extend westwards from Runcorn Gap to a proposed new dock at Garston and in 1847 gained powers to build an eastwards extension from Runcorn Gap to Warrington. Garston line services began on 1 July 1852, while the Warrington branch was opened to a temporary terminus on 1 February

1853. The Warrington & Altrincham Junction Railway, with which the St Helens company had close links, was authorised in 1851 to continue from Warrington to the Manchester South Junction & Altrincham Railway at Timperley. This opened between temporary stations at both ends of its route on 1 November 1853 and the short gap between the Garston and Timperley lines at Warrington was filled on 1 May 1854, when each was extended to the new Arpley station. On the same day the through connection to the MSJ&A at Timperley was opened.

By then the W&AJ had become the Warrington & Stockport Railway under the provisions of an 1853 Act which authorised an extension from Timperley to Stockport. In the same year it also obtained powers to build a branch from Arpley to the BL&CJ at Walton, replacing a longer connecting line authorised in 1851. The Stockport extension was not constructed, but the Walton junction branch was completed in 1855, providing a potential alternative route from Manchester to Chester, Birkenhead, and north Wales, and also a possible link with the GWR system. The W&S was thus a significant addition to the network and it was only with some reluctance that the LNWR agreed that it should be worked by the MS&L, initially in its own right and then from 1856 as an extension of the MSJ&A arrangements. In the same year a direct connection was opened between the Warrington and Garston lines at Runcorn Gap, so that a through route became available from Manchester to within five miles of Liverpool.

Despite the NSR's earlier interest, the MS&L was the first to use the Garston line against the LNWR. The latter had continued to support the Whaley Bridge company, which gained powers in 1855 to form a junction with the Cromford & High Peak Railway. This had been authorised in 1825, and though it had been included in some early proposals for through railway routes the C&HP was laid out primarily for mineral traffic, with steep inclined planes. It was opened from Cromford to Hurdlow on 29 May 1830 and completion to Whaley Bridge followed on 6 July 1831. While the line functioned primarily as a feeder to the canals with which it connected at both ends of its route, a junction with the MBM&MJ at Cromford had been opened on 21 February 1853. The Whaley Bridge connection, opened on 17 August 1857, provided a corresponding rail outlet to the north. Services between Stockport and Whaley Bridge began on 9 June 1857, and completion of the junction with the C&HP gave the LNWR, which worked the SD&WB, access to the limestone and other mineral traffic of the district. The threat to MS&L interests was further increased by the authorisation that year of an extension line to Buxton, again with LNWR support. This local issue quickly became part of a wider dispute, and within a few weeks there was open hostility.

The initial circumstances of the breach were soon lost in mutual accusations of bad faith and in an extensive war of words which has coloured subsequent accounts. The GNR and MS&L version was that, after the 'common purse' agreement with the Midland was abandoned, Huish approached Clarke at Kings Cross with a proposal for a territorial division between their two companies which disregarded the interests of the MS&L. Clarke then used this apparent evidence of duplicity to encourage the MS&L, through Watkin, to enter into a direct alliance with his company, thus giving the GNR access to Lancashire. On its side, the LNWR contended that Huish had met Clarke in his capacity as chairman of the group of officers concerned with the renegotiation of the earlier traffic agreements, and that territory was discussed solely in relation to these agreements and to proposals for new branch lines. The LNWR further argued that the only breach of faith was that by the MS&L, which unilaterally broke the 1854 agreement while it still had more than half of its term to run.

While most subsequent commentators have followed the GNR and MS&L account of the episode and cited it as a further demonstration of Huish's ruthlessness, Clarke's and Watkin's versions of these events were discredited by a parliamentary committee in 1858. Their evidence on this point shows neither in a good light, and suggests that if there was duplicity it was on the part of the GNR and MS&L general managers rather than Huish. Although there was undoubted personal animosity between Huish and Watkin, it is difficult to see what the LNWR would have gained by deliberately alienating the MS&L, especially as the financial arrangement between the two companies was not affected by the state of Euston's relations with Kings Cross. On the other hand, there were obvious advantages to the GNR in separating the MS&L from the LNWR; as later events were to prove, the MS&L also had much to gain by exploiting its nuisance value.

Wherever the origins of the dispute lay, the outcome was soon evident. With unfettered access to the MS&L's route from Retford to Manchester the GNR was able to commence vigorous competition with the LNWR for Manchester traffic in the summer of 1857. The LNWR responded by reducing Euston–Manchester timings to 4 hours 40 minutes, and by using its control of London Road station to hinder the new Kings Cross services. It also had the assistance of the Midland and L&Y in diverting exchange traffic away from the MS&L. Watkin and Clarke retaliated by carrying the competition westwards, using the routes via Warrington to run through services to Chester and to Garston, with road connections thence to Liverpool. The MS&L, with GNR support, also made preparations for Bills in 1858 to give it control of the Warrington & Stockport Railway and to provide a Garston–Liverpool line.

As usual, the competition was not sustained: the LNWR successfully opposed the MS&L's parliamentary attempt to create a Manchester–Warrington–Liverpool route and by June 1858 agreement had been reached to charge equal fares. On 12 November that year more detailed arrangements between the three companies were settled, including undertakings to exchange traffic freely and to divide London Road station between the MS&L and LNWR. But by then Huish was no longer concerned with the negotiations: he offered his resignation on 11 September 1858 and this took effect in November. At the age of 50, with a free pass for life, a gratuity of £3,000 – 18 months' salary – and a testimonial from the LNWR's staff, Huish retired as general manager and was replaced by a recruit from outside the company, William Cawkwell, the goods manager of the L&Y.

Huish's resignation has generally been linked with the failure of the offensive and defensive alliances with which his name has been chiefly linked. But, as Gourvish's study has shown, these policies were by no means the sole responsibility of the general manager – successive chairmen were closely involved in the complex diplomacy through which inter-company relations were conducted. Nor were external affairs Huish's only preoccupation: in his professional handling of what was easily the largest business undertaking in the country he demonstrated himself to be an advanced and capable manager, able to offer the board sound advice based on detailed analysis and good technical knowledge. That he had faults was

recognised both by colleagues and by his directors, but in many respects these were the other side of the personality strengths that had enabled him to stamp his authority on the internal management of the LNWR and to dominate negotiations with officers of other companies. His character traits therefore meant that he was strongly identified with what came to be perceived as a failing external policy and with the company's deteriorating financial performance. In addition, when the tide began to turn against the LNWR from the mid-1850s onwards, his management style left him with few friends, either in the company or outside. Directors, aware of their company's unpopularity with other railways, were also conscious that Huish was seen as personifying the LNWR.

The contemporary strains in the relationship between the board and its executive have already been mentioned; furthermore, it should be borne in mind that for many of the new directors seeking to assert their influence within the company Huish represented the old guard, the pre-amalgamation heritage. For example, Moon, who was six years younger than the general manager, disagreed strongly with him on a number of issues. In addition to the effects of external events and of the LNWR's deteriorating financial performance, Huish was already coming under pressure from within the company, and his resignation possibly averted a more serious internal crisis. It is no denigration of Huish's undoubted achievements and his strong commitment to the LNWR's interests to borrow a later analogy and suggest that his role was perhaps Bismarckian – by 1858 events had moved on, and it was time to drop the pilot who had steered the company, with no little success, through a period when many other railways had come close to financial disaster. As Chandos shrewdly remarked at the general meeting on 13 August 1858, alliances and agreements worked well enough when there was only a small number of companies, but became increasingly difficult to maintain in a larger and more complex system. New arrangements were therefore required, and the LNWR began to resort to more direct methods of securing its interests. In addition, the growing tendency for railway companies to act in concert to defend themselves against the threat of government intervention and to deal with mutual problems created an easier climate for settling differences within the industry – the Railway Companies' Association emerged in 1858 out of attempts by leading chairmen to mediate in the LNWR's dispute with the GNR and MS&L.

* * *

The effects of this more open policy were quickly seen. The settlements with the NSR and of the competition for Manchester traffic have already been described, and in 1859 the LNWR went on to consolidate its position by leasing the Warrington & Stockport Railway jointly with the St Helens company, which took a third share in the lease. In the same year the LNWR obtained powers to make a link between Garston and Liverpool, and in 1860 leased the Garston–Warrington line from the St Helens undertaking, which also granted the LNWR access to Garston docks. In 1861 the Warrington & Stockport was purchased outright by the LNWR. Similar measures were taken to nullify any possible future threat from the BL&CJ, which adopted the name Birkenhead Railway under an 1859 Act giving it powers to make a line from Helsby to Hooton and a short branch to Tranmere Pool. In November 1860 the Birkenhead system was leased by the LNWR and GWR and placed under joint management.

This followed an 1858 agreement which gave the GWR access to Manchester via Warrington and the L&M line. The battle with the GNR and MS&L was still undetermined at that stage and the agreement was part of a defensive cementing of relations with the GWR. The LNWR thus offered no objection when the OW&W reached an agreement with the GWR the same year which provided for the extension of mixed gauge to Paddington. However, relations were briefly strained when the OW&W amalgamated with the Newport, Abergavenny & Hereford and Worcester & Hereford in 1860 to form the West Midland Railway, and there was further tension when, after a final attempt by the successor company to promote an independent line from Oxford to London, the GWR leased the West Midland with effect from 1 July 1861. Despite this, Euston remained the London terminus for through trains to and from the Worcester line until mixed gauge was completed to Paddington on 1 October 1861.

Steps were also taken to secure the long outliers to Holyhead and Carlisle by ending their separate operation through legally-independent companies. In the case of the C&H, after a proposal for full amalgama-tion had been deferred in 1852, a new agreement was reached with effect from 1 July 1856 which provided for the C&H to be worked by the LNWR as part of its own system in return for an agreed proportion of receipts. Virtually all the staff were brought into LNWR employment, and a separate board committee was set up to administer the Chester & Holyhead district of the LNWR. This also included the Mold Railway, and another undertaking, the Bangor & Carnarvon Railway, which was authorised in 1851. This carried mineral traffic between Menai Bridge and Port Dinorwic from 10 March 1852, and was opened to Caernarfon on 1 July that year for passengers and on 10 August for freight. The C&H leased the Caernarfon line from the outset and in 1852 also completed another branch in the Bangor area, a short mineral line to Port Penrhyn, which was built without recourse to parliamentary powers. There were two other additions to the system in north Wales in the 1850s, although both were at first operationally independent. One of these offshoots from the Holyhead line was authorised under the St George's Harbour Act of 1853, which was an echo of the earlier hopes of creating a packet station in the lee of the Great Orme. However, the company limited itself to building a pier and the branch to Llandudno, which was opened on 1 October 1858. Locomotive requirements were met by hiring from the LNWR, although horse haulage was sufficient for winter traffic. The other branch, the Vale of Clwyd Railway, was authorised in 1856 to provide a link with Denbigh from the C&H main line at Foryd junction, west of Rhyl; it opened to a temporary station at Denbigh on 5 October 1858 but was not completed to its terminus until December 1860. A temporary spur to the shoreline, built to allow ballast to be extracted while the line was under construction, was brought back into use by the landowner during 1859 to provide access to his pier at the mouth of the River Foryd.

Although most of its responsibilities had passed to the LNWR, the C&H board continued to keep a watchful eye on its property. As a result of parliamentary investigations into mail services, there was renewed pressure for better links with Ireland, and with a new Post Office contract due in 1859 the directors sought to raise more capital to improve the company's fleet, which had already been expanded by the purchase of six second-hand vessels. However, they were unwilling to commit funds for this purpose without firmer arrangements with the LNWR and accordingly promoted a Bill in 1858 to authorise the latter to guarantee an issue of C&H preference shares and to permit the two companies to amalgamate. But clauses were also included which required that, if these provisions were implemented, traffic facilities should be made available to other railways which connected with the C&H. The MS&L, which was then operating a Garston–Dublin shipping service as part of its competition for LNWR traffic, had access to Chester via Walton junction, while the GWR was directly linked with the C&H at Saltney. Seeing the risk of opening the Holyhead line to competitors, the LNWR refused to implement the Act, so in November 1858 the C&H board gave notice of a Bill in the ensuing session to give it running powers from Chester to Crewe and to permit arrangements with a range of companies, including the GNR, GWR, MS&L, and NSR. Faced with this threat the LNWR board agreed to give effect to the amalgamation provisions as from 1 January 1859, and on that date the C&H was absorbed into the LNWR system. Two days later a new contract was agreed between the Post Office, the LNWR, the C&H, and the City of Dublin Steam Packet Company. Under its terms, which came into full effect on 1 October 1860, the London–Dublin time was reduced to 11 hours, and the challenge of running the mail train between Euston and Holyhead in the necessary 6 hours 40 minutes led Ramsbottom to devise water troughs and install them at Mochdre in the autumn of 1860. To permit a $3^3/_4$-hour sea crossing to Kingstown the CDSPC commissioned four new steamers, which were bought with a loan from the LNWR. The existing C&H vessels were concentrated on the North Wall service, together with the newly-built *Admiral Moorsom*, which was delivered in 1860.

Unlike the C&H, the Lancaster & Carlisle enjoyed a financially stable independence and in 1856 had agreed to provide its own locomotives and rolling stock with effect from the following year, largely to allow the LNWR to release the resources thus employed. The eventual stimulus for absorption by the LNWR was given by the complications caused by the 'little' North Western Railway. Though the latter's 1856 Bill for a revised Lune valley line was defeated, it renewed the application in 1857 and the L&C therefore countered with a proposal of its own for a branch from Low Gill to Ingleton. The Commons committee considering both schemes approved the L&C's Bill,

so the company consequently found itself in possession of parliamentary powers that gave it an alternative route south. In the same year the L&C was authorised to contribute to the South Durham & Lancashire Union Railway, which was promoted by the still-independent Stockton & Darlington Railway to provide a line between West Auckland and Tebay. The L&C also gained interests in south-west Scotland in 1857 through the incorporation of the Portpatrick Railway, to which it subscribed.

With the L&C beginning to look in other directions, and the balance further disturbed by a Midland agreement in 1858 to lease the 'little' NWR, with which the Ingleton branch would connect, Euston could no longer be confident that the line to Carlisle would remain securely under its influence. With effect from 1 August 1859, therefore, the LNWR took a 900-year lease of the L&C, guaranteeing $4^1/_2$% more than its own dividend, with a minimum of 8%. The L&C in turn absorbed the Lancaster & Preston Junction Railway and leased the Kendal & Windermere, so that the entire system passed to the LNWR. In 1860 the LNWR purchased the L&C's equipment outright, thus regaining ownership of those locomotives that it had sold to the Carlisle company when it ceased to work the line in 1857.

The interest in the South Durham & Lancashire Union Railway which the LNWR acquired from the L&C involved it briefly in the railway affairs of north-eastern England, where the NER was still attempting to complete its monopoly. Out of the North British's desire to gain an independent outlet south, the West Hartlepool Harbour & Railway Company's struggle against the NER's grip on its traffic, and the LNWR's wish to exchange traffic for the north-east over its own line to Leeds rather than via the L&Y at Normanton, there emerged a hotchpotch of ephemeral schemes to make use of the SD&LU route which would have given the LNWR access to Tyneside and to West Hartlepool. The NER eventually conceded traffic agreements which laid these projects to rest, but not before the LNWR's involvement with the West Hartlepool company had been strongly criticised at its own general meetings.

This toying with schemes to reach the north-east was one symptom that, despite the understandings of 1858, the railway world remained unsettled. A significant new consideration for the LNWR was the growing independence of the Midland: in 1857 it opened its line to Hitchin, and the GNR granted running powers to Kings Cross the following year. Although the bulk of its London traffic still moved via Rugby, the Midland's physical dependence on the LNWR was thus eased, while the continued buoyancy of its carryings and revenue, particularly from London coal traffic, gave the Midland a financial standing that contrasted sharply with its position a decade earlier when Hudson was ousted. In 1858 its dividend, like the GNR's, outstripped that of the LNWR for the first time, and in 1859 its shares were at par, compared with the 9% average discount of LNWR consols. Already the Midland was beginning to consider a route of its own into London, and the lease of the NWR started to feed its Scottish ambitions.

Against this background the LNWR's truces in 1858 with the GNR and MS&L and with the GWR left the Midland at a disadvantage, since it alone had no access to south Lancashire, while the LNWR's push towards Buxton was seen as an invasion of territory to which it held prior claim. The LNWR's revival of interest in a line from Nuneaton to Leicester and its increasing influence over the South Staffordshire Railway were also matters of concern. The L&Y, too, was beginning to feel threatened by the LNWR, especially when the latter promoted Bills in 1858 to end its need to use other companies' metals in operating between Manchester and Leeds. Although these schemes were unsuccessful, Midland and L&Y interests grew closer together. Ellis retired from the LNWR board in 1858 and in the following year the Midland reached a traffic agreement with the L&Y which gave it access to Manchester and Liverpool. The Midland also successfully opposed Bills in that session and in 1860 which would have authorised traffic arrangements between the LNWR, GNR, and MS&L; not to be ignored, the NSR opposed an alternative Bill in 1860 which would have included the Midland in a wider agreement with the other three companies.

Once again, however, the MS&L proved to be the wild card. Watkin and his directors remained dissatisfied with their company's exclusion from the area beyond the MSJ&A and suspicious of the LNWR's intentions for the Garston–Liverpool line. The MS&L also tried to block the lease of the Birkenhead Railway by the GWR and LNWR, while in the West Riding it was pursuing objectives which conflicted with those of the GNR. In an attempt to remove these continuing difficulties, Cawkwell and Clarke reached agreement with Watkin in December 1860 for a joint lease by the LNWR and GNR of the MS&L, under which the latter's ordinary shareholders would be guaranteed an eventual 3% dividend. When this was considered by a special committee of the LNWR board it was endorsed by a majority; however, it was opposed by Lord Chandos, who wrote to Denison to such effect that the GNR board rejected the proposition on 23 January 1861. Chandos meanwhile tendered his resignation both as chairman and a director at a special LNWR board meeting on 5 January; this was accepted, and was subsequently followed by the resignation of four other directors.

Some of the eventual consequences of these events will be touched upon in Chapter Five, but three should be noted at this stage. Firstly, the MS&L, freed of any LNWR restraint, proceeded to support Bills in 1861 which laid the foundation of the Cheshire Lines system and thus provided a basis for further direct competition with LNWR routes in Cheshire and south Lancashire. Secondly, the collapse of the proposed agreement left Watkin free to pursue an alliance with the Midland, which, significantly, had rejected the opportunity to join the LNWR and GNR in their negotiations with the MS&L in December 1860. This opened the way for the Midland to develop its own route to Buxton and Manchester and in turn led to its becoming a partner, with the GNR and the MS&L, in the Cheshire Lines. Lastly, of course, an immediate gap was created in the direction of the LNWR. Chandos's attitude suggests that he was distrustful of Watkin after the dispute of 1857, and also had his own opinion of the value of the MS&L to LNWR shareholders. Whether his view was correct in the long run is perhaps debatable in the light of the later damage the MS&L and Watkin were able to inflict, and it is also questionable whether his action in writing privately to Denison on a matter of company policy was consistent with his board responsibilities: in contradiction to the account of these events given in histories of the GNR, it is clear from LNWR records that Chandos's letter was sent before his resignation. However, the chairman's integrity in resigning his post on a matter of principle cannot be gainsaid, nor can the significance of these events for subsequent railway development in England.

Chandos succeeded as third Duke of Buckingham & Chandos in July 1861 and went on to resume his political career. He was replaced as chairman by his deputy, Moorsom, who had risen to the rank of vice-admiral in the reserve list. His involvement with the company went back to the early days of the London & Birmingham Railway and he had acquired a reputation as a progressive and effective director. However, Admiral Moorsom's time as chairman was short, for he died on 26 May 1861 after an operation which became necessary because of an arm wound received in battle under Nelson at Copenhagen. His death added to the difficulties facing the LNWR: besides the internal disruption caused by the resignation of Chandos and four other directors, morale had been undermined by the most serious accident the LNWR had yet experienced, a collision at Atherstone in November 1860 which caused ten deaths. Lastly, the dividend for the half-year to June 1861, £1 17s 6d, proved to rank with that for the first half of 1858 as the lowest in the company's history. The new chairman, Richard Moon, who was elected unanimously by his board colleagues on 22 June 1861, could hardly have taken over in less auspicious circumstances.

CHAPTER FIVE

Recovery and Expansion

When Richard Moon was appointed as the LNWR's fifth chairman he was 47: he had been born on 23 February 1814, the son of a Liverpool merchant of the same name. As a young man Moon had hoped to enter the Church, but his father opposed this, so after studying at St Andrews he joined the family firm. By the time he became an LNWR director in 1851 Moon had retired from the business and was living near Worcester; Liverpool links were however retained through marriage ties with the Brocklebank shipping family. Moon quickly established an influence on the LNWR's affairs after his election to the board and became chairman of the stores committee in 1852. As noted, he also chaired the board's committee of investigation in 1855, and when Moorsom replaced Chandos in 1861 Moon was appointed as his deputy. Despite this, after Moorsom's death the *Railway Times* did not at first see him as the likely successor, although *Herapath* soon commented that 'the Company have at length got the right man in the right place in Mr Moon'. A further indication that the LNWR was in new hands was the selection of Joshua Brown Westhead as deputy-chairman: he had been a director for less than five months, filling one of the vacancies caused by the January board crisis. Brown Westhead, MP for Knaresborough and later for York, remained as deputy until 1872, when he resigned because of ill-health; he was succeeded by John Pares Bickersteth, whose tenure of office was to extend beyond Moon's own retiral in 1891 and well into the next century.

Moon's forthright views on the management of the company had already had an impact during the 1850s; as chairman he was able to carry them into fuller effect, and in so doing he built up a nucleus of senior officers who provided strong executive support for the board and whose own abilities contributed significantly to the distinction which the LNWR earned during his period of office. This was reflected in their salaries: the company never stinted the remuneration of its chief officials, and despite Moon's legendary frugality he ensured that the part which they played in adding to the value of the shareholders' assets was recognised financially. At a time when few railwaymen could hope to earn more than £100 a year the LNWR paid four-figure salaries to several of its upper-echelon staff, and some of these received significant increases under Moon.

This was partly an acknowledgement of the additional responsibilities which stemmed from the streamlining and centralisation of the company's organisation. This trend was clearly emerging even before Chandos stepped down: when the veteran Henry Booth retired as joint secretary in 1859 he was not replaced, and Charles Stewart became the sole secretary, based at Euston. Stewart left in 1866 and was succeeded by Stephen Reay, previously head of the company's audit office. Despite the role that Huish had created as general manager, the secretary's post was still a key appointment, and Reay, who was appointed at an annual salary of £1,250, was to remain as one of Moon's closest advisers for more than twenty years.

Another management change that predated Moon's chairmanship was William Baker's appointment in 1859 as engineer in charge of all new works, on an initial salary of £1,000. At the same time, the maintenance of existing track and structures was reorganised under four district superintendents of permanent way, whose salaries ranged from £700 to £850. Baker's appointment, which followed the death of Robert Stephenson, replaced the previous reliance on consultant engineers for new projects and brought responsibility for all civil engineering functions within the company. A similar desire to employ in-house resources was reflected in an alteration made after Moon became chairman: in October 1861 the LNWR engaged its own solicitor and dispensed with the services of Messrs Carter, Swift & Wagstaffe, whose connection with the company went back to the

Liverpool & Manchester Railway. Although the step was taken for financial reasons and to ensure that legal advice was always on hand, there may also have been concern about possible conflicts of interest, as the same solicitors acted for the Midland Railway. Continuity was however ensured, since one of the firm's partners, James Blenkinsop, transferred to the LNWR appointment. Another organisational change followed soon afterwards: from 1 January 1862 goods handling in the London depots was taken over by the company's own staff, leaving only collection and delivery work with Pickfords and Chaplin & Horne. In this case the handover was less than amicable: David Stevenson, who had responsibility for the new arrangements, recorded in his memoirs that Chaplin & Horne went to law in an unsuccessful attempt to prevent the change, and that Benjamin Horne's hostility persisted until his death.

There was also controversy over another of Moon's early changes, the final concentration of responsibility for locomotive matters under Ramsbottom at Crewe. This was the culmination of a process which had begun at the end of 1859, when a select committee had been established to review the existing arrangements. McConnell, who enjoyed the support of several former L&B directors, argued that the financial performance of his division was affected by the then operating boundaries, under which the Trent Valley line formed part of the northern division. His initial proposal to extend his division to Crewe was rejected, but in January 1860 the board endorsed the committee's recommendation that Stafford should become the main boundary, with shared working over the former Grand Junction route between there and Bushbury.

Moon, who had consistently championed Ramsbottom's approach to locomotive design and departmental management and was a member of the select committee, opposed the boundary adjustment, and on 22 December 1859 even went so far as to resign his chairmanship of the general stores & locomotive committee, which he had held since the remit of the stores committee was extended in March 1858 to include locomotive and other rolling stock matters. However, Chandos persuaded him to resume his position the following month, and in this capacity he oversaw the implementation of one of the select committee's incidental recommendations, the rationalisation of the divisional carriage and wagon

establishments. While the immediate justification was to release the existing carriage building shop at Crewe to give more space to the locomotive works, it enabled Moon to bring into effect principles that were later to be applied to the management of the locomotive department.

As a consequence, the former southern division carriage & wagon works at Saltley assumed responsibility early in 1860 for carriage manufacture for the whole system and in exchange relinquished its wagon functions to Earlestown. The manager there, Owen Owens, became wagon superintendent for the entire line, a post which he held until 1867 when he retired and was succeeded by J W Emmett. The existing southern division carriage & wagon superintendent, a Mr Slater, was similarly given the superintendence of all the LNWR's coaching stock, in preference to Nathaniel Worsdell at Crewe, whose coach-building service had started with the L&M. Although a new post was created for Worsdell, to take charge of stores and wagon sheet manufacture at Crewe, it took several months, and repeated instructions from the directors, before he wound up his previous responsibilities. It is not clear whether these difficulties with Worsdell were a contributory factor, but Slater proffered his resignation in March 1860 and two months later the board promoted Richard Bore, manager of the carriage depot at Euston, to take over as departmental superintendent at Saltley with a salary of £400 per annum. Worsdell's supporters among the directorate, who included Hardman Earle, were however sufficiently influential to ensure that Bore was initially appointed on a provisional basis.

These were the precedents in April 1861 when Moon, by then deputy-chairman, secured the establishment of a further special committee to review the performance of the two locomotive divisions in the light of the previous year's changes. Although McConnell was a first-rate engineer, and had produced some outstanding locomotive classes, the extension of his territory failed to lead to the operating savings he had promised, and the committee tabled a highly critical report in December 1861. Glyn and another former L&B director, Robert Benson, succeeded in delaying consideration of its findings, but the next board meeting, in January 1862, adopted the report by a majority of three. McConnell accordingly resigned with effect from 31 March 1862, and on 1 April Crewe became the locomotive headquarters for the entire system, though two divisions were retained for operating purposes. Ramsbottom's salary was at the same time increased from £1,200 to £2,000 per annum in recognition of his extended responsibilities. From the start of 1864 another £1,000 was added, then in 1869 a further increase took his annual salary to £5,000.

Ramsbottom retired for health reasons in 1871, but by then he had overseen the enlargement and modernisation of Crewe works and established its reputation for the bulk production of cheap but capable locomotives. After his 'DX' goods design of 1858, of which almost 800 were in service by 1871, and a stud of 2-2-2 express passenger engines, the 'Problem' class of 1859, Ramsbottom went on to introduce in 1863 the first of fifty 'Samson' 2-4-0s for secondary passenger duties and an 0-4-0 saddle tank design for shunting. These were followed by a more powerful 2-4-0 class, the 'Newtons' of 1866, and in 1870 by Ramsbottom's final design for the LNWR, an 0-6-0 saddle tank developed from the 'DX' class. Besides turning out large quantities of new engines – in 1866 the production of 'DXs' averaged one every $2^1/_4$ working days – Crewe had to handle locomotive maintenance and also to accommodate ancillary functions, such as the brickworks, added in 1862, and the pioneering Bessemer steel plant, completed in 1865. A southward deviation of the Chester line, which opened on 26 July 1868 and was accompanied by the rebuilding of Crewe station, allowed the works area to be extended, and new manufacturing and repair shops were developed as part of the subsequent expansion. The carriage department retained separate repair facilities at Crewe, at first alongside the up main line north of the station, but later on a new site south of the line to Chester.

Wolverton continued to undertake some locomotive maintenance until 1877, but after the completion of its current orders in 1863 all new manufacture was concentrated at Crewe. This provided an opportunity for the relocation of the carriage department to Wolverton, and the facilities there were extended and adapted to enable the Saltley workshops to be vacated in 1865. However, the latter premises continued to be used for rolling stock manufacture, since they were taken over by the Metropolitan Railway Carriage & Wagon Company, which in 1862 had bought out Joseph Wright's adjacent private coachbuilding works.

These changes, which were accompanied by staff transfers from Wolverton to Crewe and Saltley to Wolverton, established the final geographical pattern of the LNWR's main works, and when the remaining southern division locomotive maintenance duties were moved from Wolverton to Rugby in 1877 the transition to a functional organisational structure was completed. However, the locomotive department's manufacturing capacity continued to be used to supply other departments, emphasising the importance of Crewe works in Moon's strategy of company self-sufficiency.

* * *

The chairman's influence was also soon apparent in the commercial and operating organisation of the LNWR. As part of the internal rationalisation that followed the 1859 amalgamations, responsibility for the company's passenger business had been restructured into six districts in January 1860, but in March 1862 these area appointments were supplemented when G P Neele was moved from Birmingham, where he had briefly served as district superintendent, to the new headquarters post of general outdoor superintendent, with an initial annual salary of £500. According to Neele's own account, one reason why he had come to the chairman's notice was the saving he achieved by using marginal time in existing locomotive rosters to cover a new service.

Another district officer to gain early promotion under Moon was George Findlay, who had joined the LNWR from the Shrewsbury & Hereford Railway in 1862 and was made chief goods manager with effect from 1 January 1866. In this capacity Findlay, then aged 39, relieved Charles Mason, the former general manager of the Birkenhead Railway, who had been appointed as Cawkwell's assistant in 1861 and also took charge of the goods department in succession to T C Mills. Under the 1866 reorganisation Cawkwell was left to concentrate on policy issues and new expenditure, while Mason, who kept his designation as assistant general manager, was given general oversight of traffic matters, both goods and passenger. Although the freight business was a separate commercial organisation, with its own district structure, depot staff, and guards, the general manager's department had effective primacy in the control of train movements, since besides directly managing the passenger traffic it was also responsible for signalling operations.

The redefinition of duties in 1866 was accompanied by a review of salaries. Cawkwell's annual remuneration, which had increased from £2,000 to £2,500 in 1863, was raised by a further £500, while Mason's went up from £1,500 to £1,800; Findlay was placed on £1,500 per annum. Neele, who had received an increase of £100 in 1865, was at first unaffected by these changes, but from July 1867 his salary became £750. Mason, who was awarded a further £200 in November 1867, backdated by a year, died prematurely in 1869, and in a virtual reversion to the pre-1866 position Findlay then became in effect Cawkwell's deputy as well as goods manager. He was designated assistant general manager in 1871 with a salary of £1,750, which was increased to £2,000 in March 1872.

Later that year Cawkwell expressed a wish to retire and was nominated for a directorship, but Moon retained some reservations about the appropriateness of the post of general manager, which he had first expressed during his opposition to Huish. Cawkwell was persuaded to continue in a temporary capacity until February 1874, but no direct replacement was then appointed: Findlay had to be content with the new position of chief traffic manager, at a salary of £2,500 per annum. He was succeeded as chief goods manager by Thomas Kay, formerly district goods manager at Manchester, while Neele, whose annual salary was by then £1,000, became general passenger superintendent. In May 1875 Neele's designation was again changed, to superintendent of the line: this followed the retiral in 1874 of Captain Bruyeres, the long-serving superintendent of the southern division. Thomas Kay retired as goods manager in 1885 and was replaced by Frederick Harrison, previously assistant to Findlay. By then, though, the latter's own status had changed, since by 1880 Moon's doubts were sufficiently allayed for Findlay to become general manager in title as well as in practice.

However, the secretary's oversight of the company's administration and finance continued as a separate departmental responsibility, as did the civil engineering, rolling stock, and locomotive functions, the latter including engine running as well as manufacture and maintenance. Corporate direction of the LNWR's affairs accordingly remained with the board, where Moon was very much in overall control, effectively acting as managing director: indeed, the railway press sometimes used this designation. The chairman, who moved to Tamworth in 1868 and to Harrow five years later, was voted the customary annual payment of £2,000 from 1862 onwards, and from time to time salaries or honoraria were also paid to various other directors in recognition of specific responsibilities. These included James Bancroft, who played a key part in many inter-company negotiations, and Cawkwell, who retained a quasi-executive role after taking up his seat at the board in 1874 and became a deputy-chairman in 1881.

Despite initial resistance to some of Moon's changes, which in 1862 and 1863 extended to organised opposition by a Manchester-based shareholders' association, the new chairman soon stamped his authority on the company, and his policies were quickly vindicated by the results that were achieved. By 1865 the combined dividend for the two half-years had recovered to $6^5/8\%$ – the highest level since 1848 – and from the following year onwards LNWR ordinary stock again paid more than the Midland equivalent. Though dividends continued to fluctuate, they never again fell below the 6% mark during Moon's period of office, and were at 7% or more for much of that time. With such tangible evidence that their chairman's initial faith in the company's underlying financial soundness had not been misplaced, the shareholders soon began to reciprocate his confidence, and in 1872 publicly acknowledged Moon's contribution to the transformation of the LNWR's affairs by voting him a testimonial to the value of £5,250.

* * *

The restoration of the LNWR's financial standing began in economic circumstances that at first were far from promising. The disruption caused by the American civil war hit Lancashire particularly hard, and though other markets in Europe and the east soon developed and were supplemented by the rapid post-war expansion of trade with the USA, the familiar cycle reasserted itself in 1866, when tightening financial conditions marked the end of the boom. This led to the failure of Overend, Gurney, a leading London bill-broking firm, and cut short a wave of railway promotion that had been induced by earlier optimism. The associated bankruptcies among contractors included that of Peto & Betts, and although the direct effects of the crisis on the LNWR were limited its impact on connecting lines had significant repercussions.

Recovery at home was affected by a run of poor harvests in the late 1860s, but after the commercial uncertainty caused by the outbreak of the Franco-Prussian war in 1870 British exports then began to benefit from the effects of the war on continental coal and iron production. Foreign demand went on to increase rapidly between 1871 and 1873 in response to renewed American expansion and to post-war rebuilding in Europe: the tonnage of iron and steel exported from Britain in 1872 was 50% higher than in 1868. While the railways profited from the general expansion in demand and in particular from the growth in mineral traffic, there was a price to be paid in increased labour and material costs: Baker's half-yearly reports for this period record the difficulties that were being experienced with new works, and the inadvisability of pressing contractors too hard. The boom ended in 1873, with financial collapses in Austria, France, and the USA; although the City weathered the international storm reasonably well, Britain's export trade was immediately damaged. This led to deepening industrial depression, and business confidence suffered a further sharp setback when the City of Glasgow Bank failed in 1878.

The railway system as a whole was of course affected by such changes in the investment climate and by the influence of the trade cycle on traffic levels and operating costs, but despite the Overend, Gurney crisis there was a rapid growth in the railways' revenue and route mileage during the 1860s. New construction slowed down in the 1870s, but even after the onset of depression the trend in receipts continued upwards until 1878, when there was a reduction in the total earnings of Britain's railways for the first time since 1858.

Though the LNWR shared in these trends, its gross revenue did not fall until 1879, when the decline was more than offset by operating savings, and this in itself illustrates part of Moon's achievement. During the 1850s the LNWR had struggled unsuccessfully to maintain its position in the face of the growth of the wider network and the development of competing routes: in 1849 the company accounted for 19% of gross railway traffic receipts in Britain, but by 1861 the proportion had fallen to 16%. After Moon took over the LNWR's relative position was largely

stabilised, despite the continued expansion of the British railway system, and in 1890 the LNWR's gross receipts still represented almost 15% of the total. While much of this was attributable to the policy of developing existing traffic that Moon propounded at the first general meeting which he chaired, the sharp post-amalgamation fall in the LNWR's share of route mileage also ceased, and indeed in the 1860s and 1870s its system grew proportionately more rapidly than Britain's railways as a whole.

When he became chairman Moon suggested that the LNWR was more than large enough, and he also frequently stressed his wish to avoid competition. The continuing growth in the company's network may appear difficult to reconcile with these views, but Moon's early statements include other remarks which hint at the factors which led him nevertheless to preside over further expansion. Firstly, he argued the LNWR's right to defend its existing traffic, pointing out, for example, how the proposed amalgamation of the GWR and West Midland would give the combined undertaking a monopoly of traffic between south Wales and the north and might also threaten the independence of projected lines in mid-Wales which would otherwise feed the LNWR. Secondly, in 1862 he emphasised his unwillingness to close the capital account 'while it could profitably be enlarged'. Although the company's share and loan capital almost trebled during Moon's chairmanship, the net return increased from 4·4% in 1861 to 5·4% in 1891, suggesting that, overall, this additional investment met the criterion of profitability. Furthermore, capital expenditure was not confined to extensions: considerable sums were devoted to improving the existing system, and while there were some significant incursions into new areas the primary justification for much of the extra mileage was either to develop the traffic of existing lines or to secure access to territory in which the LNWR already had an interest.

The initial additions to the system after Moon took over were of course the outcome of previous enactments; indeed, the first, a branch from the Shropshire Union line east of Wellington to Coalport on the river Severn, was opened on 17 June 1861, before the board had formally appointed its new chairman. Powers for this branch, which replaced a canal, had been included in an 1857 LNWR Act, but most other extensions during the early 1860s were promoted by separate companies. Among these were two undertakings authorised in 1860 and worked by the LNWR from their completion in 1862, the Bedford & Cambridge and Watford & Rickmansworth railways. The former extended the existing Bletchley–Bedford line to join the Great Eastern Railway just south of Cambridge, and incorporated within its 29½-mile route the privately-built Sandy & Potton Railway, which had been opened as a feeder to the Great Northern main line in 1857. The LNWR leased the Bedford & Cambridge at 4%, and began passenger services over the line on 7 July 1862; goods traffic was not handled until 1 August. Two months later, on 1 October 1862, the Watford & Rickmansworth Railway was opened, but in its case the working arrangements with the LNWR were not supplemented by a lease or guarantee. This proved unfortunate for the promoters when traffic expectations were undermined by the collapse of schemes for connecting lines to Uxbridge and Amersham; though the LNWR assisted by subscribing £10,000 in 1863, the W&R was placed in receivership in 1866. It was eventually bought by the larger company in 1881.

A similar example of financial over-optimism was provided by the Newport Pagnell Railway, which was authorised in 1863 to connect with the main line at Wolverton. Although the company subsequently obtained powers to extend north-eastwards, first to Olney and then to a junction with the Midland Railway, it completed its line only as far as Newport Pagnell. Goods traffic began on 23 July 1866 and full opening followed on 2 September 1867. The undertaking operated its own services but soon ran into deficit and was purchased by the LNWR in 1875 for just £50,000, £40,000 less than the shareholders' investment.

In 1863 the LNWR's interests were carried south of the Thames with the opening on 2 March of the mixed-gauge West London Extension Railway. This had been authorised in 1859 to provide a link between the terminus of the WLR at Kensington and two of the southern companies, the London, Brighton & South Coast and the London & South Western. These each took a one-sixth share in the WLER, which was floated as a separate undertaking, and the remaining capital was subscribed equally by the LNWR and GWR, the existing partners in the WLR. Part of the route north of the river was provided by filling the bed of the Kensington Canal, and the canal's former terminus at Chelsea Basin was served by a short

freight branch. The main line crossed the Thames upstream of the basin and then terminated in a series of connecting lines, two of which curved west to Clapham Junction to connect respectively with the LSWR and with the LB&SC's West End & Crystal Palace line from the new Victoria station. A third curve diverged eastward to join the Victoria line at Longhedge junction, and in 1865 the layout there was extended when the London, Chatham & Dover Railway completed a triangular junction linking Longhedge with its own line from Victoria to East Kent. On 6 July the same year a further WLER curve was opened to give an east-facing connection into the LSWR main line and thus allow through running to and from Nine Elms and Waterloo: this was laid only to standard gauge, in common with the existing westward spur to the LSWR, and after 1866 broad-gauge working was confined to the section north of Chelsea Basin.

In addition to creating useful freight transfer routes, the opening of the WLER in 1863 led to the development of a range of passenger services for interchange and local traffic. The existing West London line had been reopened to passengers by the LNWR on 2 June the previous year with the introduction of services from Camden to Kensington, primarily to cater for the 1862 International Exhibition; these were supplemented from November 1862 by Harrow–Kensington trains. A new through station was provided in anticipation of the opening of the Extension line, but Neele's *Reminiscences* suggest that the Exhibition excursion traffic, which included extended North London workings, also required the temporary reopening of the original WLR passenger station. Its replacement, which was slightly to the north, was known from 1868 as Kensington Addison Road, to distinguish it from the Metropolitan's High Street station.

Powers had been obtained in 1859 to double the track between Willesden and Kensington and to build a bridge at Wormwood Scrubbs over the main line to Paddington, eliminating the flat crossing which had existed since 1844. These works were completed in October 1860, and as part of the alterations the GWR built a west-to-south curve to replace the turntable connection that had previously been used to transfer freight traffic between its system and the WLR, which was mixed gauge south of the intersection. This new curve joined the deviated West London route at North

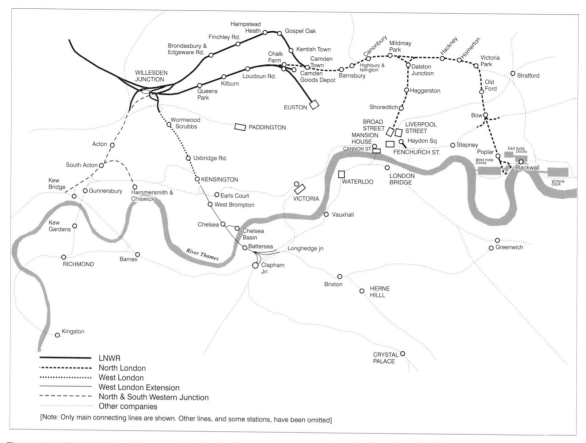

Figure 5.1 – The LNWR and its connections in the London area.

Pole junction, and the LNWR assumed sole responsibility for the standard-gauge section between that point and its own main line.

The former West London Junction station, about three-quarters of a mile east of the LNWR station then serving Willesden, was not reopened when passenger trains were restored in 1862. However, on 1 September 1866 a new Willesden Junction station was opened at the point where the connection between the Hampstead Junction and North & South Western Junction railways crossed over the main line. Platforms were provided at both upper and lower levels, linked by footbridges, and a new curve was built to allow through local services to run between the main line and the Hampstead route via the low-level platforms. A year later, on 2 September 1867, West London trains were brought into this network with the opening of additional platforms on a second high-level connection. This diverged from the HJR a few chains east of the 1866 curve, and after crossing the low-level platforms at their Euston end turned south-eastwards to join the West London line at Mitre Bridge junction.

The value of Willesden Junction as an interchange station was soon reflected in its increasing use by long-distance trains: by the 1870s it had become a standard main-line call and had largely taken over from Chalk Farm (the new name adopted in 1866 for the LNWR's Camden station, which was just south of the junction with the NLR) as the ticket-collection stop for up expresses. However, the connecting services radiating southwards from Willesden were only part of the reason for these developments: a vital element in the enhancement of the local network was the opening on 1 November 1865 of the North London Railway's new City terminus at Broad Street, reached from Dalston on the existing Camden–Poplar line. Besides subscribing to this extension, the LNWR took joint ownership of the passenger terminus and also built an adjacent goods station on its own account. This opened on 18 May 1868, supplementing the existing City depot at Haydon Square, which was by then severely overloaded.

The 'mixed Italian style' exterior of the North London Railway's City terminus at Broad Street, which was shared by LNWR local services. Note the horse omnibuses. *(National Railway Museum, NL 98)*

NLR trains via the Hampstead and N&SWJ lines were recast to run to and from Broad Street station when this opened in 1865, and called at Willesden Junction high level from 1 September the following year. A service to the NLR station at Chalk Farm (which was adjacent to the LNWR station and had similarly undergone a change of name, in its case from Hampstead Road) was maintained by quarter-hourly local workings from Broad Street, some of which were later extended over the main line to Willesden Junction low level. The LNWR's use of Broad Street was initially confined to peak Watford trains, but with the opening of the Mitre Bridge curve in 1867 a half-hourly service was instituted between Broad Street and Kensington; this was extended to Victoria over the WLER and LB&SC on 1 January 1869. A service between Waterloo, Kensington, and Richmond was introduced on the same date, with the opening of an LSWR branch which diverged from the WLR north of Addison Road. North London trains over the N&SWJ

route were also involved in these timetable rearrangements, taking advantage of a connection which the LSWR installed between South Acton and its new Kensington–Richmond line at Gunnersbury. This spur was used to provide an hourly direct service between Broad Street and Richmond, which alternated with Kew Bridge workings to maintain a 30-minute frequency north of Acton junction.

These were not the only new cross-London services which made use of the opportunities created by the developing network of lines on the capital's western outskirts. The GWR opened its Hammersmith & City branch in 1864, which connected with the WLR at Uxbridge Road and was also later linked into the LSWR Richmond line, while a further junction at Kensington was installed by the

Victoria station in London around 1880, with an LNWR train to Willesden via the West London lines standing alongside London, Brighton & South Coast trains. The LNWR locomotive may be 0-4-2 saddle tank no 1168, acquired with the Vale of Clwyd Railway. *(See E Talbot,* LNWR miscellany, *vol 2, plate 11.) (LNWR Society collection, 9232)*

Metropolitan District Railway in 1869, initially for construction traffic. From 1 February 1872, however, the LNWR's Broad Street–Victoria trains were diverted from their previous route through Battersea, running instead via this new connection and Earls Court to the District's underground platforms at Victoria. At the same time they were extended to terminate at Mansion House, barely half a mile from Broad Street. Consequently, this LNWR service soon became known as the 'outer circle', a description which distinguished it both from the 'inner circle' underground route via Notting Hill, and from a GWR 'middle circle' service inaugurated on 1 August 1872 between Moorgate and Mansion House via the Hammersmith & City line and Kensington.

However, not all contemporary schemes for improving London's railway facilities were successful. Together with the South Eastern Railway, the LNWR was drawn into supporting the North

Western & Charing Cross Railway, which was authorised in 1864 to provide an underground connection between their two systems. A joint committee of both Houses of Parliament on metropolitan railway schemes endorsed this particular project, but the change in the financial climate in 1866 led to its eventual abandonment. A similar scheme authorised in 1871, the London Central Railway, was also abortive.

Despite such failures, the 1860s and early 1870s saw a marked expansion in the railway network serving the metropolis. Another local system which underwent comparable development during these years was that in Lancashire and Cheshire. Though the first part of the 1860s was marked by the cotton famine and the resulting depression in the mill towns, the development of the Lancashire coalfield and the growth of the Mersey's seaborne trade provided strong local reinforcement of the competitive pressures that were already encouraging the building of new lines.

One such was the link between Edge Hill and Speke, authorised in 1859 to complete the alternative

Figure 5.2 – Railways in Lancashire and north Cheshire, 1861–80.

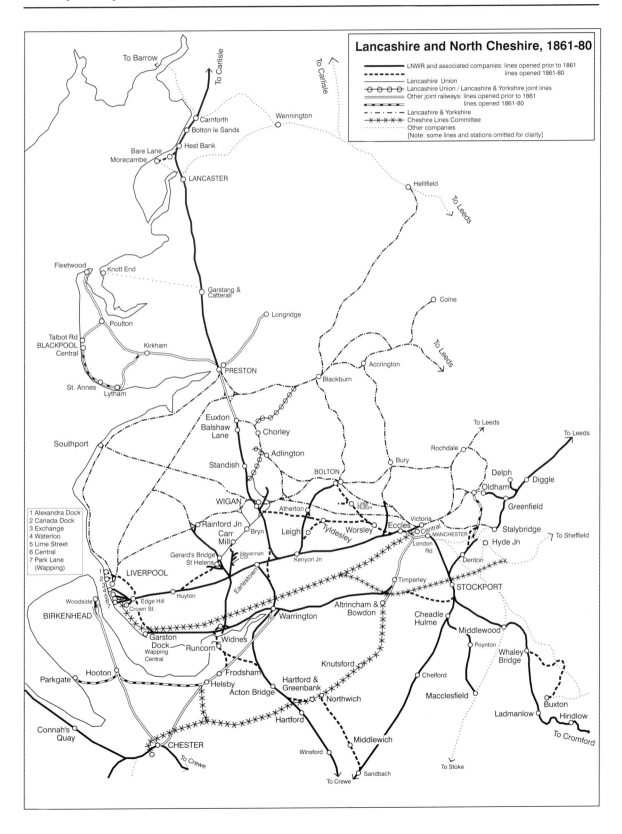

Lancashire and North Cheshire, 1861-80

LNWR and associated companies: lines opened prior to 1861
lines opened 1861-80
Lancashire Union
Lancashire Union / Lancashire & Yorkshire joint lines
Other joint railways: lines opened prior to 1861
lines opened 1861-80
Lancashire & Yorkshire
Cheshire Lines Committee
Other companies
[Note: some lines and stations omitted for clarity]

route to Liverpool via Warrington and Widnes which had been agreed as part of the 1858 settlement with the MS&L and GNR. The Speke extension opened on 15 February 1864, but by then its potential importance had greatly increased, as it also became the basis for revived proposals to shorten the route to Liverpool from the south. Plans for a bridge across the Mersey at Fiddler's Ferry, first considered by the GJR in 1835, were rejected by Parliament in 1860 on the grounds that it might interfere with navigation. However, an alternative scheme for a high-level crossing further downstream at Runcorn was approved in 1861, together with approach lines from the Garston–Warrington route at Ditton and from the main line at Aston, north of Dutton viaduct, and a short branch to Runcorn dock. At the eastern end of the new route at Birdswood (the present Weaver junction) the LNWR installed its first flying junction: the up line from Liverpool crossed over both existing west coast tracks on a skew bridge before making its trailing connection into the southbound main line.

Because of constructional difficulties, the Runcorn line was not opened throughout for goods traffic until 1 February 1869, although the section south of the bridge was used from 1 January by goods trains serving Runcorn. Passenger services began on 1 April, reducing the distance between Crewe and Liverpool by nine miles and enabling express timings

to be accelerated by up to 20 minutes. The shortening of the route to Liverpool was accompanied by major improvements to Lime Street station, which were begun in 1865 and included the building of a new LNWR hotel, opened on 1 March 1871. The station extensions also entailed cutting back the tunnel entrance at Lime Street, and this, together with improved ventilation in the tunnel itself, allowed rope haulage to Edge Hill finally to be superseded in March 1870. Locomotives had previously been used on the incline for a trial period in 1863.

Under the terms of its Act for the Runcorn line the LNWR was allowed to offset the cost of construction by charging a fare for the bridge section which was equivalent to that for the distance saved. Similar provisions were included in powers which the LNWR obtained in 1869 for a branch to connect Runcorn with Frodsham, on the Warrington section of the Birkenhead Railway; in this case, however, the intention was also to protect the GWR, the LNWR's partner in the Birkenhead system, from a loss of joint revenue as a result of the diversion of traffic from the existing route via Warrington.

The Frodsham chord opened on 1 May 1873, making the Runcorn bridge part of a more direct route

William Baker's Runcorn bridge, photographed from the Cheshire shore after the construction of the Manchester Ship Canal. *(LNWR Society collection, 702)*

Lime Street station, Liverpool, during its enlargement, showing work in progress on the construction of the overall roof. The photograph also shows a Trevithick 2-2-2 locomotive and four-wheeled carriages. *(LNWR Society collection, 1733)*

from Liverpool to Chester and north Wales. It also improved railway links between the two sides of the Mersey estuary, complementing a cut-off which the LNWR and GWR had jointly provided a decade earlier with the opening on 1 July 1863 of a branch from the Birkenhead line at Hooton to Helsby, south of Frodsham. In December 1863 the Birkenhead Railway system had been further extended with the completion of the short freight spur to Tranmere Pool, while another addition at Hooton was a single-track branch across the Wirral to Parkgate, opened on 1 October 1866. In that year the LNWR's facilities on the Liverpool waterfront were also expanded, with the completion of a line from Edge Hill to serve the new Canada Dock at Bootle. This branch was brought into use for dock traffic on 1 June 1866, but the LNWR goods station at the terminus was not opened until 15 October; passenger services were introduced on 1 July 1870.

The Bootle branch was authorised by the same 1861 Act as the Runcorn crossing, and this Act also contained powers for another cut-off to benefit trunk traffic, a direct line from Winwick, north of Warrington, to Golborne. Although less than $2\frac{1}{2}$ miles long, this new link significantly improved the west coast route, since it eliminated the awkward detour via Earlestown and the Parkside west curve. Its opening

took place on 1 August 1864, and was followed on 24 August by the formal ceremonies to mark the completion of another line authorised in 1861 which by-passed Parkside. This was the Eccles, Tyldesley & Wigan branch, which joined the main line at Springs Branch junction. Regular passenger services began on 1 September and freight traffic commenced on 1 November. In addition to improving the LNWR's through route northward from Manchester, the Tyldesley line extended the company's local catchment, and its usefulness was enhanced by two subsidiary branches which were authorised and opened at the same time. One, an east-to-north curve from Howe Bridge into the Bolton & Leigh Railway, shortened the LNWR route from Manchester to Atherton and Bolton. The other, also feeding into the original Bolton–Kenyon line, was a longer branch from Tyldesley through Leigh to a south-facing junction at Pennington.

A further offshoot from the Wigan line, from Worsley to Little Hulton, received parliamentary approval in 1865 and was opened for freight traffic on 1 July 1870. By then, however, powers had been obtained to project this branch beyond Little Hulton, with the authorisation in 1869 of a short spur westwards to serve local collieries and a more substantial extension northwards to join the Bolton & Leigh line just south of its terminus. The mineral branch was brought into use on 8 September 1873 and the Bolton extension opened for freight traffic on 16 November 1874; passenger trains via Little Hulton commenced on 1 April 1875, when a direct service was inaugurated between Manchester and a new LNWR terminus at Bolton, adjacent to the former Bolton & Leigh station at Great Moor Street.

These developments north of the L&M line improved the LNWR's penetration of an area where the L&Y was already well established. The latter had consolidated its position by amalgamating with the East Lancashire Railway in 1859, and direct conflict with the LNWR became a possibility in the early 1860s when the rapid development of the Wigan coalfield provoked considerable interest in improved transport links with the Mersey and with the mill

Urban Lancashire: a local train at Walkden, which was added to the intermediate stations on the Eccles, Tyldesley & Wigan route in 1875, fourteen years after the line's opening. *(David Joy collection: L&GRP 5033)*

towns of east Lancashire. The Lancashire Union Railways company was promoted locally for this purpose in 1863, but the L&Y countered with a scheme of its own for lines from Blackburn via Chorley to Hindley and Wigan. Although the LNWR supported the LUR, Moon was anxious to avoid duplication; as a result, parts of both schemes were authorised in 1864 following agreement that sections of the two lines should be jointly owned. Parliament approved these arrangements in 1865, together with a substitute LUR route between Wigan and the St Helens system at Gerard's Bridge. In the same year the LNWR agreed to lease the LUR for twenty-five years, with an option to purchase.

The 1865 legislation also contained clauses to improve the L&Y's access to St Helens, which were inserted because the LNWR had been authorised in 1864 to absorb the entire St Helens undertaking, replacing its existing lease of the Warrington–Garston section. The assets thus acquired included not only the original St Helens Railway and the additions mentioned in previous chapters, but also two more recent branches from the Ravenhead line, to Rainford and to Eccleston, which had opened on 1 February 1858 and in March 1859 respectively. The Eccleston branch was a short westward extension for mineral traffic only, but the Rainford line, which diverged north of Peasley Cross, carried passengers as well as

An eastbound passenger train approaching Carr Mill viaduct on the Lancashire Union line from St Helens to Wigan. The junction signals are for the freight-only Blackbrook branch extension, opened in 1880. *(LNWR Society collection, 2073)*

freight and incorporated a new St Helens station in place of the previous passenger terminus, which had been served by a short spur from the Ravenhead branch. After curving in a north-easterly direction to intersect the original Cowley Hill line near Gerard's Bridge, the new route swung north-westwards to terminate in two junctions north of Rainford village. An east-facing spur into the L&Y's Wigan–Liverpool line was brought into service at the same time as the rest of the branch, and an alternative outlet became available a month later with the opening on 1 March of an end-on junction with the ELR's newly-completed line from Ormskirk.

In order to avoid parliamentary opposition to the amalgamation Bill, the LNWR was obliged to concede favourable freight charges to local industrial users and to confirm L&Y running powers from Rainford. It also undertook to make two improvements to the St Helens system, one of which, a north-facing curve south of Peasley Cross to create a triangular junction with the Blackbrook branch, was first used on 25 March 1869. The second was a loop from the Warrington–Garston line at Widnes, to reduce movements through the level crossings on the original route. This deviation was used by goods traffic from 1 December 1869 and by passenger services from 1 March 1870. Besides these measures, the LNWR improved the Cowley Hill branch between Gerard's Bridge and Peasley junction to allow through mineral trains to avoid St Helens station, which was itself rebuilt and enlarged in 1871. In addition, a curve was brought into use at Allerton on 1 January 1873 to give direct access to Garston from the

Liverpool direction, while port facilities at Garston were enlarged with the opening of a second dock, the North Dock, on 1 June 1875.

The local network in the St Helens area was further extended by the opening of a mineral spur from the Blackbrook branch to Havannah colliery on 1 August 1870. This was in fact built under LUR powers and represented the rump of an 1866 scheme for a through connection with the St Helens–Wigan line at Garswood. The bulk of this branch was abandoned, leaving the Havannah portion detached from the rest of the LUR, which with one other exception had opened for freight traffic on 17 November 1869. The system brought into use on that date consisted of the line from Gerard's Bridge, which forked at Ince Moss, south of Wigan, to make a junction with the Eccles, Tyldesley & Wigan route and another northwards into the main line; a branch from Bryn to Pemberton, connecting with local collieries and with the L&Y; two joint sections north of Wigan; and a loop line from Ince Moss to Haigh which by-passed Wigan and was fed by spurs from the L&Y at Hindley, the LNWR Springs branch, and an ironworks near Whelley. At Haigh the Ince Moss loop trailed into the southern-most joint section, which extended from the LNWR main line at Boars Head junction to Adlington, on the Bolton–Euxton route; through traffic then used the Euxton line as far as Chorley, where joint LUR metals

Prescot, the first station on the branch from Huyton to St Helens which opened for passenger traffic in 1872. This later photograph of two local trains at the station also provides a good illustration of LNWR signal equipment – the post on the right of the picture carries co-acting upper and lower arms to assist sighting, and these are of the standard steel design with integral spectacles which was adopted in 1883. *(LNWR Society collection, 2072)*

diverged again for Cherry Tree, on the L&Y branch from Preston to Blackburn. The remainder of the joint mileage consisted of a short mineral branch from Adlington to Ellerbeck colliery; this was not completed until June 1871 and it is unclear when traffic was first carried.

Passenger trains were introduced between St Helens, Wigan, and Blackburn on 1 December 1869, and from 1 January 1872 a service was also provided over the Wigan avoiding line. However, because of disappointing receipts the latter workings were withdrawn two months later and the intermediate stations at Amberswood and Whelley were closed to regular passenger traffic. A more successful addition to the local network, also from 1 January 1872, was the extension of most LUR passenger services to and from Liverpool over a new LNWR line between Huyton and St Helens. This branch, a revival of a project that had been abandoned in the 1840s, was authorised in 1865 and used by goods trains from 18 December 1871. The opening of the Huyton–St Helens section to all traffic a fortnight later also completed the downgrading of the Parkside route,

since it provided the LNWR with a more direct outlet from Liverpool to the trunk line northwards.

The LUR sections north of Wigan were not the only additions to joint L&Y and LNWR mileage under Moon. The imposingly-titled Fleetwood, Preston & West Riding Junction Railway had been authorised in 1846, but succeeded in building only a short section linking the Preston & Wyre line with the Preston & Longridge Railway near its Deepdale terminus. This connection, which intersected the west coast main line on the level alongside the existing Maudlands crossing, was opened on 14 January 1850 but closed to regular traffic soon afterwards. In 1856 the FP&WRJ absorbed the P&L and on 1 November that year extended Longridge services over part of the 1850 link to a new station east of the Lancaster line at Maudlands Bridge. A decade later the company's original ambition of reaching the West Riding via Clitheroe was revived: this might have enabled the Midland Railway to reach Preston, so as a precaution the LNWR and L&Y jointly purchased the FP&WRJ in 1867. By 1872 a through siding had been laid at Maudlands which avoided the need to exchange freight traffic across the main line via the P&W junctions, but passenger services remained isolated until 1 June 1885, when the owning companies opened a curve to enable Longridge trains to be diverted to the main Preston station at Fishergate. Its construction involved moving the P&W Maudlands goods terminus northwards to a site west of the former FP&WRJ station, and as the new depot layout was served from the Longridge line the flat crossing at Preston could finally be eliminated.

Another local line which had no direct link with the rest of the system when it opened on 6 April 1863, the Blackpool & Lytham Railway, was added to the joint Preston & Wyre undertaking on 1 July 1871. On 1 July 1874 a connection was opened at Lytham, together with an improved junction between the main P&W line and the Lytham branch at Kirkham. This provided an alternative through route, and in 1878 the Lytham line terminus was designated Blackpool Central to distinguish it from Talbot Road station, served via Poulton.

The mileage which the LNWR shared in Lancashire with the MS&L also grew, with the joint lease in 1862 of the Oldham, Ashton-under-Lyne & Guide Bridge Junction Railway. Its 6¼-mile route, authorised in 1857, extended from a triangular junction with the MS&L main line west of Guide Bridge to an end-on connection with the LNWR's Oldham branch, and was divided into two sections by a short intervening stretch of L&Y track at Ashton. Regular passenger services, worked by the MS&L, began on 26 August 1861, but at first ran no further than Clegg Street station in Oldham, adjacent to the L&Y's Oldham Central. On 1 July 1862 LNWR trains on the branch from Greenfield were extended from their existing terminus at Oldham Mumps over joint metals to Clegg Street, and four months later, when the LNWR opened its Glodwick Road station, OA&GB passenger trains were in turn extended eastwards from Clegg Street to the new LNWR station. Goods services on the joint line did not begin until 1 February 1863.

Despite this co-operation east of Manchester, matters to the south and west were less easily resolved, with the eventual result that MS&L and its partners gained independent access to Liverpool. This process started in 1860, when the LNWR withdrew its Bill for a line from Garston to Brunswick Dock after encountering unexpected opposition in the House of Lords. This had been promoted under the terms of the 1858 settlement, and after its withdrawal the MS&L and GNR successfully brought forward an alternative Liverpool & Garston Bill in 1861. As the price of its agreement the LNWR was offered running powers over the proposed joint line, as well as over the MS&L main line from Ardwick to Sheffield and over portions of the GNR. The LNWR, which reciprocated by

allowing use of its metals between Timperley and Garston, also gained rights over two other MS&L-supported schemes: the Cheshire Midland Railway, authorised in 1860 to build a line to Northwich from the terminus of the MSJ&A at Altrincham; and the Stockport, Timperley & Altrincham Junction Railway, another 1861 authorisation. The LNWR was itself empowered in 1861 to connect into the latter line at Northenden by means of a branch from Cheadle, which opened on 1 August 1866, six months before the completion of the ST&AJ to its junction with the Warrington & Stockport line at Broadheath. Besides catering for local traffic, these new links enabled LNWR goods trains between Yorkshire and Warrington or Liverpool to travel via Stockport, avoiding the busy route through Manchester.

The LNWR similarly used its running powers over the Cheshire Midland Railway, which was completed to Knutsford on 1 January 1863, as a springboard for developing its own traffic. In 1861 it obtained powers for a branch from Chelford to the CMR at Knutsford, but in 1863 these were abandoned in favour of a connection from Sandbach to Northwich, which was opened to goods traffic on 11 November 1867 and for passengers on 1 July 1868. While longer than the route from Chelford, this approach had the advantage of closing off the gap which had been identified in the 1850s as a means of hostile incursion into LNWR territory from the south; it also gave good access to the salt deposits served by the Cheshire Midland. The completion on 1 March 1870 of a spur from the west coast main line at Hartford to the CMR's southern extension, the West Cheshire Railway, opened more of the saltfield to the LNWR and permitted the introduction of a local passenger service between Crewe and Liverpool via Northwich.

By then, however, the various Cheshire undertakings that had been used as a front for the development of alternative routes south and west of Manchester had been incorporated into a more powerful challenge to LNWR interests, through a series of agreements from 1862 onwards which transferred them to the ownership of the MS&L and GNR. The joint Liverpool & Garston line, which opened on 1 June 1864, was brought within the scope of the two companies' Cheshire Lines Committee in the following year, as was an authorised extension from Brunswick Dock to central Liverpool. But Edward Watkin, who became chairman of the MS&L in 1864, remained

2-4-0T no 1839, converted from a Trevithick tender locomotive, on the Cromford & High Peak line. The snow emphasises the sparseness of the shelter available to early footplatemen. *(LNWR Society collection, 376)*

dissatisfied with reliance on running powers over the LNWR for access to Garston, and in 1865 his company succeeded in obtaining authorisation for a separate line from Manchester to a junction with the Liverpool & Garston at Cressington, together with a connection from Timperley to join the new route at Glazebrook. In 1866 these powers were transferred to the CLC, which was enlarged the same year with the admission of the Midland Railway as a third partner.

Construction of the new Manchester–Liverpool route was first delayed while powers were obtained for a deviation at the eastern end and then by the financial crisis, so in 1868 the LNWR proposed instead that its existing Timperley–Garston line and the CLC Stockport–Timperley section should become the joint property of the CLC participants and itself. This offer was rejected, and with the financial resources of the Midland and GNR to add to those of the MS&L the CLC main line was eventually completed to Liverpool Central in 1874. As events were to prove, these shared interests in Lancashire and Cheshire did not prevent disputes elsewhere between the three partners, but the creation of the joint system added a further dimension to the LNWR's relations with the companies which participated in the CLC.

So far as the GNR and MS&L were concerned, this amounted to little more than a reinforcement of competitive stances that had already been established in the 1850s: indeed, the most recent historian of the GNR, John Wrottesley, has concluded that the company gained nothing from this and other joint ventures. And while the Cheshire Lines gave the MS&L a base for further local expansion, the LNWR was able to take counter-measures which extended beyond those already mentioned. It had expanded its interests in north Derbyshire by leasing the Cromford & High Peak Railway with effect from 25 March 1861 and this was followed by the opening of the line from Whaley Bridge to Buxton for passengers on 15 June 1863; goods traffic had commenced by 7 July. The Stockport, Disley & Whaley Bridge and its Buxton extension were absorbed in 1866 and in the same year the LNWR responded to the MS&L's Manchester–

Cressington scheme by supporting a proposed railway from Disley to Sheffield. A modified route to Sheffield, diverging from the Buxton line at Chapel-en-le-Frith, was put before Parliament in 1867 under the LNWR's own auspices, prompting the MS&L to offer substantial concessions in return for its withdrawal. The LNWR consequently gained improved running powers over the Woodhead line and the right to provide its own facilities at Sheffield, while the MS&L also undertook to send a proportion of its Liverpool traffic via the LNWR rather than via the CLC.

* * *

While some of Watkin's ambitions could thus be reined in by Euston, the third partner in the CLC, the Midland, was a significant addition to the competitive pressures on the LNWR. As mentioned in Chapter Four, the LNWR's drive towards Buxton was one of the factors in the breakdown of the former close alliance between Derby and Euston, and the Midland's response was to promote its own extension to Buxton from the Matlock–Rowsley line. This was completed in 1863, shortly before the LNWR branch opened. Although the Midland also considered reviving earlier schemes for reaching Manchester via Buxton, the LNWR's control of the Whaley Bridge route effectively blocked this approach, and instead powers were obtained in 1862 for an expensive direct connection from the Buxton line near Miller's Dale to a projected MS&L branch at New Mills, which later became joint property. The Midland completed its line to New Mills in 1867, and from there was able to reach Manchester London Road, initially via Hyde. Subsequent improvements progressively shortened the route into Manchester and also enhanced through connections with the CLC, while a branch to Ancoats, opened in 1870, gave the Midland an independent goods station in Manchester and provided a direct link into the L&Y system. In 1871, when the joint lease of the Manchester, Buxton, Matlock & Midlands Junction expired, the Midland finally absorbed that undertaking, thus extinguishing the LNWR's vestigial interest in what had become another rival line to Lancashire.

This new route to Manchester complemented the Midland's improvement of its access to London, a process that had begun in 1857 with the opening of the Hitchin extension. Agreement with the GNR enabled Midland services to use Kings Cross from 1858, though the bulk of its through mineral traffic continued to rely on LNWR metals to reach London via Rugby. However, as the Midland's financial confidence grew, accommodation difficulties at Kings Cross and congestion between Rugby and Euston led it to seek powers for an independent line from Bedford to London. This extension was authorised in 1863 and completed to St Pancras on 1 October 1868, giving the Midland its own entry to the capital and resulting in the diversion of its remaining London freight traffic from the LNWR.

The Midland also sought to emulate the LNWR's cross-London connections, and besides installing junctions with the North London and Metropolitan railways it supported schemes to link its main line with the Great Eastern Railway at Tottenham and with the North & South Western Junction Railway at Acton Wells. Although the N&SWJR's offices were at Euston, the company remained formally independent, bound to the LNWR, NLR, and LSWR only by a financial agreement. This gave the Midland the opportunity to attempt to gain control in 1870 by offering better terms, but the eventual compromise, authorised in 1871, was a joint lease of the N&SWJR by the LNWR, Midland, and NLR. While the LSWR retained running powers between Kew and Willesden, and continued to exercise these to exchange freight with the northern companies, its share of direct responsibility for this cross-London corridor was thereafter limited to its network of connecting lines south of Acton. The NLR continued to provide the local passenger service, but the Midland worked its own goods traffic over the N&SWJR, and also used the LSWR junction at South Acton to gain access to the District Railway, opening a coal depot at West Kensington in 1878.

Of the other areas where the two companies' interests overlapped, industrial west Yorkshire presented few problems, since on this edge of the LNWR's territory the Midland was in more direct competition with other railways. One minor addition to the LNWR system in the West Riding was opened on 2 April 1866: a short freight branch on the outskirts of Leeds to serve the Farnley Iron Works. In Leeds itself the LNWR was a tenant of the Midland at its Wellington passenger terminus; when the North Eastern, after initially proposing the establishment of a central

2-4-0T no 37, 'Hawk', converted from a Trevithick tender locomotive, poses on 7 October 1867, the opening day of the
Kirkburton branch, probably at the branch's junction with the
main line east of Huddersfield. *(LNWR Society collection,
9373)*

station for all the railways serving the town, reached
agreement with the LNWR in 1864 to share a new
station, the Midland accepted that this should be built
next to Wellington, with access from the north and
west over its metals. Powers were obtained in 1865,
and on 1 April 1869 Leeds New station was opened as
a joint LNWR and NER undertaking.

Another LNWR extension in the area was a line
from near Huddersfield southwards to Kirkburton,
authorised in 1863. This branch opened for passengers on 7 October 1867 and for goods on 1 January
1868, but before its completion it figured in joint
proposals with the Midland, which in 1865 had
promoted a Bill for a connecting line from Barnsley to
Kirkburton. This would have given the Midland a
route to Huddersfield, and in the same session the
LNWR and Midland jointly brought forward a
proposal for an extension from Huddersfield to
Halifax. The latter failed on standing orders, and the
Midland's Kirkburton Bill was therefore withdrawn.

That part of the scheme was not revived, since the
Midland had the prospect of alternative access to
Huddersfield by means of running powers from
Barnsley via Penistone, but the proposal for a joint
line to Halifax reappeared in 1866, together with a
rival L&Y scheme. Neither was authorised, and
though the joint Bill was brought forward again in
1867 it was withdrawn after falling victim to the
doubts that the Midland shareholders were beginning
to express about their board's expansionary policy.
The Midland revived plans for a direct line northwards from Huddersfield in 1874, but the variability
of alliances in the West Riding was demonstrated by
the fact that on this occasion the LNWR combined
with the L&Y in successfully opposing the scheme.

In the territory bounded by Birmingham,
Wolverhampton, Derby, and Leicester, interaction
with the Midland and other companies shaped the
LNWR network much more directly during the 1860s
and 1870s. The Midland was of course well
entrenched east of the Trent Valley main line, but
while the LNWR was correspondingly stronger to the
west, its dominance was limited both by the GWR's
penetration of the Birmingham–Wolverhampton
corridor and by the Midland's Derby–Bristol line,
which intersected the other main routes.

The position in the black country was also complicated at first by the fact that both the LNWR and Midland were large shareholders in the South Staffordshire Railway, which had seen some expansion during the 1850s. Besides a short connection at Dudley Port, opened on 2 January 1854 to give access from the Stour Valley line towards Dudley, and a spur to the GWR at Wednesbury which was brought into use on 1 June 1859, two extensions were authorised from the Walsall–Wichnor line into the Cannock Chase coalfield, both of which opened on 1 February 1858. One was a mineral branch to Norton Colliery; the other, from Ryecroft junction, north of Walsall, to Cannock, carried passenger traffic as well as freight. As mentioned in the previous chapter, the Cannock Mineral Railway had powers to continue from Cannock to Rugeley, and this line was leased by the LNWR from its opening on 7 November 1859; notwithstanding its title, passengers were carried from the outset.

Despite the Midland's opposition, the LNWR concluded negotiations to take over the lease of the South Staffordshire from J R McLean in 1861, and that autumn, after one of the set-piece confrontations that enliven railway history, it successfully asserted its right as lessee to exercise South Staffordshire running powers over the Midland between Wichnor junction and Burton. The LNWR's access to the traffic generated by the Burton breweries was consolidated on 1 April 1863 by the opening of its own goods terminus at Horninglow, served by a branch from the Birmingham–Derby line, and by running powers over the Midland's network of industrial branches in the town. By December 1868 the LNWR's activities in Burton were sufficient for the construction of an engine shed to be authorised, and this opened on 4 October 1869. There were similar developments at Derby, where the LNWR also opened a goods depot and engine shed during the 1860s. In 1869 the Midland agreed that the LNWR should build a mile-long branch parallel to the main line from Birmingham to give independent access to an enlarged goods station, which opened on 1 July 1871. On 1 March 1872, following arbitration over booking facilities, the LNWR further enhanced its presence in Derby by inaugurating through passenger workings from Birmingham via Walsall.

The LNWR also penetrated Midland territory further south, with the completion in 1864 of the South Leicestershire Railway. This had been authorised in 1859 as the Nuneaton & Hinckley Railway, but its name was changed in 1860 when powers were obtained for an extension to Wigston on the Midland main line, thus reviving the lapsed proposal for a link between Nuneaton and Leicester. The LNWR leased the line from 1 January 1862, when the first section opened, and brought the Hinckley–Wigston portion into service for Nuneaton–Leicester passenger trains exactly two years later. The Midland used the running powers it had been granted by the 1860 Act to introduce its own services over the route on the same day.

There were existing arrangements for LNWR merchandise traffic for Leicester to be routed via Rugby and the Midland Counties line, and Euston was at first clearly concerned not to alarm Midland sensitivities further by diverting this freight over the South Leicestershire line: although goods workings were extended beyond Hinckley from 14 November 1864 these did not initially run east of Narborough. However, on 18 November 1872 the LNWR opened its own goods depot at Leicester, reached by a spur from the Midland main line north of the passenger station. In exchange for LNWR entry to Leicester from Wigston junction, the Midland had been given access to Coventry via Nuneaton, and to facilitate this the South Leicestershire's 1860 Act required the provision of a direct junction between the Hinckley and Coventry routes south of Nuneaton station. Though this chord was built, necessitating a bridge under the Trent Valley main line, it is doubtful whether it was ever brought into use as a through connection: it later served as a siding to link Nuneaton engine shed with the Leicester line.

On 1 November 1864 the Midland opened its branch from Whitacre to Nuneaton, completing a direct route between Birmingham and Leicester, and Nuneaton gained further significance during the promotional activity of the mid-1860s, when lines northward into the Leicestershire and south Derbyshire coalfield were promoted both by the Midland and by an LNWR-supported company. Although the Midland's Bill was preferred when the two proposals came before Parliament in 1866, the price of success was an amendment enabling the LNWR to participate in the authorised scheme. A further Act in the following year accordingly reconstituted the Ashby & Nuneaton Railway as a joint undertaking. In addition, the 1867 Act confirmed LNWR

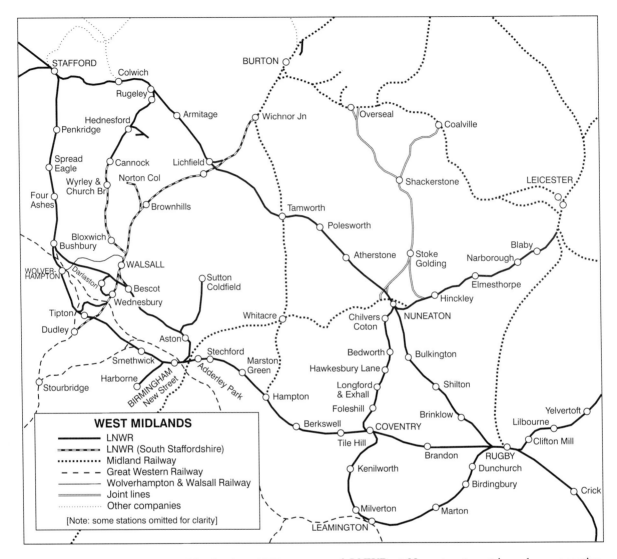

Figure 5.3 – Railways in the west midlands prior to 1875.

running powers to Burton and Derby from Wichnor and also from Tamworth, where a north-to-west connection between the Midland and Trent Valley lines had been opened on 12 June 1847, before the Trent Valley route carried public traffic. The Midland gained reciprocal running powers over the South Staffordshire system and to Wolverhampton. In the same year, 1867, the LNWR finally absorbed the South Staffordshire, the Midland having previously disposed of its shares in this company.

A further Ashby & Nuneaton Act in 1868 author-ised various additions and deviations, and the joint line as built ran from junctions with both the Midland

and LNWR at Nuneaton to a triangular connection with the Midland's Leicester–Burton branch at Overseal & Moira. The undertaking also included two branches, from Shackerstone to another junction with the Burton line at Coalville, and from Stoke Golding to Hinckley; the latter, however, was never used by regular traffic, and was effectively abandoned. The remainder of the system opened in 1873, for mineral trains on 1 August, for general merchandise on 18 August, and for passengers on 1 September. The parent companies operated separate services from their respective stations at Nuneaton, but until 1890 the Midland did not allow its partner to work passenger trains beyond the limits of the joint system; mineral running powers were restricted to some collieries reached from the Leicester–Burton branch.

This extension of LNWR influence east of the Trent Valley main line was partially balanced by Midland gains in the territory north of its Tamworth–Birmingham route, though these took longer to evolve. The LNWR had initially staked its claim to this area with the opening of a branch from Aston to Sutton Coldfield on 2 June 1862, and behind this flank it quickly set about consolidating its position in the black country and Cannock Chase. Using powers taken over with the South Staffordshire, two new branches were constructed from the Walsall–Dudley line and brought into service on the same day, 14 September 1863. One, from a north-facing junction at Wednesbury, curved west and north through Darlaston before connecting into the Grand Junction line in the Birmingham direction at James Bridge. The other ran south-west from Wednesbury to join the Stour Valley line west of Tipton; the junction there faced north-west, thus allowing the introduction of direct services between Walsall and Wolverhampton. North of Walsall, the LNWR took over responsibility for building the Cannock Chase Railway, which had been authorised in 1860 to provide a link between the Cannock Mineral Railway and the Marquis of Anglesey's colliery interests. This line extended eastwards from Hednesford to Rawnsley, with a spur to Heathy Leasows to connect with the Littleworth Tramway. The Cannock Chase Railway was opened on 7 October 1862, and it is believed that the Littleworth Tramway, which was authorised under canal powers in 1854 but constructed by the LNWR, was brought into service around the same time. After completion, both lines were worked by the colliery companies which they served.

The principal threat to the LNWR's catchment to the north of Birmingham at first appeared to come not from the Midland but the GWR, and the pattern was set by the Stourbridge Railway, which had been incorporated in 1860 to connect Old Hill with the OW&W line at Stourbridge. In the following year a further Act authorised an extension north-eastwards to join the LNWR at Smethwick, but in 1862 the GWR obtained powers for a short connection into its own main line at Handsworth. This proved to be the first of several contemporary schemes for links into the Snow Hill–Wolverhampton route at the expense of the Stour Valley or Grand Junction lines. In 1864 the Cannock Chase & Wolverhampton Railway was authorised to build a route into the coalfield from the GWR at Wolverhampton, and in the following year the Wolverhampton & Walsall Railway's Act gave powers for a connection between the GWR and the South Staffordshire system north of Walsall. In 1866 the West Bromwich & Walsall Railway was incorporated with the intention of providing a further link between the GWR and Walsall, though in its case LNWR opposition succeeded in restricting the project to a short connecting line between West Bromwich and Bescot. Another 1866 authorisation was the Harborne Railway, a suburban branch from the Stour Valley line. Its promoters initially sought to follow the Stourbridge company's example by also seeking a junction with the GWR, but this part of the proposal was abandoned because of opposition by the city authorities to a further line through inner Birmingham.

With the change in the financial climate these projects had mixed fortunes. The Stourbridge Railway was leased by the GWR in 1866 and absorbed in 1870; despite this, the LNWR was able to operate through services to Kidderminster over the Smethwick connection when the Old Hill–Handsworth extension opened on 1 April 1867. The Cannock Chase & Wolverhampton failed to build its main line to the GWR, but survived in modified form as an independent mineral railway linking the Cannock network at Rawnsley with Anglesea Sidings on the Walsall–Lichfield line. The West Bromwich & Walsall scheme was abandoned and the same fate threatened the Harborne Railway, which made no progress until the LNWR subscribed £20,000 in 1870. It was not completed until 1874, opening for all traffic on 10 August. Although the Harborne line was worked by the LNWR from the outset, the company retained its separate identity.

Financial problems also delayed completion of the Wolverhampton & Walsall Railway, which in 1866 had been authorised to extend its line to connect with the Stour Valley line as well as with the GWR at Wolverhampton. The same Act also empowered the LNWR to subscribe, and £100,000 of the W&W's paid-up share capital of £220,000 had been provided in this way by the time the line was opened on 1 November 1872. The company also relied on the LNWR to work its traffic from the outset, but disappointing financial results soon led the W&W to dispute the terms of the operating arrangement. To avoid further litigation the LNWR offered to purchase the smaller company outright, and parliamentary powers were obtained which made the sale effective from 1 July 1875.

However, the transaction was agreed only after a number of acrimonious meetings of the W&W shareholders, since a faction, led by the chairman, the Earl of Lichfield, had argued that the undertaking should instead be sold to the Midland, which possessed running powers over the W&W and was able to use them by virtue of the 1867 agreement allowing it to operate over the South Staffordshire system. In addition, the Midland's absorption in 1874 of the Wolverhampton, Walsall & Midland Junction Railway, which had been authorised in 1872, offered the prospect of a direct connection from the Birmingham–Derby main line into the W&W. The latter was therefore of greater strategic value to the Midland than the LNWR, which was by then developing other proposals for its network in the area. To avoid a parliamentary contest the LNWR offered to resell the W&W, and ownership was accordingly transferred on 1 July 1876, although the Midland did not take over the working of the line until a month later. Its independent route to Walsall was eventually completed on 1 July 1879 with the WW&MJ's opening to Ryecroft junction; the link between the Derby line and Wolverhampton via the junction with the W&W at North Walsall had been brought into use for freight traffic six weeks earlier, on 19 May. In 1880 the Midland opened its own goods station in Walsall, reached by a spur from the South Staffordshire line.

The pattern of events in the east and west midlands during this period typified the fluidity of the LNWR's relations with the Midland Railway, which fluctuated between co-operation, friction, and outright rivalry. However, the most spectacular expression of these changing attitudes was found at the northern extremity of the two companies' systems, where the LNWR had fallen heir to the Low Gill–Ingleton scheme through its 1859 lease of the Lancaster & Carlisle. It also took over the latter's powers for a short branch from Hest Bank to Morecambe, which was opened to a junction near the Midland's existing station on 8 August 1864. Meanwhile the Ingleton line had been brought into service for goods traffic on 24 August 1861 and for passengers on 16 September the same year; the reopening of the Clapham–Ingleton

section by the Midland Railway on 1 October 1861 had completed the long-awaited third route to Scotland.

Hopes of significant traffic development over this new connection soon proved abortive. The LNWR, faced with major expenditure in bringing the L&C track up to standard, saw no need to assist competitive services at its sole cost, so in 1863 it began discussions with the Midland about sharing the financially onerous L&C lease. Preliminary agreement was reached in 1864, but negotiations broke down the following year after the LNWR insisted that Carlisle should be included among the local stations where jointly-agreed charges would apply. The Midland feared that this stipulation might also affect the rates it could set for its Anglo-Scottish traffic and therefore withdrew, turning instead to the North of England Union Railway, which was seeking powers for a line from Settle through the Pennines to NER territory. The Midland took over this undertaking, and in 1866 brought forward a Bill which adapted the NEUR scheme and extended its proposed route northwards via Appleby to Carlisle. The Settle & Carlisle Bill was actively supported by the North British and Glasgow & South Western companies, which considered that their traffic via Carlisle was constrained by the LNWR's close relationship with the Caledonian, and also by the L&Y, which saw how its position would be strengthened by an alternative route to Scotland. Despite the LNWR's strenuous opposition, the line was authorised, and in 1867 the Midland and GSWR sought to build on the parliamentary success of the previous session by promoting an amalgamation Bill. Though this failed, the main reason for its rejection was the fact that there was as yet no direct physical connection between the two systems. A single trunk undertaking stretching from London and Bristol across the border to Glasgow therefore remained a possibility.

As mentioned on page 94, however, the Midland's shareholders were beginning to have second thoughts about increasing their commitments. In the aftermath of the Overend, Gurney collapse the extensions to London and Manchester were becoming unwelcome financial burdens, and the company's dividends were declining. In 1868, therefore, revised terms for joint use of the L&C were agreed with the LNWR, and a Bill was introduced the following year to confirm this agreement and authorise the abandonment of the

Settle & Carlisle. But the other railways that had supported the Midland three years earlier now vigorously opposed its change of heart, and Parliament refused to sanction the abandonment. The Midland thus found itself compelled to build a line it no longer wanted, and on 1 May 1876 its route to Carlisle was opened throughout for passenger traffic; freight working had begun the previous summer.

Midland trains entered Carlisle over the line from Newcastle, which they joined at Petteril Bridge junction. NER passenger services had begun using Citadel station in 1863, using a new chord on the up side of the

The site of the former St Nicholas crossing at Carlisle in July 1877, photographed after the completion of the first phase of the layout modifications. The picture was taken from the new west coast main line embankment south of the station, and the formation leading to the superseded flat crossing can be clearly seen in the left foreground. The raised tracks in the upper part of the picture give access to the LNWR goods station, and bridge respectively (left to right) the NER chord into Citadel station; the NER canal branch; and the LNWR approach to the new joint goods lines. *(Courtesy of Denis Perriam)*

main line which had been installed in 1862 to replace the original connection on the down side. As part of these works the L&C tracks had been slewed slightly westwards, but they continued to intersect the canal branch south of the station, and on 10 July 1870 six passengers were killed when an NER freight train collided with a southbound west coast express on this crossing. With Midland workings soon to be added, this accident emphasised the need for further improvements at Carlisle, and powers were obtained in 1873 for independent goods tracks and for alterations to the passenger station and its approaches. The Midland bore a large share of the cost of these changes and in return the Citadel station committee was reconstituted to include its representatives, together with those of the other tenant companies. The additional and altered lines were built under a single contract but assigned to various ownerships, and the changed layout was brought into service in two stages, on 8 July and 6 August 1877. The LNWR portions consisted of raised approach tracks both to Citadel and its adjacent freight depot, and a dive-under giving

The original Whitehaven Junction Railway station at Workington. The station was rebuilt when the layout was extended in the mid-1880s. *(David Joy collection)*

access to the new through goods line, which ran to the west of the passenger station. It shared ownership of the goods line with the Caledonian, GSWR, and Midland, and the four companies established a separate joint committee to administer this addition to the Carlisle network.

The Midland's ambitions to extend beyond the 'little' North Western Railway also had a bearing on railway politics elsewhere in Cumberland and the neighbouring counties. Because of the difficult terrain west of the L&C main line, the system in Furness and west Cumberland had developed in virtual isolation, with the Maryport & Carlisle providing the only external connection. Its route was continued south of Maryport by the Whitehaven Junction Railway, which had been opened to Workington on 19 January 1846 and to Harrington on 18 May the same year. Goods traffic was operated over the final section to Whitehaven from 15 February 1847, and passenger services were extended on 19 March; meanwhile an eastward projection from Workington had been

provided with the opening of the Cockermouth & Workington Railway on 28 April 1847. To the south, the Furness Railway had opened the first parts of its network in the Barrow area in 1846; this was extended into Cumberland by the Whitehaven & Furness Junction Railway, completed in 1850, but until the opening of the Bransty tunnel on 30 September 1852 the only physical link with the northern lines was via harbour sidings at Whitehaven. Despite the rapid exploitation of the region's iron ore and other mineral deposits, the initial route southwards from the Furness system was by sea to Fleetwood or Morecambe, or by road; there was no rail alternative to the detour via Carlisle until 1857, when the Ulverston & Lancaster Railway was completed to its junction with the L&C at Carnforth.

The Furness absorbed the U&L in 1862 and in the following year obtained powers, jointly with the Midland, for a line from Carnforth to the NWR at Wennington. This transformed the position, for it gave another main-line company potential access to the mineral traffic of the area, as well as to the port of Barrow, the Midland's prime objective. The LNWR responded by obtaining powers in 1864 to subscribe to and enter into traffic arrangements with the

Cockermouth, Keswick & Penrith Railway, which had been authorised in 1861 to provide an alternative route into west Cumberland. These powers were shared with the North Eastern Railway through the latter's acquisition of the Stockton & Darlington Railway, which in 1862 had reached Clifton, south of Penrith, by means of its Eden Valley subsidiary.

The CK&P opened for goods on 1 November 1864 and for passengers on 2 January 1865, and from the outset it was worked by the two larger companies. The NER handled the heavy mineral traffic between its system and Cockermouth, and to avoid the need for its trains to reverse at Penrith it built a south-facing chord from the west coast main line to the CK&P, which opened on 5 September 1866. The LNWR worked the other services, and quickly enlarged its toe-hold in west Cumberland by acquiring the Whitehaven Junction and Cockermouth & Workington railways in

1866. This formed part of a territorial division with the Furness, which in the same year absorbed the Whitehaven & Furness Junction. Besides gaining a direct stake in the district's industrial traffic, the LNWR also obtained access to the ports of west Cumberland, as the WJR had opened harbour branches at Whitehaven in 1848, at Maryport in September 1858, and at Workington, probably in 1860. With the opening in 1864 of the new Lonsdale Dock at Workington, north of the river Derwent, the C&W, too, had gained direct access to harbour facilities via a spur which crossed the WJR to reach the dock sidings.

Once established in the area, the LNWR began to show interest in another local concern, the Whitehaven, Cleator & Egremont Railway, which had

Figure 5.4 – Railways in Cumberland.

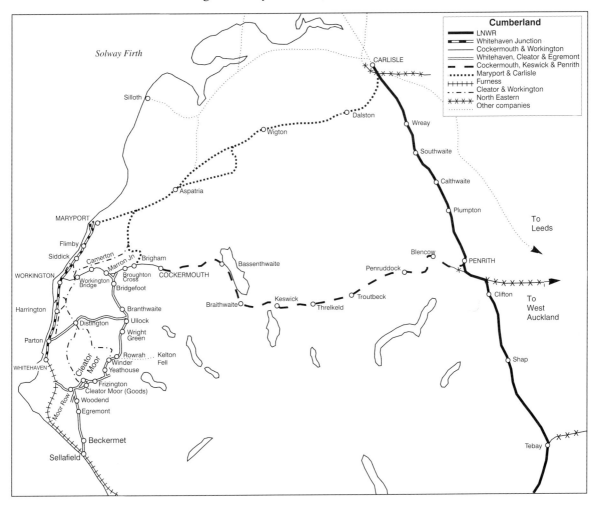

The joint station at Cockermouth, where the LNWR line from Workington met the Cockermouth, Keswick & Penrith Railway. This pre-grouping view shows an unidentified 'Cauliflower' 0-6-0 entering the station with an eastbound passenger service. *(David Joy collection)*

been incorporated in 1854. It diverged from the Furness Junction line at Mirehouse, just south of Whitehaven, and its main line to Egremont, together with a branch from Moor Row to Frizington, had opened for freight traffic on 11 January 1856; passenger services on both routes began on 1 July 1857. An extension from Frizington to near Lamplugh was brought into use for goods in November 1862 and for passengers on 12 February 1864, while a further northward extension to a triangular junction with the Cockermouth line was opened in 1866: mineral traffic probably commenced on 15 January and passenger services began on 2 April. In the same year work started on a short mineral branch to Bigrigg, south-west of Cleator Moor, which was completed in 1867, and a through route south was provided by the opening on 1 August 1869 of a link between Egremont and Sellafield, owned jointly with the Furness.

Subsidence of part of the Frizington line at Cleator Moor led to the authorisation of a northerly deviation in 1863, which seems to have been brought into use for goods traffic the following year but was not approved for passenger services until April 1866; the original route, via Crossfield, was retained as a freight-only loop. Similar problems further north led to the building of another short deviation, beyond Frizington: this was used by goods trains from April 1874 and for passenger traffic some two months later, leaving the stub of the old line as a mineral branch to Eskett.

Despite the difficult terrain through which it was built and some early disagreements over access to Whitehaven, the WC&E quickly prospered from its rich mineral traffic, and with dividends of 9% it could afford to remain independent when the LNWR made approaches in 1867. But while the company went on to even greater profitability in the early 1870s, its prospects were threatened by the authorisation in 1876 of a competitor for the local mineral traffic, the Cleator & Workington Junction Railway. The WC&E responded by promoting defensive extensions to the coastal ironworks south of Workington; however, these impinged upon LNWR territory, prompting a renewed offer from Euston to absorb the Cumbrian undertaking. Agreement was reached in November 1876 on the basis of a guaranteed dividend of 10% and the necessary legislation was promoted, but this development in its turn alarmed the Furness Railway – even though the latter was itself closely involved with the Cleator & Workington project, it considered that such an extension of LNWR influence would breach the local demarcation that had been established in 1866. To avoid parliamentary opposition to its acquisition of the WC&E, which took effect on 1 July 1877, the LNWR agreed that the undertaking should subsequently be transferred into joint ownership. Amended powers were accordingly obtained in the following session which vested the WC&E in the LNWR and Furness from 1 July 1878 and placed the existing joint section between Egremont and Sellafield on the same footing as the rest of the system.

The Cleator & Workington opened between Cleator Moor and Siddick junction, north of Workington, in 1879. Its subsequent extensions included a line northwards to link directly with M&C metals, and a branch from Distington to Rowrah to capture the traffic of the independent Rowrah & Kelton Fell Railway, which on its opening in 1877 had connected with the WC&E. Notwithstanding such complications, the pragmatism which typified railway affairs in this remote part of England soon reasserted itself: there was a tradition of interworking between the west Cumbrian systems, and by 1881 LNWR locomotive duties included some turns over the C&W line as part of arrangements with the Furness to balance engine mileage on WC&E account.

The joint undertaking was itself enlarged with the opening for mineral traffic on 2 May 1879 of a branch from Ullock to Parton, which intersected the C&W at Distington. The western section was the only surviving element of the WC&E's 1876 attempt to reach the coast, and extended a line from Ullock to the Gilgarron estate which had been authorised in 1875. On 11 November 1879 the short Mowbray branch, which diverged between Frizington and Eskett, was brought into service, and on 1 March 1880 another minor branch was opened from Gillfoot on the

Cleator Moor station on the Whitehaven, Cleator & Egremont section around the turn of the century, with an LNWR tank heading a joint passenger train. *(David Joy collection)*

The LNWR extension to Blaenau Ffestiniog under construction in 1879, with a contractor's locomotive at the temporary passenger station at the southern end of the Festiniog tunnel. Narrow-gauge track and slate wagons can be seen on the right of the picture. *(Public Record Office, RAIL 410/1403 A159)*

Egremont line. Apart from a short-lived passenger service between Parton and Distington, introduced on 1 June 1881 and withdrawn on 8 December 1883, these later branches carried freight traffic only, and subsequent additions to the WC&E system were built as sidings.

* * *

In the pattern of its railway development, west Cumberland had many similarities to Wales, where mineral resources likewise provided a stimulus to new projects despite the obstacles of topography and remoteness. The LNWR played a considerable part in this expansion and indeed by the end of the 1860s was the largest railway undertaking in the principality. In north Wales the projection of branches from the Chester & Holyhead line continued: the first to be added under Moon was the Conway & Llanrwst

Railway, which had been authorised in 1860 and was leased by the LNWR at 4% under the terms of an 1863 Act. The branch, which joined the main line at Llandudno Junction, was carrying goods traffic by July 1862, although the formal opening did not take place until 16 June 1863: regular passenger services began the next day. In 1865 the LNWR obtained powers for an extension to Betws-y-Coed: this was open for freight by February 1868, and passenger services commenced on 6 April that year. A further extension was authorised in 1872, requiring a tunnel more than two miles long to reach Blaenau Ffestiniog and connect with the narrow-gauge Festiniog Railway and the slate quarries which it served. Because of this it was originally intended to adopt the Festiniog's 1' 11½" gauge for the extension, and work started on this basis; in 1873, however, it was decided to build the line to the standard gauge. As a result of this change and of the difficulties of constructing the Festiniog tunnel, then the second longest on the LNWR system, opening to a temporary terminus at Blaenau Ffestiniog was delayed until 22 July 1879, though the section as far as Dolwyddelen, east of the tunnel, was brought into use for goods traffic earlier that year. The short continuation to the permanent LNWR station at Blaenau Ffestiniog was opened on 1 April 1881, more than two years before the GWR completed its route into the town from the south.

The extension to Blaenau Ffestiniog completed the LNWR's virtual encirclement of Snowdonia and its slate deposits, leaving only the southern flank in other hands. Even on this side, LNWR influence might have extended further, as the Carnarvonshire Railway was incorporated in 1862 to build a line from the terminus of the Bangor & Carnarvon Railway to Porthmadog. However, as the Aberystwith & Welsh Coast Railway had also obtained powers for the section between Porthmadog and Afon Wen as part of its projected extension to Porth Dinllaen, the Carnarvonshire restricted itself to the portion north of Afon Wen. For the section between Caernarfon and Pen-y-groes the company decided to adapt part of the 3' 6" gauge Nantlle Railway, which had been opened in 1828 to link the slate quarries and copper mines of the Nantlle vale with Caernarfon harbour and which nurtured separate ambitions to reach Cardigan Bay. Powers to formalise the acquisition were obtained in July 1867, and the line between Pant, south of Caernarfon, and Afon Wen was opened soon afterwards, on 2

September. However, this was not the first traffic to be worked over the line: virtually a year earlier, on 6 September 1866, an excursion from Porthmadog to Caernarfon was derailed at Bryncir with the loss of six lives. Other excursions had operated during August of that year, together with some goods trains, even though construction was still in progress.

Relations with the AWCR's successor, the Cambrian Railways, at first remained close: the Carnarvonshire hired locomotives from the Cambrian until its stock was delivered, and extended its trains from Afon Wen to serve Criccieth, Porthmadog, and Penrhyndeudraeth during the few weeks between its own opening and the completion of the coastal line between Barmouth Junction and Pwllheli on 10 October 1867. However, the Carnarvonshire was affected by the financial difficulties which were then endemic among smaller companies and was taken over by the LNWR in 1869. The absorption was confirmed by an Act of 1870 which also sanctioned the vesting of the Carnarvon & Llanberis Railway in the LNWR. This company, authorised in 1864, had been worked by the LNWR from its opening on 1 July 1869 between Llanberis and Morfa, on the east side of Caernarfon. The two local railways were officially linked with the main system on 5 July 1870 with the opening of a connection through the town; however, some LNWR goods traffic had passed over this line while it was still in the contractor's hands. Pant and Morfa stations were closed when the through route opened, and the original Nantlle terminus and sidings at Caernarfon quay had been converted to standard gauge by February 1872. To ease the movement of slate traffic the LNWR also widened and partly realigned the western section of the Nantlle Railway, between Tal-y-sarn and a new junction with the Carnarvonshire line at Pen-y-groes; this reopened for freight on 22 May 1872 and for passengers on 1 October that year. The station at Tal-y-sarn was designated Nantlle and, as it would have been too costly to convert the remainder of the route for locomotive operation, this became the transhipment point for the western stub of the original 3' 6" gauge line, which was retained to serve local slate quarries.

At Gaerwen, five miles due north of Caernarfon across the Menai strait, the Anglesea Central Railway branched from the Holyhead main line towards Amlwch, on the north coast of the island. The ACR was authorised in 1863 and opened for goods traffic as

Pen-y-groes station circa 1885, with a posed group including station and permanent-way staff, together with a 'DX' 0-6-0 and its crew. *(By permission of the National Library of Wales: John Thomas collection, S33)*

far as a temporary station at Llangefni in December 1864; passenger services commenced on 12 March 1865. On 1 February 1866 the Llangefni–Llanerchymedd section was opened to all traffic, and goods services were extended to Amlwch by the autumn of that year; however, it was 3 June 1867 before the section north of Llanerchymedd was opened for passengers. The ACR initially operated independently, but by 1871 the LNWR was supplying rolling stock and locomotives and in 1876 it purchased the undertaking for £80,000, £25,000 less than had been paid by its shareholders.

These LNWR acquisitions in north-west Wales were among a number of nominally independent lines that been promoted in the late 1850s and early 1860s to open up further areas of the principality to railway traffic. Some, like the Aberystwith & Welsh Coast,

eventually became part of the sprawling Cambrian network, while others found their way into the GWR or LNWR folds. A few remained independent, but even among these a number of promotional connections can be traced through overlapping directorships, shared professional advisers, and common contractors. The Neath & Brecon, for example, had close ties with the Anglesea Central, while through one of their directors there was also an indirect link with another group of companies that shared the same secretary, solicitor, and London head office; though most were English undertakings, they included the Carnarvon & Llanberis.

The most pervasive of these early connections, however, resulted from the constructional and financial ventures of Thomas Savin and his various associates. These not only played a considerable part in shaping the Cambrian Railways but also extended well beyond the latter's eventual constituents. For example, the close initial links between the AWCR and the Carnarvonshire reflected Savin's role in the promotion and construction of both undertakings.

Together with David Davies, his then partner, Savin had previously been involved in the building of the Vale of Clwyd Railway, and Savin and Davies also played an important part in establishing its continuation, the Denbigh, Ruthin & Corwen Railway. This was incorporated in 1860 and was intended to connect with a line from Llangollen to Corwen, authorised the same year. Since a GWR-inspired branch from the Shrewsbury & Chester line to Llangollen was already under construction, the authorisation of the DR&C presented an opportunity to interest Paddington in acquiring the Vale of Clwyd as the last link in a chain reaching from Ruabon to the north Wales coast at Rhyl. Savin persevered in the attempt to lease the DR&C and Vale of Clwyd to the GWR after the dissolution of his partnership with Davies in the autumn of 1860, so the LNWR responded by supporting the proposed Mold & Denbigh Junction Railway, which was intended to outflank the Vale of Clwyd by providing an alternative route to Denbigh. Savin in turn promoted a rival project, but the GWR's readiness to negotiate with him quickly waned, perhaps not surprisingly in view of the fact that he was at the same time involved in other proposed lines which were in direct opposition to schemes which it supported.

The M&DJ was authorised in August 1861, but by then LNWR interests had already gained control of the Vale of Clwyd Railway: this was formalised by a lease which took effect from September 1861. In the following year parliamentary powers were obtained to regularise the status of the Foryd branch and for construction of a new pier at the mouth of the Clwyd. Both were in use for goods traffic by August 1864 and a passenger station was built to serve Foryd pier, but although the *Railway Times* reported the branch as opened on 1 October 1865 it does not appear to have seen regular passenger traffic. In 1868, under the terms of an Act of 1867, the LNWR absorbed the Vale of Clwyd. The connecting DR&C was opened as far as Ruthin on 1 March 1862 and extended to a temporary terminus at Corwen by October 1864; on 1 September 1865 it was completed to the junction with the GWR, which had reached Corwen from Llangollen on 8 May. Until 31 July 1865 services were operated by the LNWR; Savin then worked the line under contract, but following his bankruptcy in

A 'Special DX' 0-6-0 heading a down passenger train on the Caernarfon town line, past standard-gauge wagons on the converted Nantlle Railway sidings and sailing vessels loading slates at the quay. *(LNWR Society collection, 415)*

36230. Carnarvon Castle from Slate Quay.

1866 the DR&C handled its own traffic until 1878. In
that year a new working agreement was reached with
the LNWR, and complete absorption followed in
1879.

Although the collapse of Savin's ambitions had
removed the LNWR's reasons for supporting the
Mold & Denbigh Junction, its promoters went ahead
with construction and with ambitious plans for extension. However, the financial crisis of 1866 left the
company in debt to landowners and its contractor and
it was not until 12 September 1869 that the line was
opened for traffic from Mold to its junction with the
Vale of Clwyd at Trefnant, north of Denbigh. Double
track between the junction and Denbigh was
completed the following year. The LNWR worked the
M&DJ from the outset but it remained a separate
undertaking, and as late as 1914 its proprietors were
contending that their interests suffered because the
LNWR gave preference to the Vale of Clwyd route.

On 1 September 1869, a few days before the
opening of the M&DJ, the LNWR completed a short
line of its own into the Clwydian hills, the freight-only
Cwm branch from Prestatyn to Dyserth. This had been
authorised in 1866 by an Act which also gave powers
for a further addition to the company's network in
north Wales, a mineral line from Tryddyn junction,
east of Mold, to Coed Talon; a minor deviation was
authorised in the following year. The branch incorporated part of the formation of the private Nerquis
Railway, which was purchased in 1868. The first
section, from Tryddyn junction to Oak Pits colliery,
was opened on 16 May 1869 and on 8 July 1870 the
line was completed to a south-facing junction at Coed
Talon. The Nerquis Railway's existing alignment
provided the northern side of a triangular connection
with the Ffrith branch.

As mentioned in Chapter Three, the Ffrith branch
was originally planned to extend south of Coed Talon,
but the situation in the industrial area around
Wrexham had subsequently been complicated by the
opening in 1862 of the GWR-worked Wrexham &
Minera Railway and by the authorisation in the same
year of the Wrexham, Mold & Connah's Quay
Railway. The latter's promoters included Savin and
his colleagues in many of the Cambrian companies,
Benjamin and Robert Piercy and George Whalley MP,
who as part of their wider plans had given notice in
1860 of an intended line from Ellesmere to the Ffrith
branch, via Ruabon. They failed to proceed with this

Bill in 1861 and instead brought forwards revised
proposals in the next session for a more easterly route,
from Bettisfield via Wrexham to Buckley. Despite
competition from a GWR-inspired Mold & Wrexham
project and the loss of the section south of Wrexham
and some intended branches, the WM&CQ emerged
from Parliament in 1862 with powers for a line linking
Wrexham with the Buckley Railway, which in 1860
had been authorised to adapt an earlier mineral
tramway for locomotive operation. Running powers
over the Buckley Railway to its northern terminus at
Connah's Quay gave access to the Dee estuary and to
the C&H main line, while the WM&CQ itself also
formed junctions with the LNWR's Mold branch near
Hope and with the GWR at Wrexham.

The opening of the WM&CQ in 1866 thus linked
the two main-line systems, but although the company
was a candidate for absorption by the LNWR on more
than one occasion it remained independent until it
found its way into Watkin's sphere of influence and
ultimately became part of the Great Central Railway.
Its route was however soon paralleled by another
connection between the GWR and LNWR which
revived earlier proposals for a southward projection
of the Ffrith branch. In 1865, faced with a further
scheme for a line between Mold and Wrexham, this
time as part of the M&DJ's abortive plans for expansion, the LNWR supported a rival Bill by the
Wrexham & Minera Railway for an extension from
Brymbo to the Ffrith branch, together with a spur
from the latter to join the Mold line at Llong. These
powers were granted, but in 1866 the spur westwards
to Llong was superseded by the authorisation of the
LNWR's Tryddyn branch, while the remainder of the
line was vested jointly in the LNWR and GWR as the
Wrexham & Minera Extension Railway. Construction
began in 1870 under the supervision of the owning
companies' joint committee and on 29 January 1872
instructions were given to open the line for freight
traffic. The original W&M was leased by the GWR in
1871 and joint ownership extended northwards from
the junction at Brymbo for just under three miles; a
further mile of LNWR track, brought into service at
the same time, completed the link with Coed Talon
and the Mold line.

South of the coalfield, the Oswestry, Ellesmere &
Whitchurch Railway, promoted by Whalley, Savin,
and the Piercy brothers with support from the LNWR,
was successful in a parliamentary contest in 1861 with

a rival GWR scheme; as noted above, however, initial proposals for a branch from Ellesmere to the Ffrith line were abandoned, as was an intended continuation from Ellesmere to Wem, on the Shrewsbury–Crewe line. Although the GWR succeeded in restricting the WM&CQ to the section north of Wrexham when the parliamentary battle was rejoined in 1862, its own Bills for lines from Oswestry and Rednal to Ellesmere and Whitchurch were rejected, while the OE&W obtained powers for its Wem branch. In 1864 the WM&CQ was eventually authorised to extend southwards from Wrexham to the OE&W, but these powers, and those for the Ellesmere–Wem branch, were later abandoned, allowing the GWR to maintain its monopoly of the route south from Wrexham until a Watkin-inspired line to Ellesmere was completed in 1895.

Paddington's interest in north Shropshire was not however purely defensive: it was also prompted by aspirations to obtain improved access to Manchester and to the Potteries. Its hopes of extending via Ellesmere were baulked by the parliamentary defeats of 1861 and 1862, but the GWR gained an isolated outpost in north-east Shropshire in 1863 with the opening of the Nantwich & Drayton Railway, which it worked from the outset. This was one of several contemporary proposals for lines radiating from Market Drayton; while most proved ephemeral, the completion of the Wellington & Drayton Railway in 1867 gave the GWR a route from Wellington to Nantwich, with running powers thence to Crewe. A further outlet was added in 1870, when the North Staffordshire opened a branch from Silverdale to Market Drayton. Although these links provided the GWR with useful new through connections, the LNWR was able to counter by creating its own direct route between Shrewsbury and Chester with the opening on 1 October 1872 of a branch from Whitchurch to Tattenhall junction, east of Chester.

These manœuvres, together with those in Denbighshire and Flintshire described earlier, found echoes in events south and west of Shrewsbury, where the LNWR made its largest incursions into new territory. This stirring of activity in Wales and the marches, which reflected the overlap of existing LNWR and GWR spheres of influence in the region and the resulting opportunities for independent promoters to exploit gaps in the network, at first seriously threatened the accord that had been established

between Euston and Paddington in the late 1850s. However, the two companies pulled back from open confrontation and instead ratified a comprehensive traffic agreement in 1863 which was given physical expression in the construction of the previously-deferred connections between their systems at Leamington and Banbury, and also of a junction at Oxford. This ending of hostility can be attributed to three main factors: the priority that the GWR gave to completing its amalgamations with the West Midland and South Wales railways, which made it anxious to avoid parliamentary opposition; its financial exhaustion, which obliged it for a while to issue shares in place of cash dividends; and the LNWR's willingness to offer joint control of key routes.

This last point is important, since it bears out Moon's contention that his company was not seeking to establish a new monopoly in central and southern Wales: indeed, he was at times lukewarm in his personal support for extension into these areas. As noted earlier, however, he was prepared to justify expansion to retain existing traffic, and this was the trigger which reactivated Euston's interest in the territory beyond the Severn. The GWR's 1861 agreements with the South Wales and West Midland railways gave it effective control of both existing routes into south Wales, via Gloucester and via Hereford, a development which alarmed the independent standard-gauge companies in the Welsh valleys as well as the LNWR. In addition, the WMR – which numbered Edward Watkin among its directors – had gained a route to Shrewsbury by leasing the Severn Valley Railway in 1860, and also nurtured ambitions to reach the Irish Sea. These factors, together with the contemporary schemes for branches from the GWR's Shrewsbury–Chester line, posed a potential threat to LNWR access to large parts of Wales.

Euston's response took the form of a series of agreements which secured its interests beyond Shrewsbury. The LNWR had already subscribed £30,000 in 1860 to the Oswestry & Newtown Railway, which was originally promoted in association with the GWR but as a result of financial difficulties was by then under the effective control of Davies and Savin. In 1861 this subscription was backed up with traffic agreements with the O&N and the connecting Llanidloes & Newtown. By that stage Davies had parted company with Savin over the latter's plans for extensions to Aberystwyth and the north coast of Cardigan Bay; though the GWR took advantage of the rift to offer favourable terms to the intervening Newtown & Machynlleth Railway, which Davies then still controlled, its lease was not ratified, and the Machynlleth line was worked by Savin on behalf of the O&N from its opening in 1863. On 23 April 1864 a comprehensive traffic agreement consolidated the various arrangements between the LNWR and the Savin companies in mid-Wales; this presaged the formation of the Cambrian Railways later that year and provided the basis for a close relationship with the LNWR which lasted until the grouping.

The two systems connected directly at Whitchurch and Afon Wen, and later also at Builth Road when the Cambrian took over the Mid Wales Railway, but their initial link was via the Shrewsbury & Welshpool Railway, which was authorised in 1856 and diverged from the Hereford line three-quarters of a mile south of the joint station at Shrewsbury. On 13 February 1861 the S&W main line opened as far as Hanwood, the junction for a branch to Minsterley which opened on the same day. The rest of the S&W to its junction with the O&N at Buttington, north of Welshpool, was brought into service on 27 January 1862. The LNWR worked the S&W from its opening and in 1864 leased the line at 4%. However, the Act giving the necessary authorisation also permitted the GWR to share in the lease; this took effect on 1 January 1865, adding the Welshpool line to the catalogue of joint LNWR and GWR interests.

A similar arrangement had already been made for the route from Shrewsbury to Hereford. As part of the negotiations for the formation of the West Midland Railway in 1860, running powers over the Newport, Abergavenny & Hereford section had been conceded to the S&H, but the latter's directors, fearing the effects of the proposed further amalgamation of the WMR with the GWR and aware also of the possibility of a hostile bid from this quarter, approached the LNWR early in 1861 to take over their line when Thomas Brassey's lease expired the following year. Terms were quickly agreed for a lease at 6%, but the LNWR also offered the GWR and WMR the opportunity to participate. They refused this offer and instead opposed the Bill which the S&H and LNWR brought forward in 1862 to sanction their agreement. After the failure of this parliamentary opposition, the offer of a joint lease was belatedly accepted, so with effect from 1 July 1862 the S&H passed to the LNWR and the

GWR, the WMR sharing the latter's half interest until their amalgamation took effect in 1863. The Tenbury Railway, which diverged at Woofferton and had been worked from its opening on 1 August 1861 by Brassey on behalf of the S&H, was included in the joint undertaking. The lessees took over the line's existing rolling stock and locomotives, while the LNWR also inherited the services of George Findlay, who had run the S&H extremely successfully on behalf of Brassey and in addition managed some of Savin's lines. Findlay was appointed as LNWR district superintendent at Shrewsbury, but also continued his involvement with the Cambrian companies until his promotion to Euston in 1865.

Despite their earlier disagreement, the LNWR and GWR quickly settled down to develop the S&H. Double track was extended south of Ludlow, while at Shrewsbury a new curve was opened on 1 May 1867 to allow direct running to and from the Wellington line without reversal. In the previous summer another through connection had been provided with the completion of two miles of track linking Rotherwas junction, on the Hereford–Gloucester route, with the Newport line at Red Hill junction. This opened for goods traffic on 16 July 1866 and for passengers on 1 August, allowing through trains to use the S&H station at Barr's Court in preference to the less satisfactory Barton station. Although the Red Hill loop was south of the joint section and connected with GWR metals at both ends, it was built and owned by the LNWR, which, as joint lessee of the S&H, had inherited running powers over the former Newport, Abergavenny & Hereford Railway. The latter, however, did not actually extend to Newport: it terminated south of Pontypool in a junction with the Monmouthshire Railway's eastern valleys line, which it used to reach Mill Street station in Newport. The NA&H's running powers into Newport were available only to the GWR, but in 1863 the LNWR concluded its own agreement with the Monmouthshire, enabling it too to work through to Newport. Separate LNWR passenger trains ceased at the end of 1865 as a result of a decision to operate joint services over the Hereford line, but in 1874 the GWR opened an alternative route from Pontypool Road to Newport High Street. The LNWR accordingly reinstated its trains between Shrewsbury and Newport

Figure 5.5 – The LNWR in south Wales.

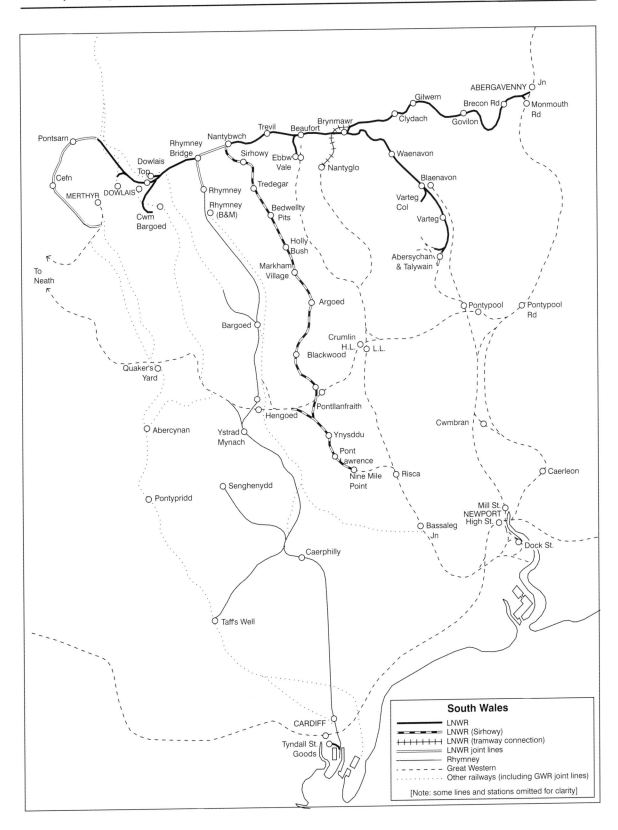

Legend:

South Wales

▬▬▬	LNWR
▬▪▬▪	LNWR (Sirhowy)
┼┼┼┼┼	LNWR (tramway connection)
═══	LNWR joint lines
───	Rhymney
─ ─ ─	Great Western
· · · · ·	Other railways (including GWR joint lines)

[Note: some lines and stations omitted for clarity]

Mill Street on 1 January 1875, and this service continued until 1879 even though the GWR took effective control of the Monmouthshire Railway later in 1875.

The GWR's initial resistance to LNWR control of the S&H was not due simply to its concern at the improved links its rival would gain with existing lines in south Wales. In a further adroit move, the LNWR had reached agreement in November 1861 to lease the Merthyr, Tredegar & Abergavenny Railway, which had been authorised in 1859 and was still under construction, incorporating parts of earlier tramroads in its steeply-graded route. Though the MT&A could only be reached by running powers, it laid the basis for the LNWR's access to the collieries and ironworks of Monmouthshire and Glamorgan via the heads of the valleys, and eventually enabled the company to gain access to Cardiff in addition to Newport. The first portion, between Abergavenny and Brynmawr, was ceremonially opened on 29 September 1862; public services commenced on 1 October, the day that the LNWR's lease took formal effect. The remainder of the authorised line, to Nantybwch, was opened on 1 March 1864 and in the same year the Rhymney Railway obtained powers to extend from Rhymney to Nantybwch. The Rhymney company was facing strong competition from the Brecon & Merthyr, and the LNWR was able to reach an agreement which not only provided for the extension to be made jointly but also gave it running powers to Cardiff for goods traffic. These arrangements received parliamentary sanction in 1867 and on 1 August 1871 the joint extension was opened for goods traffic; passenger services began on 2 October. The agreement with the Rhymney enabled the LNWR to open a separate goods station at Tyndall Street in Cardiff on 1 October 1875 which was reached by half a mile of its own track.

By then the LNWR had become firmly entrenched in the railway geopolitics of south Wales. Through access to the MT&A was improved by the opening on 20 June 1870 of a north-to-west spur from a new Abergavenny Junction station on the Hereford line, replacing the reversal required by the previous junction, which faced the GWR's Monmouth Road station. Further connections into the valleys were provided by a branch from Beaufort to Ebbw Vale, which opened for passengers and goods respectively on 1 September and 31 October 1867, and by a short

extension of the Sirhowy Railway to Nantybwch, brought into service for goods traffic on 12 October 1868 and for passengers on 2 November. The Sirhowy undertaking, which had been built as a tramway in the early years of the century and converted under powers obtained in 1860, depended on the Monmouthshire Railway for access to Newport. When the Monmouthshire was acquired by the GWR in 1875 the Sirhowy responded by approaching the LNWR, and an Act authorising a lease was obtained in 1876. The LNWR thus gained a second route to Newport, which it reached by running powers from the Sirhowy's southern terminus at Nine Mile Point.

Another connection with the former Monmouthshire system was later provided via the Brynmawr & Blaenavon Railway, which was incorporated in 1866 and leased by the LNWR in the same year. The Blaenavon line, which reached a summit of 1,400' at Waenavon, the highest on the LNWR system, was opened for freight traffic on 1 November 1869 and for passengers on 18 December. Although the terminus at Blaenavon was close to the Monmouthshire Railway's eastern valleys line from Pontypool, there was no direct link at that point. However, two LNWR extensions were authorised in 1874, one a mineral branch to Varteg Hill colliery which opened on 17 December 1877 and the other to join the Monmouthshire's Cwmfrwyd branch near Abersychan. The position there was complicated by the fact that the Monmouthshire itself obtained an Act in 1874 to provide a new connection into the Cwmfrwyd branch from Trevithin junction, north of Pontypool, and these powers overlapped with those of the LNWR in the vicinity of Talywain. The LNWR's single-track extension to a new station at Abersychan & Talywain was opened on 1 May 1878, together with a mineral spur from Garndiffaith junction to the Cwmfrwyd branch. On 18 September 1879 the Monmouthshire line from Trevithin junction was completed, linking with the LNWR by a short jointly-owned section south of Talywain. Joint ownership also extended 28 chains westwards from Talywain junction to give another connection into the existing network of mineral lines in the area.

With the opening of the Monmouthshire line a GWR-operated passenger service was introduced between Newport and Abersychan & Talywain and by agreement some of these trains were extended to and from Brynmawr, superseding most of the previous

Above: 0–6–2 'Coal Tank' no 3151 photographed in the early 1920s near Cefn on an up LNWR freight working over the single-track Morlais junction–Penywern junction section. *(LCGB Ken Nunn collection, H937)*

Right: The GWR station at Merthyr with 'Coal Tank' 0–6–2 waiting to depart on an LNWR service in the early 1920s. *(LCGB Ken Nunn collection, H3008)*

LNWR local workings. This pattern of passenger operation persisted thereafter, since the main value of the Abersychan extension to the LNWR was in increasing its share of the local mineral traffic, which justified the provision of a locomotive shed at Blaenavon in 1881. Freight to and from Newport was exchanged with the GWR at Talywain junction and the short section between there and Garndiffaith junction was doubled in 1885. As part of this remodelling, ownerships appear to have been adjusted to give the GWR full control of the mineral line to the west of Talywain junction and to extend the joint section northwards through Abersychan & Talywain station to just south of Garndiffaith junction.

Besides gaining these southern outlets, the MT&A route was also pushed further west with the opening on 1 January 1873 of a link between Rhymney Bridge, on the joint Rhymney/LNWR section, and the Brecon & Merthyr at Ivor junction, giving access to Dowlais; an intermediate junction at Dowlais Top provided a northward connection into the B&M. The latter's metals also enabled the LNWR eventually to reach Merthyr: in 1874 an extension was authorised from Penywern, just north of Ivor junction, to join the B&M's Merthyr branch at Morlais junction. Though the new section was less than $1^{1}/_{4}$ miles long, almost half was in tunnel, and it was not opened for traffic until 1 June 1879. The B&M line, which had been completed to Merthyr on 1 August 1868, became joint property south of Morlais junction under powers obtained in 1875, and running powers over the GWR secured entry to Merthyr High Street station. The junctions at Merthyr and Dowlais also gave the

LNWR access to the local industrial tramway systems, but a more direct connection into the most extensive of these, the Dowlais Iron Company's network, was provided with the opening of the Cwm Bargoed mineral branch, east of Dowlais, on 14 June 1881.

Dowlais and Merthyr were not, however, the western limits of the LNWR's ambitions in south Wales: Swansea was also an objective, and in 1864 the company was able to make use of inherited running powers over the former NA&H Pontypool–Aberdare branch to reach the Vale of Neath Railway and thus gain access to Swansea. Warned by the precedent of the MT&A, the GWR quickly agreed terms for amalgamation with the Vale of Neath, but although the *Railway Times* of 18 November 1865 suggested the possibility of a joint lease the LNWR was by then already building up an alternative route to Swansea and west Wales. As part of its agreement with the Shrewsbury & Hereford it succeeded to that company's close association with the Knighton Railway, which had been authorised in 1858 to build a line from Craven Arms to the Radnorshire border town which gave the company its name. This was opened as far as Bucknell on 1 October 1860 and completed on 6 March 1861, though mineral trains were operated to Knighton before then. In 1859, after a fierce parliamentary battle with the rival Mid Wales scheme, the Central Wales Railway had obtained

powers to extend the route as far as Llandrindod, and the portion between Knighton and Knucklas was in use for mineral traffic by August 1862.

The Knighton Railway was at first operated by Thomas Brassey under traffic agreements with the S&H, which also extended to the Central Wales Railway. When Brassey's contract expired on 30 June 1862 the two companies turned to the LNWR, and a backdated working agreement was eventually concluded in 1863. Freight services were extended to near Penybont in the autumn of 1864 and the formal opening to Llandrindod took place on 10 October 1865: public traffic commenced on 1 December. A further continuation, the Central Wales Extension, had been authorised in 1860, and this too was opened in stages and worked by the LNWR. The first section, as far as Builth Road, was brought into use on 1 November 1866; in the following year services were extended to Garth on 11 March and then to Llanwrtyd on 6 May, while the final portion, to Llandovery, was opened for goods traffic on 1 June 1868 and for passengers a week later. Under the terms of the 1863 Act authorising their working agreements, the Central Wales and Knighton companies then amalgamated, and the combined undertaking was absorbed by the LNWR in 1869, together with the CWER.

At Builth Road the route crossed over the Mid Wales Railway, which had been completed between Llanidloes and Brecon in 1864. Exchange platforms were provided, and a chord linking the two lines was brought into service in February 1867. Though this curve was transferred to LNWR ownership in 1870, it

Knucklas viaduct, on the Central Wales Railway. *(LNWR Society collection, 9118)*

was built by the MWR under powers obtained in 1862 and was the one positive outcome of that company's ambitions to secure additional outlets from the Wye valley route to which it had been confined by its previous parliamentary contests with the Central Wales promoters. This rivalry had been prompted by the contemporary interest in shortening railway distances between south and west Wales and the midlands and north of England, which was also reflected in the authorisation of several other Welsh lines. However, the financial crisis of 1866 left the MWR and Central Wales companies in undisturbed possession of their largely unpromising terrain: the MWR itself abandoned two branches, while another survivor from this period, Davis's Manchester & Milford Railway, forsook the ambitions implicit in its title by giving up its intended route to Pencader from Llanidloes in favour of the easier but less direct approach from Aberystwyth. A similar retrenchment was forced upon the Neath & Brecon Railway, which in 1864 obtained powers to extend to the CWER at Llangammarch: though its Act authorised an operating agreement that would have made the N&B effectively part of the LNWR system, the company's hopes of achieving a connection with the Central Wales route were subsequently dashed by the bankruptcy of its contractor. The N&B was instead forced to concentrate on completing its line to Brecon and was ultimately drawn into the orbit of the Midland Railway, which in 1865 took control of the Hereford, Hay & Brecon Railway.

However, a continuation southward was already available from the CWER's intended terminus at Llandovery by means of the Vale of Towy Railway, which had obtained powers in 1854 for a line between there and Llandilo. This in turn connected with the Llanelly Railway & Dock Company, which was authorised as early as 1833 and had reached Llandilo in January 1857. The Llanelly company leased the Vale of Towy undertaking from its opening on 1 April 1858, and in 1861, after the prospect of through traffic had been bolstered by the authorisation of the CWER the previous year, also obtained powers for new routes to Carmarthen and Swansea. The Carmarthen line diverged at Llandilo and terminated in a junction with the broad-gauge Cardigan & Carmarthen Railway at Abergwili, north of the town; the 1861 Act conferred running powers from this junction, but it was necessary for the Llanelly company to obtain

further parliamentary authorisation in 1862 to allow it to install mixed-gauge track between Abergwili and the C&C's junction with the South Wales Railway at Myrtle Hill, south of Carmarthen. The branch was opened for goods traffic on 1 November 1864 and for regular passenger services on 1 June 1865, though excursions were run between Llandilo and Carmarthen on the three previous days. Later that summer, on 2 August, goods trains began operating over the extension from Pontardulais to Swansea. A subsidiary line to Penclawdd diverged at Gower Road, and as the works were sufficiently advanced for the directors to travel over this branch on 22 August 1865 it is probable that it opened for goods shortly afterwards. Passenger traffic over the Swansea and Penclawdd lines did not however commence until 14 December 1867, when the Llanelly's Swansea Victoria terminus was opened.

The delays in completing the Swansea section for passenger traffic were the consequence of the company's worsening financial situation, which was also reflected in the postponement and later abandonment of a branch to the Mumbles, authorised in 1865. The Swansea and Carmarthen extensions had been kept separate from the original undertaking and were typical of many schemes at that time in being heavily dependent on the contractor's ability to refinance the cost of the works during construction. The Llanelly contracts were won by the firm of Watson & Overend, which also built the Mid Wales Railway and operated it after its opening in 1864. During the late summer and autumn of 1865 Watson & Overend became increasingly overcommitted and eventually defaulted in January 1866, despite the attempts of the Llanelly board to assist by raising additional loans. This left the railway company to meet the contractor's outstanding obligations for interest payments and for land and rolling stock purchases, in addition to the the substantial expenditure still necessary to complete the Swansea extension. Although the Carmarthen line was by then open, the directors discovered that the rolling stock in use on the branch was the property of the MWR and had to be replaced. With Savin's default following that of Watson & Overend, the stage was set for further collapse: despite the coincidence of names, there was no personal connection between Watson & Overend and Overend, Gurney, but the latter firm had been actively involved in discounting railway securities and indeed it was a court case involving Mid

Wales securities which finally precipitated its own failure.

Although some funds were made available from the original Llanelly undertaking, the Swansea extension was soon in receivership. In these circumstances the LNWR's drive southwards via the Central Wales route offered a lifeline, both because of the extra revenue which its traffic would bring and through the prospect of additional assistance in completing the Swansea section. A deputation from the LNWR board inspected the Llanelly Railway in July 1867, and this was followed by arrangements for a loan of up to £40,000 (which was negotiated in the names of the chairman, deputy-chairman, and secretary rather than the LNWR itself) in exchange for running powers over the Llanelly network and a joint lease of the Vale of Towy line. When the CWER opened for passenger traffic on 8 June 1868 the LNWR could thus extend its services to both Swansea and Carmarthen; from the following year it was also able to provide through carriages to Pembroke Dock by virtue of the Pembroke & Tenby Railway's running powers over the former South Wales Railway main line between Whitland and Carmarthen, which the GWR honoured by converting one broad-gauge track on this section to standard gauge.

While the original Llanelly undertaking prospered from to the additional traffic which the LNWR brought on to the system, the unsecured investors in the Swansea and Carmarthen extensions were left without dividends because of the prior charges borne by these lines' accounts. These burdens included interest on debts to the other part of the company in addition to the costs of external borrowing. In 1870 an independent receiver was appointed for the Swansea section in place of the company secretary, while the Llanelly board's decision not to underwrite interest payments on Carmarthen debentures also forced that section into receivership. These events led to a complete financial reconstruction which resulted in the incorporation of the Swansea and Carmarthen lines as an entirely separate company in 1871. This proved to be a Trojan horse, for the Swansea & Carmarthen Railway immediately agreed that the LNWR should take over the working of its system. The Llanelly directors then sought to repudiate the earlier agreement with the LNWR, but the law lords determined in 1873 that the latter's running powers remained valid. In the same year the LNWR

purchased the S&C lines south of Pontardulais for £310,000, leaving the Llandilo–Abergwili branch to be reconstituted as the Central Wales & Carmarthen Junction Railway. In 1874 the LNWR obtained powers for a short extension of the Penclawdd branch to Llanmorlais; this was completed for freight traffic in 1877, although passenger services were not extended to the new terminus until 1 March 1884. The LNWR was also authorised in 1876 to build a separate goods station at Llanelly, but these powers were eventually abandoned in 1890.

The GWR leased the remainder of the Llanelly system in 1873, giving it control of the Pontardulais–Llandilo section, together with an equal voice in the Vale of Towy Railway, which in 1884 was vested jointly in the two main-line companies. This extension of Paddington's interests was followed by complete absorption of the Llanelly undertaking in 1889. However, the existing running powers safeguarded the LNWR's continued access to south-west Wales via the Central Wales route and maintained its competitive advantage over the less direct GWR alternatives for traffic to and from Shrewsbury and the north. In addition, by purchasing the section south of Pontardulais, the LNWR had secured its position in Swansea before the Midland could complete its own difficult cross-country approach via Brecon in 1874.

* * *

The expansion of the LNWR's activities during the 1860s and 1870s was not confined to England and Wales. Although the 1860 Post Office contract had confirmed the City of Dublin Steam Packet Company's hold on the sea portion of the London–Dublin mail route, the LNWR retained a vital role in transport links with the Irish capital through its contract for the connecting Euston–Holyhead rail services, its financial and traffic agreements with the steamer company, and its decision to develop the Holyhead–North Wall route for complementary cargo and passenger sailings. In 1863 and 1864 delivery was taken of two new paddle steamers, the *Alexandra* and *Stanley*, which had been designed specially for the North Wall crossing. These joined the *Admiral Moorsom* of 1860 and the remaining C&H vessels – two of the 1847 quartet, the *Anglia* and *Scotia*, had been sold to the confederate states in 1861 as blockade runners – and most of the second-hand tonnage had also been disposed of by the early 1860s, leaving only the *Sea Nymph* and *Telegraph* to supplement the *Cambria* and *Hibernia* and the newer steamers.

In 1863 the LNWR leased part of the inner harbour at Holyhead and brought improved berthage and shore facilities into use in 1866. At the beginning of that year a new marine superintendent, Captain C B C Dent, had taken over following the death of Captain R H Risk, who had himself been appointed in 1862 after the death of Captain Thomas Hirste, the former C&H superintendent, in 1861. Dent – who was engaged initially at a salary of £400, £50 more than his predecessor – supervised the LNWR's marine activities at Holyhead until the 1890s, progressing meanwhile in naval rank to Admiral, and vessels and services were quickly developed under his vigorous management. In 1868 two further paddle steamers were delivered, the *Countess of Erne* and *Duke of Sutherland*; the slightly larger *Duchess of Sutherland* followed in 1869 and her sister ship, the *Edith*, joined the fleet a year later.

During the 1860s the company's interests in Irish services also began to extend into other areas. Through the Lancaster & Carlisle Railway, the LNWR had acquired a financial stake in the Portpatrick Railway, which opened between Castle Douglas and Stranraer on 12 March 1861 and was completed to Portpatrick on 28 August 1862. An infrequent steamer service already linked Stranraer with Larne, but to provide improved connections the LNWR joined with the Portpatrick and other interested railways in underwriting daily crossings by the Stranraer & Larne Steamboat Company, specially formed for this purpose. The new service commenced on 1 October 1862 and on the same day a branch to Stranraer Harbour was opened. However, the losses soon proved too much for the sponsoring railways and the service ceased at the end of 1863.

The Portpatrick Railway had meanwhile become embroiled in the rivalry between the GSWR and the Caledonian, and the latter, with the support of the LNWR, undertook to work the line under a 21-year agreement which took effect in 1864. Next year the Caledonian in turn experimented with a shipping service from Stranraer, in its case direct to Belfast, but this too was short-lived. After various other efforts, including an attempt to revive the short crossing from Portpatrick to Donaghadee, a regular service was

eventually established in 1872 by the Larne & Stranraer Steamboat Company, in which the Portpatrick Railway had a financial interest. At first the route was operated by a single paddle steamer, the *Princess Louise*, but she was joined by the *Princess Beatrice* in 1876.

By that stage competition for traffic to and from the north of Ireland had increased considerably. Besides the traditional crossing from Liverpool, there were also sailings between Fleetwood and Belfast, while in 1867 a new connectional route was inaugurated when the Midland began working boat trains over Furness metals in conjunction with the Belfast services of the Barrow Steam Navigation Company. In response, the L&Y and LNWR obtained powers in 1870 jointly to take over the Fleetwood–Belfast route from the North Lancashire Steam Navigation Company, acquiring one vessel from the company and purchasing another second-hand to maintain the service until the delivery of the *Princess of Wales*, the first of a fleet of five paddle steamers built for the joint owners.

In 1870 the LNWR also secured authorisation to operate vessels between Holyhead and Greenore, on Carlingford Lough, and the commencement of this service on 1 May 1873 marked not only the start of a new shipping route to the north of Ireland but also the opening of what amounted to an Irish outpost of the company's railway system. This was the Dundalk & Greenore Railway, which had been incorporated in 1863 to provide a connection between the Irish North Western Railway and a proposed new harbour at the mouth of Carlingford Lough. The D&G had the support and encouragement of the LNWR, and although at first there was no direct financial contribution a number of shares were held by LNWR nominees. However, the D&G suffered the after-effects of the financial collapse of 1866, so in 1867 the LNWR obtained powers to subscribe to the D&G and to appoint directors. In 1868 the head office moved to Euston and the LNWR secretary, Stephen Reay, took on the same position with the Irish company; in the following year Richard Moon became its chairman. By the time the D&G opened for service on 1 May 1873 it was in effect part of the LNWR, which had provided the bulk of the capital for the undertaking and had built its 5' 3" gauge rolling stock and locomotives. The LNWR also opened an hotel at Greenore, and operated a local steamer service between Greenore and Warrenpoint, on the northern shore of the lough.

Dundalk station, Great Northern Railway of Ireland, with a Dundalk, Newry & Greenore Railway train headed by Crewe-built 0-6-0 saddle-tank no 6, 'Holyhead'. *(LNWR Society, 2052)*

Through carriages linked Belfast with the Holyhead sailings under an agreement with the INWR to share the costs of the shipping service, and this arrangement was continued after the amalgamations of 1876 which created the Great Northern Railway of Ireland. Local railway connections from Greenore were extended on 1 August 1876 when a line was opened north-westwards to Newry, and the opening of a junction there with the Newry & Armagh section of the GNR(I) on 1 July 1880 completed a shorter route between Greenore and Belfast. The Newry & Greenore Railway had originally been authorised in 1863 as a separate undertaking, though empowered jointly with the D&G to develop Greenore harbour. However, despite extensions of time, the N&G failed to recover from the financial collapse of 1866, and its interest in the harbour was allowed to lapse. On 21 July 1873, soon after the opening of the Dundalk line, the N&G's remaining powers were transferred to the D&G, which was authorised to change its name to the Dundalk, Newry & Greenore Railway. The same Act permitted the LNWR to increase its subscription to the combined under-taking and in the following year the LNWR took over the borrowing powers of the DN&G.

The Holyhead–Greenore route was inaugurated

with vessels transferred from the North Wall service, but two purpose-built paddle steamers, the *Eleanor* and *Earl Spencer*, were delivered by Laird Brothers in 1873 and 1874 respectively. One of the earlier vessels, the *Edith*, sank on 8 September 1875 after colliding with the inbound *Duchess of Sutherland* shortly after departing from Holyhead for Greenore; she was ultimately raised in December 1877 and returned to service as a cargo vessel. Meanwhile a new steamer, the *Isabella*, had been ordered for the Greenore service; her significance in LNWR marine history is that she was the company's first steel-hulled vessel, built by Lairds with steel supplied from Crewe. After delivery in 1877 the *Isabella* was at first used for North Wall sailings, but in 1880 she took up station on her intended route.

* * *

Although the DN&G provided a further example of the LNWR's tendency to become drawn into financial responsibility for associated lines, the board was by then becoming increasingly selective in committing the company's funds to other railways. Strategic investments continued to be made in schemes in Scotland and Ireland which could generate through traffic: for example, shares in the Callander & Oban Railway were added to the LNWR's portfolio in 1878, while Euston's role in developments in Dublin will be described in the next chapter. However, some interests in established companies were sold: the LNWR disposed of its Caledonian shares in 1862 and ran down its holding of Scottish North Eastern securities after 1867 when that company amalgamated with the Caledonian.

In England and Wales, the policy of absorbing smaller undertakings continued, but after assisting the Harborne Railway in 1870 the LNWR virtually ceased to take shares in connecting companies: the solitary exception was the Charnwood Forest Railway, described in the following chapter, in which £50,000 was invested in 1883. As a result, some minor railways in England which under previous policies might have been considered candidates for LNWR support were instead left to fend for themselves. One, the Garstang & Knott End Railway in Lancashire, only raised sufficient funds to complete part of its intended route from its junction with the main line at Garstang & Catterall; it opened on 5 December 1870, but services had to be withdrawn in 1872 for financial reasons. After approaches to both the LNWR and L&Y were rejected, the line reopened in 1875, initially in receivership, and operated as a separate undertaking until the grouping. Another feeder into the main line linked Blisworth with the Banbury branch at Cockley Brake junction: it opened between Blisworth and Towcester on 1 May 1866 as the Midland Counties & South Wales Railway and was completed under the more modest title of the Northampton & Banbury Junction Railway on 1 June 1872. Although the undertaking was worked from 1876 with stock hired on a mileage basis from the LNWR, it remained operationally and financially independent. The connecting East & West Junction Railway, which with its various extensions sought to revive the N&BJ's earlier ambitions to provide a cross-country route to Wales, completed a link between Towcester and Stratford-upon-Avon in 1873; traffic was however suspended in 1877. The E&WJ reopened in March 1885 and though it provided a route from Euston to Stratford which appeared as such in the LNWR public timetables, it too remained independent, ultimately merging with the N&BJ in 1910 as the Stratford-upon-Avon & Midland Junction Railway.

Continuing obligations to existing companies, together with the selective new investments mentioned above, left the LNWR with substantial holdings in other railways, though the amount shown against this heading in the capital account was reduced from £6·2m at 30 June 1861 to half of that sum at the end of 1872. Part of this reduction was due to disposals, but the bulk reflected the capital restructuring and consolidation carried out under Moon, which simplified the LNWR's financial affairs and disentangled the web of leases, guarantees, working agreements, and subscriptions that had been built up during the course of expansion. From 1862 onwards it became the practice wherever possible to dissolve subsidiaries that had been acquired on the basis of long leases or guarantees, allowing the shares held by the LNWR in such companies to be extinguished; other shareholders were issued with guaranteed stock to provide an equivalent income. By the end of 1870 more than £5m of new capital had been issued in this way: while some represented recent construction, such as the Bangor & Carnarvon or Central Wales lines, much of it could be attributed to the incorporation of earlier undertakings within the LNWR's own accounts.

For investment under its own Acts, or to meet fresh subscriptions to other companies, new 5% preference stock was created from 1863 onwards and the premiums from this stock were carried to the credit of the capital account. Further tranches of debenture stock were also issued to retire earlier loans or take up unexercised borrowing powers. Additions to ordinary stock were relatively small, so the capital account consequently became more highly geared during the 1860s and early 1870s. As interest rates tended downwards after the mid-1860s, the changing capital structure worked together with the growth in net receipts to the benefit of dividends, helping LNWR ordinary stock to rise to 50% or more above par by the early 1870s. By 1871 the *Railway Times* was able to comment that the company's shares had fluctuated less than Consols over the previous three years, clear testimony to the effectiveness of Moon's financial policies in restoring the LNWR's status as the leading investment among the Stock Exchange's 'Home Rails'.

CHAPTER SIX

High Moon

The first half of Moon's period of office saw a rapid increase in the LNWR's route mileage: between 1861 and 1876 the system grew by just under 600 miles, almost matching the expansion during the company's first fifteen years. A further 134 miles were added over the next five years, but growth was already slackening and during the ten years ending in 1891 the increase was only 141 miles. While the lengthy stages from the planning of a line to its eventual opening make it difficult to draw firm chronological divisions in the growth of the system, a turning point in the LNWR's development can be discerned during the 1870s. Until then the processes of acquisition and extension that had begun during the 1840s and were resumed with new vigour under Moon continued to add significantly to the territory served by the company. With one exception, which will be described later, the route mileage added from the late 1870s onwards consisted of branches and connections to consolidate the network and assist existing traffic flows, rather than extensions into new districts. This altered emphasis was partly a consequence of the extent to which earlier schemes had filled the obvious gaps in the railway map, leaving fewer opportunities for expansion. However, it also reflected changes in the economic background, together with a substantial shift in public and political attitudes to the railway companies which at times directly affected the LNWR's approach to new investment.

The fluctuations of the trade cycle remained evident during these years: after the setbacks of the 1870s, the international economy recovered between 1879 and 1883 under the influence of renewed American railway building and the growing demand for steamships. There was a further downturn after 1883, which reached a trough in 1886, but shipbuilding activity in particular recovered in the later 1880s, presaging a new boom in 1890. Such trends continued to influence the receipts of the LNWR along with other railways, but the effects of these fluc-

tuations, although often felt severely in particular industries or localities, became less significant as the century went on. This was largely a result of continuing economic expansion: as patterns of production and of international trade became more complex, individual factors played a smaller part in the total picture, while the accumulation of resources provided a more substantial buffer against short-run disturbances in overseas markets. In the domestic economy, the growth in the population of Great Britain from 26·1m in 1871 to 33·0m in 1891 gave an underlying buoyancy to the demand for travel and transport, which was reinforced by urbanisation and greater economic interdependence: food, industrial raw materials and manufactured products were increasingly traded both inter-regionally and internationally. Railways, of course, played a vital part in these developments: the total volume of freight carried by rail within Britain expanded from 92·6m tons in 1861 to 166·5m tons in 1871 and reached 305·9m tons in 1891. In the international economy, the opening up of Europe and the more distant continents by railways complemented the effects of improved merchant shipping, while steamships also had an impact on the British transport market by increasing the severity of competition which the railways faced from coastal services.

But despite the growth in economic activity, commentators in Britain became increasingly concerned at the failure of prices and profits to recover after the 1873 collapse, and the period between then and 1896 became known as the 'great depression'. This description of course contained elements of over-simplification: besides conflating a number of separate trends, it failed to reflect the fact that, as prices fell, real earnings rose, encouraging consumer demand. This in itself provided increased traffic, and there were other positive aspects for the railway companies. Firstly, while wages did not fall in proportion to the cost of living, lower prices helped to put an end to the upward tendency in labour costs that

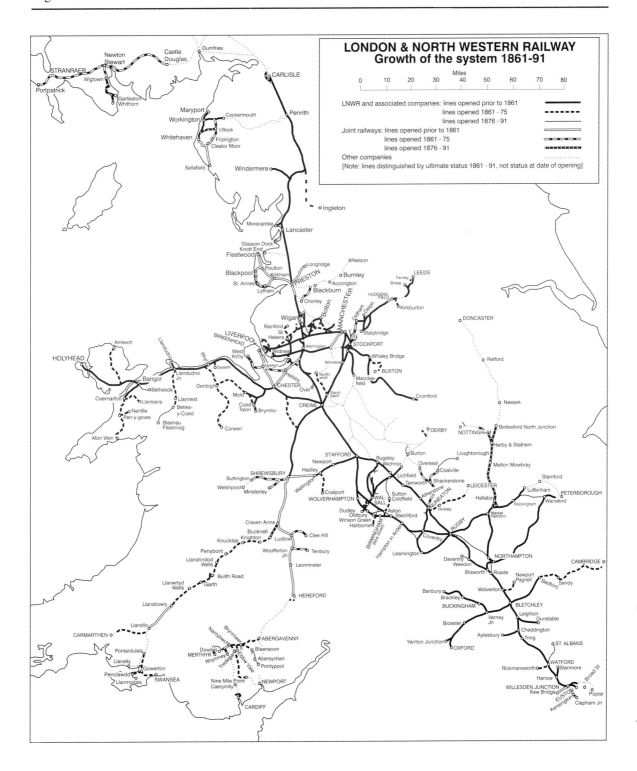

Figure 6.1 – Growth of the LNWR system 1861–91.

was evident prior to 1873. Secondly, the prices of the railways' basic raw materials, coal and iron, fell after 1873, thus directly reducing operating and engineering costs. Lastly, interest rates moved significantly downwards during the late 1880s, reducing the impact of prior charges on divisible profits and making it easier to raise money for new investment. However, regardless of the balance for individual sectors of the economy such as the railways, the sense that something was going badly wrong with Britain's overall economic performance was sufficient to provoke widespread concern and to stimulate parliamentary and academic inquiries into causes and possible solutions.

It has also been claimed that, despite the short-run benefits for the railways of the changes experienced during this period, the longer-term effects were nevertheless harmful, encouraging the over-lavish provision of facilities and blunting the incentive for operational economies. The LNWR certainly continued to invest substantially, though the scale of this should not be exaggerated: financial restructuring in 1879 added £10m of nominal capital to the LNWR's accounts and when the effects of this are eliminated actual expenditure from 1877 to 1891 inclusive was less than that for the preceding fifteen years. Nor is there any evidence that Moon relaxed his customary vigilance over revenue expenditure: while, as will be described later, there were changes in the composition and volume of traffic which made increases in train mileage virtually inescapable, such increases were constantly scrutinised and offsetting savings were actively pursued. For example, in 1878 some lines were closed on Sundays (including the direct route to Liverpool via Runcorn), while several junctions were relocated during the 1880s to reduce signalling requirements. Though with hindsight it might be suggested that the LNWR and other leading undertakings could have achieved a still better return for their shareholders by investing more sparingly and by even stricter control over traffic costs, it is important not to overlook the very strong pressures on the companies to meet increasing demands and to respond to changing political and social expectations.

Indeed, one direct consequence of the altered economic situation after 1873 was that the railways' charging policies became the focus of keener scrutiny. While some reductions were made – Moon referred at general meetings in 1885 and 1886 to the concessions

the LNWR had made to its main customers, and to the difficulties of competing with shipping rates – this was not sufficient to stem criticism from a wide variety of sources. Coal-owners and ironmasters, faced with falling domestic and export prices, questioned the freight rates they had to pay; farmers struggling against increasing competition in their home market attacked railway commercial practices which gave favourable rates to bulk loads of imported produce; Manchester interests compared their transport costs with those of coastal towns, and in 1885 finally succeeded in obtaining authorisation for a ship canal.

Railway charges accordingly became an increasingly important political issue, and brought a new dimension into the relationship between government and the railways, which had become more settled after the regulatory activity of the 1840s and 1850s. A Royal Commission on Railways was appointed in 1865 with wide terms of reference, but its main positive outcome was the 1868 Regulation of Railways Act, which standardised railway accounts on a basis which owed much to the LNWR's existing practice. The Commission also took up the question of railway safety, which remained a matter of public and parliamentary concern. Although the LNWR had begun to adopt Saxby's patent interlocking of points and signals in 1864, it did not escape serious accidents: the worst disaster in the company's history occurred at Abergele on 20 August 1868, when the down 'Irish Mail' collided with wagons that had run away during shunting operations. The accident was turned into a catastrophe by the fact that two of the wagons contained casks of paraffin, and the collision and ensuing fire resulted in thirty-three deaths. There were three major accidents in 1870: the Carlisle collision, mentioned on page 99; the loss of three lives at Tamworth on 14 September, when the up 'Irish Mail' was mistakenly diverted into a siding; and a collision in fog between a passenger train and derailed coal wagons at Harrow on 26 November, with seven fatalities. All of these incidents revealed deficiencies in signalling or operating arrangements which the LNWR took steps to remedy, but the next serious accident, to the overnight 'Tourist' express to Scotland at Wigan on 1 August 1873, with the loss of ten lives, was never satisfactorily explained. While the immediate cause was the high-speed derailment of part of the train on facing points, these were interlocked and

'Precedent' class 2-4-0 no 2187 'Penrith Beacon' at the Newark brake trials in 1875, heading a rake of coaches fitted with the Clarke & Webb chain brake. *(LNWR Society collection, 9806)*

the signalling system appeared to be in order: the outcome was the adoption of facing point locks as an additional precaution on main passenger lines.

Queen Victoria felt strongly on the subject of railway safety, and following the Wigan derailment and other accidents in 1873 she wrote to Mr Gladstone to suggest, among other measures, that a director should be compelled to travel on each train: evidence that the monarch was sadly out of touch with the realities of railway operation and management. Nevertheless, the Board of Trade in turn issued a circular to all the companies on the need for improved safety precautions, to which Moon replied very fully, detailing the LNWR's expenditure on safety measures. A Royal Commission on Railway Accidents was then appointed, but its recommendations resulted in no more than a requirement for statutory returns on the subject of continuous brakes. The railways organised a demonstration of the available braking technologies at Newark in 1875, but faced with the variety of methods neither the Board of Trade nor the Royal Commission was prepared to recommend a single standard.

This followed a pattern that had already been established in the 1860s. The previous Royal

Commission had come to the conclusion that the primary responsibility for safety lay with the companies and that direct interference by the government would inhibit the railways' own efforts to improve standards. This view, which Moon strongly supported, was reinforced by the unhappy result of the one additional safety measure embodied in the 1868 Act, which gave the Board of Trade powers to require the installation of communication cords. This was put into effect in 1872, but the system which was stipulated proved so unsatisfactory that the requirement was quickly withdrawn. While the Board of Trade's duty to inspect passenger lines before opening enabled it to determine the criteria for new works, successive governments preferred to rely on publicity and the power of public opinion rather than compulsion to ensure that improved safety measures were applied to existing lines and rolling stock. A private member's Bill in 1873 which sought to make interlocking mandatory on all passenger lines resulted instead in the compromise that companies should make annual returns of their signalling arrangements, and in 1874 the railway inspectorate's powers to call for accident returns and to carry out inquiries were increased. But in the absence of specific recommendations the companies were free to adopt individual approaches to matters such as signalling, brakes, and working instructions.

Although the Railway Clearing House provided a forum for developing some common standards, the lack of uniformity over brakes continued to bedevil the British railway industry, and this was one area where the LNWR did not contribute to best practice, preferring Webb's adaptation of Clarke's chain brake to the vacuum or Westinghouse systems. After persisting with the chain brake – the deficiencies of which were amply recorded by Neele – it then began to install the simple vacuum system in 1882, and it was not until 1888 that the LNWR finally adopted the automatic vacuum brake. In the following year, after the Armagh accident, the government at last made automatic brakes and interlocking compulsory on passenger routes, but by then the opportunity for either the Board of Trade or the railways themselves to establish common standards had been missed.

With the exception of braking, however, the LNWR's record on safety and related issues was generally good by contemporary standards, and when liability for employees' accidents became the subject of legislation in 1880 the company's provision was already sufficient to allow it to contract out of the statutory scheme. While maintaining the hostility to organised labour representation which was the hallmark of nineteenth-century railway industrial relations, the LNWR was a good, if paternalistic, employer, and had established superannuation, savings, and insurance schemes at an early stage. In addition the board took steps to ensure the provision of schools and churches as well as housing for its employees at centres such as Crewe and Wolverton. Moon was however increasingly critical of the demands made on railways through the rating system to provide poor relief and local amenities for the community at large: in 1890 rates and taxes cost the company almost £280,000, compared with £85,000 in 1861. Proportionately, this growth was little more than the increase in the LNWR's revenue over the same period, but the chairman's strong views on fiscal matters and the company's inability to control this

particular element in its expenditure made local rates a frequent topic at general meetings.

References to the contributions that the railways were already making to the broader economic and social fabric of Victorian Britain were not, however, sufficient to reduce the pressure for direct interference in their charging powers. The first step came in 1873, when the Regulation of Railways Act authorised the appointment of Railway Commissioners with a specific jurisdiction in cases brought under the provisions of the Railway & Canal Traffic Act, 1854. While this was of limited immediate effect, it provided a focus for complaints about traffic charges and facilities and was followed in 1881 by the appointment of a Select Committee on Railways to examine the entire question of railway pricing policy. The Railway Companies' Association was able to co-ordinate its members' evidence to ensure a well-presented case on matters such as terminal charges and discounted rates for bulk consignments, so the Committee's report did little to satisfy traders and farmers who had been looking for parliamentary action to reduce freight charges. In 1883, however, the Cheap Trains Act compelled the companies to make special provision for workmen and for certain categories of government traffic in return for concessions in passenger duty, thus extending the precedent of state interference in passenger fares that had been set by Gladstone in 1844.

Attempts to widen the scope of legislative review to include goods rates were at first abortive in the confused political situation of the mid-1880s, when the railways were able to make common cause with other interest groups to resist such assaults on property rights. However, the economic pressures which united the agricultural and industrial lobbies also had the effect of leaving the railways increasingly isolated as a political force, and a new Railway & Canal Traffic Act was eventually passed in 1888, with cross-party support. Under its provisions each railway company was required to prepare and publish a revision of its freight classifications and charges; the Board of Trade was next empowered to hear objections to each company's proposals, amending them further if it deemed this to be appropriate, before submitting the revised classifications and charges for parliamentary determination. In addition, the Act increased the extent of legal jurisdiction over charges and traffic facilities, replacing the Railway

Commissioners, who had been appointed on a temporary basis, with a permanent Railway & Canal Commission. While these processes had only begun to take effect by the time Moon retired in 1891, he rightly saw the change in the statutory framework as a major new limitation of the companies' freedom of action. Unwittingly, though, his own efforts to restore the level of the LNWR's dividends had perhaps played a part in this, by strengthening the hand of those who contrasted the relative prosperity of the railways with reduced profits elsewhere in the economy and argued that this imbalance justified legislative intervention.

Another way in which parliamentary action directly affected the LNWR during Moon's chairmanship came through the reaffirmation during the 1870s of the previous hostility to railway amalgamation. While the Midland's intended amalgamation with the GSWR had been temporarily blocked in 1867, it seemed likely that the proposal would be revived, especially as the two largest Scottish companies, the North British and the Caledonian, were also showing interest in a merger. Against this background, and with the prospect of the loss of some Scottish traffic to the Midland when the Settle line was completed, the LNWR looked for ways of strengthening its own position. Despite the L&Y's support for a third route to Scotland, and an earlier flirtation with the Great Eastern Railway, its interests coincided most closely with those of the LNWR, and this found practical expression in 1871, when Crewe began to supply locomotives of the 'DX' class to the L&Y. By that stage the two boards had decided to bring forward an amalgamation Bill in the 1872 session: as the L&Y's profits had held up well despite the depression of the late 1860s, the agreed terms provided for its shareholders to receive 12s 6d more in annual dividends for each £100 stock than their LNWR colleagues. Moon defended this on the basis that the difference was so small that it was not worth jeopardising the benefits that would come from amalgamation, but for once his financial judgement was perhaps questionable: L&Y dividends were approaching a peak which was never subsequently matched, whereas from 1873 onwards the LNWR outperformed its intended partner.

However, the proposed merger, together with that between the Midland and the GSWR, revived the old fear of monopolies. Parliament reflected this in 1872 by appointing a joint committee of both Houses to consider the general question of railway amalgamation, and as a consequence the contentious Bills were deferred. In 1873, in accordance with the recommendations of the previous session's Select Committee on Railway Companies' Amalgamations, a further joint committee was established to consider specific amalgamation schemes. This committee was intended to be permanent, but sat only in that year: however, during its existence it rejected both the LNWR and L&Y and the Midland and GSWR proposals. While there were initial thoughts of bringing forward the LNWR and L&Y Bill in a future session, the two companies instead decided on the more limited solution of renewing and strengthening their existing agreements. The LNWR's assistance was briefly extended into carriage building when a fire at Miles Platting in 1873 disrupted the L&Y's own workshops, but in 1875 the independent locomotive builders obtained an injunction to prevent the LNWR from supplying engines to another railway, on the grounds that this was *ultra vires*. Up to that point Crewe had supplied eighty-six 'DXs', ten 'Newtons' and five 0-4-0 tanks to the L&Y. In addition to the legal action, several railway manufacturers emphasised their hostility by diverting their freight traffic away from the LNWR, and this appears to have been influential in persuading the board not to contest the matter further. Despite this further setback the two companies continued to develop their partnership in traffic matters and, as will be seen, in their joint undertakings. Although they maintained a friendly rivalry which was underscored by occasional differences on specific issues, the examples of co-operation were a more significant pointer to the future.

However, the parliamentary decisions of 1873 did not put an end to amalgamation proposals: as in the 1850s, other schemes were approved once the initial concern had subsided, the most notable of which was the GWR's amalgamation with the west country lines in 1876. Nor did it prevent the LNWR from continuing the process of absorbing leased or worked lines which were already effectively part of its system. The vesting of smaller individual undertakings continued, but the drawback of existing practice was that separate categories of stock were necessary to meet the differing obligations to the shareholders in the absorbed companies. The audit committee argued in 1876 that this proliferation of relatively small issues placed the LNWR at a disadvantage in the stock market, and that the company – and its shareholders – would command better terms if these securities were consolidated. Moon warmly endorsed this recommendation, which carried forward principles that had already been adopted in standardising the preference and debenture stocks, so in 1877 powers were obtained to merge the various subsidiary issues and also to replace the existing 5% preference stock with a 4% issue. In 1878 arrangements were agreed with the shareholders of those subsidiary undertakings that had maintained a separate existence, and the company's capital was reconstructed into only four classes of security, with a total nominal value of £92·4m. In addition to the £32·7m of ordinary stock and £20·5m of 4% debenture stock, the new capital account included £15·1m of guaranteed stock and £21·3m of preference stock, each with a 4% coupon. The remaining loan debt was gradually replaced by debenture stock.

As part of the implementation of these proposals, most of the remaining subsidiaries were formally wound up in 1879, including the Chester & Holyhead and Lancaster & Carlisle. Though many of the affected undertakings were already practically defunct, the L&C had continued as a holding company with its own directors, and two of their number were added to the LNWR board in 1879 when the L&C was dissolved. There were a few subsequent absorptions of smaller lines, and the process of rationalisation was taken further during the 1880s when the LNWR and L&Y rearranged their shared undertakings. In 1883 the LNWR absorbed the Lancashire Union and assumed its interests in the joint sections north of Wigan, and in 1888 the North Union and Preston & Wyre railways were also wound up as separate companies. The P&W network remained joint, but the Euxton–Wigan and Euxton–Bolton sections of the former North Union Railway became the sole property of the LNWR and L&Y respectively, leaving the Euxton–Preston portion in common ownership. The Preston & Longridge, which had been vested jointly in the two companies in 1866, was unaffected.

So far as the LNWR was concerned, therefore, the amalgamation movement of the 1870s led only to the establishment of a closer alliance with the L&Y and the redrawing of its corporate and financial structure to include most of the subsidiary companies that already formed part of its network. Other proposals that would have resulted in significant alterations to

existing spheres of influence proved abortive before even reaching the parliamentary stage. In 1875 there were suggestions that the Midland and LNWR might jointly absorb the North Staffordshire, and the GNR and MS&L also expressed interest in forming part of the consortium. This scheme foundered, as did subsequent direct negotiations between the North Staffordshire and the MS&L. In 1877 there were discussions about a joint lease of the MS&L by the GNR and Midland, but once again Watkin – whose personal preference was for a union with the GNR – proved too demanding, and the scheme was abandoned.

This last proposal formed part of the complex territorial manœuvring in the 1870s between the MS&L, GNR, and Midland, with the GER another interested party by virtue of its line from London to Peterborough and its hope of ultimately reaching Doncaster. The MS&L's ambitions were eventually satisfied by its extension to Marylebone, but before that stage was reached the corridor between the existing GNR and Midland main lines (which had figured in proposals developed by Watkin in 1870 for a Doncaster–Market Harborough route) had been largely occupied by two new north–south lines. Local ironstone deposits provided one justification for these projects, but the underlying reason for their promotion was the competition between the Midland and GNR for coal traffic to London, exacerbated by the MS&L's search for new outlets. One of the ironies of this competition between its eastern neighbours was that the LNWR was able to make a further addition to its territory at the invitation of the GNR and regain a stake in mineral traffic from the coalfields north of Nottingham which it had largely lost when the Midland completed its line to St Pancras.

The GNR first sought LNWR support in 1872 by offering running powers over a proposed branch from Nottingham to Burton which would carry it into Midland territory; in the same session it also obtained authorisation for a line from Newark to Melton Mowbray. In the 1873 session the GNR went further, seeking powers to extend from Melton Mowbray to a junction with the LNWR's Rugby–Stamford branch near Market Harborough and to construct the entire line from Newark jointly with the LNWR. This Bill was opposed by the Midland and MS&L, which brought forward a rival scheme for a route from Kettering to Worksop and Askern, on the NER.

Neither proposal succeeded, although the GNR gained parliamentary approval for a line from Melton Mowbray to Leicester which had been rejected in 1872. In 1874, however, a further Act authorised the LNWR's participation, together with the extension south from Melton and another branch, while the Midland obtained powers the following year for a link between Manton and its main line at Rushton, north of Kettering. Although this represented only a portion of the larger scheme that the Midland had proposed jointly with the MS&L in 1873, it created a new through route from Kettering to Nottingham, using part of the Syston–Peterborough branch and a line from Melton Mowbray to Nottingham which had been authorised in 1872.

Their 1874 Act empowered the GNR and LNWR jointly to build a railway from the Rugby–Stamford line at Welham junction, east of Market Harborough, to Bottesford, where connections would be formed with the Nottingham–Grantham branch and with the GNR's projected line to Newark. The Act also authorised an east spur at the southern end of the line, from Hallaton to Drayton junction, and a branch from Stathern to Saxondale junction, seven miles from Nottingham. The joint system incorporated sections authorised in 1872, although the portion between Bottesford and Newark and the Leicester branch were left under GNR ownership. The LNWR gave its partner running powers to Northampton and to Peterborough, and as its contribution to the project undertook to build a direct line from Seaton to Wansford, on its Blisworth–Peterborough branch. This would obviate the detour via Stamford and the use of Midland metals to reach Peterborough. It also obtained powers to double the connecting Northampton–Market Harborough branch and completed this work in 1879. The GNR reciprocated with a spur to link the LNWR and east coast main lines at Peterborough, and by granting running powers from Bottesford to Doncaster via Newark and from Saxondale junction to Nottingham then onwards over the GNR lines into the coalfield.

Responsibility for construction was divided, and the contracts for the portion of line south of Tilton and for the branch from Stathern to Saxondale junction were carried out under the supervision of the LNWR. This proved to be one of the last major projects undertaken by William Baker, the company's engineer: he died on 20 December 1878, at the age of 62, and was succeeded by his assistant, Francis Stevenson. Ballast train workings between Newark and Melton Mowbray via Bottesford began on 23 May 1879, but the section from Saxondale junction to Melton Mowbray was the first to be used for public traffic: the GNR introduced two daily goods trains between Colwick and Melton Mowbray from 30 June 1879, with provision for trip working when required from Stathern junction northwards along the Bottesford line to serve Redmile. Passenger traffic over these parts of the joint system began on 1 September with the introduction of connecting Nottingham–Melton Mowbray and Newark–Harby & Stathern services, worked by the GNR. Progress south of Melton was delayed by slips in embankments, but on 13 October 1879 the route was opened for freight traffic as far as Burrow & Twyford (renamed John o' Gaunt in 1883). Through goods trains to and from Market Harborough via Welham junction commenced on 1 November and on 1 December the LNWR began working goods services to Doncaster. Passenger trains between Nottingham and Northampton were introduced on 15 December, but regular use of the east fork from Hallaton to Drayton did not begin until 2 July 1883, when the GNR inaugurated a Leicester–Peterborough service. At Bottesford, the northern end of the joint line, a south-to-west curve was included in the layout, but this quickly fell into disuse since the branch to Saxondale junction provided a more direct route for Nottingham traffic. However, the GNR added a south-to-east chord, which it opened on 1 September 1880 for a new passenger service between Grantham and Harby & Stathern. Another short spur was provided at Melton Mowbray, in this case as part of the joint mileage. The spur, known as Sysonby junction, connected with the Midland Railway, and was probably built in 1879. However, it appears to have seen little use at first and was severed on 31 October 1882; it was then brought back into service on 16 April 1883 for Midland ironstone traffic but closed completely on 18 April 1887.

The LNWR's main contribution to the passenger train mileage over the joint line was a Northampton–Nottingham service, which included one through working from and to Euston. It also provided some peak summer workings to east coast destinations via Newark, supplementing the regular GNR services to Newark, Grantham, and Peterborough. But the joint line's principal value to

'Whitworth' class 2-4-0 no 609 'Earl of Chester' on Great Northern metals at Radcliffe-on-Trent with a Northampton–Nottingham service via the GNR & LNWR joint line. *(National Railway Museum, LPC 16844)*

the LNWR was for freight traffic, enabling it to gain a share of the coal traffic from south Yorkshire, Nottinghamshire, and Derbyshire, and also to expand its network of express merchandise services. The company established a separate district organisation to cover the territory north of Northampton and east of Rugby, and built locomotive sheds at Doncaster and Colwick to meet the requirements of its new traffic flows. In 1888 it also opened a separate goods station at Manvers Street in Nottingham, reached by a short section of its own track.

Further west in the Trent basin the LNWR's independent mileage at Burton was increased in 1882 with the completion on 3 July of a branch alongside the Trent & Mersey Canal from Shobnall junction to

Stretton junction, on the North Staffordshire's Uttoxeter line. Earlier, in July 1880, the LNWR had opened another goods depot in the town, Kottingham & Moor Street wharf, which was reached over Midland metals. Elsewhere in the east midlands the LNWR gained entry to Loughborough in 1883 via the Charnwood Forest Railway, authorised in 1874 to connect with the Shacklestone–Hugglescote branch of the joint Ashby & Nuneaton Railway. The LNWR subscribed to the CFR and worked it from its opening on 16 April 1883, but the smaller company retained its separate identity despite financial difficulties which left it in receivership for some years.

As mentioned, the Seaton–Wansford connection, which linked the Rugby–Luffenham and Blisworth–Peterborough branches, had been promoted in association with the GNR & LNWR joint line; as part of the negotiations for the Bill, Lord Exeter, owner of the Stamford & Essendine Railway, secured an agreement that the junction with the S&E's Sibson branch at Wansford, which had opened in 1867 but was taken out of use in 1870, should be reinstated. By the time this was done, on 1 March 1878, the S&E had been leased by the GNR, which used the junction to give local connections via Stamford. The Seaton–Wansford section was opened for goods on 21 July 1879 and for passengers on 1 November, and besides catering for traffic between the joint line and Peterborough it also improved links between the west midlands and the eastern counties. The LNWR used the new route to inaugurate weekday through coaches between Birmingham and Norwich on Monday 2 November 1879.

Another cut-off which had a role in developing services via the joint line but which also served a wider purpose was the connection between Roade and Northampton. This was used by goods trains from 1 August 1881 and by regular passenger services from 3 April 1882, although it carried Northampton race specials a few days earlier. Besides improving access to Northampton from the south, the line from Roade formed part of a loop which rejoined the main line at Rugby, and indeed had been authorised as such under an 1875 Act which also gave powers for widening between Bletchley and Roade. Quadruple track had been gradually extended northwards from London, and the completion of additional tunnels at Watford in 1874 and Primrose Hill in 1878 removed the last constrictions between Euston and Bletchley. But Kilsby tunnel was a more substantial obstacle, and the Northampton loop enabled duplicate tracks to be provided throughout between Bletchley and Rugby without the heavy costs that would have been involved in quadrupling the original route via Weedon. The additional lines south of Roade and the extension to Rugby from Kingsthorpe junction near Northampton were opened for goods traffic on the same day as the Roade–Northampton link, 1 August 1881; local passenger trains began running over the Northampton–Rugby section four months later, on 1 December, and the slow lines between Bletchley and Roade were brought into use for passenger traffic on 31 July 1882. Though the Blisworth–Northampton branch was retained for local services – and was required as a diversionary route in 1882 and again in the winter of 1891–2 because of problems with the deep cutting at Roade – completion of the loop enabled Northampton at last to be served by through main line trains. As a result, Northampton Castle

became the town's principal station; a connecting spur from Bridge Street station, opened for goods in 1879 and for passengers on 1 December 1881, permitted Peterborough trains to serve both stations.

The duplication of the main line to Rugby formed part of a programme of widenings approved by the shareholders in 1870 to cope with the rapid growth in traffic. A short section of the Liverpool & Manchester route between Edge Hill and Huyton had been quadrupled in 1871 and in 1876 relief lines were provided between Stafford and Crewe, while additional tracks were brought into use on the North Union line north of Euxton in 1880 in conjunction with the rebuilding of the joint station at Preston. During the 1880s further widenings were put in hand, including the Warrington–Winwick and Golborne–Springs Branch sections of the west coast main line, part of the L&M east of Barton Moss, and the approaches to both Liverpool and Manchester from the south. The extension of quadruple track into Lime Street in 1885 involved opening out more of the tunnel, and major engineering works were similarly required on the route into Manchester London Road. This included the widening of Stockport viaduct to carry two extra tracks, which were brought into service in 1889: besides completing quadruple track between Stockport and Ardwick, the Stockport widenings also fed into the Heaton Norris–Guide Bridge line, which was quadrupled as far as Denton junction in the same year.

There were also major improvements north and east of Denton, designed to increase capacity on the busy cross-Pennine route and to reduce the LNWR's need to use sections of other companies' lines. A short branch from Denton to Crowthorne junction, on the OA&GB, had been opened for goods traffic on 14 February 1876 and for passenger services on 1 April, giving the LNWR access to the joint line and its junction with the L&Y at Ashton without reversal at Guide Bridge. On 1 March 1882 a direct link was opened from the Crowthorne junction line at Ashton Moss to Droylsden, providing a west-facing connection with the L&Y and creating a convenient through route between Stockport and the north side of Manchester. Later the same year another short branch from Denton was completed, to Dukinfield on the MS&L line to Stalybridge. This line, opened for goods on 2 October 1882 and for passengers on 1 November, was authorised in 1879, following an abortive attempt during

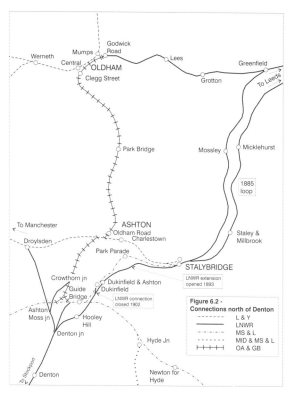

Figure 6.2 – Connections north of Denton.

the previous session to gain powers for a separate route from Reddish to Saddleworth. While the latter scheme would have freed the LNWR entirely from the need to rely on running powers over the MS&L to reach the Yorkshire line from Stockport, the shorter branch authorised in 1879 achieved one of the objectives of the earlier proposal by keeping through services clear of the complex junctions at Guide Bridge.

A comparable improvement was made at the eastern extremity of the cross-Pennine route, and brought into service on the same day as the Ashton Moss–Droylsden link, 1 March 1882: this was a line from Wortley to Canal junction, which gave direct access to Leeds New station and by-passed the congested approach over Midland track via Whitehall junction. However, the previous route remained important for freight purposes, since it served the LNWR's interchange sidings at Copley Hill and the joint Leeds Central goods station; in addition, a short branch gave access to a new goods station at Whitehall Road, also jointly owned with the L&Y, which had opened on 1 December 1880. With the

diversion of regular passenger services via the Canal junction line, a new Wortley & Farnley station was opened to replace the previous station on the old route, and another related change was the deviation of the connection into the Farnley goods branch. A new north spur, authorised in 1881 and opened on 31 May 1885, enabled the branch to be controlled from Wortley & Farnley and allowed the closure of the signal box at the former south-facing junction.

One bottleneck on the route between Stalybridge and Leeds, the single-track Standedge tunnel, had been eased by the opening of a second bore in 1871, but to give further capacity the double line between Stalybridge and the western end of the tunnel at Marsden was supplemented by two tracks on a new alignment on the eastern side of the valley. This loop was used for goods trains from 1 December 1885 and for passenger services from 3 May 1886, when four intermediate stations were opened for local traffic. On the Leeds side of Standedge tunnel the existing route was followed when work started in 1882 to provide additional tracks as far as the junction with the L&Y at Heaton Lodge, but while the section between Hillhouse and Heaton Lodge was brought into use in 1884, rebuilding of Huddersfield station and widening of the joint section through Springwood tunnel had to be carried out in stages. A second tunnel was opened in October 1886 and the original tunnel was then closed for repairs until 1888, when widening was completed from Golcar to Springwood. In 1889 quadruple track was extended westwards to Slaithwaite and in July 1891, soon after Moon retired, a further extension, between Slaithwaite and Marsden, was brought into service. By then work had already started on a third Standedge tunnel, to complete four continuous tracks across the Pennines.

LNWR services between Manchester and Leeds used a section of the L&Y east of Heaton Lodge, portions of which were widened in 1884. These services also relied on the L&Y route between Manchester and Stalybridge, and growing congestion at Victoria station led the LNWR to obtain powers for a separate station immediately to the west. This station, Manchester Exchange, was partially opened on 30 June 1884 and completed in July 1885. The quadrupling of portions of the L&M line west of Manchester has already been mentioned; further capital expenditure was similarly devoted to increasing capacity elsewhere in Lancashire, and much of the additional mileage was made up by short extensions and junction lines. One such was a $1^1/_2$-mile connection between the Lancashire Union and west coast main lines north of Wigan, from Whelley to Standish junction, which opened on 5 June 1882. This was later complemented by a series of new links south and east of Wigan which extended the range of routes available to through traffic. Three of these connections were brought into use for goods traffic on 25 October 1886: the Platt Bridge junction railway, from the main line at Bamfurlong to the LUR at Amberswood west junction; the Hindley junction railway, an east-facing curve out of the Eccles, Tyldesley & Wigan line at Bickershaw junction into the MS&L-worked Wigan Junction Railway at Strangeways east junction; and the latter company's spur from Strangeways west junction to Amberswood east junction on the LUR. The WJR, which opened in 1879 between Glazebrook and Strangeways colliery and reached Wigan in 1884, possessed parliamentary powers for both east- and west-facing connections with the LUR at Amberswood, but the eastern junction had not been formed when the LNWR deposited its plans in 1882 for a link from the Eccles line to the LUR. These proposed a separate right-of-way from Bickershaw junction through to Amberswood east, parallelling the WJR alignment from Strangeways; however, only the Bickershaw–Strangeways section

was authorised, and the WJR was left to complete the connection. Consequently, the LNWR was obliged to rely on running powers to regain its own metals at Amberswood east junction, but despite this the Hindley connection created a valuable alternative route which by the summer of 1887 was being used for express passenger services between Manchester Exchange and Preston. These joined the west coast route at Standish junction, and the Platt Bridge link also enabled the LUR to serve as a loop from the main line, avoiding the double-track section between Wigan and Standish. As part of subsequent capacity enhancements, which were completed on 1 October 1889, the layout at Bamfurlong was further modified to include a burrowing connection into the Platt Bridge junction railway.

Another addition to the complex network in the Wigan area was provided by a freight-only branch from the Leigh line at Pennington, which had been promoted in response to the WJR's penetration of the Westleigh coalfield. This branch, which incorporated a former private colliery railway, terminated in a triangular junction with the main Eccles–Wigan route at

Manchester Exchange, with 2-4-2T no 338 on a westbound train. On the turntable is GWR 2-4-0 no 3240, which would have worked from Chester over the joint Birkenhead Railway line to Warrington and reached Manchester under running powers. *(LNWR Society collection, 411)*

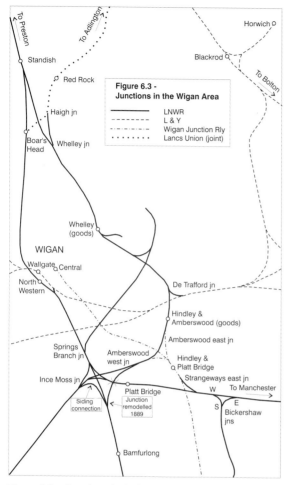

Figure 6.3 – Junctions in the Wigan area.

through route, allowing mineral trains to and from Widnes to be kept clear of the busy route via Peasley Cross. An improved link between St Helens and the Liverpool & Manchester line, primarily for passenger traffic, was provided with the opening on 30 May 1885 of the Sutton Oak curve. This duplicated the existing connection at St Helens Junction, but reduced conflicting movements by burrowing under the Widnes line to gain direct access to Sutton Oak junction.

The continuing growth of the port of Liverpool resulted in the building of an offshoot from the Canada Dock branch to Alexandra Dock, which opened for goods traffic on 1 January 1880 and for passengers on 5 September 1881. An east curve from the Canada Dock line at Edge Lane towards Broad Green was opened on 11 June 1883; this was followed in 1887 by the completion of a flyover loop from Wavertree to Edge Hill to serve the complex of goods sidings north of the passenger lines. At the northern extremity of the Liverpool network a connection between the Alexandra Dock branch and the L&Y at Bootle was opened on 1 May 1886, enabling an Edge Hill–Southport passenger service to be provided in connection with main line trains. This new service included some through carriages between Euston and Southport, replacing workings via Wigan which had been inaugurated in 1880 via a connection between the west coast main line and the L&Y south of the latter's Wallgate station.

There were also developments on the Wirral side of the Mersey. On 1 April 1878 the joint passenger service to and from Birkenhead was diverted over a short branch from the existing line at Green Lane to a new terminal station adjacent to the Woodside ferry landing stage. The previous terminus at Monks Ferry was relegated to freight traffic and its ferry link with Liverpool was withdrawn. One of the three steamers from the Monks Ferry service, which was railway-owned, was sold to the London, Tilbury & Southend Railway; the other two vessels were later redeployed by the LNWR on its Carlingford Lough service. The Birkenhead Railway network was expanded further on 19 April 1886 with the opening of an extension of the Hooton–Parkgate branch northwards along the Dee estuary to West Kirby, where a connection was made with the suburban services of the independent Wirral Railway. In 1888 these were extended from Birkenhead to Liverpool through the

Bickershaw and was used for mineral traffic from 9 February 1885; full opening for goods traffic followed three weeks later, on 2 March. A short subsidiary branch from Pennington to Diggles colliery was probably opened at about the same time. Earlier that year, on 1 February, two deviations of the original Bolton & Leigh line were brought into use, avoiding the inclines on the northern section of the route and completing its progressive conversion to double track. An additional connection between the Bolton and Wigan lines had been provided two years previously, with the opening of a north-to-west spur to complement the existing Atherton east junction. This new curve had been installed by February 1883.

Further west, the opening on 2 February 1880 of a short extension of the Blackbrook branch to Carr Mill junction on the St Helens–Wigan line created another

Mersey Railway tunnel, which had opened two years earlier.

A more modest harbour which gained railway facilities during the 1880s was Glasson Dock, on the southern side of the Lune estuary: a branch from Lancaster was opened for goods traffic on 2 July 1883 and for passenger services a week later. North of the Lune the opening on 19 May 1888 of a spur to Bare Lane completed a triangle between the main line and the Hest Bank–Morecambe branch. This allowed direct services between Lancaster Castle station and Morecambe, where the LNWR had opened its own Euston Road terminus on 10 May 1886. An earlier connection out of the west coast main line was the short Over & Wharton branch in Cheshire, opened on 1 June 1882, which served local salt and iron works and also provided a more convenient passenger station for Winsford than the main line station of that name. Further east in the same county, a direct link between the Cheadle and Whaley Bridge routes south of Stockport was opened for goods trains on 1 December 1883 and for passenger traffic on 1 July 1884, enabling services between the Buxton line and Merseyside to avoid Stockport.

A new branch in north Wales, from Bangor to Bethesda, was also opened to passengers on 1 July 1884; although this line was built primarily for slate traffic, freight services did not commence until 1 September 1884. On 26 May the following year another spur from the Buxton branch, the Middlewood curve, was opened as the joint property of the LNWR and North Staffordshire. This gave an east-to-south connection with the Marple–Macclesfield line, itself jointly owned by the MS&L and NSR. Connectional facilities between the Buxton and Marple routes had been established on 1 April 1879, when high and low level stations were opened at Middlewood, but the building of the curve allowed freight traffic to be interworked. In addition, the LNWR used the junction during the summer months for through carriages between Euston and Buxton via Macclesfield and the NSR established a local passenger service between Macclesfield and Buxton, which also operated on a seasonal basis only after December 1885.

The first additions to the LNWR's network in the west midlands during the late 1870s and the 1880s were for mineral traffic. The Leighswood branch, opened on 14 November 1878 from a junction with

the South Staffordshire line between Rushall and Pelsall, was initially operated by the Leighswood Colliery Company, and it was 1880 before LNWR locomotives took over the working of the branch. Another short mineral line, brought into service on 25 April 1879, extended the Norton Colliery branch to join the Walsall–Rugeley line at Hednesford, and a further link in the network of routes serving the Cannock coalfield was provided when the Littleworth extension railway opened on 15 August 1881. This line, barely half a mile in length, gave a southward connection from the Littleworth Tramway into the Norton branch extension, and though built under LNWR powers it too, in common with the Tramway and its existing outlets to the north, was worked by colliery company locomotives. Another freight line opened in 1881, the Griff Colliery branch, diverged from the Coventry–Nuneaton route north of Bedworth, serving brickworks as well as the mine from which it took its name. This branch was operated by the LNWR from its opening on 22 June, but in 1889 Midland freight trains also began to work over the line.

In the west midlands, as in Lancashire and Cheshire, several connections were built to enhance the usefulness of existing lines. On 1 March 1881 two curves were opened from the original Grand Junction route: one, eastwards from James Bridge, connected with the South Staffordshire at Pleck junction, while the other ran from Portobello to join the Walsall & Wolverhampton line at Heath Town. Similar connections had been mooted on previous occasions, but the authorisation of these lines in 1877 provided a substitute for the full W&W route, which had been transferred to Midland ownership the year before. The LNWR's running powers between Heath Town and Wolverhampton enabled it to use the new connections for passenger and freight services between Walsall and Wolverhampton, and gave a shorter end-to-end distance than either the W&W itself or the LNWR alternative via Wednesbury and the link to the Stour Valley line north-west of Tipton. A new curve at Tipton, allowing through running to and from Birmingham, was opened on 1 January 1883, but was used only for goods traffic: indeed, the original Wednesbury–Tipton connection lost its passenger trains on 1 November 1890, partly because of tramway competition but also because the provision of the direct Walsall–Wolverhampton service had deprived it of much of its previous traffic.

This was not the only casualty of the new route via Heath Town: the addition of Walsall–Wolverhampton trains to the Grand Junction line gave an improved service to James Bridge station, which was less than a mile from Darlaston station on the South Staffordshire loop from Wednesbury to James Bridge. Despite local opposition, passenger services were withdrawn from the loop on 1 November 1887 and James Bridge became the station for Darlaston. Another connection which increased the use of the Grand Junction line was a revival of the 1830s proposal for a direct link into the Euston line east of Birmingham, which was authorised in 1877 in the form of a connection between Aston and Stechford. This opened for goods traffic on 7 September 1880, and when passenger services began on 1 March 1882 the route via Aston was used for the Wolverhampton portions of some London expresses and also to provide through carriages between Euston and Walsall.

Aston's importance as a junction was increased by two other lines. One was a short branch to Windsor Street goods terminus, which opened on 1 March

The terminus of the Harrow & Stanmore line, opened in 1890. *(LNWR Society collection, 579)*

1880 to relieve the existing facilities at Curzon Street. The other was an extension of the Aston–Sutton Coldfield branch northwards to join the former South Staffordshire line at Lichfield, which was brought into use for goods traffic on 1 September 1884. On 3 November a new Lichfield City station was opened, slightly to the south of the original station on the Walsall–Wichnor line, and local passenger trains were extended from Sutton Coldfield to Lichfield on 15 December. The LNWR also inaugurated a service between Birmingham and Derby over the new line on 1 July 1885, in anticipation of the Midland Railway's diversion of its through expresses to run via Selly Oak from 1 October. Although this enabled Bristol–Derby services to call at New Street, the principal LNWR trains via Sutton Coldfield continued to offer a reasonable alternative for passengers between Birmingham and Burton or Derby.

The LNWR's competitive position in the Birmingham area was also assisted by the improvement of its route to Leamington under the provisions of an 1881 Act. This authorised a direct line from Berkeswell to a junction at Kenilworth with the original branch from Coventry, together with doubling of the Kenilworth–Leamington section. The double-track section was brought into use on 2 March 1884

Birmingham New Street station, photographed in September 1885 a few months after the completion of its rebuilding and extension. The locomotive adjacent to the carriages standing in platform 1, on the up side of the station and flanking the LNWR's Queen's Hotel, is an ex-southern division 'Small Bloomer' 2-2-2, then numbered 1816. *(National Railway Museum, CR C142)*

and the Berkeswell loop was opened for goods traffic on the same day; passenger services began on 2 June. This gave the LNWR a direct Birmingham–Leamington line which matched the GWR route via Solihull, and several smartly-timed Rugby–Birmingham local workings were introduced via Leamington and Berkeswell. Some doubling east of Leamington was also completed in 1884, but further plans for improving south Warwickshire's rail connections were already emerging. The first stage, a branch from Weedon to Daventry, was authorised in 1885 and opened on 1 March 1888. This was followed in 1890 by the authorisation of a direct connection between Daventry and the Rugby–Leamington branch near Marton, offering the prospect of a secondary route from Euston to Birmingham which would be only three miles longer than the main line.

The Daventry–Marton extension was not begun until after Moon retired, but apart from the independently-promoted Harrow & Stanmore Railway, which

was worked by the LNWR from its opening on 18 December 1890, the final addition to the company's network while he was chairman was also in the west midlands. This was a series of connecting lines between the Stour Valley and Grand Junction routes, authorised in 1883, which greatly increased operating flexibility and enabled goods trains to avoid New Street. The two main lines were linked between Perry Bar and Winson Green, with triangular junctions at each end; in addition a freight-only branch was built to serve Soho Pool. Goods traffic between Perry Bar north junction and Soho Pool began on 3 October 1887, while the through connections towards Wolverhampton at Soho junction

Figure 6.4 – LNWR FREIGHT REVENUE AND TONNAGE, 1871–91
Source: Railway returns and LNWR accounts

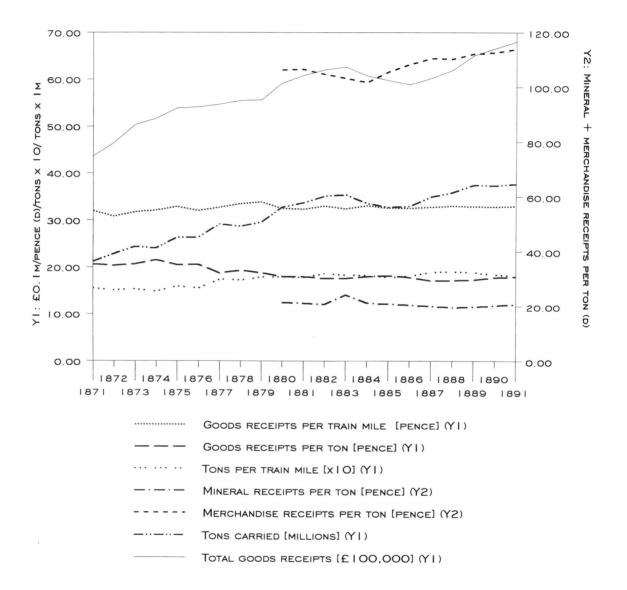

Legend:

.... GOODS RECEIPTS PER TRAIN MILE [PENCE] (Y1)

— — — GOODS RECEIPTS PER TON [PENCE] (Y1)

· · · · · · · TONS PER TRAIN MILE [x10] (Y1)

—·—·— MINERAL RECEIPTS PER TON [PENCE] (Y2)

— — — — MERCHANDISE RECEIPTS PER TON [PENCE] (Y2)

—··—··— TONS CARRIED [MILLIONS] (Y1)

———— TOTAL GOODS RECEIPTS [£100,000] (Y1)

and towards Aston at Perry Barr station junction were brought into use on 1 March 1888. The south-facing junction with the Stour Valley line was opened on 1 April 1889, together with extra tracks between Winson Green and Harborne junction. On the same day the new link lines and an intermediate station at Soho Road were brought into use for passenger trains, which included a circular inner-suburban service and some re-routed Walsall workings. These additions complemented developments at New Street station, which had

been virtually doubled in size with the opening of additional platforms on 8 February 1885. In a subsequent phase, completed in 1896, the eastern approaches to Birmingham were widened and remodelled, eliminating conflicts between LNWR and Midland trains and allowing each company to work its traffic separately at New Street, which became a joint station in 1897.

* * *

Such improvements in capacity were, of course, primarily a response to the growth in traffic and to the service densities that were required to accommodate it. LNWR route mileage increased by 20% between 1876 and 1891,[1] but train mileage increased by more than 31% over the same period. Although the total number of train miles run was subject to a number of influences, the most basic was the amount of traffic offering. During these years train mileage grew in two distinct waves, which coincided with economic upswings: the period up to 1883, and then again from 1887 to 1891. The LNWR's gross revenue followed the same pattern, and train mileage, like revenue, dipped sharply during the depression of the mid 1880s.

The correlation of traffic and train mileage was at its most straightforward for freight, although in the absence of ton-mile statistics some elements have to be inferred from the relative variations in tonnage, revenue, and train mileage figures. Minerals accounted for the overwhelming bulk of freight tonnage, but the different characteristics of mineral and general merchandise traffic are emphasised by the fact that the latter always contributed a greater share of revenue. In boom years, both mineral and merchandise tonnage and revenue rose sharply: between 1880 and 1883 merchandise tonnage grew by 9%, and minerals by 8·3%; total freight revenue increased by 6%. However, the volume of mineral traffic was such most of the absolute increase in loadings came from this sector. In 1880 25m tons of minerals were handled: in 1883 carryings reached 27·1m tons, before falling to 24·8m tons in 1885 and then peaking at 29·2m tons in 1889. The pressures on freight charges and the special rates which applied to many bulk flows make extrapolation from trends in revenue somewhat speculative, but the tendency for average receipts per ton of mineral traffic to fall back before the peaks in total annual tonnage implies that initially the greatest expansion came in short-haul traffic. Average receipts per ton recovered slightly in 1883 and between 1889 and 1891, suggesting that, as might be expected, the demand for iron and coal at the height of the booms was sufficient to generate longer hauls.

From a financial perspective, the benefits of these peaks were offset by the fact that the commodities which contributed the greatest volume of freight traffic were also the railways' staple raw materials. This accordingly contributed to an increase in costs per train mile during the booms, though up to 1891 the rise in gross revenue was sufficient to offset the effects of higher unit costs. But besides being transmitted directly from the wider economy to the LNWR's accounts through coal and iron prices, the dynamic interaction between supply and demand also affected operating ratios in other ways. In the upswings, revenue per goods-train mile peaked in 1882 and 1888, despite the slight fall in average revenue per ton; conversely, revenue per train mile declined in both 1883 and 1889, although average revenue per ton increased and absolute levels of freight tonnage and revenue were higher. The inference is that, as traffic grew, revenue was at first maximised by improving loadings on existing services, but benefits were then eroded by the need to provide additional capacity. The opposite tendency was shown during the depression of the mid-1880s: freight revenue in 1884 was 3·4% less than in 1883, but goods-train mileage was cut by 4·9%, resulting in an increase in revenue per train mile. However, once this marginal mileage had been eliminated it proved more difficult to respond to the continuing fall in freight receipts, and average revenue per goods-train mile declined again from 1885 to 1887.

The effects of economic fluctuations can therefore be traced through the statistics of LNWR freight traffic, although the impact varied at different stages in the trade cycle. A further complication is that train capacity, a basic factor in the relationship between freight tonnage and train mileage, was not a constant. Direct evidence is fragmentary, but there is no doubt that, regardless of the short-run variations inferred above, goods trains in the 1880s were generally longer and heavier than in the previous decade: although average revenue per ton declined throughout the 1870s, the ratios of both tonnage and gross revenue to goods-train mileage improved steadily from 1870 to 1879. According to the *Railway News* of 20 January

[1] The definition of route mileage used here is miles owned, jointly-owned, worked or leased by the LNWR and worked by the company's engines. If foreign mileage worked over is included, the total increase between 1876 and 1891 was 25%. However, the more detailed statistics first published for 1913 (when foreign mileage accounted for 29% of the total route miles worked over, compared with 23% in 1891 and 20% in 1876) indicate that only 6% of the LNWR train mileage in that year resulted from working over other companies' lines.

1917, a typical LNWR coal train weighed 541 tons in 1875, whereas its 1887 equivalent was 636 tons.

Heavier trains were in turn reflected in locomotive design. After taking over at Crewe in 1871, Webb's immediate concern was to improve the efficiency and capacity of the works, so the demand for additional engines was at first satisfied by continuing the production of Ramsbottom designs, including the final batches of the 'DX' goods class, which had made its initial appearance in 1858. In 1873, however, the first of Webb's own classes appeared, the 0-6-0 '17" Goods'. Although related to the 'DX' design through a small-wheeled saddle-tank derivative produced in 1870, the Webb 0-6-0 had a higher boiler pressure than its Ramsbottom predecessors, and this, in combination with its 4' 3" diameter wheels, made it a robust and powerful machine. The class became a new standard – 500 were built between 1873 and 1892 – and was remarkable for the simplicity and cheapness of its design. However, despite Webb's justifiable reputation for economy, his new goods engines incorporated a cab, which, although small, was an advance on Ramsbottom's spartan standards. And while all but the first few of the class emerged in the distinctively-hued LNWR black which in 1873 replaced green as the company's locomotive colour, the decision to adopt so austere a livery is usually attributed to Cawkwell, the general manager, rather than Webb.

The next development of the LNWR 0–6–0 locomotive came in 1880, when Webb produced a design with 18" cylinders and 5' driving wheels. These '18" Goods', of which 310 were eventually built, carried the LNWR crest on their centre splashers, hence their alternative official designation as 'Crested Goods', and more popularly as 'Cauliflowers'. Their other distinction was that they were the first class to incorporate the Joy radial valve gear instead of the variants of the Stephenson link motion previously used by the LNWR. The configuration of the Joy gear allowed Webb to include a central axle-box for the vulnerable crank axle, and this layout became the Crewe standard.

The 'Cauliflowers' were designed for main-line express goods working, but their speed also made them suitable for passenger trains, and the same adaptability was shown by the 'Special DXs', Webb's rebuild of the Ramsbottom 0-6-0s with new higher-pressure boilers. Five hundred of the original 'DXs' were rebuilt in this form, providing a useful supplement to the Webb 0-6-0s. In 1881, the year that the first 'Special DX' appeared, Crewe also turned out an 0-6-2 tank variant of the '17" Goods', 300 of which were produced between then and 1897. Though, as their name implied, these 'Coal Tanks' were introduced primarily for freight traffic, these too found their way into passenger service. Webb's other tank designs were mainly intended for passenger traffic, apart from a small class of oil-burning 0-4-0 dock shunters introduced in 1880.

These developments gave the LNWR an expanding stud of capable and economical six-coupled engines, allowing many older locomotives to be replaced or rebuilt. The new classes thus contributed directly to improved freight train performance through their greater capacity, and this in itself played a part in containing costs. In addition, Webb's progressive modernisation of Crewe, and his pursuit of economy in both the construction of locomotives and in their operation and maintenance, also helped to control the total expenditure attributable to the locomotive department. In 1884 the capital stock of locomotives was fixed at 2,323, with a value of £3·57m, so that all new building had to be accommodated within the revenue account. But despite this, and despite the increasing weight and speed of trains, locomotive costs per train mile were generally lower in the 1880s than in the 1860s, and the comparison remains favourable even when allowance is made for changes in coal prices.

Other improvements also contributed to more efficient goods operations. The gradual quadrupling of the busiest main lines, and the development of alternative routes such as the connections by-passing Wigan or Birmingham, eliminated some of the fitful progress between relief sidings that was the lot of daytime freight trains on busy passenger routes. Running loops, made acceptable by the introduction of facing point locks, provided an alternative to full quadrupling, and extra siding space was installed at other key places where through relief lines were not feasible. Such measures gave greater line capacity and helped to improve the scheduling of freight trains. A major innovation off the road was the commissioning between 1875 and 1883 of the 'gridiron' sidings at Edge Hill, to assist in handling goods at Liverpool, where there had been a four-fold expansion in outward traffic between 1850 and 1873. The sidings, laid out to the design of Harry Footner, one of the company's assistant engineers, were the first in Britain equipped to sort and marshall mixed goods traffic by gravitation alone, and their installation permitted immediate savings in shunting locomotive requirements. They also provided a safer working environment for yard staff – the annual rate of fatal accidents to shunters on Britain's railways, over 5 per 1,000 at the end of the century, testified to the human cost of traditional methods of wagon handling.

There was also considerable investment in new or enlarged goods stations at major centres, primarily to enable the LNWR to respond to the business community's requirements for rapid despatch of a growing volume of small consignments. Acworth's classic account of depot activities at Manchester London Road and Broad Street in his *Railways of England* is one of several contemporary descriptions which demonstrate the extent of the demands made on the railways as businesses relied increasingly on the distribution network in order to reduce stockholding. Acworth's observations and similar comments at shareholders' meetings showed that the railways were well aware of the burdens this placed upon them: expensive city centre warehousing and the labour-intensive services demanded by traders hardly helped to improve the overall return on goods operations, but were part of the uneasy compromise between the companies' commercial and competitive objectives, their common carrier obligations, and the public service expectations of the legislature and the business community. However, land acquisition outlays could be minimised by using the undercrofts of passenger stations, as at London Road, even if this entailed employing hoists, capstans, and turntables to move wagons, while careful planning of depot layouts and goods loading could reduce costs through better working practices and improved vehicle utilisation.

Moon also continued to pursue the objective of achieving savings by reducing the company's reliance on outside contractors: on 31 December 1877 Chaplin & Horne's agency for collecting and delivering parcels and goods in London ended, and the firm's men, horses, and vehicles were transferred to the LNWR under the superintendence of the veteran David Stevenson, who was recalled to London from his post as district goods manager at Rugby. Despite the scale of the reorganisation, the company benefited not only from bringing cartage and canvassing under its direct control, but also from the advertising provided by having its own fleet of

Francis Webb, wearing his chain of office as Mayor of Crewe, a position which he held from 1886 to 1888. *(LNWR Society collection, 1172)*

vans running through the streets of London. In addition, the establishment of a network of parcels and goods receiving offices increased the LNWR's direct representation in the metropolis, and the issue of passenger tickets was quickly added to the services offered by these outlets. Another agency, that of Carver & Co in Liverpool and Manchester, was taken over by the LNWR on 1 May 1888. However, Pickfords retained its goods cartage contract in London and some other towns – it was not given up until 1901 – and as part of the 1878 changes the firm's London goods depots also began to accept parcels, thus increasing the catchment of the LNWR's parcels service. Free parcels collection was offered in London and other major centres from 1880 onwards, but by then the Post Office was a

An LNWR horse dray posed at Stafford with a consignment of ice. *(LNWR Society collection, 1410)*

prospective competitor for smaller packages. Legislation was eventually passed to allow the establishment of a parcel post service in 1883, and in anticipation of this the Railway Clearing House rates for parcels traffic were reduced in 1882. As inland parcel post was charged by weight alone, irrespective of distance, this left the railways with an advantage for shorter-distance consignments, where their graduated scales were lower than postal rates. Although some traffic was diverted to the parcel post, even this did not represent a complete loss to the railways, for while the companies were obliged to carry Post Office parcels they were guaranteed 55% of the gross income. The LNWR's total parcels revenue – which included receipts from livestock carried by passenger services and the dwindling business in the conveyance of private road vehicles – therefore continued to expand despite this extra competition. Having risen from £329,222 in 1871 to £514,838 in 1881, total income from parcels reached £755,663 in 1891.

* * *

Parcels earnings were included in passenger train revenue, which rose in aggregate by almost 40% between 1871 and 1891. Though cyclical fluctuations had some effect on this part of the business, their impact was much less marked than on freight traffic: after a sharp increase in the 1860s, passenger receipts grew relatively smoothly during the two succeeding decades, and 1879 was the only year when there was an actual fall in passenger journeys. However, behind the overall growth in revenue was a major change in its composition. Parcels traffic played a part in this – its share of total passenger train earnings increased from 10% in 1871 to 15% in 1891 – but the most significant change was in the proportion of revenue contributed by the various passenger classes. In 1871, third-class traffic comprised just under a third of all coaching receipts (including parcels and mail); by 1878 the proportion was more than half. From then onwards it increased more slowly, reaching 58% by 1891. Conversely, first- and second-class revenue, respectively 23% and 28% of the total in 1871, had declined to 14% and 8% by 1891. And while these changes took place against a background of steady growth in total passenger earnings, they went beyond a simple alteration in relative shares: second-class

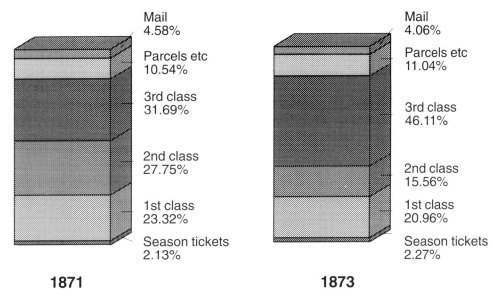

Composition of coaching revenue

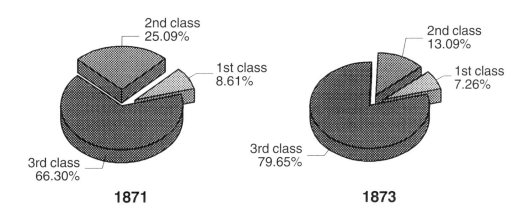

Proportion of passenger journeys by class

Figure 6.5 – LNWR COACHING REVENUE AND PASSENGER JOURNEYS, 1871 AND 1873

revenue declined in absolute terms after 1871, and first-class followed suit after 1874. Parcels income exceeded that from second-class passengers in 1879; five years later it had also overhauled first-class receipts.

The changing composition of passenger revenue was in turn the result of trends in traffic volumes, journey lengths, and fares. From 1852 onwards, third-class and parliamentary-fare passengers had accounted for more than half the journeys made on the company's system, but because their journeys were relatively short and at low fares their contribution to gross revenue remained less than that of the other classes. However, in common with other railways, the LNWR experienced a rapid increase in the volume of its third-class business during the 1860s. Although receipts per passenger actually fell, the number of third-class passengers grew to such an extent that by 1867 the revenue which they contributed was greater than that from first-class passengers, even though the latter paid an average fare per journey which was almost five times higher.

Some of the reasons for the growing democratisation of railway travel have already been touched upon: they included increasing urbanisation and higher real incomes, as well as more general holiday provision. But while the underlying factors affecting passenger demand were rooted in wider social and economic trends, the pace of change during the 1870s was also directly influenced by steps taken by the Midland Railway, firstly in admitting third-class passengers to all its trains from 1 January 1872 and then in withdrawing second-class facilities altogether in 1875. Faced with these initiatives by one of its main competitors, the LNWR could not avoid responding and from 1872 onwards it began to relax the traditional restrictions on third-class travel. In addition to gaining access to the principal express services on the LNWR system, third-class passengers were also offered through bookings and tourist fares for longer journeys. As a result, third-class revenue jumped from 32% of total passenger-train earnings in 1871 to 42% in 1872 and 46% in 1873, while over the same two years second-class revenue fell from 28% to 18% and then 16%.

Though none of the other major lines followed the Midland in adopting a two-class structure in 1875, there was an immediate impact on competitive routes, since the Midland gave effect to its policy by lowering first-class fares to the previous second-class levels. Consequently, in addition to reducing first-class charges, other companies were obliged to revise their second-class rates to maintain a differential. The new fares were applied on LNWR routes to the east midlands, Carlisle, Liverpool, and Manchester from 1 January 1875, and to the west midlands from 1 March. One result was a short-lived recovery in second-class journeys in 1875, and a slightly smaller increase in first-class traffic; however, this increased volume was insufficient to offset lower average fares, so that the decline in first-and second-class revenue was not stemmed.

In common with most of his contemporaries, Moon deprecated the Midland's changes, and the costs and benefits of providing for the various categories of passenger traffic became a recurring theme at general meetings. The chairman's innate conservatism encouraged him to persist in the view that three classes should be retained, but there were contrary opinions and as time went on the continuing growth in third-class traffic and revenue reinforced the commercial logic of the Midland's decision. Even in the short term, the extra third-class traffic generated by the relaxation of restrictions in 1872 more than offset any abstraction of higher-fare revenue, while the contrasting failure to generate any net financial benefit from the lowering of first- and second-class fares in 1875 suggests that by this stage demand from these classes was relatively inelastic. However, it should not be forgotten that the Midland's changes were part of its campaign to win passengers on the trunk routes between London, Lancashire, the West Riding, and Carlisle, so views within competing companies were coloured by the effects on existing traffic. Measured by market impact, the Midland's tactics were certainly successful: its passenger traffic grew by more than 50% between 1871 and 1876 and generated a revenue increase of 38%, whereas the LNWR's passenger receipts grew by only 19% over the same period. However, the Midland's performance also reflected a 25% increase in route mileage, compared with the LNWR's 11%, and even with the additional traffic which it attracted to its system the Midland failed to catch up with its rival in terms of indicators such as revenue per passenger, per route mile, or per train mile. Overall, its relative financial position weakened during the 1870s.

The growth in the total volume of passenger traffic

was accompanied by an expansion in passenger-train miles. On the LNWR, passenger numbers grew more rapidly than train miles up to the mid-1870s, but both grew at approximately the same rate from then onwards. Accordingly, the ratio of passenger journeys to passenger-train miles increased from 2·1:1 in 1861 to 3·0:1 in 1876, before falling back slightly to fluctuate around 2·8:1 for most of the remainder of the century. However, the increasing proportion of third-class traffic, together with the extension of special tourist and excursion fares, resulted in a decrease in revenue per passenger-train mile (exclusive of parcels etc) from £0·230 in 1861 to £0·200 in 1871; it recovered to £0·225 in 1876 before declining to £0·170 in 1886 and then rising slowly once more, reaching £0·175 in 1891. Including parcels revenue, which rose over the period, and mail receipts, which declined, total earnings per passenger-train mile were £0·218 in 1891, compared with £0·275 in 1861 and £0·243 in 1871.

Separate cost figures for passenger and freight trains are not available after 1868 (when company estimates suggested that freight services cost about a third more per mile to operate than passenger trains). In that year total traffic expenditure averaged £0·143 per train mile; the average then fell to £0·130 in 1871 before reaching a peak of £0·163 in 1875. Over the next ten years costs declined to £0·139, before increasing again to £0·153 by 1891. In 1868 profit per passenger-train mile had been £0·126, after allowing for some capital items, and though in the subsequent absence of separate cost statistics it is not possible to extrapolate directly, the revenue and operating figures quoted above suggest that the margin per passenger-train mile was under increasing pressure after 1876. However, the growth in the total volume of passenger business was sufficient to ensure that revenue – and profits – continued to expand.

The last point is important, since it provides a perspective on the worsening operating ratios experienced by most of Britain's railways during the 'great depression'. As with freight traffic, increasing public expectations and the growth in competition – most vividly demonstrated by the Midland's passenger policy – put the companies under pressure to improve the facilities which they offered to their customers, and this undoubtedly diluted the profits of even the strongest undertakings. Although the LNWR was relatively successful in containing its operating

expenses, Moon frequently reminded shareholders of the additional costs they had to bear in meeting the demand for better passenger accommodation and services. Findlay, in his book *The working and management of an English railway*, gave an example of this: the number of passengers carried per ton of coal fell by 22% between 1870 and 1888, because of the increased weight and speed of trains. But as long as net revenue continued to grow, and the cost of new borrowing remained significantly lower than the company's total return on capital, actual or anticipated competitive pressures and the increasing demands of public and parliamentary opinion provided a powerful stimulus for expanded and improved passenger facilities.

Part of the response was the new rural and suburban branch lines described earlier. On existing routes it took the form of increased services, the provision of additional intermediate stations, and the modernisation and enlargement of others. The major developments at Birmingham New Street, Liverpool Lime Street, Leeds, and Manchester have already been mentioned, and other stations such as Preston, Carlisle, and Huddersfield were rebuilt as part of layout improvements. On the approach to London, the last double-track bottleneck was eliminated on 28 April 1878, with the opening of a second tunnel at Primrose Hill. This was followed by the provision of bay platforms at Willesden Junction low level, allowing North London trains to be extended northwards over the main line between Chalk Farm and Willesden from 2 June 1879. Two new intermediate stations, Queens Park and Loudoun Road, were opened, and these were also served by the LNWR's Euston–Watford suburban service, which from the same date was increased on weekdays to a regular hourly frequency, supplemented at the peaks. Facilities at Willesden Junction high level were improved in 1885, with the opening on 20 July of a curve between the West London platforms and the N&SWJ line at Acton Wells; this permitted the closure of the separate Richmond platforms, simplifying connections between cross-London services and main-line express and suburban trains.

Improvements at Euston itself were more difficult to achieve because of the restricted site. During the early 1870s a limited amount of extra capacity was obtained by building two new arrival platforms alongside Seymour Street, east of the original London &

This 1907 view shows the joint station at Preston, a quarter of a century after its rebuilding. *(National Railway Museum, HOR F15)*

Birmingham layout. A decade later office and hotel accommodation was increased, but there was no substantial addition to the station's operational area until 1888. In that year, following agreement with the landowner, the Bedford estates, work commenced on a westward extension which involved the removal of the carriage sheds and a relocation of Cardington Street. These works, together with alterations at Camden, were pushed ahead vigorously during the closing years of Moon's chairmanship, and increased accommodation for suburban traffic was also provided by building a two-sided wooden platform between the L&B arrival and departure roads. This was completed in 1891, but it was not until 1892 that the much-needed additional main line departure platforms became available.

By then the LNWR's passenger services had been transformed. The recasting of principal express services had begun in 1875, as a response to the increased train loads resulting from the widened availability of third-class facilities. Longer formations exacerbated the problems posed by the chain brake, since a brake van was required for every nine vehicles. In June 1875 separate 'horse and carriage' trains were established on the main line, to relieve expresses of horse-boxes and other miscellaneous vehicles. From the same date additional Euston–Birmingham workings were provided to lighten longer-distance services and reduce marshalling at Rugby. Apart from a solitary up express which was scheduled to take 2 hours 57 minutes, the best trains between London and Birmingham had hitherto been allowed between 3 and $3^{1}/_{4}$ hours; the new services introduced in 1875 were slightly faster, and by 1882 a 2 hour 50 minute timing, with five intermediate stops, was being operated by one train in each direction over the longer route through Northampton. A year later an up express was timed at 2 hours 35 minutes via the direct route.

Services to the west midlands encountered competition only from the GWR; while its best London–Birmingham time of 2 hours 42 minutes for the longer journey via Oxford compared favourably with LNWR schedules, other services from Paddington were more lethargic. To Manchester, however, there was keener competition, both from the MS&L and GNR partnership and from the Midland, whose route to London Road was improved with the opening of the Romiley–Ashburys cut-off in 1875. The LNWR was obliged by its agreement with the North Staffordshire Railway to operate two daily up and down expresses via Stoke, but although this route was shorter than that via Crewe, it was slower and entailed more intermediate calls. The LNWR had hitherto been content with best timings of 4 hours 55 minutes down and 5 hours up on its Manchester services, but in response to further Midland improvements in 1880, when St Pancras expresses were diverted to Manchester Central, one Euston–Manchester train in each direction was scheduled to take 4 hours 40 minutes, a timing which had previously been attained during the dispute with the MS&L in 1857. In November 1882 the 11.10 am departure from London Road via Crewe was retarded to 11.15 am, retaining its 3.50 pm Euston arrival, and in the following year $4^{1}/_{2}$-hour timings were established to meet renewed competition from the Kings Cross expresses. The latter were further accelerated in 1884, and this was matched in 1885 by reducing the best Euston timing to $4^{1}/_{4}$ hours.

Many of the Euston–Manchester services were combined with Liverpool portions, and though these also faced competition from Midland and Kings Cross services, and to a lesser extent from Paddington–Birkenhead trains, the LNWR had a clearer advantage in distance on its route to Liverpool. While Euston–Lime Street services participated in the general acceleration of LNWR expresses, their journey times were usually 10–15 minutes longer than those of the equivalent Manchester trains. Besides the less strenuous competition for Liverpool traffic, this difference also took account of the slightly longer distance – $193^{1}/_{2}$ miles from Euston, compared with 189 miles to Manchester via Crewe, or $183^{1}/_{2}$ miles via the North Staffordshire route – and the slow final approach to Lime Street from Edge Hill. Despite this, the fastest Euston–Liverpool schedule of 1883, $4^{1}/_{2}$ hours, matched that to Manchester, but during the remainder of the 1880s the best Liverpool timing improved by only a further 5 minutes.

The St Pancras and Kings Cross expresses reached Liverpool over the Cheshire Lines route, and the MS&L also took advantage of this line to introduce a regular hourly interval express service between Liverpool and Manchester in 1877, taking 45 minutes for the 34 miles with one intermediate stop at Warrington. In October the same year the LNWR responded with a similar schedule over the $31^{1}/_{2}$ miles between Lime Street and Exchange: all trains called at Edge Hill, and some stopped additionally at Newton or St Helens Junction. Further semi-fast services, taking 50–60 minutes for the journey, were introduced in 1880, giving a regular half-hourly frequency between the two Lancashire cities for most of the day. Most of the hourly expresses ran to or from Leeds, but the even interval principle was not extended eastwards and timings on this part of the route saw little improvement, despite the competition from the L&Y for traffic between Manchester and the West Riding.

Although the routes between Euston and the west midlands and south Lancashire carried the densest and commercially most important of the LNWR's long-distance passenger flows, the most dramatic effects of competition were demonstrated in the development of cross-border services during the 1870s and 1880s, and here again the intervention of the Midland was a major factor. Schedules between Euston and Scotland had improved only slightly from the early days of the west coast route: by 1871 there were still only four trains in each direction, and the best, the overnight 'Limited Mail', took just over $10^{1}/_{2}$ hours between London and Edinburgh, with the Glasgow portion taking 10 minutes longer; Aberdeen was reached in 15 hours 40 minutes. In the following year the principal down day service, at 10 am, was accelerated to reach Glasgow in $10^{1}/_{2}$ hours, while in June 1875 third-class passengers were admitted to west coast Anglo-Scottish expresses. This was in anticipation of Midland competition, and with the opening of the Settle route in 1876 there were further improvements to services between Euston and Scotland. The through workings which linked Liverpool and Manchester with Scotland were also improved in response to the new Midland and L&Y service via Hellifield. In 1877 the fastest

Euston–Edinburgh timing was 9 hours 50 minutes, and when Glasgow Central station opened in 1879 it was reached in 10 hours from Euston. The slower daytime services, the 5.15 am newspaper train and the 7.15 am and 11 am departures, took from 45 to 90 minutes longer. In 1885, with the introduction of a separate train for postal traffic, overnight schedules were also rearranged: the old 'Limited Mail' was retained as the principal night passenger express, reaching Edinburgh in 10 hours and Glasgow 10 minutes later, but it was supplemented by other year-round and seasonal services. The best overnight timing to Aberdeen was reduced to just under 14 hours.

The Midland's Anglo–Scottish expresses were handicapped by the longer GSWR line between Carlisle and Glasgow and the slow Waverley route to Edinburgh, but remained competitive with the west coast services to those points. The distance from either Euston or St Pancras to Edinburgh via Carlisle was however greater than that from Kings Cross via Newcastle, and the easier alignment of much of the east coast route reinforced this advantage. Following the opening of the Settle & Carlisle line, the timing between Kings Cross and Waverley was reduced by 30 minutes to 9 hours, but the east coast partners apparently had so little to fear from the more westerly routes that their prime daytime trains, the 10 am departures in each direction, continued to carry only first- and second-class passengers, leaving third-class travellers reliant on slower services. By 1887 east coast third-class timings were bettered by the 10 am west coast expresses, so in November that year third-class passengers were admitted to the equivalent departures from Kings Cross and Waverley to restore that route's competitive advantage for this class of traffic also.

The LNWR and Caledonian response was delayed until 1888, when with little notice the 10 am from Euston was accelerated from 1 June to reach both Edinburgh and Glasgow in 9 hours. Their rivals reacted with an 8½-hour timing to Edinburgh from the same date, and when the August west coast timetables were published with a matching Euston–Edinburgh schedule a further 30 minute reduction was announced for the Kings Cross route. From Monday 6 August the 10 am from Euston ran as an Edinburgh train only, with the Glasgow portion following separately, and for a few days the two partnerships vied to

achieve the fastest London–Edinburgh timing, running lightweight formations with little regard to published schedules. On 13 August Edinburgh was reached in 7 hours 38 minutes from Euston, an end-to-end average of 52·4 mph; the following day an east coast time of 7 hours 32 minutes was recorded, 52·1 mph. For the remainder of August a regular 8-hour schedule was operated between Euston and Edinburgh, 15 minutes more than from Kings Cross; from September the west coast timing reverted to 8½ hours, with the east coast maintaining a 15-minute advantage. There were also permanent accelerations to Perth and Aberdeen, and in the summer of 1889 the Euston–Glasgow timing was reduced to 8½ hours. In less than two decades, therefore, there was an improvement of over 2½ hours, more than 25%, in the fastest west coast Anglo-Scottish timings. In addition there were significant additions to the range of services, the most important of which was the introduction of a 2 pm departure in July 1889 with timings comparable with those of the 10 am express.

These improvements in LNWR passenger services were accompanied by a modernisation of rolling stock, though progress compared less favourably with a number of other companies because of the idiosyncrasies which marked some practice during the later Moon years. The parliamentary returns – which are not always easy to reconcile with the figures reported to shareholders – show that the LNWR fleet of coaching vehicles, 3,346 in 1865, expanded to 4,340 in 1871, 5,637 in 1881 and 7,249 in 1891, with passenger stock making up about two-thirds of this total. According to Findlay, the number of passenger seats increased by 89% between 1871 and 1888, from 93,190 to 176,974. As the stock of passenger carriages grew by only 65% over the same period, the seating figures indicate an increase in average vehicle capacity. This was partly a reflection of the falling proportion of first- and second-class accommodation: in 1871 these two classes accounted for 52% of all passenger seating, whereas by 1888 they represented only 26% of the total. However, vehicles also became larger and more expensive: the capital embodied in coaching stock increased significantly, from £866,292 in 1871 to £1,534,391 in 1888 and £1,673,461 in 1891. In addition, because of the LNWR's conservative accounting principles, a further share of the cost of upgrading the carriage fleet was met from revenue, through renewals. As with locomotives, this practice

A twin saloon set on six-wheeled 34' underframes, as built in 1882. Note the off-centre gangway connection between the two coaches, which were designated respectively as ladies' and gentlemen's saloons. The ladies' saloon is nearest the camera. *(LNWR Society collection, 1881)*

left a significant proportion of duplicate stock, which although written out of the capital account remained available for secondary duties.

Up to the 1870s, LNWR passenger vehicles, like those of other British railways, were built on two or three axles, and Wolverton produced large numbers of 27' 6" three-axle coaches on a rigid wheelbase. In 1874, however, the GNR led the way with bogie stock, quickly followed by the Midland Railway, which imported Pullman coaches from America, and in addition ordered bogie vehicles to its own design: in 1875 some 53' carriages on six-wheel bogies were built for the opening of the Settle & Carlisle route. The LNWR was also moving towards more sophisticated passenger accommodation: in June 1873 a regular sleeping car service was introduced on the overnight 'Limited Mail' to and from Glasgow and in 1875 these facilities were extended to the Holyhead and Liverpool routes. However, the sleeping carriages retained a three-axle underframe and they were restricted to a 32' length, reputedly because this was within the maximum that could be handled on the traverser in the Euston carriage sheds. The same dimension was used from the mid-1870s onwards for a wide range of coaching stock constructed at Wolverton, including new carriages built at the joint expense of the LNWR and its Caledonian partner for their through Anglo-Scottish services. The 32' vehi-

cles were carried on a 20' wheelbase, and many were equipped with Webb's patent radial truck on one of the outer axles to give some lateral play on curves. The design was then stretched in the early 1880s to 33' and 34' variants, the latter including a small fleet of first-class saloons which were built as twin-car sets with an intermediate gangway. Some of these twin saloons were later adapted to provide the LNWR's first dining cars, which were introduced on 1 March 1889 between Euston and Manchester and on the Liverpool route the following month.

The twin 34' configuration was also used in 1881 for new sleeping carriages for the 'Irish Mail', but at the beginning of 1883 42' sleepers were brought into service on the overnight Glasgow service. Although bogie stock was by then well established on several other leading railways, Wolverton accommodated the extra length by adding a second outer radial truck. This four-axle underframe was adopted for subsequent construction for principal LNWR and WCJS services, including gangwayed postal vehicles introduced in 1885, and its use was at first continued by

Charles A Park, who was recruited from the North Eastern Railway and succeeded Richard Bore as carriage superintendent from the beginning of 1886. According to Acworth, writing in 1889, a 42' third-class carriage could be built for £600, whereas the lavatory tri-composite version cost £800. These were serviceable vehicles which offered significantly better accommodation than the six-wheelers of the 1860s, but their running was inferior to that of the bogie stock of the Midland and other competitors, while the shorter chassis lengths which remained standard on the LNWR became an increasing limitation as capacity requirements continued to grow together with long-distance passengers' expectations of improved accommodation and amenities.

These developments in coaching stock, along with the extension of third-class facilities and the traffic growth that accompanied it, resulted in an increase in the weight of express trains which paralleled the growth in freight train loadings. Findlay quoted the example of the 10 am from Euston, which on a typical day in 1863 was 312' in length and weighed 123 tons with the engine; by 1887 it was 652' long, and weighed 268 tons. Not only were main-line passenger trains becoming heavier, but they also ran faster and

further between intermediate stops, thus adding to the demands on the locomotive department.

As already noted, Webb's improvement of the freight stud also contributed to passenger haulage, since the 'Cauliflowers', 'Special DXs' and 'Coal Tanks', though designed primarily for goods requirements, were capable mixed-traffic locomotives. For passenger service, Webb at first continued the production of Ramsbottom 'Newtons' and 'Samsons', and in addition began the reboilering of the McConnell 2-2-2 'Bloomers'. Only in 1874 did the first of his own express locomotive classes appear, with the introduction of the 'Precursors' and 'Precedents'. Both had the 2-4-0 wheel arrangement favoured by his predecessor and were fitted with the same boilers as the '17" Goods' locomotives, but there were significant differences between the two classes. The 'Precursors' were intended for service on the demanding gradients of the Carlisle line and were accordingly built with 5' 6" driving wheels. While this gave them a higher nominal tractive effort, they proved to be underboilered for the express duties north of Crewe for which they had been intended. By 1877, therefore, the twenty original 'Precursors' had been redeployed on other services, notably on the Manchester–Leeds route, and a further twenty were built in 1878 and 1879.

Their sister class, the 6' 6" 'Precedents', proved more satisfactory for front-rank expresses, and

A 42' eight-wheeled sleeping carriage with radial outer axles. *(LNWR Society collection, 1541)*

seventy were built between 1874 and 1882. In 1887 Webb introduced a new version, with stronger frames and 150 lb boiler pressure instead of the original 140 lb, and between 1887 and 1894 these 'Improved Precedents' took the place of Ramsbottom 'Newtons' in the capital stock. A smaller-wheeled variant introduced in 1889 began the similar replacement of the 'Samsons'. These nominal rebuilds, which became colloquially known as 'Jumbos' (a nickname first applied to the original 'Precedents'), were extremely versatile, and one of the earliest of the class, 'Hardwicke', earned particular distinction over the difficult route between Crewe and Carlisle during the races of August 1888. Another, 'Charles Dickens', built as a 'Precedent' in 1882 and later rebuilt to the new standard, worked a return trip between Manchester and Euston virtually every weekday until 1902 and was credited with over 2·3m miles in service when withdrawn in 1912. But though many of these 2-4-0s survived until well into the twentieth century, their longevity was primarily due to their later usefulness for secondary services – by the early 1880s Webb was already moving towards a radically different design standard for express locomotive classes in response to the increasing demands of main-line

An unidentified 'Improved Precedent' class locomotive heading an up express near Harrow in 1906. *(LNWR Society collection, 9223)*

passenger duties.

This new approach took the form of compounding, using steam twice by exhausting the high-pressure cylinders into a low-pressure cylinder. The double-expansion principle was already well-established in marine engineering, but the first successful application to railway practice was by Albert Mallet in France in 1876. In view of Webb's preoccupation with economy and efficiency it is not surprising that he was the first British locomotive engineer to follow Mallet's example by seeking more power through compounding, rather than by relying solely on increases in the size of firebox and boiler, and much of his subsequent career was identified with the attempt to develop compound designs to keep pace with the requirements of the LNWR's principal passenger services. Although some of these classes were relatively successful, subsequent commentators have regarded Webb's concentration on double expansion for his later express locomotives as something of a blind alley. Moreover, while most of his designs appear to have met the objective of economy in fuel consumption, there is a certain irony in the fact that Webb's first compound classes appeared at a time when coal prices had fallen to their lowest level for more than two decades.

Webb began to experiment with compounding in 1878, when he modified a Trevithick 2-2-2 by reducing the diameter of one cylinder and feeding its exhaust to the second cylinder, which operated at lower pressure. Encouraged by the success of this conversion, Webb went on to produce in 1882 a proto-type compound, 'Experiment', with two high-pres-sure outside cylinders and a low-pressure inside cylinder. As with the 'Cauliflowers', Webb employed Joy valve gear, but the configuration required for outside cylinders left no room for coupling rods. Accordingly, though 'Experiment' was similar in outline to the earlier simple 2-4-0 designs, it was in fact a 2-2-2-0, with the high-pressure cylinders powering the rear wheels and the inside low-pressure cylinder driving the central axle.

Twenty-nine more engines of the 'Experiment' type were built in 1883 and 1884, but in practice they proved to be inferior to the 'Precedents'. Webb's second 2-2-2-0 compound design, introduced in 1884, was however an improvement: this class, the 'Dreadnoughts', was given a larger boiler with higher pressure, 175 lbs compared with the 150 lbs of the 'Experiments', and slightly smaller driving wheels. The higher tractive effort and greater weight of these locomotives, together with a modified reversing gear which simplified the control of the high- and low-pressure cylinders, overcame the sluggishness which had marred Webb's first compound class. Forty 'Dreadnoughts' were built between 1884 and 1888, and then in 1889 Webb produced the most successful of his three-cylinder 2-2-2-0 designs, the 'Teutonics', of which ten were built. With their even larger boilers and 7' 1" driving wheel diameter – 10" more than the 'Dreadnoughts', and 6" more than the 'Experiments' – these locomotives were reputed to be extremely free running on the open road, and were also noted for their mechanical reliability: Bowen Cooke quoted mileages in excess of 85,000 between overhauls.

Webb also experimented with compound tank engines, but none of the three prototypes he built in 1886 and 1887 went into production, and his other tank locomotive designs were all simple expansion.

The first of his passenger tank classes, a 2-4-0 for light suburban and branch line duties, was produced in 1876, and fifty of the class were turned out between then and 1880. This design was succeeded in 1879 by a 2-4-2 class, with larger bunker capacity to give extended range: 180 of these were built, and most of the 2-4-0Ts were also reconstructed to the same dimensions. Like the 2-4-0Ts, some of the 2-4-2Ts were fitted with condensing gear to enable them to work over the District Railway on Mansion House services. Webb then went on in 1890 to use the 2-4-2 configuration for a tank engine version of his 1874 'Precursors': 160 of this class were subsequently built, including 40 categorised as rebuilds of the earlier tender design. The 5' 6" driving wheels and capacious bunkers of these locomotives made them suitable for a wide range of duties, including some of the main passenger turns on the demanding Central Wales route.

* * *

In common with the LNWR's other principal services, those to and from Ireland also saw considerable development and modernisation during this period. Initially the LNWR's Holyhead–North Wall sailings had offered little competition for the passenger traffic carried by the City of Dublin company's mail steamers: the railway vessels were slower, carried goods and livestock as well as passengers, and their schedules were affected by tidal restrictions in Dublin harbour. According to Neele, the CDSPC captains disdained the rival fleet as 'pig boats', and it is clear that the LNWR was left with the lower end of the market: while the Kingstown mail sailings excluded third-class passengers, the North Wall service offered only the basic distinction between deck and cabin accommodation. In 1873, however, the dredging of the Liffey enabled fixed schedules to be adopted on the Holyhead–North Wall route, and this was the prelude to vigorous efforts to upgrade the service. In 1876 the LNWR took delivery of two new 16-knot paddle steamers from Lairds of Birkenhead, and on 1 July that year these vessels, the *Shamrock* and the *Rose*, inaugurated a day express service, 'free from the taint of cattle traffic'. The connecting boat trains, while slower than the premium-fare 'Irish Mail', enabled the LNWR to offer a through daytime Euston–Dublin schedule which provided a reasonable

Above: In this photograph taken in the closing years of the century, an unidentified 'Dreadnought' 2-2-2-0 pilots a later 'Jubilee' class compound northwards through Tamworth while 2-4-2T no 290 takes water during its station stop with an up local train. *(LNWR Society collection, 1328)*

Below: A 2-4-2T on express duties on the Central Wales line. *(Mitchell Library: Langmuir collection)*

North Wall, Dublin, in 1886, with the *Shamrock* alongside the *Duchess of Sutherland*. The LNWR-owned passenger station is behind the quayside shed, with the company's hotel to the right. *(LNWR Society collection, 789)*

alternative to the Kingstown route. A further pair of new vessels, the *Lily* and the *Violet*, was supplied by Lairds in 1880, enabling a corresponding night service to be established. These later ships were faster and slightly longer than their 1876 predecessors, but a more significant difference was that, following the example of the *Isabella* in 1877, they were built of Crewe steel and thus shared her advantage of lighter draught. While the slower cargo boats continued to be available to passengers, the day and night expresses offered superior cabin accommodation at fares which were little more than second-class charges on the mail steamers.

Efforts were also made to improve shore facilities on either side of the Irish Sea. Railway facilities in Dublin had developed like those of London: the various trunk routes had independent termini which were dispersed on the two sides of the river. Unlike London, however, there were no local junction lines, which made road transfer necessary for all inter-system journeys. This affected American as well as domestic Irish traffic, since Queenstown harbour, near Cork, was a port of call for transatlantic services.

Travelling by rail and sea via Holyhead, Dublin, and Queenstown was faster than the through passage by ocean liner from or to Liverpool, and before the end of the 1860s the LNWR was advertising this as the 'quick route to America'. However, although the mails went this way and were guaranteed a speedy interchange, the extra connections – which included the need to cross Dublin by road between the Westland Row terminus of the Kingstown boat trains and the Great Southern & Western's Kingsbridge station – were a more substantial obstacle for transatlantic passengers and their baggage.

The first step towards improving rail links within Dublin had been taken in 1864 with the opening for goods traffic of the Midland Great Western Railway's Liffey branch, which curved round the north of the city to terminate on the east bank of the Royal Canal at North Wall, adjacent to the LNWR berths. The MGWR extension passed under the approaches to the Amiens Street station of the Dublin & Drogheda Railway, and in 1869 the latter company also obtained powers for a branch to North Wall, known as the Drogheda curve. The LNWR was empowered to contribute two-thirds of the cost of the D&D scheme, which would connect directly with its steamer terminal; it also supported a GS&W proposal, authorised in 1872, to gain access to North Wall from the main line just west of Kingsbridge by means of a $2^{1}/_{2}$-

mile connection into the Liffey branch at Glasnevin junction. The GS&W was granted running powers over the MGWR as far as West Road junction, near North Wall, and from there it was authorised to build an easterly spur to the quayside. As the route of this spur intersected the Drogheda curve, it also offered the prospect of connecting all the lines on the north bank of the Liffey. The LNWR's eventual contribution to the GS&W project was £117,500, and the English company appears to have undertaken most of the works on behalf of its Irish partner. The LNWR also seems to have participated directly in the construction of the D&D branch, besides providing the associated quayside terminal facilities on its own account.

The opening of North Wall passenger station on 1 September 1877, together with the Drogheda curve and the GS&W extensions, enabled LNWR sailings to connect directly with trains serving the three main-line systems radiating westward and northward from Dublin. Through a series of amalgamations the D&D route north had by that stage become part of the Great Northern Railway of Ireland, and in 1878 financial arrangements between the new company and the LNWR were simplified by transferring the ownership of the southern section of the Drogheda curve, beyond its junction with the GS&W at Church Road. The LNWR accordingly ceased to be a shareholder in the GNR(I) and instead became the direct owner of half a mile of 5' 3" gauge route, as well as passenger, goods, and cattle stations at North Wall. Train services, however, were provided entirely by the connecting Irish companies.

In addition to supporting these developments at Dublin, the LNWR also invested in new works at Holyhead. The CDSPC sailings continued to use the Admiralty pier at the northern extremity of the old harbour, but with the transfer of the LNWR steamers to the inner harbour in 1866 the railway company gradually improved both the channel and the shore installations used by its services. In 1869 an independent company obtained more comprehensive improvement powers; however, these were not exercised, so the LNWR was itself authorised in 1873 to develop the inner harbour and to build a graving dock for its vessels. The eventual scheme, started in 1877, provided rail-served quays on both sides of the harbour, laid out in a 'V' configuration, so that arriving and departing passenger steamers could berth

alongside their respective connecting trains on the east and west sides of the terminal. A substantial hotel, which replaced the former coaching inn acquired with the C&H, was included in the station building, adding to the LNWR's already extensive chain of modern hotel properties. The new facilities at Holyhead were opened by the Prince of Wales on 17 June 1880 and a fortnight later the overnight express service was inaugurated to complement the day sailings.

The improved railway steamer services and shore facilities thus amounted to a much more significant challenge to the City of Dublin company, and in 1882, in anticipation of the expiry of the Post Office contract the following year, the LNWR submitted its own tender for the sea passage. Besides the crossing to and from Kingstown, the railway bid also offered the North Wall route as an alternative, since this would allow the mails to be transferred directly to and from trains serving most parts of Ireland. The postmaster-general accepted the LNWR offer for the Kingstown route, with the option of diverting the service to North Wall at a later date, and on the strength of this the board planned new tonnage for the fleet.

However, the CDSPC's loss of its share of the previous contract provoked a political outcry from Ireland, and the LNWR was prevailed upon by the government to withdraw its tender. The Dublin company was instead entrusted with the mail crossing for a further twelve years from October 1883 and responded to the challenge from the LNWR's through rail connections at North Wall by combining with several of the Irish trunk lines to promote the City of Dublin Junction Railways. This project, to link Westland Row with the systems north of the Liffey, was authorised in 1884, but the GS&W, no doubt influenced by its close ties with the LNWR, withdrew from the scheme, as did the MGWR. However, the CDJR was built by the Dublin, Wicklow & Wexford Railway, with financial guarantees from the GNR(I) and CDSPC, and eventually opened between Westland Row and Amiens Street in December 1890. In 1894, after a dispute with the MGWR, a south-to-west connection was completed north of Amiens Street which enabled through carriages to be operated between Kingstown harbour and the GS&W and MGWR systems in addition to those already provided over the GNR(I).

The government's change of heart did not prevent the LNWR from pressing ahead with modernisation of its fleet. Two additional passenger steamers, slightly enlarged versions of the *Lily* and *Violet*, had been proposed for the mail contract; though only one such order went ahead in 1882, the new vessel's name, *Banshee,* reflected her intended purpose by being borrowed from one of the previous Admiralty packet boats on the Kingstown route. However, when delivered from Lairds in 1884 she joined the four existing purpose-built steamers on the North Wall express sailings, reducing the need to draw on the cargo or Greenore services for stand-by capacity. In the

Holyhead harbour in 1880, probably photographed at the opening of the extension works on 1 July. The *Lily* is on the right of the picture, against the arrival quay, and the *Earl Spencer* is next to her, on the departure side. Facing her, alongside the old terminal shed, is the *Isabella*, with a selection of older vessels beyond. *(See A W H Pearsall & H H Davies,* The Holyhead steamers of the LNWR, *p 4.) (National Railway Museum, CR A219)*

circumstances in which the *Banshee* had been ordered there were advantages in adapting an existing well-tried design, but she proved to be the last paddle vessel commissioned into the LNWR's Holyhead fleet and also the last with single-expansion engines. The company made its first venture into marine compounding in 1881 with the *Eleanor*, a steel-hulled paddle steamer built by Lairds for the Greenore run. She was a replacement for the 1873 vessel of that name, which ran aground in Carlingford Lough in fog on 27 January 1881; though initially it had been hoped to refloat her, subsequent gales led to her complete loss.

For another contract placed in 1882, two cargo boats ordered from Duncans of Port Glasgow, the LNWR for the first time specified screw propulsion, again with compound machinery. These vessels, the *Holyhead* and *North Wall*, were delivered in 1883; the *Holyhead*, however, was lost in a collision on 30

October that year and was replaced in 1885 by the *Irene*, built to a similar design by Harland & Wolff of Belfast. The next pair of twin-screw cargo boats took development a stage further by incorporating triple-expansion engines: these steamers, the *Olga* of 1887 and the *Anglesey* of 1888, were built respectively by Lairds and Harland & Wolff. An earlier vessel, the *Duchess of Sutherland*, was also fitted with twin screws and triple-expansion machinery when she was rebuilt in 1888, and the same combination was used in the *Cambria*, a tug obtained from Lairds in 1889 to provide assistance at Holyhead. She revived the name of the last Chester & Holyhead vessel, which had been sold in 1881, but the new *Cambria's* railway career was considerably shorter than her namesake's: she was disposed of in the early 1890s.

Moon ruefully told the shareholders on 17 August 1886 that steamers went out of fashion very quickly, and by the end of that decade the only pre-1870 vessel still in LNWR service was the rebuilt *Duchess of Sutherland*. The increasing attention devoted to marine matters was demonstrated by the growth in the capital invested in the fleet: in 1880 this stood at £332,748 and by 1891 it had grown to £424,898, net of allowances for disposals. In addition the LNWR's steamship insurance and depreciation fund, which was a charge against revenue, also financed part of the replacement programme. However, not all of the calls on the insurance and depreciation fund were due to modernisation: shipping losses in the 1880s were high, although with relatively few fatalities. In addition to the first *Eleanor* and the *Holyhead*, the casualties included the veteran *Admiral Moorsom*, which sank on 16 January 1885 after a collision at sea, and the *Earl Spencer*, which grounded on Holyhead breakwater in fog on 8 January 1888. She was however successfully refloated, and continued in service until 1896.

On the joint routes to the north of Ireland the main changes were organisational. As part of the arrangements for the dissolution of the Preston & Wyre company a share of the costs of the Fleetwood–Belfast service appeared as a direct item in the LNWR's accounts from 1887 onwards, but after the delivery of the Barrow-built paddle steamer *Prince of Wales* in 1886 there was a lull in progress on this service. Both the rail and sea portions of the route to Belfast via Larne, however, had a more complex history during the closing years of Moon's chairman-

ship. The opening of the Settle & Carlisle line in 1876 had provided an alternative route to south-west Scotland from England, and with the Portpatrick Railway's working agreement with the Caledonian due to expire in 1885 its board began to canvass Midland and GSWR interests as well as the Caledonian and LNWR alliance. Agreement was reached in 1883 that the four trunk railways should acquire the Portpatrick company jointly, but a Bill for this purpose was withdrawn in 1884 when terms could not be settled for use of the GSWR's connecting line between Dumfries and Castle Douglas.

Meanwhile the independent Wigtownshire Railway, which diverged from the Stranraer line at Newton Stewart, had sought inclusion in the arrangements in an attempt to resolve its own financial problems. Its route had opened as far as Wigtown for goods traffic on 3 March 1875 and on 7 April for passengers, extending on 2 August that year to a station later known as Millisle, near Garliestown. On 3 April 1876 a short branch was brought into service from this point to the harbour at Garliestown and on 9 July 1877 the company completed its main line to Whithorn.

When discussions about the future of the Portpatrick Railway were resumed in the autumn of 1884, the Wigtownshire company – which had petitioned against the previous Bill – was brought into the new negotiations. Under the terms of the Portpatrick & Wigtownshire Railways (Sale and Transfer) Act of 1885 the two lines were vested in the LNWR, Midland, Caledonian, and GSWR, and a joint committee was established to manage them. By adding joint mileage in Scotland to its existing system, the LNWR thus achieved the distinction of being the only railway undertaking with route owner-ship interests in England, Wales, Scotland, and Ireland: it remained the only company in this position until the Midland acquired the Belfast & Northern Counties Railway in 1904. And though these Scottish lines were administered from Carlisle, where the Portpatrick & Wigtownshire committee was based, the LNWR's direct involvement came close to extending across the border soon after the inception of the new arrangements. Initially the Caledonian and GSWR operated Portpatrick & Wigtownshire train services on behalf of the committee, but when fresh tenders for supplying motive power were invited in 1887 the LNWR's offer proved to be the lowest and

was at first accepted. The Scottish partners, however, were allowed to amend their bids, so the operation of the joint system remained with them.

The main reason for the involvement of the LNWR and Midland in the P&WJC was, of course, its connection with the short sea crossing to Ulster. The Portpatrick Railway had been the majority shareholder in the Larne & Stranraer Steamboat Company, and after the establishment of the joint committee the LNWR's marine superintendent was asked to act in a similar capacity for the L&SSC. Accordingly, the annual surveys of its two vessels, the *Princess Beatrice* and the *Princess Louise*, were transferred to Holyhead. In a further adminstrative change, management of the steamboat company passed in 1887 to a committee of eight of its directors, half of whom were nominated by the P&WJC.

In 1889 the need to purchase new tonnage led the railway interests to decide to buy out the remaining private shareholders in the L&SSC, wind up the existing undertaking, and replace it with a new company owned by the four P&WJC participants and two Irish railways, the Belfast & Northern Counties Railway and the Carrickfergus & Larne Railway. The last-named, however, was absorbed by the BNCR in 1890, and the new shipping company was never established. Instead, the existing managing committee, the membership of which had been reduced to six in 1889 with the replacement of the four non-P&WJC directors by two BNCR representatives, took over effective responsibility for the L&SSC's ships on behalf of their parent undertakings, and also ordered a new paddle steamer from Denny's yard at Dumbarton. This, the *Princess Victoria*, was delivered in 1890, replacing the *Princess Louise*. Initially she was registered in the name of the secretary of the managing committee, but under an 1893 agreement, retrospective to 1890, ownership of the Stranraer–Larne shipping interests was regularised by the formal establishment of the Larne & Stranraer Steamship Joint Committee. The LNWR had a 20% interest in the joint fleet, as did each of its three P&WJC partners and the BNCR.

* * *

Sir Richard Moon. There are few pictures of Sir Richard: this official portrait was taken in July 1887, when he was 73. *(LNWR Society collection, 9223)*

Moon played a key role in the negotiations which established the P&WJC, and he served briefly as its chairman before handing over to his LNWR board colleague, Miles MacInnes. The latter, who was elected as MP for Hexham in 1885, was well placed to chair the joint committee since he lived just outside Carlisle. Moon himself had moved in 1882 from Harrow to Copsewood Grange, near Coventry, but continued to devote himself full-time to the company's affairs. This service was acknowledged in the jubilee honours of 1887, when he was created a baronet. In the same year he became the first freeman of the borough of Crewe as part of the celebrations of the town's own fiftieth anniversary as a railway centre.

By that stage Sir Richard Moon was firmly established as the doyen of English railway chairmen: of his immediate contemporaries, Sir Daniel Gooch, his opposite number on the GWR board since 1865, died in 1889, and only Sir Edward Watkin, chairman of the MS&L from 1864, went on to surpass Moon's length of office. Lady Moon died on 31 January 1891 and Sir Richard, who was greatly affected by the loss of his wife, announced soon afterwards that on medical advice he would retire both as chairman and a director of the LNWR at the company's general meeting on 20 February 1891. Among those who paid tributes at that meeting were W H Smith, the chancellor of the exchequer, and Lord Colville, chairman of the Great Northern, and on the following day *The Times* devoted a leading article to his achievements.

After his retiral Sir Richard kept in touch with the company, and spoke from the floor at the general meeting on 17 February 1893, characteristically choosing a financial subject for his intervention. At one point he confided to Neele that if things went wrong the board would have to send for him again, but an illness in 1897 left him a semi-invalid and on 17 November 1899 he died at home at Copsewood Grange, aged 85. His eldest son, Edward, predeceased him in 1893, so the baronetcy passed to Sir Richard's grandson, who was then living in America. However, the younger of his two surviving sons, Ernest, maintained a link with the LNWR and served on the audit committee from 1907 to the end of the company's independent existence.

The tributes that were paid to Sir Richard Moon when he retired were renewed in his obituary notices, although with the lapse of time more echoed a point that some commentators had made in 1891, that his attributes were of the old school and that he would have found it increasingly difficult to adjust to the changing railway world of the 1890s. All obituarists, however, concurred in acknowledging his integrity, his commitment to the company, and his ability to command the loyalty of its staff. Moon's devotion to LNWR affairs, coupled with his intensely reserved personality, set him apart from most of his contemporaries, and this has perhaps affected his subsequent reputation. Many of the anecdotes that have survived about him relate his frugality, while the fact that most British railway history has been written from the perspective of competing companies has reinforced the general portrayal of Moon as a stern and unsympathetic individual. But besides the testimony of LNWR officers such as David Stevenson and G P Neele, other aspects of his character can be discerned from even so prosaic a source as the company's proceedings, and two examples provide contrasting vignettes. One was in the immediate aftermath of the Abergele accident of 20 August 1868: the general meeting was held the following day, and the official record describes how Moon, speaking 'under strong emotion', curtailed the business in acknowledgement of the circumstances. On a lighter note, he amused the general meeting on 16 February 1886 by describing an encounter with an elderly clergyman and his wife who shared a journey with him: 'the lady had not been in the compartment five minutes before she asked him to enlarge their station.'

As Neele records, there was no official monument to Sir Richard Moon. He himself would have eschewed such acknowledgement: he accepted his baronetcy only at his family's urging, and he refused a monetary testimonial when he retired. While he was realistic enough to forecast the problems that lay ahead, his memorial was the financial strength of the undertaking that had been the centre of his endeavours since the 1850s, and the standard by which he would have chosen to be judged was the objective one of the LNWR's half-yearly accounts. By background and outlook Moon regarded the stewardship of the company's affairs as an individual responsibility, expressed in commitment, probity, and attention to detail: it is a measure of his distinction that for thirty years he applied these personal attributes with such success to the direction of the largest business undertaking in Britain.

CHAPTER SEVEN

A New Era and a New Century

Sir Richard Moon's successor was Lord Stalbridge, the fourth son of the second Marquis of Westminster. Richard de Aquila Grosvenor was born in Dorset on 28 January 1837, and after education at Westminster School and Cambridge entered Parliament in 1861 as Liberal member for Flintshire. Lord Richard was appointed to Lord Wolverton's vacancy on the LNWR board in 1870 but meanwhile pursued his political career, becoming a privy councillor in 1872 and serving as chief whip throughout Gladstone's second administration, which extended from 1880 to 1885. In 1886 he was elevated to the peerage as Baron Stalbridge. Despite his parliamentary commitments he took a keen interest in railway matters and was no stranger to the footplate.

Lord Stalbridge's appointment as chairman was soon followed by the emergence of a new generation of principal officers. There had already been one important loss before Moon retired: Stephen Reay, the LNWR's secretary during most of his chairmanship and one of his closest advisers, had died in harness in November 1888. His immediate successor, Francis Harley, held office only briefly before ill-health compelled him to hand over to his assistant, Thomas Houghton, in 1890. Other major staff changes took place in the early years of the new chairmanship. The general manager, George Findlay, who was knighted in the birthday honours of 1892, fell ill later that year and died unexpectedly on 26 March 1893 aged 64. He was thus survived by his predecessor, William Cawkwell, who continued to serve as one of the company's two deputy-chairmen until his death in November 1897. A further member of Sir Richard's group of close confidants, G P Neele, retired as superintendent of the line in 1895 at the age of 69; he lived until 4 January 1921. Although the engineering departments remained under their existing heads until the new century, another chief officer who followed the old chairman into retirement was Admiral Dent, who stood down as marine superintendent in 1893.

With the exception of Admiral Dent's post, which was filled by recruiting Captain W H Binney from the Pacific Steam Navigation Company, the senior appointments made under Lord Stalbridge involved no breach in the continuity of the LNWR's management traditions. The new general manager, Frederick Harrison, who was himself knighted in 1902, had started his railway career under Findlay at Shrewsbury and moved with him to Euston in 1864. After seven years at headquarters Harrison then held district positions at Liverpool and Chester before returning as assistant superintendent of the line in 1875. In 1885 he became chief goods manager, and was appointed as general manager at the age of 49. His previous post was taken by Frank Ree, whose initial career had been with the company's continental agents; he entered mainstream LNWR service in 1873 and was district goods manager at Liverpool when he was promoted in June 1893. He then again succeeded Sir Frederick Harrison when the latter retired in 1909 and was thus the third consecutive chief goods manager to attain the post of general manager. Robert Turnbull, previously assistant superintendent of the line, took over from G P Neele in 1895 and there was similar continuity in the secretary's post, Thomas Houghton being succeeded in 1902 by Walter Haywood, his assistant. Haywood retired for health reasons in 1904; the new assistant secretary James Bishop, who had previously served as the chairman's private secretary, then stepped up in turn. Appointments in the engineering departments followed a largely similar pattern, so Lord Stalbridge's chief officers were firmly schooled in the traditions of the high Victorian period of the LNWR's history.

Despite this strong internal continuity, the succession of younger officers to key positions during the early stages in the new chairmanship coincided with major changes in the economic, political, and social environment in which the company operated. While it would be wrong to underestimate the forces for change that were at work during Moon's period of office, many only began to have a significant effect after his departure. The most immediate of these was the railway rates campaign: although his predecessor was fully alive to the potential threat which this posed, Lord Stalbridge, as chairman both of the LNWR and of the Railway Companies' Association, was faced with the reality of the outcome. After consideration in Board of Trade hearings, the provisional order embodying the proposed new classifications and maximum rates applicable to the LNWR was brought before a joint committee of both Houses of Parliament in 1891, which imposed some further reductions. The outcome of these processes, the LNWR Provisional Order Confirmation Act, received the Royal Assent on 5 August 1891 and was due to take effect on 1 August 1892. The company, like other railways, was therefore left with only a few months to revise all its existing rates to ensure they did not breach the new, lower, maxima.

While the deadline was extended to 1 January 1893 in response to the railways' representations, they were left with a sense of grievance. Their maximum rates, which had been sanctioned in their enabling Acts and thus formed part of the basis upon which shareholders had invested their money, had been reduced in response to political pressure. Moreover, the railways also felt that they had acted responsibly during the Board of Trade hearings and subsequent parliamentary proceedings, and had sought to reach fair compromises with trading and agricultural interests. Faced with a prospective loss of revenue and also with what they regarded as an unreasonable timetable for revising the multiplicity of special rates – the LNWR alone had 30 million rates to review – the companies decided that they would simply charge their new maxima from 1 January 1893. With hindsight, this was a major political mistake, for it led to an immediate outcry and the appointment of a further select committee. Its recommendations, embodied in legislation in 1894, departed entirely from the spirit of the 1888 Act by effectively denying the companies the right to apply the new maximum rates so recently approved by Parliament. Instead, if a user objected, any charge above the actual level prevailing in 1892 had to be justified before the Railway & Canal Commission. An important test case in 1899 imposed additional restrictions by limiting the extent to which

general increases in costs could be used to support changes in particular charges. The railways therefore emerged from the 1890s with their commercial freedom tightly constrained and with their political influence further eroded by their ill-judged response to the implementation of the 1888 legislation.

This virtual freezing of railway freight charges came at a difficult time. The Baring crisis of 1890 had cut short the economic boom and the first years of Lord Stalbridge's chairmanship were marked by depression. When recovery came in the mid-1890s it was accompanied by the significant price increases which marked the ending of the 'great depression', while inflation was further reinforced by the outbreak of the Boer war in 1899. The LNWR's expenditure on locomotive coal in 1901 was £903,608, compared with £403,405 in 1895: after allowing for traffic growth, the cost of coal per train mile more than doubled. Permanent way materials cost £170,403 in 1895; in 1899 the bill was £276,591. Although such costs fluctuated from year to year, the trend was upwards; more significantly, as food and other consumer prices began to rise, the pressure on wage rates also began to increase.

For the railways, these pressures were increased by the Regulation of Railways Act of 1893, which gave the Board of Trade powers to regulate hours of work, and by the growing strength of railway trades unions. A threatened railway strike in 1907 was averted by the intervention of David Lloyd George, then president of the Board of Trade: while the settlement stopped short of the formal recognition which the unions sought, it resulted in the establishment of the wages conciliation system, which in 1910, the first full year of operation, cost the LNWR an estimated £70,000 for adjustments in hours and gradings. However, this was just a further stage in a long upward trend in labour costs which was the result both of higher wage rates and of the additional staffing needed to satisfy new statutory requirements and meet changes in working practices. Board of Trade statistics which aggregated the returns from the leading English railways show that the average weekly wages of railway employees (including overtime) increased by over 10% between 1896 and 1911, while staff numbers grew by 25%. Direct comparisons are not available, but the LNWR's workforce of around 78,000 in 1899 had increased to 86,500 by 1912, while wages took almost 30% of operating revenue in 1911 compared with just under 27% in

1891. Although the latter change may seem relatively small, the net balance available for distribution to ordinary shareholders in 1911 was only 24% of operating revenue.

A familiar element in increased costs was one which had frequently exercised Sir Richard Moon, local rates and taxes. These continued to be a source of complaint at general meetings, the more so as the growing responsibilities of local authorities and the rising expectations of the communities which they served increased the charges borne by railways. The LNWR, in common with other companies, did what it could to challenge the valuations put on its property – for example, in 1907 it appealed against an increase from £7,460 to £11,000 in the assessment of its line in a parish in the Penrith Union and won a reduction to £6,180. But nothing could be done about rises in rate poundages other than to urge upon shareholders the need to protect the railway's financial interests when they voted in local elections. The LNWR's rating burden increased from £277,631 in 1891 to £643,223 in 1911: while small in relation to total revenue, the growth in this imposition was particularly keenly felt when profit margins were being squeezed and when some rateborne expenditure helped to assist buses and tramways to compete for short-distance passenger traffic.

The late Victorian and Edwardian years therefore proved to be a more hostile climate for railway operation. However, because of the continued growth in traffic and the concern of individual companies or particular areas to develop their potential, there was at first no shortage of new schemes, and total railway mileage in Great Britain grew by 15% between 1891 and 1911, from 17,328 miles to 20,015 miles. While some of this represented expansion into more rural areas, it also reflected continuing competition for trunk traffic, and the LNWR was exposed to rival routes on both the west and east. A major new threat which Lord Stalbridge inherited was the MS&L's extension to London: this scheme was before Parliament in 1891, and though it was defeated that session by the vigorous opposition of the GNR, the Midland, and the LNWR, the MS&L finally obtained its powers in 1893. Under its new title, the Great Central Railway ceremonially opened its line to Marylebone on 9 March 1899, thus finally realising Sir Edward Watkin's ambition of an independent line between Manchester and London. Watkin, who had

retired as chairman of the MS&L in 1894, attended the opening despite ill-health; he died early in the new century, on 13 April 1901.

The London extension was primarily a challenge to the GNR and Midland: although the GCR continued to pursue local expansion in south Lancashire and the Wirral, the immediate competitive effects of the Marylebone line on the LNWR were limited, and, as will be seen, were offset by improved traffic facilities in the Nottingham–Sheffield corridor which had been part of the price of the LNWR's agreement to the first stage of the MS&L's southward extension. However, the GCR's difficulties with its access to London over the Metropolitan Railway led it to forge an alliance with the GWR, which represented a more real threat to LNWR interests. The GWR participated with the GCR in the creation of a new cross-country route via the Woodford–Banbury link, which was opened in 1900. In addition, part of its Princes Risborough branch was incorporated in a new joint line between Northolt and Ashendon in Buckinghamshire which was used both as an alternative approach to Marylebone and to provide a better route between Paddington and Birmingham. The latter was completed in 1910 with the opening of the extension from Ashendon to Aynho junction on the existing line via Oxford, giving the GWR a route from London to the west midlands which was two miles shorter than that from Euston and consequently also strengthened its competitiveness beyond Wolverhampton.

The Aynho cut-off was just one aspect of the GWR's transformation during the 1890s and 1900s, symbolised by the final abandonment of the broad gauge in 1892. While the improved Birmingham service represented the most direct assault on the LNWR's interests, these were also affected by the opening of Fishguard harbour in 1906 as part of the improvement of the GWR route between Britain and Ireland. The new competition via Fishguard was mirrored further north, where the Midland mounted a vigorous challenge for northern Irish traffic. These developments are described in more detail later in this chapter, but the Midland's activities were among several steps which it took to bolster its net revenue in response to GCR competition: for example, it sought to increase its share of the Anglo-Scottish market by upgrading the service over the Settle & Carlisle line 1901. The potential threat to LNWR traffic was reinforced by parliamentary powers which the Midland had obtained in 1898 for a direct line to Bradford which would also have shortened the route from St Pancras to northern Ireland and to Scotland. In the event this did not materialise because the Bradford scheme was largely unrealised. However, in 1902 the Midland improved its approach to Manchester Central by opening a new line from New Mills to Heaton Mersey, resulting in St Pancras–Manchester timings which were better than those from Marylebone and were barely slower than the LNWR route.

The LNWR therefore faced increased competition on many of its main routes during Lord Stalbridge's chairmanship. It was also exposed to additional forms of competition through the development of urban tramway systems and through the opening of the Manchester Ship Canal in 1894. A further portent was the establishment in 1906 of a lorry service for export traffic from the Potteries to Liverpool. But while the emergence of new modes of transport had some effects on the LNWR, its interaction with other railways remained a central concern. As will be seen, the company's relations with two of its leading contemporaries were radically modified during the Edwardian era, and this was part of a more extensive adaptation of the LNWR's internal and external policies which reflected changes not only in the immediate competitive framework but also in the wider financial and political setting.

* * *

The new chairman's period of office began promisingly enough: dividends for 1891 were at 7%, and while this did not quite match the standards of Moon's final two years they suggested that the lean times of the mid-1880s had indeed been left behind. However, economic depression took its toll of receipts in 1892 and 1893 and was reinforced by strikes in the coal and cotton industries. Although train miles were reduced in response and other economies were made, operating expenses remained relatively high, and the ordinary dividend fell to £2 12s 6d for the first half of 1895, the lowest level since 1863. The combination of strong recovery and falling interest rates restored profits in the later 1890s, giving an annual dividend of $7\frac{1}{8}$% from 1896 to 1899, but costs also increased rapidly and a brief pause in the growth in goods receipts in 1901 was sufficient to pull the dividend

back to $5\frac{1}{2}$%. Recovery was slow and spasmodic: though the dividend for Lord Stalbridge's last full year of office, 1910, was $6\frac{5}{8}$%, it was clear that the financial climate had changed. From a 1900 peak of $198\frac{3}{4}$, LNWR consolidated stock fell to $129\frac{1}{4}$ in 1908, and the best price in 1910, $137\frac{7}{8}$, compared very poorly with the 1900 low of $174\frac{3}{4}$.

Some of the pressures on costs and revenue that contributed to this changed performance have already been mentioned. It should also be noted that part of the change in the stock-market valuation of the LNWR was due to a technical factor: the 1890s had been a decade of exceptionally low interest rates, so the return to higher yields after 1899 was reflected in an adjustment in prices. In addition, considerations such as labour unrest and political uncertainty had their effect on market sentiment, while new opportunities overseas in the 1900s also undermined the attractiveness of 'Home Rails' to investors. But the performance and policies of the major British railways also came under increasing criticism which served to undermine their financial standing still further. While all the main-line companies were affected by the changing circumstances, and the LNWR responded better than most, such a deterioration in the position of the country's leading railway undertaking and largest joint-stock company was bound to excite interest.

Accordingly, the LNWR was singled out for attention, and in a series of increasingly acrimonious general meetings its directors and management came under heavy attack. Part of the criticism came from individual shareholders who were concerned at the apparent lack of control over costs, but from 1900 they were reinforced by representatives of some of the investment trusts that had built up holdings in LNWR stock. This group, led by Nathaniel Spens, William Burdett-Coutts MP, and the Hon George Peel (grandson of Sir Robert Peel), backed up their criticism of LNWR policy by drawing on George Paish's comparisons of American and British railway operating procedures which were published in *The Statist* from 1900 onwards. This opposition was formalised through the establishment of a Railway Shareholders' Association, which claimed that unnecessary competition, over-lavish facilities for traders, and poor train loading were the causes of the weak financial performance of British railways, and argued that co-operation between companies and the adoption of

American management information techniques were necessary in order to restore shareholders' earnings. In making this case the Association was able to point to the improved results on the North Eastern Railway, where George Gibb's reforms had included the introduction of ton-mile statistics.

At first the skirmishing was reasonably polite: although one shareholder at the August 1902 general meeting borrowed a Disraelian phrase by attacking the directors as 'extinct volcanoes', Spens preserved the proprieties by moving the vote of thanks to the chairman at the end of the meeting. After an exchange of circulars, however, matters came to a head at the next half-yearly meeting when Burdett-Coutts, seconded by a former director, Lord Brassey, moved an amendment requiring the board to supply information sought by the dissident shareholders. This amendment was defeated only because of the proxies held by the chairman, allowing the Association to claim a moral victory. A renewed attack in 1905 was defeated by a larger proxy vote, but allegations that the company's staff had been used to canvass support for the board led to legal action which went as far as the Court of Appeal before it was determined in 1907 that it was not illegal for the company's resources to be used in this way. By then, however, the main focus of the argument had shifted elsewhere as a result of the Board of Trade's establishment in 1906 of a departmental inquiry into railway accounts and statistics. Here the technical arguments for and against the use of ton-miles and passenger-miles were debated at length and with some heat, but in a delphic judgement the committee concluded that, while there was a strong case for adding ton-mile figures to the existing statutory railway statistics, they would only be effective if the companies supported their use. In the absence of such support the committee did not recommend the imposition of an obligation to compile ton-mile data, so the requirement was not included in the immediate changes made by the Railway Companies (Accounts & Returns) Act of 1911. However, the Board of Trade was given reserve powers to increase the level of statistical reporting, thus leaving an opportunity for the later introduction of ton-mile returns.

By this time the argument about ton-miles had become a largely symbolic debate between the advocates of scientific management and those who stressed the value of experience and traditional rule-of-thumb methods. Within LNWR general meetings the issue had in any case been overtaken by events, since the recovery in dividends which began in 1904 removed much of the criticism of the board and the company's senior management. Spokesmen for the Railway Shareholders' Association – which in 1905 had been weakened by the defection of some supporters, including Lord Brassey – justified their group's position by arguing that its pressure had contributed to the improved performance. Lord Stalbridge and his colleagues countered this by claiming that the initiative had come from within the company and that the improvements in its financial position vindicated the existing management. While in retrospect it can be seen that there was a great deal of justification for the board's position, the personalisation of the dispute and the extent to which it led to the adoption of entrenched positions certainly did not assist the company's standing in the more difficult financial circumstances of the Edwardian age. This was unfortunate, since it obscured the real progress that was being made and the extent to which the LNWR was coming to terms with twentieth-century operating conditions.

The general manager had in fact visited the United States in 1896 to observe railroads there, and Lord Stalbridge claimed that a positive policy of improving train and wagon loads dated from that year. By 1900 shareholders were being told of experiments with larger trucks and more powerful locomotives, and these were followed by innovations such the opening of the Crewe transhipment shed in 1901 to concentrate wagon loads. Lord Stalbridge stated in 1903 that the average loading of wagons handled by the company's staff had improved by 43% since 1895, while the evidence of Carl Grasemann, the southern divisional goods manager, to the Departmental Committee on Railway Accounts & Statistics showed that the LNWR had an extremely well-developed system of reporting by exception to ensure that loadings were kept under constant review. Although mineral traffic, most of which moved in private owners' stock, was more difficult to control, the company's experiments with 20-ton and 15-ton trucks and the steps it took to ensure that its own wagon-handling equipment could cope with larger vehicles gave a positive lead to collieries and to other wagon owners which helped to contribute to the major improvement in freight-train productivity after 1900.

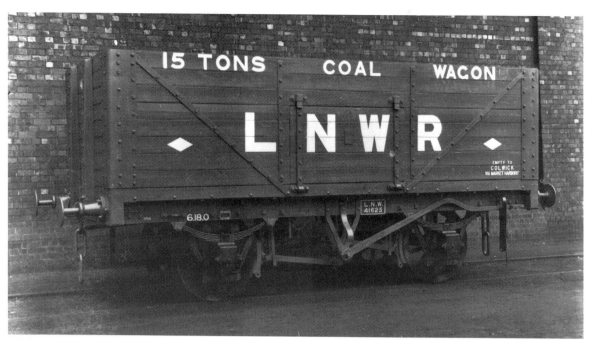

An LNWR 15-ton wagon. *(LNWR Society collection, 9584)*

The LNWR's revenue per goods-train mile increased by 55% between 1900 and 1911, even though receipts per ton remained virtually constant.

* * *

The improvement in methods of handling freight traffic was just one aspect of the LNWR's response to external pressures during Lord Stalbridge's chairmanship. These pressures were also reflected in the way the company's system developed and, more fundamentally, in its dealings with other companies. In the two decades preceding 1891 the route mileage of the LNWR grew by 28%. By contrast, expansion under Lord Stalbridge was a modest 4%: when he retired at the beginning of 1911 the company owned, part-owned, leased, or worked 1,966 miles, only 76 miles more than at the end of 1891. The smallness of this increase reflected both a decrease in LNWR promotional activity – authorised mileage grew by just 43½ miles – and the lack of major absorptions after 1890. Indeed, only two undertakings were incorporated within the company during this period, and both were already worked by the LNWR. One was the Central Wales & Carmarthen Junction, bought for £137,500 with effect from 1 July 1891. The other was the 2½-

mile Harrow & Stanmore Railway, which had been worked by the LNWR from its opening in 1890 and was taken over on 1 July 1899.

Two other companies were acquired jointly with the GWR. The first, the Ludlow & Clee Hill Railway, was a mineral branch from the Shrewsbury & Hereford Railway which had been opened in 1864. The LNWR and GWR had worked the line since 1867 and eventually purchased it in 1892. The second was the Brynmawr & Western Valleys Railway, which obtained powers in 1899 to build a 1⅛-mile connection between the LNWR Abergavenny–Merthyr line at Brynmawr and the terminus of the GWR's Nantyglo branch, by-passing a private mineral railway that the LNWR had leased since 1881. In 1902 the LNWR and GWR jointly took over and exercised the powers of the Brynmawr & Western Valleys company. The line was opened to goods traffic in August 1905 and regular passenger trains commenced on 28 May the following year, mostly provided by the GWR as a continuation of its existing Newport–Nantyglo service.

An earlier addition to LNWR and GWR joint metals had taken place on 15 June 1891, when a 36-chain section of Birkenhead Railway track was brought into use at Rock Ferry to complete a short extension of the Mersey Railway from its previous southern terminus at Green Lane. This offered passengers to and from Liverpool a direct rail interchange as an alternative to the Woodside ferry crossing, and the usefulness of this connection was enhanced in June 1892 when the Mersey Railway was extended from James Street in Liverpool to a low-level island platform under the CLC's Central station. Apart from some short-lived GWR experiments between 1894 and 1900 with through workings (which in 1899 included a Central Low Level–Folkestone portion), the service between Rock Ferry and Liverpool was operated by the Mersey Railway as a self-contained shuttle. In 1903 the entire Mersey system was electrified, including the Birkenhead Railway's portion of the Rock Ferry spur. A further minor increase in joint mileage took place at Hereford, where a curve opened on 2 January 1893 provided a south-facing link between the Gloucester and Newport routes. As the Midland's Brecon line made a triangular junction with the latter, its trains were able to use the new curve to gain access to the joint station at Barr's Court. This allowed the GWR's Barton station, which had been used by the Midland since 1874, to be closed to passenger traffic from the same date. The Midland had a direct interest in another line that was opened later the same year: this was a freight branch in Leicestershire from Narborough to Enderby, which was brought into service on 24 July. Although Narborough was on the LNWR's Nuneaton–Leicester line, the branch was authorised by a Midland Railway Act in 1890 and added to the existing responsibilities of the two companies' joint committee.

Another joint network which saw some extension was the Preston & Wyre system, in which the LNWR had retained a one-third stake after the rationalisation of the interests which it shared with the Lancashire & Yorkshire Railway. On 1 July 1899 a spur was opened at Poulton to permit through running between Blackpool and Fleetwood: this amounted to a reinstatement, since the Blackpool branch had originally formed a triangular junction at Poulton. Powers had been obtained in 1892 to slew the main Fleetwood line from its previous direct course in order to ease the 6-chain radius of the Blackpool junction, and the case for this alteration was forcefully demonstrated the following year when an LNWR Blackpool–Stockport train entered the curve at excessive speed and was derailed with loss of life. Work on the deviation commenced in 1894 and was completed on 28 March 1896; the opening of the south-to-west curve in 1899

restored the previous triangular junction on a new alignment and to a larger scale. A further development in the Fylde, again reflecting Blackpool's importance as a resort, was the building of a 6$\frac{1}{2}$-mile line from Kirkham which avoided the detour via either Poulton or Lytham. This opened on 21 April 1903 and gave access to Blackpool Central station by a junction with the Lytham route at Waterloo Road.

The first new opening on the LNWR proper under Lord Stalbridge was a line from Buxton to the Cromford & High Peak Railway at Dowlow. This was authorised in 1887 and opened for goods traffic on 27 June 1892, together with a new connection westwards from Hindlow to the original route at Harpur Hill. The junctions at Buxton, comprising a direct link with the Stockport line at Fairfield and a chord from Buxton station which was authorised separately in 1891, superseded the existing connection at Whaley Bridge: as a consequence the original C&HP route north of Ladmanlow (including the Bunsall and Shallcross inclines) was abandoned on the same day, apart from a short stub which was retained to serve the Peak Forest Canal at Whaley Bridge. The section between Dowlow and Harpur Hill which was replaced by the new junction lines was also closed on 27 June 1892.

The High Peak Junction scheme had originally been authorised in 1874, but these powers had been allowed to lapse before their revival in 1887. In order to give the LNWR better access to Buxton from the south and to cater for increasing limestone traffic, its 1890 Act had provided for the improvement of further sections of the Cromford line and the building of a new branch from Parsley Hay to Ashbourne on the North Staffordshire system. The upgrading of the C&HP section was undertaken first, allowing the inauguration of a passenger service between Buxton and Parsley Hay on 1 June 1894. Work started on the 13$\frac{1}{2}$-mile Ashbourne line in 1896 and this opened for traffic on 4 August 1899. From 1 October that year the LNWR used the branch to provide a more direct through service between Euston and Buxton than had previously been available via Macclesfield and the Middlewood curve. This new service ran via the Ashby & Nuneaton line and Burton, relying on running powers over the Midland and NSR between Moira west junction and Ashbourne.

Another example of the way in which joint systems and running powers were used to develop the LNWR's network of services was provided to the east

The inaugural train on the Parsley Hay–Ashbourne branch on 4 August 1899, pictured near Hartington. The train is headed by 'Cauliflower' 0-6-0 no 930 and 'Precedent' 2-4-0 no 2004, 'Witch'. *(LNWR Society collection, 9998)*

of the peak district. The price of Euston's agreement to the Annesley extension, the first stage of the MS&L's push southwards, had been the granting of running powers for goods traffic over the new line, supplementing its existing powers via Woodhead. The LNWR was able to reach Annesley when the extension opened in 1892 by using its running powers over the GNR from Saxondale junction. It thus obtained a more direct route to Sheffield from the south, via the GNR & LNWR joint line, and also gained access to the rich coalfield served by the MS&L extension. Although Sheffield was remote from its main system, the LNWR consolidated its position there by opening Nunnery goods station on 1 May 1895, linked with the MS&L main line by 56 chains of its own track. On 2 February 1903 the LNWR expanded its facilities in Sheffield with the opening of the new City goods station, served by an extension of the Nunnery branch.

There were also changes in the arrangements with the MS&L on the other side of the Pennines. On 1

August 1893 a new portion of line between Dukinfield and Stalybridge was brought into use for goods traffic; passenger services commenced on 7 August. This supplemented the LNWR's existing running powers over the MS&L branch from Guide Bridge by creating a separate approach to Stalybridge from the south. An intermediate station, Dukinfield & Ashton, was opened on 2 October 1893, but some LNWR local services continued to use the earlier route via Ashton (Park Parade) until 2 June 1902, when the 1882 connection at Dukinfield was closed to all traffic. In addition to reducing its use of GCR metals, the LNWR provided some relief to the Sheffield company's locomotive fleet – which was put under extreme pressure by the opening of the Marylebone extension – by sharing the working of MSJ&A services from 1899.

Development of the capacity of the LNWR's own system continued during the 1890s, but in contrast with previous decades few new routes were added, and these were mostly minor extensions. Besides the lines already mentioned, additions included the Seaton–Uppingham branch, brought into use for goods on 17 August 1894 and for regular passenger traffic on 1 October; the Norton Green Colliery–Five

Ways mineral line in south Staffordshire, opened on 13 January 1894; the Daventry–Marton junction extension described in Chapter Six, which opened on 1 August 1895; a goods spur from the Watford–Rickmansworth branch to serve the Croxley paper mills, brought into use on 4 May 1899; and a short junction curve, opened on 20 July 1899, which provided a south-facing connection out of the link from the St Helens–Sutton Oak line at Peasley to the Blackbrook branch. In addition, a branch from Weaste to Manchester docks was opened for general goods traffic on 4 November 1895 after serving as a contractor's line during the construction of the Manchester Ship Canal.

The building of the Ship Canal also necessitated diversion of both the west coast main line and the Birkenhead Railway at Acton Grange, south of Warrington, and of the Warrington–Stockport line at Latchford, east of Warrington. These new alignments were brought into use on 9 July 1893 and on 16 July the following year the Birkenhead tracks were extended north from Acton Grange junction across the Canal to Walton new junction. To maintain access to Arpley the old junction at Walton was retained, reached by a steeply-graded loop from the new route

at Acton Grange. Connections were also installed into the Ship Canal railway from Walton old junction and at Latchford.

There was a major addition to the LNWR system in 1900 with the opening of the 13½-mile Leeds new line between Heaton Lodge and Wortley, which completed the improvement of the LNWR route across the Pennines to Leeds via Huddersfield. The opening of the additional Standedge tunnel on 6 August 1894 had removed the last double-track bottleneck between Stalybridge and Heaton Lodge; however, at the latter point the LNWR joined the L&Y main line and relied on running powers as far as Ravensthorpe, where its own metals were regained for the approach to Leeds. Because of the difficulty of widening the Dewsbury line (which included Morley tunnel), and to avoid the congestion and junction conflicts of the L&Y route, the LNWR proposed a separate line from Bradley, just south of the junction at Heaton Lodge, which would run via the Spen Valley

The southern portals of the Standedge tunnels at Diggle. The double-track entrance on the left of the picture is the new tunnel opened in 1894; in the centre is the original 1847 single-line tunnel; and at the extreme right is the second bore which was added in 1871. *(David Joy collection)*

and Gildersome to to rejoin the original route at Wortley. Despite opposition from the L&Y, powers were obtained in 1892 and work started in 1896. The route was difficult, involving heavy gradients and two tunnels, and the eventual cost of over £66,000 per mile was more than three times that of the contemporary Ashbourne–Parsley Hay branch. However, the new line provided an unobstructed entry into Leeds, burrowing under the L&Y just east of Heaton Lodge and terminating in a flying junction with the Dewsbury line at Farnley. A short section at the southern end, as far as Battyeford, was opened for local goods services in September 1899; the rest of the line was opened for goods traffic on 9 July 1900 and passenger services commenced on 1 October.

The Leeds line was the last major scheme completed under Francis Stevenson, chief civil engineer of the company since 1878. Stevenson died on 1 February 1902 aged 75, a few days after completing his half-yearly report on works in progress, and his achievements and personality were warmly acknowledged at the ensuing general meeting. He was succeeded by Edward Bayliss Thornhill, the assistant engineer (new works), whose career with the company had started in 1862. Thornhill retired in 1909, and was succeeded in turn by his assistant for new works, Ernest Trench, who had joined the LNWR in 1893 but spent some time with the Midland Railway before becoming chief engineer of the North London in 1903 and then rejoining the LNWR in 1906.

The first lines opened after Thornhill had taken over were two short branches completed in 1903. One was extremely short-lived: this was a $^1/_2$-mile spur from Willesden to Park Royal to serve the Royal Show, which operated for passengers from 13 June to 4 July, with a slightly longer life for goods traffic. The other was a direct connection between the Tyldesley and Bickershaw lines near Leigh, which opened for goods traffic between Pennington east and west junctions on 2 June 1903. On 1 October this line was brought into use for passenger services between Leigh and Wigan, which also used the formerly freight-only Bickershaw branch between Pennington west and Bickershaw west junctions.

The next openings came in 1908. On 16 March part of the former Penllwyn tramway was reinstated for freight traffic between Ynysddu Lower and a new connection with the Sirhowy line west of Nine Mile

Point, and on 1 July the first portion of the Red Wharf Bay branch in Anglesey was opened, between Holland Arms on the Amlwch line and Pentraeth. The latter was not however the first passenger opening in north Wales under Lord Stalbridge: on 1 January 1892 the LNWR had introduced a limited service between Mold and Coed Talon and from 15 November 1897 this was extended over the joint Wrexham & Minera Extension Railway to the GWR station at Brymbo. The Prestatyn–Dyserth freight branch also acquired a passenger service on 28 August 1905, operated by the first of the LNWR's new steam railcars. An extension of this branch to Newmarket was authorised the same year under light railway procedures, but the extension was not completed.

The remainder of the 6$^1/_2$-mile Red Wharf Bay branch was brought into service on 24 May 1909. This was the second passenger opening that month: on 1 May local trains had begun to use the Styal loop between Wilmslow and Longsight, which had been authorised as long ago as 1898. In addition to opening up a new area for Manchester commuting traffic, the Styal line, which was used by goods trains from 8 February 1909, also relieved the main Manchester–Crewe line without incurring the heavy costs of providing additional tracks through Stockport. As part of the programme of increasing capacity on the southern approaches to Manchester further widening was carried out south of London Road station and a subsidiary terminal at Mayfield was opened on 1 April 1910.

The lines described above were not, however, the only additions to the LNWR's authorised mileage between 1891 and 1911. Several minor schemes were allowed to lapse and the same fate befell a major project authorised in 1898 which would have completely transformed operation of the Lancaster & Carlisle route. This was an improvement to the main line over Shap, involving an 8$^1/_2$-mile deviation between Tebay and Shap station and a summit tunnel. Another important scheme, to give extra capacity on the Euston suburban lines, was also postponed and eventually substantially modified after its authorisation in 1907: this project will be described later.

* * *

This relatively modest expansion of the network after 1891 was partly a result of earlier progress: the

A heavy northbound goods train posed on Shap incline behind 'A' class compound 0-8-0 no 2534, which was built in 1895. The deviation line authorised in 1898 would have run close to the existing route, but with easier gradients and a summit tunnel. *(LNWR Society collection, 9338)*

absorptions and extensions under Moon had given the LNWR virtually complete coverage of its own territory and left little scope for viable expansion. It also reflected the fact that new technologies were now available – tramways, and, as the new century progressed, motor buses and lorries – so that the case for extensions into new suburban or rural areas became less compelling. The LNWR itself began to operate motor buses in 1905, establishing a new route between Connah's Quay and Mold and replacing the horse bus between Holywell town and its station with a motor vehicle. The latter joined a steam lorry which went into service on the route after being exhibited at the Royal Agricultural Show at Park Royal. In 1906 buses were introduced between Watford and Croxley Green and between Watford and Harrow via Bushey, and services were subsequently developed further both in north Wales and in the outer London suburbs. However, the introduction of the Croxley Green and Holywell road services was followed in 1907 by parliamentary powers for the construction of new branch lines, so it is clear that the LNWR saw buses as having a role in establishing a potential railway route and not simply as an alternative. Broader explanations have therefore to be sought for the limited growth in route mileage during this period, particularly after 1900.

One major factor was a change in the terms in which the company could raise money. Postponement of capital expenditure in the face of decreased profits or adverse conditions in the financial markets was, of course, not new: for example, construction of the Ashbourne & Buxton did not begin until 1895, five years after authorisation, while the delays in implementing powers for the Buxton junction and the Styal loop have already been mentioned. But with shareholders sensitive to the effects of additional capital expenditure on their dividends and the City actively hostile to new railway issues from 1900 onwards, the board was increasingly reluctant to raise capital on a large scale, so that the funds that were available were largely earmarked for essential improvements to the existing system. After a successful conversion of existing debenture stock in 1893 the only major new issue placed by the LNWR was £4·8m of 4% preference stock which was raised in two tranches in 1902 and 1908. The fact that this capital was raised as preference rather than ordinary stock was itself significant, since the board had previously dismissed arguments from Nathaniel Spens and others that the company would be able to raise funds more cheaply by increasing the preferred element in its stock. The board had instead contended that it would not be in the interests of ordinary shareholders to increase prior charges. A further issue of ordinary stock had been approved at the February 1901 general meeting, so the decision a year later to substitute preference stock was an indication of how the market had turned. While an easing of interest rates in 1908 helped the placing of the second block of new capital, the large premiums that had been a feature of LNWR issues became a thing of the past, and debentures issues in 1910 and 1911 realised less than their par value.

With new funds more difficult to raise, capital expenditure fell sharply from its 1900 peak of £1·65m. There was a slight recovery in 1907, but by the end of the decade the LNWR was spending less than £400,000 annually on capital account. Moreover, the expenditure that was undertaken was increasingly financed on a deficit basis and covered by other balances, including the new device of a general reserve account, which was opened in 1906 and stood at £350,000 by the end of 1910. The capital deficit increased from £1·27m in 1891 to £3·72m at the end of 1910, and before the 1908 stock issue it reached £3·86m.

Investment schemes could only proceed cautiously in such straitened conditions, and priority had to be given to essential improvements and to providing rolling stock to keep abreast of traffic growth. Circumstances therefore limited the scope for major new projects: for example, while the Shap deviation would have given substantial operating benefits, it was promoted in the context of the Midland's proposed improvements in west Yorkshire, which would have strengthened the competition for Anglo-Scottish traffic. With the Midland slow to implement its plans and the operational case for the LNWR deviation weakened by improvements in motive power, there was no pressing justification to begin work when capital was more urgently needed to remove bottlenecks elsewhere. A particular problem that required immediate attention was at Atherstone, where Warwickshire County Council succeeded in November 1898 in obtaining an injunction to compel compliance with a provision in the 1845 Railway Clauses Consolidation Act that trains should not exceed 4 mph at level crossings over turnpike roads. This affected some 149 trains daily in winter and 160

in summer, and extended express journey times by about 5 minutes. The LNWR at first considered diverting the main line away from Atherstone in retaliation, but the problem was ultimately resolved by building a bridge.

Major schemes that were undertaken included the widening of sections of the Chester & Holyhead and Trent Valley routes, the reconstruction of the entire Crewe layout between 1896 and 1906, including the provision of separate goods lines, and the gradual improvement of Euston and its approaches. As part of the Crewe improvements an electrically-operated signalling installation was designed by Webb and the company's signal engineer, A M Thompson, and the 'Crewe system' was also applied in the Euston scheme and at Manchester London Road. An important marine project was the provision of a third dock at Garston, primarily for coal shipments, together with a tidal lock to give better access for larger vessels. This scheme had been under consideration since the 1880s but was not authorised until 1902. Work started in 1904 and at the dock's ceremonial opening on 24 February 1909 it was named after the chairman.

Projects such as these were vital for the development of the LNWR's existing business and were therefore given priority in the company's capital expenditure programmes. But even if funds had been more readily available other pressures were at work which militated against a more expansionary policy. One of the arguments of the Railway Shareholders' Association and other critics of British railway performance was that needless competition contributed to poor results by diluting traffic flows and encouraging over-provision of services and facilities. With charges virtually fixed and with rising wages putting margins under pressure, this argument began to carry increasing weight, while public attitudes started to change as traders and politicians came to appreciate that competition was not necessarily in the interests of passengers and traders if it perpetuated high operating costs. In 1899 Parliament gave approval for the working union of the London, Chatham & Dover and South Eastern railways, and this signalled the start of a renewed move towards closer arrangements between companies. Lord Stalbridge, as chairman of the Railway Companies' Association from 1894 to 1900, was well placed to assess this changing climate of opinion, and the LNWR's pivotal place in the railway network ensured that his board colleagues

This official photograph looking north towards Crewe station shows the new Crewe south junction signal box shortly after the commissioning of the electrically-operated signalling system in 1906. Despite the modernity of its equipment, its design perpetuated much of the outline of the classic large LNWR signal box. *(National Railway Museum, CR A492)*

were also keenly aware of the issues involved. In the face of renewed competition from the Midland Railway, which was itself responding to the effects of the GCR line to Marylebone, and of the actual and potential threats posed by the GWR cut-offs, the issue for the LNWR was how best to adapt to the altered situation.

The first step was in a not-unexpected direction. Although the 1872 attempt to amalgamate with the L&Y had been blocked in Parliament, the two companies had continued the close working relationship which was dictated by the geography of their systems and by their joint interests, and this was reflected in a series of pooling arrangements. However, the limited period of each agreement meant that competition was not entirely eliminated, since as the expiry date approached each company sought to attract more traffic in order to gain a better future share of pooled

receipts. With the 1894 agreement due to expire at the end of 1904 a more radical approach was therefore adopted. The new document was drawn up to run for fifty years and contained not only the usual pooling clauses but also provisions to ensure comprehensive co-operation in traffic handling and routing and the elimination of competitive canvassing for goods business. The new agreement came into force at the beginning of 1905 and immediately began to generate savings: cartage resources were shared in Liverpool and elsewhere and traffic was sent by the most direct route rather than by that which gave the greatest mileage advantage to the receiving company. For example, consignments for Lancaster received by the L&Y in Liverpool were simply handed to the LNWR for through transit instead of being forwarded to Preston for transhipment there.

The railway companies were keen to emphasise that the public benefited from such rationalisation: certainly, the results of the closer working relationship between the LNWR and L&Y were soon demonstrated in additional facilities as well as in reduced goods transit times and operating savings. Interavailability of tickets was introduced – a great boon for passengers in view of the complex network of alternative routes in Lancashire and west Yorkshire – and new through carriage workings were established, such as those between east Lancashire and Euston via Manchester Victoria. Opportunities were also taken to adapt existing passenger services if this offered advantages: for example, after 1904 the direct L&Y lines to and from Preston were increasingly preferred to the LNWR routes via Standish for the Manchester and Liverpool portions of Anglo-Scottish trains.

By the end of 1905 there were already suggestions that the principles that had been established on the east-west axis might be applied to the much larger tract of territory between London and Carlisle where the LNWR's lines interlaced and overlapped with those of the Midland. Initially, the situation seemed less promising: whereas the L&Y and LNWR had a tradition of co-operation, much more was at stake in the rivalry with the Midland. The brief revival of racing to Edinburgh in 1901, though more of a contest between the Midland and the east coast route, was a reminder of the threat posed to the LNWR's Carlisle and Scottish traffic, while the New Mills cut-off and the development of the port of Heysham directly increased the Midland's competitiveness on the routes to Manchester and to northern Ireland. While the LNWR had also placed pressure on the Midland with measures such as the Ashbourne–Buxton line and the use of its freight running powers over the Great Central, as more critical attitudes emerged the railway press and shareholders became quick to decry anything that suggested a more aggressive policy. For example, the *Railway Times* in 1904 accused the LNWR of deliberately aggravating wasteful competition by accelerating its Euston–Manchester service, and the board's claim that the improvements were

justified met with some scepticism at general meetings.

Against this background, and with the prospect of stronger competition on its other flank from the improved GWR route to Birmingham and the Mersey, the LNWR was in a potentially difficult position; equally, however, the Midland was exposed to the GCR and to shareholder pressure that had not been allayed by a stock conversion operation in 1897. The appointment of Guy Granet, the former secretary of the Railway Companies' Association, as assistant general manager of the Midland in 1905 and then as general manager in 1906 brought a new outlook to the conduct of that company's policy, and the need for review was emphasised in 1907 when the GCR and GNR reached agreement for a working union that was little short of amalgamation. This was rejected by the Railway & Canal Commission in 1908, but the two companies then reached terms with one of the major objectors, the Great Eastern Railway. With some encouragement from the Board of Trade, a Bill was prepared for the 1909 session to authorise a wider working union between the 'three Greats', as the consortium became known.

The Midland had been offered an opportunity to join the GCR and GNR grouping; however, although exclusion from such a coalition would have posed a substantial competitive threat to his company, Granet appears to have concluded that its interests would be better secured by looking to the west. By July 1908 agreement was reached between the Midland and LNWR for the comprehensive pooling of competitive traffic for at least a hundred years. The Lancashire and Yorkshire area was initially excluded because of difficulty in reconciling the terms of the new agreement with the 1904 arrangements, but the L&Y threatened to challenge the validity of the Midland and LNWR scheme. As a result an agreement was established between all three companies from 1 January 1909, again for a minimum period of a hundred years. Although less far-reaching than the 'three Greats' proposal, the 1908 and 1909 documents both included provision for future recourse to Parliament to seek a fuller partnership, and, like the 1904 agreement, laid the foundation for close working arrangements between the participants. A key incentive for this was the provision that only 20% of pooled receipts should be retained by each company for expenses; informed commentators suggested that this was basic to the success of the agreements because the percentage was too small to offer any inducement to work traffic if it could be handled more cheaply by a partner.

So far as the Midland and LNWR were concerned, the first results of the new agreement were apparent by the end of the summer of 1908. Some overlapping branch passenger services in Leicestershire were eliminated and a start was made in adjusting exchange points for through goods traffic. This was followed by arrangements for the London booking offices of each company to sell the other's tickets. By the following summer tickets were widely interavailable on the LNWR, L&Y, and Midland systems, including the sea routes to Belfast, and from October 1909 the separate Midland and LNWR sleeping car services between London and Stranraer were combined, operating from St Pancras in the winter of 1909 and then transferring to the Euston route a year later. As with the earlier LNWR/L&Y agreement, cartage services were shared and despatches rationalised, and other steps were taken to reduce costs and offer more through trains. These included a new service from Leamington to Nottingham and through coaches from L&Y stations in Yorkshire to St Pancras. Examples of savings were the withdrawal of the Carlisle–London meat train operated by the Midland in competition with the LNWR and the routing of Heysham–Carnforth iron ore traffic via Hest Bank instead of the circuitous Midland route via Wennington. Further consequences were the sharing of goods depot and booking office facilities, entailing the transfer of employees between companies in some places. Although the railway unions were concerned at the staffing implications and some traders felt aggrieved because of reduced facilities, the beneficial effects of the 1908 and 1909 agreements were soon widely recognised: the *Railway Times* reported on 1 January 1910 that the Midland and LNWR had saved £400,000 in the first six months of the previous year, largely as a result of the agreement, while receipts and profits per train mile on the LNWR began a renewed upward trend in 1909 despite the impact of higher wages after the 1907 dispute.

Net revenue also benefited from the results of another agreement. The North London Railway had been badly affected by tramway competition and the reduction in its dividend from $7\frac{1}{2}\%$ in 1899 to $3\frac{1}{2}\%$ in 1908 had a significant financial impact on the LNWR, which owned 60% of its ordinary stock. By an agree-ment confirmed by the boards of the two companies in December 1908 and effective from 1 February 1909, most senior officers of the North London were retired, their places being taken by their LNWR equivalents. The LNWR also took over responsibility for supplying rolling stock and permanent way materials. Although the NLR remained nominally independent, managerially and operationally it became in effect part of the LNWR. By 1910 costs had been reduced by 14% from the 1908 levels and the NLR was able to pay a 5% dividend.

By the time Lord Stalbridge retired, therefore, the value of working agreements had been demonstrated on the LNWR in two separate ways. The arrange-ments with the L&Y and Midland had shown that the pooling of competitive traffic could significantly reduce costs without damaging facilities for the public: indeed, the companies could reasonably claim that they had enhanced rather than diminished their services. The North London agreement reflected a different situation: the difficulties faced by a purely urban railway in remaining viable in the face of tramway competition. The effective absorption of the NLR by its majority shareholder not only showed that worthwhile economies of scale could be achieved; it also gave the smaller company access to the resources that were needed to ensure its development. In helping to secure wider political and public acceptance of the case for closer working arrangements between railway companies, these examples were reinforced by the results of similar agreements between the major Scottish railways and between the GWR and LSWR. Despite this, the proposal which had encour-aged the *rapprochement* between the Midland and the LNWR, the 'three Greats' Bill, failed in Parliament in 1909 because of government vacillation, one outcome of which was the appointment that year of the Board of Trade Committee on Railway Agreements & Amalgamations, with Ernest Moon as one of its members. By the time the committee took evidence Sir Frederick Harrison, who had negotiated the agree-ments with the L&Y and Midland, had retired as general manager and joined the LNWR board, so the company's evidence was given by his successor, Frank Ree. Both Ree and Granet made clear that their companies, together with the L&Y, had already accepted the concept of a natural territorial unit and that amalgamation was the logical outcome. Their position was shared by most of the other railway witnesses and was generally endorsed by the committee. Its report largely laid the basis for the 1923 grouping, just as the 1909 agreement substantially defined the English and Welsh boundaries of the London Midland & Scottish Railway.

* * *

One of the benefits claimed for the new agreements was the freeing of management time from intercompany rivalry and negotiation, allowing more attention to be devoted to improving efficiency and developing traffic potential within each system. As has been seen, the importance of improving productivity was clearly recognised by the LNWR board and there were frequent references to new techniques and to labour-saving devices in Lord Stalbridge's speeches to general meetings. In his address to shareholders on 16 February 1906 he also stressed the importance of investing in advertising as a means of

developing traffic. While this reflected the changing commercial atmosphere of that era, it was perhaps also a mark of the difference between the new chairman and his more austere predecessor that the LNWR's advertising and public relations efforts made great strides under Lord Stalbridge. In addition to superb pictorial posters, items such as postcards, calendars, lantern slides, and bookmarks began to appear to supplement tourist guides and other more traditional publications as means of encouraging travel. The company also mounted displays at the national and international exhibitions that were a feature of the age. These measures were backed up by a flow of information to the railway and daily press which kept the LNWR's name before the public and has allowed some more obscure facts and figures to survive. For example, the *Railway Engineer* reported in 1899 that around 20,000 bicycles were carried by train services out of Euston in the three summer months, while an article on the LNWR's Grand National excursions in the *Railway Times* of 25 March 1911 revealed that 967,416 meals were served in the company's restaurant cars during 1910.

Although publicity could influence the market for LNWR services, its effectiveness depended ulti-

An example of LNWR publicity: this postcard of Webb 'Greater Britain' class 2-2-2-2 compound no 2054 'Queen Empress' in its Jubilee livery is overprinted with particulars of its visit to the United States in 1893.

Sent to the Chicago Exhibition in 1893 where it gained the gold medal for excellence of workmanship and subsequently ran a L. & N.W. train from Chicago to New York, the only British train ever run in America. Specially painted white and with the Royal Arms in honor of Queen Victoria's Diamond Jubilee in 1897 Has run 473,759 miles to end of Sept. 1904

COMPOUND PASSENGER ENGINE "QUEEN EMPRESS". BUILT 1893. DRIVING WHEELS 7 FT. DIAMETER.

A twelve-wheeled clerestory dining car, built at Wolverton for West Coast Joint Stock service in 1892. *(LNWR Society collection, 2041)*

mately on the quality of the product and here again there was considerable progress under Lord Stalbridge. While this was part of a general trend on Britain's railways as customers became more demanding and the means were developed to meet these demands, the LNWR made its own contribution to this improvement, although in terms of the speed of its principal passenger trains the LNWR probably followed rather than led. This was not due simply to conservatism or to the fact that on many of its routes the LNWR had an advantage in distance which made it unnecessary to match the performance of its competitors: it also reflected the density of traffic on the main line out of Euston, which made it difficult to accelerate individual trains without some sacrifice of total line capacity.

On one of the main competitive routes, that between London and Scotland, speed was indeed only intermittently a problem. The racing to Edinburgh in 1888 had been concluded by an understanding that services would observe an 8½-hour timing between the two capitals. However, the opening of the Forth bridge in 1890 gave the east coast companies a shorter route to Aberdeen and in 1894 they accelerated their 8 pm night express to reach the latter point in 11 hours 35 minutes. The following year the west coast partners responded by improving their service with effect from 1 July, which provoked further acceleration of the Kings Cross service and led to a flurry of racing that gave an outlet for the press's 'silly season' energies. G P Neele clearly took a jaundiced view of these activities – he saw little point in rushing overnight

passengers to arrive in Aberdeen at an early hour in the morning – but as he was on the point of retiring as superintendent of the line the issue became one for his successor. While the matter was eventually resolved by an agreement that the east coast service would run to Aberdeen in 35 minutes less than the LNWR and Caledonian, the latter emerged as effective victors and followed the active competition with a run at an end-to-end average speed of 63·3 mph for the 540 miles from Euston to Aberdeen. Despite this demonstration of what could be achieved, a revision of Anglo-Scottish daytime schedules in 1896 set the London–Edinburgh minimum at 8¼ hours. This remained the agreed fastest timing for the rest of the pre-war period, except during a brief renewal of competition in 1901 which was provoked by the acceleration of the service between Edinburgh and St Pancras.

Although Anglo-Scottish timings in general remained fairly leisurely, other improvements were made in the service. The 2 pm west coast train had acquired a dining car in 1891 and in July 1893 its Glasgow portion was transformed by the introduction of a rake of new west coast joint stock corridor coaches, built at Wolverton under Charles Park. These coaches set a new standard for LNWR express services and as more were brought into service the Edinburgh portion of what became know as 'the

Wolverton works: this view from 1894 shows the carriage body shop. *(LNWR Society collection, 833)*

Corridor' was re-equipped. The new stock also spread to other Anglo-Scottish circuits, including trains between Lancashire and Scotland.

This new west coast stock was distinguished by being first and third class only: in May 1893 second class was withdrawn from Anglo-Scottish services, a step that had become inevitable when the Caledonian Railway joined the increasing number of companies that had followed the Midland's example in abolishing second-class bookings. Lord Stalbridge, however, followed Sir Richard Moon in doggedly defending its retention by the LNWR, although the amount of second-class seating was reduced and new stock was built with conversion in mind. In 1897 second-class fares were lowered to 1·1d per mile on most of the system: while this succeeded in reversing the gradual decline in patronage for a short time, the change merely gave further ammunition to those who argued that the continued provision of second-class accommodation was uneconomical. The chairman justified the policy in terms of public demand for an intermediate class, and suggested a figure of 2 million

passengers per annum as the threshold for maintaining second class. However, the fact that it was abolished on the LNWR on all but a few suburban services soon after Lord Stalbridge retired, when annual patronage was still in excess of 3 million passengers, implies that the long survival of the second class owed more to his personal views than to commercial logic. West coast services apart, therefore, Wolverton continued to provide three classes in the new sets that were turned out under Park's superintendence for the principal services. Besides the widespread use of corridor connections and the standardisation of bogies in place of radial trucks – including the introduction of three-axle bogies for dining saloons, sleeping carriages, and some other special stock – design developments included the final elimination in 1892 of the non-automatic brake, the adoption in 1896 of Stone's electric train lighting system, and the installation of communication cords as required by the Board of Trade. Park also oversaw the construction of a new royal train set: this entered service in 1903 and included saloon carriages which were available for public charter when not required for state duties.

When Park retired at the end of April 1910 his

successor, Henry Douglas Earl, inherited an express coaching fleet which had largely been transformed. This was matched by radical changes in the locomotive stud and Earl's later career was affected by the steps that were taken to achieve this. He had been works manager at Crewe from 1888 to 1903 and might have had some expectation of succeeding Webb as locomotive superintendent; instead, he was appointed wagon superintendent at Earlestown and served there until moving to the Wolverton post. His brother-in-law George Whale took over responsibility for locomotive matters in succession to Webb, with the title of chief mechanical engineer. Although this designation had been increasingly applied to his predecessor, Whale's was the first appointment to this title.

Most of Whale's previous service had been in the outdoor department of the locomotive superintendency; he was running superintendent for the northern division from 1877 to 1899 and from then until 1903 had overall responsibility for running matters under Webb. The appointment of an outdoor rather than a works man to succeed Webb was a mark of the increasing frustration being felt by the board and the general and traffic management of the company with the locomotive department; it also took place in circumstances which were little short of tragic in their intermingling of Webb's professional and personal decline.

There was no hint of this when Stalbridge took over at Euston. Webb was by then well into his stride in building locomotives that were economical both in first cost and operation and were effective with the traffic of the day. The 'Teutonic' class of 1889 had

'Jubilee' class 4-4-0 locos under construction at Crewe in 1899, with no 1908, 'Royal George', nearest the camera. *(National Railway Museum, CR MA247)*

taken his compound express passenger design to new levels of performance, while the 0-8-0 engines introduced in 1893 contributed significantly towards improved freight train loadings. However, his attempt to design compound passenger locomotives of still greater capacity, the large-boilered 'Greater Britain' and 'John Hicks' classes of 1891 and 1894, was not the success that had been hoped, and Webb was on surer ground with his contemporary rebuilding of earlier 2-4-0s to produce the 'Jumbos', an outstandingly workmanlike contribution to the fleet. New classes of passenger and goods tank engines, also resting on earlier successful designs, similarly added to the effectiveness of the locomotive stock during the 1890s.

The real gap was in express locomotives capable of handling the heavier weights of the newer coaching stock at speeds which matched the traffic department's aspirations. Webb's next essay at meeting this need was the production of two four-cylinder 4-4-0s in 1897, one a compound, the other single-expansion. The compound variant became the prototype for his new 'Jubilee' class and a further eighteen were produced in 1899 and 1900; an enlarged version, the 'Alfred the Great' class, appeared in the latter year and went into production in 1901. Two further related designs followed: a four-cylinder 0-8-0 goods compound; and a 4-6-0 mixed traffic class which did not appear until 1903.

While the design principles embodied in these compounds produced an extremely successful heavy freight locomotive, the passenger classes once more failed to match expectations. In October 1901 the general manager signalled his disquiet with Crewe's contemporary output by ruling that passenger trains with the equivalent of more than seventeen six-wheeled vehicles (an eight-wheeled bogie coach was counted as $1\frac{1}{2}$) were to be doubled-headed. Webb was by then aged 65 and his increasingly erratic personality was undoubtedly causing difficulties both for management and his subordinates. Rumours of his impending retirement began to circulate the following year and though it was agreed that he would step down on 1 July 1903 his mental health finally collapsed in May of that year. Whale had already been appointed to succeed him and effectively took over immediately. Webb died in 1906 and by then was so discredited that his death attracted little recognition from the company or his profession. But, as Brian Reed has shown, his

achievements were far greater than his later contemporaries acknowledged, while the relative failure of his last passenger designs was allowed to overshadow his commitment to the LNWR and to Crewe. Webb's bequests to municipal and railway charities reflected a generosity of spirit which unfortunately was not reciprocated by his former employers and senior colleagues.

The appointment of Whale rather than Earl was a sign that the board's priorities lay with locomotive running rather than with production; although Whale more than amply fulfilled the remit he was given, he was himself 60 when he succeeded to Webb's post and he too paid a price in terms of his health, dying within a year of his retiral in 1909. Whale's successor, C J Bowen Cooke, came from a similar background: he had become southern divisional superintendent under Whale in 1899 and moved to Crewe to replace him as running superintendent in 1903. Earl's successor as works manager was Arthur Trevithick, one of Francis Trevithick's sons. Trevithick too had a running background but had been assistant works manager since 1899; like his predecessor, he was passed over when the chief mechanical engineer's post became vacant and he followed in Earl's footsteps by taking over the wagon superintendency when Earl moved to Wolverton in 1910.

Whale's immediate task was to fill the demand for a reliable first-rank express locomotive; though he completed some of Webb's orders, including the production run of the 4-6-0 compounds, his thoughts were conditioned by his running experience and he selected the 'Jumbos', rather than the later compounds, as the basis for development. Within a matter of months the first of a new design of 4-4-0 single-expansion engines was in service, borrowing the name 'Precursor' from an earlier Webb class. These production of these locomotives, which quickly

Whale 'Precursor' class 4-4-0 no 412 'Marquis' at Manchester London Road with a southbound express. This locomotive, built in 1904, was the LNWR participant in the 1909 exchange with the Great Northern Railway. *(LNWR Society collection, 1085)*

This commercial postcard shows a 'Benbow' class 4-4-0 compound, rebuilt by Whale from Webb's 'Alfred the Great' class, heading a westbound train over Saddleworth viaduct. The Delph branch trails in from the left of the picture. *(Mitchell Library: Langmuir collection)*

became the mainstay of the LNWR's principal passenger workings, was accompanied by the scrapping of earlier Webb compounds; while the rapidity of the transition caused problems both in the organisation of work at Crewe and in providing motive power during the summer of 1904, it was evidence of the urgency to stamp a fresh mark on the locomotive department.

Whale followed the 'Precursors' with a 4-4-2 tank derivative and a 4-6-0 class, the 'Experiments', introduced in 1905. In their initial form the latter did not have the success of the 'Precursors' but they provided the basis for a mixed-traffic 4-6-0 which was produced in considerable numbers from 1906 onwards. The remainder of Whale's output consisted of rebuilds of Webb designs, including the 'Benbows' (a modification of the 'Alfred the Great' 4-4-0s) large and small boilered 2-8-0 compounds converted from 0-8-0s, and single-expansion conversions which retained the 0-8-0 wheelbase.

With the most pressing gaps filled by his prede-

Great Northern 4-4-2 no 1449 at Euston in June 1909, awaiting departure on the 10 am to Glasgow during the 1909 locomotive exchange. *(LNWR Society collection, 9194)*

cessor, Bowen Cooke was able to adopt a more studied approach to his responsibilities and among his first actions in 1909 was the arrangement of locomotive exchanges with the GNR, Caledonian, and LB&SC. This was followed by a further exchange in 1910, instigated by the GWR. These exchanges demonstrated to Cooke that there was further scope for improvement in LNWR locomotive practice and his particular contribution was the adoption of superheating. Like Webb in 1897, Bowen Cooke produced two 4-4-0s for comparative trials; these appeared in July 1910, appropriately named after the new king and his consort. Nine more of the non-superheated 'Queen Mary' version were built in 1910 but were later converted to conform with the superheated variant which went into production in 1911. One of the new 'King George V' class, 'Coronation', was supposedly the 5,000th engine to be built at Crewe and was earmarked to haul the royal train as part of the coronation celebrations. The other major new class introduced under Lord Stalbridge was a 4-6-2 tank, the only Pacific design on the LNWR: this was a development of the successful 'Precursor' tanks, but the extra pair of wheels gave lower axle weights and hence greater availability. The initial build in 1910 was non-

'Jubilee' compound 4-4-0 no 1918 'Renown' awaiting departure from Broad Street station in London on the evening of 1 February 1910 with the inaugural 5.25 pm down 'City to City' departure for Birmingham and Wolverhampton. *(LCGB Ken Nunn collection, 465)*

superheated but from 1911 onwards a superheated version was produced. Again, the earlier designs were later converted.

In retrospect it can be argued that LNWR locomotive progress during this period did not match the standards that were achieved on some other lines; Brian Reed's assessment was also that the high degree of management efficiency and cost control that had been built up at Crewe by Webb was lost under his successors. Nevertheless, Whale and Bowen Cooke met the task that was set them: they provided a range of fast and capable express and mixed-traffic designs which eliminated much of the double-heading which had dogged Webb's final years and enabled the traffic department to respond with confidence to passengers' increasing expectations.

On the principal internal services the first moves towards acceleration had been taken in 1902, when a 2 hour 5 minute schedule was established for the Birmingham service and 3¾-hour and 3 hour 55 minute timings were offered to Manchester and Liverpool respectively. In August 1902 a solitary 2-hour timing appeared on the Birmingham route, and in May 1904 3½-hour Manchester and 3¾-hour Liverpool schedules were introduced. In March 1905,

with new motive power in good supply, there was a further general acceleration of the main services, including the introduction of three up and four down Birmingham expresses with 2-hour schedules. GWR competition was of course a factor in the improvement of the west midlands services: a 2 hour 25 minute Paddington–Snow Hill express had been introduced in 1899 despite the penalty of the longer route via Oxford. With the opening of the Aynho cut-off imminent the LNWR decided in 1910 to use its new relationship with the North London Railway to supplement the Euston service with a morning express from Wolverhampton to Broad Street, returning in the evening. These 'City to City' expresses offered a 2¼-hour New Street–Broad Street journey and were aimed specifically at the business market: in addition to dining cars they offered an on-board typing service, a facility which was extended to one of the Euston services a few months later.

Apart from the Anglo-Scottish trains, the other

The Denny-built *Anglia* on sea trials in the Clyde prior to joining the LNWR fleet in 1902. *(University of Glasgow archives)*

express services operated out of Euston were those in connection with the shipping routes to Ireland and North America. Here too competition played a part and although the characteristics of the Irish Sea and transatlantic crossings were very different their fortunes became closely entangled for a while. The underlying position on the short sea route to Dublin was unchanged by the award of a fresh mail contract to the City of Dublin Steam Packet Company's Holyhead–Kingstown sailings in 1895, to run for twenty years from 1 April 1897. However, the completion of the City of Dublin Junction line from Westland Row to Amiens Street on 1 May 1891 had placed the convenience of the through connections between Kingstown and other parts of Ireland on a par with those offered by the North Wall route. Furthermore, as part of its tender the City of Dublin company had undertaken to provide an accelerated service and brought the first of four new twin-screw steamers on to the route in 1897. The LNWR had

offered a half-hour acceleration of the Euston–Holyhead connection for its part of the new mail contract and had already added dining facilities to the daytime 'Irish Mail' in 1895. In order to maintain the attractiveness of its own steamer service the LNWR also commissioned a comparable fleet of twin-screw vessels from the Denny yard. The first of these, the *Cambria*, went into service in 1897; the launch of the *Anglia* and *Hibernia* in 1900 and the *Scotia* in 1902 completed both the modernisation and the revival of the names of the first quartet of railway steamers on the Holyhead route.

Connecting rail services for the North Wall sailings were also improved. The night service was the first to be accelerated, from 1 May 1897, to give a Euston departure at 10.15 pm instead of the previous 6.30 pm, but arriving at Dublin only $1\frac{1}{2}$ hours later than previously, at 7.30 am local time. There were similar improvements to the up night service and in July 1898 the down and up day services were accelerated by $1\frac{1}{2}$ hours and 1 hour respectively. Further accelerations followed and by 1908 the 11 am departure from North Wall was giving a 7.55 pm arrival at Euston. With the connecting trains for the LNWR day and night steamers each scheduled to give a later departure from Euston than the 'Irish Mail' there were thus four express services daily between London and Dublin which offered a high standard of passenger amenity on both the rail and sea portions of the journey. In addition the LNWR improved connections with other principal points on its network.

In 1907 Captain Binney, the LNWR's marine superintendent, retired because of ill-health and was replaced by Commander G E Holland, who had previously served with the Royal Indian Marine. This naval background perhaps stood him in good stead the year after his appointment, for the rivalry with the CDSPC took on a new and more direct form. Ostensibly in response to increased harbour dues at Dublin, the LNWR decided to operate its daytime service to and from Kingstown with effect from 1 April 1908; this provoked legal action by the City of Dublin company, which claimed that under the terms of the mail contract its steamers had exclusive right to the facilities at Carlisle Pier, Kingstown. Although the LNWR won the case and was awarded costs, the CDSPC then resorted to physical obstruction, using its vessels to hinder access by the railway steamers. The LNWR was itself forced to go to law, and eventually succeeded in restraining the Steam Packet company, though as usual with issues relating to the Holyhead service there was strong Irish political interest, coupled in this case with concern by the Dublin harbour authorities at the loss of part of their traffic. With matters resolved in its favour the LNWR was able to run a daytime service to Dublin via Kingstown in overall timings that matched those of the mail contract, but with early afternoon departures in both directions. The night sailings continued to use North Wall, as did the cattle and cargo service, which from 1900 was also gradually re-equipped with new twin-screw vessels: the *South Stack,* introduced in 1900; the *Snowdon* in 1902; the *Slieve More* in 1904; the *Slieve Bawn* in 1905; and the *Slieve Bloom* and *Slieve Gallion* in 1908.

By this stage, however, the rivalry with the Steam Packet company was not the only factor influencing the LNWR's services to Dublin. The GWR had a long-standing association with sailings from New Milford to southern Ireland, but in 1898 the position was transformed by its acquisition of the North Pembrokeshire Railway and the Fishguard & Rosslare Railways & Harbour Company, the latter

jointly with the Great Southern & Western Railway. The Fishguard & Rosslare was a somewhat speculative undertaking with interests on both sides of the Irish Sea, which it proposed to develop by exploiting Fishguard's potential as a cross-channel port. In 1893 it had obtained powers to make a connection with the North Pembrokeshire Railway, which was in turn authorised in 1895 to build an extension to link with the LNWR at Abergwili junction; however, the latter scheme appears to have been primarily a ploy to encourage GWR interest.

The involvement of the GWR and the GS&W, which had hitherto been a close ally of the LNWR, put the Fishguard & Rosslare undertaking into a different context, particularly in view of its powers for a direct line from Rosslare to Waterford. The new crossing of St George's Channel therefore offered the prospect both of an alternative short sea route to Dublin and of a more direct approach to southern Ireland. Since Cork was the third largest city in Ireland and also lay on the American mail route via Queenstown, the threat offered by the Fishguard project could not be ignored. While the railway press suggested that the LNWR might seek running powers from Carmarthen to gain access to Fishguard from the midlands and north of England, it restricted its intervention to the other side of the Irish Sea. In 1902 the LNWR sought unsuccessfully to amend its current Bill at a late stage in the parliamentary processes to authorise it to subscribe to the Dublin, Wicklow & Wexford Railway. These powers were however granted in 1903, together with the right to nominate a director of the Irish company: the company's Irish manager, Henry Burgess, took up this place. The LNWR thus not only secured the most direct route from Rosslare to Dublin against the possibility of a GS&W take-over, but also injected sufficient capital into the DW&W to enable it to complete its line to Waterford and thus challenge the GS&W monopoly there. In recognition of its expanded territory the DW&W changed its name to the Dublin & South Eastern Railway in 1906; on 30 August the same year the Fishguard–Rosslare service was inaugurated.

The position on routes to the north of Ireland similarly became more complex. As described in Chapter Six, by 1885 the LNWR had interests in three shipping services to northern Ireland: its own route from Holyhead to Greenore; the Fleetwood–Belfast service operated jointly with the Lancashire & Yorkshire

The *Rosstrevor,* the LNWR's first screw steamer, running the measured mile on the Firth of Clyde off Skelmorlie before taking up service on the Greenore route in 1895. *(University of Glasgow archives)*

Railway; and the Stranraer–Larne route, which after 1889 was under the control of the Larne & Stranraer Steamship Joint Committee. The Midland Railway, another of the partners in the Larne route, also operated between Barrow and Belfast jointly with the Furness Railway, while further competition was provided by independent companies, most notably the Belfast Steamship Company's sailings from Liverpool.

The joint crossings were the first to be improved. The development of the Stranraer route after 1889 has already been described, while the upgrading of the Fleetwood service began in 1892 with the commissioning of the *Duke of Clarence*, the first of a fleet of Denny-built screw steamers. In 1894 the tidal restrictions at Fleetwood were overcome, permitting a fixed sailing time and substantial acceleration of the overnight schedule from Euston to Belfast. The LNWR improved its own service between Holyhead and Greenore the following year, placing its first wholly-owned screw steamer, the *Rosstrevor*, on the

route in June 1895. Two sister ships, the *Connemara* and *Galtee More*, followed in 1897 and 1898, to be joined in 1908 by the *Rathmore*. Greenore passengers also benefited from the improved Euston connections provided by the night 'Irish Mail' trains, while services on the LNWR's Dundalk, Newry & Greenore offshoot and over the connecting Great Northern lines were also enhanced: from 1903 the GNR(I) stabled a locomotive at Greenore to work the accelerated Belfast boat train. In 1904 the Stranraer route was further upgraded, with the introduction of the first Irish Sea turbine steamer, the *Princess Maud*. Five years later the joint service from Fleetwood gained two turbine vessels, the *Duke of Cumberland* and the *Duke of Argyll*. Like the *Princess Maud,* these were from Denny's Dumbarton yard.

By then, however, the equilibrium between the existing crossings to the north of Ireland had been disturbed by other factors. The first manifestation of this was the L&Y's purchase in September 1902 of the Drogheda Steam Packet Company, which operated from Liverpool to Drogheda and Londonderry. More significant, however, was the Midland Railway's successful negotiation that autumn to acquire the Belfast & Northern Counties Railway, which received parliamentary approval in 1903. Besides adding the

Belfast company's share in the Larne shipping service to the existing interest which it held through the Portpatrick & Wigtownshire joint committee, the Midland gained control of an extensive railway network in Ulster which connected with the ports of Belfast, Larne, and Londonderry. Since it was at the same time constructing a new harbour at Heysham, the Midland emerged as a substantial competitor for Irish traffic; indeed, when Heysham opened on 1 September 1904 steamer services were inaugurated to Dublin and Londonderry as well as to Belfast. The LNWR's role in serving the north of Ireland – always more diffuse than on the trunk route to Dublin via Holyhead – therefore became less secure, despite the improvements in the Greenore service and in the joint crossings in which it had a share.

So far as transatlantic traffic was concerned, the LNWR's direct involvement was of course confined to connecting services, though Liverpool shipping interests were represented on its board. With the Midland keen to exploit its Cheshire Lines link with Liverpool, competition for American traffic via the Mersey was well established: Neele described how canvassing on board ship could result in an entire London-bound complement opting for one route rather than the other, though generally the LNWR, with its faster route, could expect the lion's share of inbound passengers.

More serious for the LNWR, however, was the possibility of a shift in the main transatlantic axis away from Liverpool. In 1892 the LSWR had acquired the Southampton docks and it embarked on a vigorous improvement programme which was rewarded in 1893 when the sailings of the former Inman Line moved there under the new flag of the American Line. The direct rail-sea transfer, the lack of tidal restrictions, and the possibility of serving Continental traffic by calling at Cherbourg, all gave Southampton strong advantages, and the threat that Cunard and the White Star Line might also move their operations south prompted the Mersey Docks & Harbour Board to dredge the tidal bar to permit fixed sailing times. In collaboration with the LNWR the Harbour Board obtained powers in 1893 to add a passenger station to its dockside railway network,

Two 0-6-0 saddle tanks awaiting departure from Liverpool Riverside station with a boat train. Access to the station was over a swing bridge, limiting the weight of locomotives used on these services. *(LNWR Society collection, 218)*

reached via a new spur from the Waterloo goods branch, which ceased to be rope-worked in February 1895. From the same month, pending completion of the new station, free road transfer was provided between Lime Street and the Pierhead. Riverside station was first used on 12 June 1895 by a special working and on 15 June the inaugural scheduled boat train from Euston to Riverside was operated to connect with the outbound *Campania*; passengers arriving from New York on the *Umbria* the same evening were met by a train for the south. These American boat specials were regarded as front-rank trains: in 1907 specially-designed sets, with dining facilities for all three passenger classes, were put into service on the route in time for the *Lusitania's* record-breaking maiden voyage.

However, the pull of Southampton remained strong, and in 1907 the White Star Line supplemented its services from Liverpool to New York and Boston with a new express service from Southampton. While the Liverpool sailings' customary call at Queenstown offered a means of shortening the overall transatlantic journey time for mails and for those passengers prepared to make the double transfer to cross Ireland, the LNWR's hold on this traffic was threatened by the Rosslare route. Furthermore, liners using the English Channel route could shorten the Atlantic crossing by calling at Plymouth. In an endeavour to improve the position of its Liverpool route the White Star Line decided to experiment with a call off Holyhead: on 20 June 1909 the liner *Cedric*, inbound from New York, made the first such stop, and was met by three LNWR specials. However, Cunard responded to this by instituting a call at Fishguard, where the first service was provided on 30 August 1909 by the *Mauretania* on her way to Liverpool. To the alarm of Irish interests the company decided to call at Fishguard instead of Queenstown on eastbound voyages from the beginning of 1910, a pattern which persisted until the war. Fishguard was also adopted as a port of call by Booth Line sailings between Liverpool and South America and for the South African and Australian services of the Blue Funnel Line.

For a short while there was argument over the respective merits of Holyhead and Fishguard as 'auxiliary' ports for Liverpool – Fishguard, while nearer New York and convenient for the south of Britain, was less accessible from the north and midlands than Holyhead, which also had potential for

Canadian sailings. In practice, however, Holyhead was a less satisfactory calling point for larger vessels, and services could not be provided reliably in winter. Furthermore, since it was an Admiralty port, government funding would be required for any improvements there, whereas the GWR's investment for Irish services at Fishguard had included a breakwater which also gave suitable anchorage for ocean-going liners. Despite reports in 1910 that work would be undertaken at Holyhead to enable the large White Star liners then under construction to go on to the Liverpool station, new berths were in fact provided at Southampton for the *Olympic* and *Titanic* and the company withdrew its Holyhead calls altogether in October of that year. The attempt to use Holyhead to support the Liverpool route was therefore undermined by the superior alternative of Fishguard, which also affected the LNWR's interests in the Queenstown route. More fundamentally, however, Liverpool's role was itself under threat from the growing importance of Southampton; while Cunard remained loyal to the Mersey until 1920, the LNWR's own contributions to the improvement of transatlantic services could not reverse the underlying trend.

Southampton itself began to appear in LNWR schedules from 1905, with the establishment of through carriages from Liverpool and Manchester to Southampton, Bournemouth, and Weymouth via Willesden, Kensington, and Clapham Junction. These supplemented a similar service inaugurated over the West London route in July 1904 which provided carriages between Liverpool and Manchester and the Sussex resorts of Eastbourne and Brighton; from 1 March 1905 a separate train was established, known as the 'Sunny South Special'. Through services via Kensington were also expanded to take in South Eastern & Chatham destinations, but from 1 October 1910, as a result of the new co-operation with the Midland Railway and in response to a joint GWR and LSWR service between Birkenhead and Manchester and the south coast, the Bournemouth train was diverted via Cheltenham and the Somerset & Dorset line. In the following summer the Southampton and Portsmouth service was similarly diverted south of Birmingham to run via the Midland & South Western Junction Railway.

These south coast workings were part of a gradual expansion of LNWR cross-country services, which had begun in 1884, when, in conjunction with the

The aftermath of the Shrewsbury derailment on 15 October 1907. *(LNWR Society collection, 9730)*

NER, two daily trains were introduced in each direction between Liverpool and Newcastle. In July 1888 through expresses were established between Bristol and Crewe, with portions to and from Liverpool and Manchester, and in some cases Scotland. This service was operated jointly with the GWR and ran via the new Severn tunnel and Hereford. In 1893, by agreement with the NER, LNWR trains from Liverpool began to work beyond Leeds to York and Hull, and in the same year the overnight service via the Severn tunnel was extended to Plymouth and Penzance, a development made possible by the abolition of the broad gauge. Daytime portions to Devon destinations were added subsequently, and by 1907 the usual pattern of longer-distance working was for the Scottish section to operate as far as Bristol and for more westerly stations to be served from Liverpool or Manchester. Such through carriages were part of the formation of the 1.20 am departure from Crewe on 15 October that year, which suffered the LNWR's most serious accident of the new century when it derailed at high speed on the 10 mph restriction at Crewe junction, Shrewsbury. There were eighteen deaths and thirty-one other casualties, and as the train crew were among those killed the cause of the accident was never satisfactorily established.

In addition to these through workings, improved Oxford–Cambridge services were established in 1905, while in 1908 the LNWR co-operated in the provision of another west-east link, a GWR and GER summer service from Cardiff to Yarmouth and Lowestoft. This ran via Cheltenham and Leamington and then used the LNWR route via Rugby to reach the GER system at Peterborough. The service lasted for only two summers, but to permit its introduction a second connection was opened on 10 July 1908 between the GWR and LNWR lines at Leamington, south of the two companies' stations. Another innovation that year at Leamington has already been mentioned: this was the joint Midland and LNWR through service to Nottingham via Coventry and Leicester which was introduced on 1 October.

Faster and better-equipped main line services and a greater range of cross-country services were two aspects of the changing pattern of railway passenger

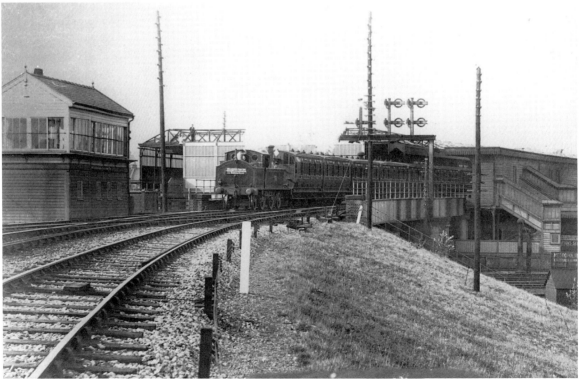

operations in the years before the first world war. They reflected a greater demand for travel – in Britain as a whole the number of railway passenger journeys grew by 57% between 1891 and 1911 – which in turn rested on trends which have already been mentioned: a growing population, higher disposable incomes, and social factors such as the increasing extent of holidays with pay: year by year the number of passengers carried during the August bank holiday week set new records. While it can be questioned how far the enhanced services provided for this increased demand were financially rewarding – shareholders and the railway press were frequent critics of the excursion and weekend fares that brought long-distance journeys within the scope of those of modest means – rising public expectations, as well as the spur of competition, made it difficult for railway managements to resist the pressure for passenger facilities. For example, municipal protests quickly forced concessions when the LNWR attempted to restrict excursion services and fares to Morecambe at peak summer weekends in 1907.

Similar pressures affected local services, and the new suburban and rural passenger routes opened during this period have already been mentioned. In the west midlands, one earlier casualty, the Tipton–Wednesbury service, was reinstated with effect from 1 July 1893. While tramway competition caused some service reductions on inner-suburban routes, the general picture was one of expansion and new stations were provided in several areas to serve residential developments. On the principal suburban routes bogie stock was gradually introduced, while the introduction of steam railcars in 1905 provided a more economical way of serving lightly-used lines and offered opportunities for opening unstaffed halts to develop traffic. Seven such units were built, the last in 1910; however, there was a departure from the principle of self-contained railcars in 1908 when a purpose-built push-pull set was provided for locomotive operation on the Red Wharf Bay line. Such 'motor trains' were quickly adopted by the LNWR as a more flexible means of operating local services.

Opposite above: LNWR steam railcar no 3 at Bicester in 1906. *(LNWR Society collection, 383)*

Opposite below: Willesden Junction high level from the south, showing a 2–4–2T departing from the 1894 island platform on an Earls Court working. *(LNWR Society collection, 1383)*

In the London area, increasing traffic densities and the pressures these imposed on complex networks resulted in some withdrawals to offset against improvements. In 1893 the through Willesden–Waterloo service was cut short at Kensington Addison Road in response to congestion on the LSWR, while on 1 November 1900 trains between Willesden and the Chatham line at Herne Hill were withdrawn. And though the District Railway provided electric locomotives for the Broad Street–Mansion House service when its line was electrified in 1905, through workings ceased on 1 January 1909 in order to avoid the traction change at Earls Court. They were replaced by a Willesden Junction–Earls Court service.

The West and North London routes provided useful local services and helped to feed express services calling at Willesden Junction, but because of the priority given to long-distance trains the LNWR had been relatively slow to encourage the growth of main-line commuter traffic. However, despite the relief given by the remodelling of the high level station at Willesden in 1894 and the widening of the Euston approaches in 1905, the pressure of outer suburban traffic built up to the point where more drastic action was required – between 1884 and 1904 there was a 200% increase in Watford–London traffic. The company's response to this growth in demand, announced at the August 1906 general meeting, was a proposal for a new electric line between Watford and Euston, largely alongside the existing main line but with a diversion via Watford High Street at the northern extremity and a branch to Croxley Green. The most ambitious part of the scheme, however, was the plan for the southern terminus. Instead of following the existing route into Euston, the intention was to tunnel from Hampstead into a single-track loop under the main line station, thus enabling incoming trains to return without reversal. Underground pedestrian links with Euston Road and with the tube stations then under construction were also proposed.

Suburban electric services were of course not new to Britain at that stage, and Webb had provided a model layout for a LNWR board discussion of electrification as early as 1902. This was followed by a proposal to electrify the Newport Pagnell branch as a pilot project, but although approved and under active discussion in 1904 the scheme was allowed to lapse. When the Watford project received parliamentary authorisation in 1907 details of power supply and electric rolling stock had not been finally settled: the estimated cost of £2·2m was only for civil engineering, stations, and permanent way. However, cost proved to be the stumbling block in the difficult stock-market conditions of that year, and though Lord Stalbridge defended the overall viability of the project it was decided to implement it gradually as financial circumstances permitted. As a result, the surface sections were put in hand on a piecemeal basis: work on the Willesden–Sudbury portion began in 1907 and the Sudbury–Harrow section was started the following year, as was the reconstruction of Watford Junction station. By the end of 1910 the Harrow–Watford and Willesden–Kensal Green portions were also under construction, together with the Croxley Green branch and several of the proposed new stations.

Parts of the new suburban line were brought into use in 1912 with steam traction, but Lord Stalbridge did not live to see this. He retired as chairman at the February 1911 general meeting; though he remained a director, ill-health quickly overtook him and he died at his London home on 18 May 1912 in his seventy-sixth year. Many tributes were paid to him when he retired and in his obituary notices, for he had been an effective and valued chairman and a respected figure in the railway world. Despite the distinction of his predecessor, Lord Stalbridge had quickly made his own mark and successfully led the company through the difficulties which faced it in the 1890s and 1900s. In a period of office which proved to be second only to Moon's in length, he oversaw the recasting of the LNWR's external relationships, the overhaul of its operating methods, and the modernisation of much of its equipment. Lord Stalbridge, who was born in the year that the Grand Junction and the first portion of the London & Birmingham were opened and who on his appointment as a director in 1870 succeeded to the board seat vacated by the LNWR's founding chairman, was able to hand over to his successor a railway that was getting to grips effectively with the demands of the twentieth century.

CHAPTER EIGHT

Peace and War

The board of the LNWR appointed Gilbert Henry Claughton, one of the deputy-chairmen, to succeed Lord Stalbridge in February 1911. Claughton, whose father was Bishop of St Albans, was born on 21 February 1856; after serving an apprenticeship with Beyer Peacock he studied at King's College in London before taking up a post with the Earl of Dudley, to whom he was related through his mother and who had extensive colliery interests. He became chief mineral agent to the Dudley estates in 1891 and was also active in local government in the area, serving four terms as mayor of Dudley and chairing the finance committee of Staffordshire County Council for a number of years. He stood unsuccessfully as Conservative parliamentary candidate for Dudley in 1906, the year after his co-option to the LNWR board to replace the late Henry Ward. Claughton also held directorships in the United Counties Bank (later part of Barclays) and in the North British & Mercantile Insurance Company, as well as in local gas and water supply undertakings. He became one of the LNWR's two deputy-chairmen early in 1910, succeeding John Pares Bickersteth, who died the previous year. Shortly after his appointment Claughton was called upon to take the chair at the February 1910 general meeting in the absence through ill-health of both Lord Stalbridge and the senior deputy, the Hon Charles Napier Lawrence. He acquitted himself well, chairing the proceedings confidently and with the quiet humour that was to be evident in his conduct of many subsequent meetings. It seems probable that he was chosen as deputy-chairman with the succession in mind, since he had age on his side and an impressive background in industry and public affairs, and within months of his appointment as chairman Claughton had shown that his contribution would be as distinguished as that of his predecessors.

After the vicissitudes of the Edwardian years, the new chairman and his colleagues at first had grounds for optimism when considering the future. The move towards pooling and agreements had effectively eliminated the threat of further competition from other railways, and while the Departmental Committee on Railway Agreements & Amalgamations had suggested in its report in June 1911 that government controls should be extended in response to these trends, this recommendation was not implemented. The recovery from the depression of 1908, already reflected in receipts and dividends by the time Lord Stalbridge stepped down, continued strongly, allowing economic activity to reach an unprecedented peak in 1913. Although close observers of foreign and domestic politics might have felt disquiet at the growing tension in international relations and at the increasing pressure for Irish home rule, outwardly at least these developments did little to disturb national confidence.

A more immediate threat came from the renewal of labour unrest. The conciliation system had secured industrial peace on the railways in 1907 and the limited concessions made by the companies had been accepted by the railway unions, albeit reluctantly, in the light of the relative depression of traffic and receipts in 1908. However, with the recovery in operating profits and the continued increase in the cost of living, the revised agreements achieved through the conciliation machinery began to appear less attractive to the railwaymen. Against a background of growing militancy throughout the trade union movement, reinforced by particular fears among railway workers that the new pooling agreements posed threats to their job security and conditions of service, labour dissatisfaction increased. In the torrid summer of 1911 there were strikes by seamen and dockers, which were followed by outbreaks of localised action by railway workers. In an effort to reassert control over their members, the railway craft and manual unions warned on 15 August 1911 that a national railway strike would be called unless their rights to

The LNWR chairman, Gilbert Claughton, is at the right of this picture, taken in 1911, which shows him with a group of veteran drivers at Crewe. *(National Railway Museum, CR A559)*

negotiate were recognised.

The government let the companies know that troops would be made available to protect the railways and to keep traffic moving, but its only response to the unions was the offer of a Royal Commission to examine the workings of the conciliation system. Faced with this intransigence the union leaders implemented their strike call on Thursday 17 August. Although the home secretary Winston Churchill exhibited his customary eagerness for armed confrontation, the strike was immediately effective and only a few trains ran: in the week of the dispute the LNWR's receipts were 29·6% less than usual, while the scale of the disruption showed the new strength of the unions.

In his work in the coal industry the LNWR's new chairman had demonstrated an ability to achieve rapport with labour interests and his skills were soon called upon in the railway dispute. The economic disruption caused by the strike added to the pressures

the government was already facing because of the Agadir crisis, so the prime minister Herbert Asquith felt obliged to intervene. On Saturday 19 August Claughton and Granet, who had been given full negotiating powers by the Railway Companies' Association, met first with ministers and then with the union leaders to discuss a settlement. After receiving assurances that the proposed Royal Commission would act speedily and would reflect labour interests in its membership, the unions agreed to call off the strike. Claughton achieved a further coup by obtaining ministerial agreement to a precondition that the railways would be permitted to increase their charges to pass on any additional costs arising from changes in the conciliation scheme.

The Royal Commission reported in a matter of weeks, but its recommendations did not fully meet the unions' aspirations. However, Claughton was again instrumental in negotiating a compromise agreement which removed the threat of a further strike and gave more flexibility in the application of the conciliation system. Furthermore, by his willingness to negotiate direct with union representatives, the chairman of Britain's largest railway company had effectively conceded recognition of their right to act on behalf of their members, a principle which had hitherto been formally denied on the LNWR as on most other railways. Although some companies distanced themselves from Claughton's position, his readiness to acknowledge the reality of the situation earned him the respect and trust of the union leaders and showed how far the LNWR had come in adapting to the changing climate of industrial relations. On the union side this new-found strength was reinforced in 1913 when the National Union of Railwaymen was formed by the amalgamation of three of the existing railway unions.

The railways' continuing vulnerability to the effects of industrial action was dramatically demonstrated in March 1912 when a prolonged national coal strike caused considerable disruption and loss of revenue: the LNWR, in common with other companies, was forced to suspend services to conserve fuel stocks and in the first half of 1912 operated 2m train miles fewer than in the equivalent period of 1911. This provided the occasion for the final abandonment of second-class facilities on the LNWR: these had been withdrawn from all but a few London suburban routes after 31 December 1911 and were suspended altogether during the coal strike to enable better use to be made of the restricted services that could be operated. Despite parliamentary questions, second-class bookings were not restored when the emergency ended.

In the following year the LNWR was also particularly affected by an extended strike of Irish transport workers which reduced cross-channel traffic. But apart from a major strike on the North Eastern in December 1912, the revised conciliation scheme was generally sufficient to maintain peaceful industrial relations on Britain's railways in the immediate pre-war period, although the price for the companies was a renewed growth in railwaymen's average earnings and in the share of receipts taken by wages: in 1912 wages exceeded 30% of the LNWR's traffic receipts for the first time. Employment costs were also increased by Lloyd George's national insurance provisions, which took effect that year. However, in 1913 the Railway & Canal Traffic Act implemented the government's earlier undertaking to Claughton by allowing the railways to reflect increased labour costs in their charges. Ministers were hesitant about this legislation and attempted to embody some of the recommendations of the Departmental Committee on

Railway Agreements & Amalgamations in an early version of the Bill, but the companies stood their ground and they followed the passage of the Act by giving notice of a 4% increase in goods charges from 1 July 1913. In the confused political situation of that year the government sought to defuse hostility to the increase by announcing the appointment of a further Royal Commission, under Lord Loreburn, to examine the relationship between the railways and the state. By that stage there was a wide body of support for railway nationalisation and it was generally assumed that this would be one of the main issues which the Commission would examine.

* * *

In his speech to the general meeting on 27 February 1914 Claughton welcomed the establishment of the Royal Commission, arguing that the more the government, the traders, and the public knew about what the railways were doing the more favourably they would emerge from such an enquiry. So far as the LNWR was concerned this confidence was certainly justified, for the immediate pre-war years marked a new peak in the company's performance. Traffic and receipts grew to record levels in 1913, despite the effects of industrial unrest. While costs also increased, net revenue was bolstered by the volume of traffic and was sufficient for a dividend of 7% in 1913, the best since 1899.

Although share prices remained depressed, the more favourable economic conditions which underlay the improved financial results encouraged the board to take up new projects once more. Work started in 1911 on two new lines which had been authorised by the LNWR's 1907 Act: a branch to Holywell and a direct connection to the Nuneaton line from east of Coventry. The Holywell branch was partly on the formation of a former private railway and work proceeded so rapidly that the $1\frac{1}{2}$-mile line opened for all traffic on 1 July 1912. The $3\frac{1}{2}$-mile Coventry loop, which was a more substantial undertaking, was not completed until 10 August 1914. It was built solely for freight traffic: its purpose was to enable mineral trains from the collieries south of Nuneaton to avoid Coventry station and also to give better goods services to the expanding industries on the north-eastern side of the city. There had already been two other minor additions to the freight network: on 1 January 1912 the joint Enderby branch was extended by 13 chains and exactly a year later a further short section of the Penllwyn tramway in south Wales was reinstated as a spur to Wattsville. One mineral proposal which failed to reach fruition was the Wolverhampton & Cannock Chase Light Railway, authorised in 1901; this scheme was transferred to the LNWR and amended under a light railway order of 1913 but made no further progress until 1922, when preliminary expenditure was incurred for a short colliery spur from the Cannock branch following a further amendment to the order in 1921. The spur was completed in 1923 by the LNWR's successor and the remaining powers were allowed to lapse.

The other new mileage of this period came from the gradual implementation of the London suburban scheme. On 15 June 1912 local steam trains began operating over the extra tracks between Willesden and Harrow and the new intermediate stations in this section opened on the same date. The Croxley Green branch was also opened for passenger traffic on 15 June, although goods services did not commence until 1 October that year. The remaining new outer suburban lines and stations were brought into use on 10 February 1913 with the completion of the additional tracks between Harrow and Watford. This portion included the loop from the main line to serve Watford High Street and a western spur at Colne junction which permitted trains to work to and from Croxley Green without reversal at Watford.

By this stage, however, the plans for the development of the southern portion of the suburban lines had been substantially modified. The new arrangements with the North London Railway offered an opportunity to review the scope of the scheme, and as more than 90% of passengers from the Watford line were bound for destinations other than Euston itself it was felt that a wider choice of London stations would be desirable, a conclusion that was perhaps also influenced by the fact that the Metropolitan Railway gained powers in 1911 for a branch to Watford. In November that year, following agreement with the London Electric Railway for an extension of its tube line from Paddington to a junction at Queens Park, the LNWR accordingly announced major changes in its suburban electrification proposals. Instead of the original proposal for a low-level terminal loop under Euston, it had been decided to continue the suburban tracks from Queens Park through an additional

Primrose Hill tunnel to burrowing junctions at Chalk Farm. These would make direct connections with the existing Euston slow lines and with the North London Railway, which would also be electrified from that point to add Broad Street to the proposed network. In addition, electrification was to be extended to the Hampstead Junction line and from Willesden to Earls Court, Kew Bridge, and Richmond. A power station at Stonebridge Park near Wembley would supply traction current for the 600 volt dc third and fourth rail system that would be necessary for compatibility with the London underground.

Including sections already served by District Railway electric trains, the modified proposals involved $41^1/_2$ electrified route miles, compared with the $18^1/_2$ miles of the original scheme, but Claughton told the shareholders on 16 February 1912 that the total project costs would be some £250,000 less than had been envisaged in 1907. The key to the revised plan was the inclusion of through workings to Broad Street and to the LER Bakerloo line in addition to Euston: besides making a wider range of destinations available to Watford line commuters, this enabled the technically elegant but costly terminal loop to be discarded. Once Broad Street was incorporated in the electrification scheme, the extensions south from Willesden Junction were a logical operational and commercial addition which would give further connections into London's growing network of electric railways.

Authority for the revised proposals, including powers for the LNWR to advance £1m to the London Electric Railway and to electrify other companies' lines, as well as to supply electricity for industrial purposes, was granted in the LER and LNWR Acts of 1912. Under the supervision of F A Cortez Leigh, who had been appointed as the company's electrical engineer in 1910, work went ahead rapidly, allowing the first electrified section, between Earls Court and Willesden Junction high level, to be brought into service on 1 May 1914. Current was purchased from the GWR's Park Royal power station pending the completion of Stonebridge Park, while rolling stock was initially hired from the District Railway. In August 1914, however, the first batch of the LNWR's three-car electric sets began to enter service. The initial order of four trains was built by the Metropolitan Carriage, Wagon & Finance Company, with Siemens electrical equipment. The contract for

This damaged photograph is one of the few surviving pictures of the LNWR's experimental petrol-electric railcar, and shows it at Pen-y-groes after its transfer to Nantle branch workings in 1915. (*Gwynedd Record Office, XS 1497/14/4*)

power cars for the main fleet of thirty-eight sets was placed with the same builder, but specified Oerlikon equipment, while the order for their trailers went to Wolverton. A more limited experiment with a new form of traction was made in west London at about the same time: a petrol-electric railcar was obtained in 1913 and saw service on the Hammersmith branch of the North & South Western Junction line before being transferred in 1915 to the Nantlle branch in north Wales.

The London electrification project and the new lines elsewhere helped to account for the recovery of the LNWR's capital investment during the first years of Claughton's chairmanship: from a total of £348,029 in 1911 expenditure grew to £639,550 in 1912, £839,310 in 1913, and £1,233,250 in 1914, the highest level for more than a decade. Other schemes, of course, contributed to these totals: works to widen the Trent Valley line between Armitage and Rugeley and the Chester & Holyhead between Abergele and Llandulas were started in 1911 and 1913 respectively, while additional loops were provided at several other points on the system. A major project began at Euston in 1912 to centralise booking facilities, improve refreshment accommodation, and provide additional office space. Walsall and Nuneaton stations were reconstructed, and investment at Nuneaton also included junction remodelling and the provision of a new locomotive shed. However, the Euston and Nuneaton schemes were both delayed by strikes in the building trades in 1914. In addition to the new stations included in the London suburban scheme, about twenty stations or halts were opened elsewhere on existing lines, many when push-pull services were introduced. Goods accommodation was increased at a number of places, including Warrington, Monument Lane in Birmingham, and Ellesmere Port on the Birkenhead joint railway. The expansion in traffic also required the provision of extra siding capacity at Heaton Norris and various yards in the west midlands.

Another reflection of the growth in goods traffic was the expenditure of £36,000 in 1913 and 1914 on the installation of a telephone network for train control purposes. Following the Midland's pioneering work in this field, the LNWR's first application of centralised control of goods train movements was at Springs Branch, Wigan, in September 1912. The system was gradually extended to other main nodes in the freight network and a chief control office was later established at Crewe. New wagons were also required: over £100,000 was invested in extra goods stock in 1913 and this was supported by an expansion of the wagon works at Earlestown. Other projects undertaken on departmental account included a new locomotive coaling plant at Edge Hill and the removal of the company's sleeper creosoting works from Willesden to a larger site at Northampton.

The modernisation of the LNWR's steamer interests also continued. Following the success of the

Commer bus, LNWR fleet no 45, purchased in 1913 for the expansion of the group of Cannock Chase local routes operated from Brownhills station. (*LNWR Society collection, 581*)

Princess Maud on the Stranraer route, a sister ship, the *Princess Victoria*, was delivered in 1912, allowing the disposal of the two 1890s vessels owned by the joint committee. In the same year the LNWR took delivery of the first turbine vessel for its own services, the *Greenore*. She was built by Cammell-Laird at Birkenhead for the Holyhead–Greenore service and attained 21 knots during trials. Her name had previously been carried by the Carlingford Lough local steamer, which was renamed *Cloghmore*. A further change in the fleet in 1912 was the withdrawal of the veteran steamer *Edith*, then serving as a cargo boat: she had been converted from paddle to screw propulsion in 1892. A second turbine steamer for the Greenore service, the *Curraghmore*, was laid down at Denny's in 1914, but work was suspended because of the war and she was not delivered until 1919.

Although the upgrading of the fleet had beneficial results – the Greenore service made a small profit for the first time in the second half of 1912 – the revised form of statutory accounts required after 1912 showed, as some shareholders had long suspected, that the company's shipping operations made an overall loss, with gross receipts of £216,797 in 1913 failing to cover revenue costs by some £24,622. This, however, was after deduction of £46,667 for insurance and depreciation; since the balance on the steamboat insurance and depreciation fund in 1913 was almost £700,000, compared with a total outstanding capital investment of £1,065,864, the position could be regarded as not too unhealthy, especially when taken together with the £33,377 profit on the LNWR's docks and harbours. Moon had frequently defended the company's Irish shipping services on the basis of their contributory revenue: the results published in 1913 suggest that this position was jusfiable in view of the long railway hauls between Holyhead and the LNWR's main English traffic centres.

The contributory revenue case could also be argued for the company's road passenger operations, which the accounts showed as making a £1,908 loss against receipts of £27,425 in 1913. While expenses still included some provision for horse-drawn passenger vehicles, the LNWR's motor bus operations in the London suburbs and north Wales had undergone considerable development by that stage, and a further group of routes, serving the Cannock Chase area of Staffordshire, was introduced in 1912. In the first six months of that year over 700,000

passengers were carried by the company's motor vehicle fleet, which also included several small single-deck vehicles that had been purchased to replace the earlier horse-drawn 'family omnibuses' provided in London for small groups travelling to or from Euston. In 1914 the LNWR's commitment to the development of road services was demonstrated by the appointment of F W Dingley to the new post of road motor superintendent, with both technical and commercial responsibility for a fleet of over a hundred vehicles. However, while lorries and vans outnumbered buses among the LNWR's road motors, the overwhelming bulk of goods and parcels cartage was still carried out with horse-drawn vehicles. The company's superintendent of horses, who was responsible for over 6,000 animals, therefore had little immediate cause for concern as a result of this new appointment.

The 1913 accounts show that the LNWR's other ancillary businesses – canals, hotels, and refreshment services – made a positive contribution to net revenue. Despite the importance of such activities, however, the combined non-railway turnover was only 5% of operational receipts, so progress remained firmly

One of the small horse-buses used by the LNWR to transfer passengers between Euston and other London termini. *(National Railway Museum, CR C807)*

dependent on the main railway business. The changes in the statutory returns make exact comparisons difficult, but gross operating revenue in 1913 was £1·1m more than in 1911. Such an increase – almost 7% – needs little qualification as a measure of the growth in the company's activity.

Some of the capital projects undertaken to assist in handling this extra traffic have already been mentioned. Repairs and renewals on revenue account also expanded to meet demand, while specific provision for depreciation, which was a well-established feature of the steamboat account, began to be built into some other operating accounts from the second half of 1911. More than £1m had been set aside for this purpose by the end of 1914 and this even included a small sum for locomotive depreciation, although it remained the company's practice to charge most new engines to revenue as renewals. Since serviceable 'replaced' locomotives continued to be held on the duplicate stock, the total fleet increased from 3,003 at the end of 1911 to 3,068 three years later. In addition, motive power capacity was increased as older classes in the capital stock were replaced by new or modified designs.

The first of the new classes to enter service during Claughton's chairmanship was in some respects a stop-gap. After the success of his superheated 4-4-0 Bowen Cooke planned a more powerful four-cylinder 4-6-0 express passenger locomotive but the axle-loading initially envisaged was not acceptable to the civil engineer. To maintain output a two-cylinder superheated 4-6-0 design was developed from the 'Experiments' and ten of this new 'Prince of Wales' class were produced at the end of 1911. Bowen Cooke followed these with two heavy freight designs: an 0-8-2 tank version of the 'G' class simple 0-8-0s, and a further 0-8-0 tender variant, the superheated 'G1' class. Production of these classes, together with further 'George V' 4-4-0s and 4-6-2 tanks, kept Crewe busy until the first of the new four-cylinder 4-6-0 class emerged at the beginning of 1913. Its design incorporated Walschaerts valve gear, a departure from Crewe's standard Joy pattern, and a Belpaire firebox, which Crewe had first tried on two 'Jubilees' in 1904 and was then adopted by Bowen Cooke for his 4-6-2 tanks. From May 1913 further examples of the new 4-6-0s began to appear and after some adjustment of cylinder diameters the 'Claughtons' became established as the LNWR's front-rank heavy express passenger locomotives.

The class took its name from the prototype, which bore the name 'Sir Gilbert Claughton', reflecting the baronetcy which the chairman had been awarded in June 1912. This early honour was recognition both of the importance of his post and of Claughton's personal stature in the business world, particularly in the field of industrial relations. His name was joined by others as further locomotives in the class appeared and among the 'Claughtons' named in May 1913 were two more acknowledging recent honours, both knighthoods. The first had been awarded to the general manager in the new year list of 1913: Sir Frank Ree thus joined his immediate predecessors, Sir George Findlay and Sir Frederick Harrison, in receiving such recognition. The esteem in which the LNWR was held was also reflected in the second knighthood, that of Robert Turnbull, superintendent of the line since 1895. This was awarded on 21 April 1913 during a visit by King George and Queen Mary

to Crewe. After being received at the station by the town's mayor, LNWR signalman Frederick Manning, the royal party inspected Crewe works and then went on to Crewe Hall for the investiture ceremony.

These knighthoods marked the culmination of two distinguished careers. Early in 1913 Sir Frank Ree had announced his intention of retiring in the following year and when the board offered the post of general manager to Turnbull he too indicated his wish to retire. The extent of the management talent that had been developed on the LNWR was shown by the fact that the current general managers of no fewer than five of its leading English contemporaries had seen service on the Premier Line. The L&Y was in the hands of John Aspinall, who had begun his career in 1868 as one of Ramsbottom's pupils at Crewe; the GNR and SE&C were managed respectively by Charles and Francis Dent, sons of the late marine superintendent, who had followed their father into LNWR employment; the North Staffordshire was under W D Phillipps, formerly superintendent of the north-eastern district ; and in 1912 the LSWR had recruited as its new general manager Herbert Walker, who was the outdoor goods manager for the southern division of the LNWR prior to this appointment.

However, Turnbull's decision not to accept the general managership left a succession problem within the company, since the only other commercial officer of comparable status was Carl Grasemann, who had followed Sir Frank Ree as chief goods manager. Grasemann had joined the LNWR in 1876 after working for five years in a ship-broking firm and had risen to become outdoor goods manager for the southern division in 1893, the position which he held until his appointment as chief goods manager in 1909. Although it had been expected that he would also succeed Ree as general manager, his health had broken down in 1911, so he could not take on the rigours of the general manager's post.

The directors therefore had to look outside the company to find a candidate of appropriate experience and rank to take over from Ree. Their choice, however, was an old Euston man: Guy Calthrop, who was born in 1870 and entered LNWR service in 1886, gaining his initial experience in the traffic department. He was appointed as Robert Turnbull's chief outdoor assistant in 1895 and in 1901 he became assistant to the general manager. In 1902 Calthrop successfully applied for the general superintendent's post on the

Caledonian Railway; in 1908, at the comparatively early age of 38, he was promoted to general manager, but left Scotland two years later to become general manager of the Buenos Ayres & Pacific Railway. Calthrop was offered the LNWR post in May 1913 and accepted with effect from the summer of 1914, when it was expected that Sir Frank Ree would stand down. But any hopes the board might have entertained of a smooth transition were to prove abortive: events during the period between Calthrop's appointment and his assumption of office resulted not only in a series of major changes in the company's senior staff but also in a fundamental alteration in the basis upon which the general manager exercised his responsibilities.

The first changes were in the goods department, where Grasemann retired because of his health at the end of June 1913. His retirement proved short, for he died that December at the age of 57. His successor as chief goods manager, F T Kinsman, had started his railway career at Holyhead in 1869; he was appointed outdoor goods manager for the northern division in 1893 and in 1911 had been transferred to London to act as chief goods manager during Grasemann's illness. Kinsman became chief outdoor goods manager in September of that year and it was from this post that he was promoted at the beginning of July 1913. However, his substantive tenure as chief goods manager was brief, as he retired on 31 December 1913. He in turn was succeeded by I T Williams, who was born in 1853 and had joined the company in 1876. By 1907 he was traffic superintendent at Broad Street and in 1911 he became an assistant to the general manager, with special responsibility for the conciliation scheme and for industrial relations. The creation of this post was an acknowledgement of the growing importance of labour matters as a high-level management function, while the selection of Williams for the appointment reflected the aptitude he had already demonstrated in his handling of personnel issues.

Williams's promotion to chief goods manager had barely taken effect when the sudden death of Sir Frank Ree on 17 February 1914 at the age of 62 gave a further example of the heavy toll which senior executive responsibility could exact. The general manager had not been in good health, but the unexpectedness of his death shocked the railway world and left the LNWR board with an immediate problem. In the circumstances Sir Robert Turnbull was prevailed

upon to accept the general managership until Calthrop was able to take up his appointment. Turnbull's existing post of superintendent of the line was left unfilled; while this may have been done to allow Calthrop a voice in the appointment, another indication of the extent to which senior management resources were being stretched came at the end of June 1914 when Turnbull's immediate deputy, Ffolliott Vere Denning, had to retire as assistant superintendent of the line because of what was described as a serious breakdown in his health. This left Lancelot Worthy Horne, the assistant to the superintendent of the line, as effective head of the traffic department. Horne's family connections with the LNWR went back to pre-amalgamation days, for he was a grandson of one of the partners in Chaplin & Horne. He was born in 1873 and had joined the LNWR in 1892, moving to the superintendent's office in 1895. After eighteen months at Euston he held a variety of district posts before being appointed goods manager at Liverpool in 1909. The following year he became district superintendent at London and in 1911 was made assistant to the superintendent of the line, the post which Denning had held until his promotion in 1909. However, Horne was not formally appointed as superintendent of the line until 16 October 1914, more than three months after Denning's retiral. This was after Sir Robert Turnbull himself had retired, for Calthrop took over as general manager with effect from 1 October 1914.

But staff changes had by then been overshadowed by a more fundamental influence on the company's affairs: the outbreak of war with Germany on 4 August 1914, less than a month after Calthrop's arrival in England from the Argentine. As a result, the ultimate control of the LNWR, as part of the machinery of war, had already passed from the board of directors which had appointed the new general manager to his post.

* * *

Appreciation of the potential importance of Britain's railways in wartime was well established. Legislation was available which gave the government powers over the system in the event of war, while professional railwaymen had developed links with the military authorities which reflected their expected role both in mobilisation at home and in providing support to an expeditionary force overseas. An engineer volunteer corps had been established as early as 1859 to give specialist assistance to the Royal Engineers and in 1865 the Engineer & Railway Volunteer Staff Corps had been established to provide a nucleus of senior managers and engineers from the railways, docks, and civil engineering and contracting firms. It was initially envisaged that in time of war this corps would undertake the management of the home railway system on behalf of the War Office. Sir George Findlay, who was a Lieutenant-Colonel in the Engineer & Railway Volunteers, devoted a chapter of his *Working and management of an English railway* to the question of railways and defence; he also lectured on the same subject at the Woolwich military academy. To supplement the links between the military authorities and the railways that were established through the volunteer movement, the LNWR provided placements for regular Royal Engineer officers to enable them to gain practical experience of railway operating.

In 1896 an Army Railway Council was established, which in 1903 was renamed the War Railway Council in deference to the Admiralty. The Council was made up of army, naval, Board of Trade, and railway representatives; its duties included advising the military authorities on railway matters, drawing up arrangements for the mobilisation of troops by rail, and establishing a staff of army officers to provide local liaison between the services and the railways. These arrangements were first put to the test in the Boer war, which involved substantial troop movements through Liverpool, and the experience in South Africa refined subsequent planning on matters such as armoured and hospital trains. The Boer war also gave the LNWR its first exposure to the direct demands that would be made on its workforce during prolonged hostilities: 1,760 employees enlisted, including a contingent of engineer volunteers from Crewe. Of the LNWR men who served in South Africa, 92 were killed and 280 invalided home. The company kept posts open for those on active service and spent £19,000 assisting their families; as a further contribution to the war effort the directors released Frederick Harrison for a period in 1900 to allow him to serve on a Royal Commission examining hospital provision for the wounded in South Africa.

Through an executive committee established in 1903 the War Railway Council developed contingency plans for mobilisation which included detailed schedules for railway movements of troops, horses, guns, and supplies. The individual companies' timetables were collated by the LNWR and LSWR on behalf of the War Office, so that a complete programme was available should it be required. In 1911 planning arrangements were further revised in the light of the establishment of home military commands: each was assigned a 'secretary railway company' to co-ordinate its movement requirements and the LNWR took on this role for the Western Command. Large-scale manoeuvres in the autumn of 1913, involving the transport of some 38,000 men, enabled the arrangements to be tested.

These procedures ensured that both the railways and the military authorities were prepared for mobilisation. In addition, arrangements for the overall control of the railway system in wartime conditions were also being refined. Besides the general provisions of the Cheap Trains Act of 1883, which obliged railways to convey troops and stores at fixed charges, two more specific legislative instruments were available: the Regulation of the Forces Act, 1871, which empowered the secretary of state for war to take possession of any railway in the United Kingdom in the event of an emergency, and the National Defence Act, 1888, which required railways to give priority to military traffic. The latter had been enacted because of concerns that the sweeping powers of the 1871 Act would impose major financial obligations on the government and would also be too disruptive of normal management arrangements to enable the system to function effectively. While Sir George Findlay had written his study on the assumption that the 1888 legislation would be applied, opinion within the railways subsequently tended to favour use of the 1871 powers, since they alone would enable the various undertakings to be worked as a unified system and could provide a basis for prioritising civilian as well as military traffic. In a report of 1911 the general managers of the leading companies recommended that in the event of emergency they should be formed into a committee, under the chairmanship of a minister, to carry out the powers available in the 1871 Act. Frank Ree elaborated these views for the Committee of Imperial Defence the following year and suggested that the pooling of receipts and expenses could provide a basis for the financial administration of the railways under emergency conditions. In order to enable the demands of the various government departments to be harmonised, he also proposed the establishment of a separate consultative committee in addition to the War Railway Council and the committee of general managers.

Ree's proposals were accepted by the government and in November 1912 the Railway Executive Committee was formed under the nominal chairmanship of the president of the Board of Trade, but with Ree himself as acting chairman for all day-to-day business. The general managers of the Caledonian, Great Central, Great Northern, Great Western, London & South Western, Midland, and North Eastern railways made up the remainder of the committee, with the addition of the general manager of the South Eastern & Chatham from May 1913. The LNWR's Westminster office at 35 Parliament Street provided the Railway Executive Committee's headquarters and the company also supplied the committee's first secretary, Lancelot Horne. Ree's other recommendation, that a consultative committee should be set up, was implemented in January 1913 by the establishment of the Communications Board. This was chaired by the quartermaster general and comprised representatives of the Board of Trade, Home Office, Admiralty, War Office, and the Railway Executive Committee.

With Sir Frank Ree's death in February 1914 the acting chairmanship of the Railway Executive Committee passed to his deputy on the Committee, Herbert Walker, and the secretaryship was also taken over by the LSWR in the person of Gilbert Szlumper, Walker's assistant. By then the Committee was well into the task of revising mobilisation arrangements and preparing detailed operational instructions for the railways' part in a war which seemed more and more likely. Sir Robert Turnbull took up the LNWR's place on the Railway Executive Committee until Calthrop succeeded to this as well as to the general managership on 1 October 1914. Sir Robert was appointed to the board of the LNWR in December 1914 – with the added distinction of being nominated to the special place reserved for the Duke of Sutherland or his appointee – and continued to serve the Committee in a personal capacity. The LNWR influence on the Railway Executive Committee therefore remained strong, while the Committee's achievements were themselves a posthumous tribute to Sir Frank Ree's role in its establishment. Under the able guidance of

Herbert Walker (whose contribution was recognised by a knighthood in 1915) this small group of railway general managers, supported by a few specialist subcommittees and a modest secretariat, was not only highly effective in mobilising the railways' resources for the war effort but also extremely influential in shaping the post-war future of the industry.

* * *

When war was declared on 4 August 1914 the provisions of Section 16 of the Regulation of the Forces Act, 1871, were brought into effect at midnight on the same date, giving the Railway Executive Committee control of virtually all railways in Great Britain. Financial arrangements had already been agreed in outline: it had been accepted that the controlled lines should be treated as a single financial entity and that compensation should be based on the difference between aggregate net receipts during the period of control and the equivalent period of the previous year. Reimbursement would be made to the individual companies in proportion to their share of total net receipts in the pre-war period. As 1913 had been a boom year for the railways, the government initially applied the proviso that total compensation should be reduced by the percentage that aggregate net receipts in the first half of 1914 fell short of those in the equivalent period of the previous year. This clawback was abandoned with effect from 1 January 1915 in return for the companies' undertaking to meet 25% of the war bonus granted to railway employees who came within the conciliation scheme. The war bonus – of 3s per week for men earning less than 30s per week and 2s per week for higher-paid workers – was the first response to the rapid increase in living costs because of war conditions, and was negotiated under a wartime 'truce agreement' between the railway unions and the companies. In November 1913 the employees' side had given the requisite notice of their intention to seek a revision of the conditions of the 1911 conciliation scheme. Negotiations were already under way when hostilities started, but on 1 October 1914 both sides agreed that because of the war the existing scheme should continue in force. Payment of bonuses – which grew to 33s per week by 1918 – was a means of responding to wartime inflation without disturbing underlying grading structures and conditions. However, while the government met the cost of all the subsequent increases this device had profound long-term consequences for the companies.

As the war went on and as what had initially been envisaged as a short-term arrangement to cover a temporary emergency became the continuing basis of railway finance, further adjustments were made to the compensation provisions. These included an allowance of 4% on new capital projects brought into use after the beginning of 1913 and government agreement to reimburse the costs of maintenance that was deferred because of wartime conditions. However, the basic principle of payment of a standard pre-war revenue was applied throughout the war and during the subsequent period of control. As a result, changes in traffic levels and operating costs ceased to have any relevance to the earnings of individual companies and their shareholders, while the influence of boards of directors over the operation of their undertakings virtually disappeared, since general managers took their instructions from the Railway Executive Committee

Financial aspects and the separate interests of individual companies were thus subordinated from the outset to the need to control the system as a whole for wartime purposes, and the value of the careful preparations that had been made by the Railway Executive Committee was immediately shown. Even before war was formally declared the railways were required to demonstrate the adaptability that was to be essential in the succeeding years, for besides coping with peak summer traffic the companies were busy at the beginning of August 1914 in moving territorial army units to their usual annual training. It was only when the international situation became critical on 3 August that it was decided to cancel these arrangements, so with virtually no notice the railways were called upon to return the territorial units to their home depots on 3 and 4 August. General mobilisation then began on 5 August, involving the LNWR alone in the running of 550 special trains; this was followed from 10 August by the complex task of moving the expeditionary force for embarkation at Southampton, complete with horses, baggage, and equipment. And while these troop movements were being handled, the navy's requirements also had to be met: although the fleet was already on a war footing, full mobilisation involved the transport of large quantities of steam coal, as well as personnel and stores. Most of the fleet's coal came from south Wales; though at first

some could be sent by sea, the Admiralty immediately hired 4,000 wagons for its traffic. The pattern of moving coal by special trains from south Wales to the east coast ports was thus set from the outset, and between 2 August and 30 September 165 Admiralty coal trains passed over the LNWR.

Once mobilisation was complete the system of arranging troop movements through secretary companies was abandoned in favour of direct liaison between each command and the railway where troops were being entrained. After a year of working in this fashion, however, it was decided to revert to the previous system. Besides resuming its duties as secretary company for Western Command the LNWR also took over responsibility for Eastern Command from the SE&C and acted in the same capacity for the Central Force. In addition to handling troop movements over its own system, the LNWR thus played an important wider role in their organisation; like the other railways it also had the task of conveying wounded soldiers to hospitals in Britain and in common with most major companies it provided ambulance trains for this traffic.

Besides the requirements generated by the British army's operations on the continent, other particular transport tasks fell to the LNWR as the war went on. One was in response to a short-term emergency, the Easter Rising of 1916, which required the despatch of two divisions to Ireland via Liverpool, involving sixty-four troop trains. Initially it was intended to march the men from Lime Street station to the Landing Stage, but on police advice the trains were routed direct to Riverside station. The operating restrictions over the Waterloo branch and the single-track approach to Riverside via the Mersey Docks lines were a severe constraint, but the LNWR was able to meet military needs by drafting in extra staff to hand-signal the workings.

Another flow through Liverpool was in the opposite direction and was a longer-standing requirement. This was the onward transport of divisions arriving by sea, initially from Ireland and from the empire but also from America after the United States entered the war in 1917. The rapid build-up of American forces – in all over 844,000 US servicemen and nurses arrived through Liverpool – and the growth in the size of Atlantic convoys soon made handling these movements a major task in its own right, requiring the participation of all the railway companies which served the Mersey ports. However, the bulk of the demand was met by the LNWR, which provided 1,684 out of the 2,333 special trains for American troops and also had the overall responsibility for planning and regulating these movements, including co-ordinating their timings with those of trains carrying troops disembarked on the Clyde.

The channel ports were the principal link with the European theatre of war; the west coast ports and the railways serving them provided the main conduit for the arrival of troops and military and civilian imports from overseas. East coast ports and the anchorage at Scapa Flow in the Orkneys provided the main focus for the Royal Navy's activities, although the threat from German submarines also necessitated naval operations from west coast harbours. Admiralty traffic thus placed another major demand on the LNWR, which provided a key link in the transport chain to many of the main naval bases even thought it did not serve them directly. Coal traffic has already been mentioned; while the GWR had the task of concentrating trainloads from south Wales at Pontypool Road, and working them northwards over the Shrewsbury & Hereford joint line, the bulk of these 'Jellicoe specials' were handed over to the LNWR at Warrington to be hauled over Shap to Carlisle, whence they were forwarded to Grangemouth, the port for the coaling ships of the Grand Fleet. In all 13,631 Admiralty coal trains were worked from south Wales between 27 August 1914 and 31 December 1918, carrying more than 5m tons of coal; on one day in November 1918 14,000 tons were despatched to Grangemouth. Every practical relief route was used – some coal was even worked north over the single-track Mid Wales line – but the bulk of this traffic had to find its way over the west coast main line *en route* to Scotland.

The threat of German attack to shipping movements along the east coast also made it necessary for naval personnel, ammunition, stores, and mail to be carried by rail over the long distances between England and the north of Scotland. The passenger flow become so intensive that on 15 February 1917 the LNWR instituted a regular through train between Euston and Thurso for naval traffic. From 21 May 1917 this service was rerouted north of Carlisle in order to provide a call at Inverkeithing and was scheduled to cover the 717 miles to Thurso in 21½ hours. Connections to and from other major naval depots

were provided intermediately. The train ran every weekday until 30 April 1919 and carried some 475,000 passengers, an average of about 300 for each working. The operation of this service entailed a total of 388,700 train miles over LNWR metals alone; in addition, the company established standard paths for naval leave trains operating between Scottish ports and Plymouth or Portsmouth.

Besides carrying passenger and freight traffic on behalf of the services, the railways had to deal with the increased demand for goods transport which resulted from the expansion in industrial activity to meet wartime needs. They were also affected by the disruption of normal transport flows, in particular the virtual cessation of coastal shipping and the diversion of overseas trade away from south and east coast ports. In addition, the volume of exports was reduced, while imports increased, especially from America. As a result, a greatly increased burden was thrown on Liverpool and other west coast ports, so the LNWR found itself having to handle traffic flows which differed substantially from the pre-war pattern. For example, during the second half of 1913 the LNWR had worked a monthly average of 36 trains of empty wagons into Liverpool to meet traffic requirements; with the reduction in export traffic and the increase in imports through the Mersey the average reached 276 trains per month in 1917. After an initial reduction caused by the need to give priority to troop trains and by the disruption to peacetime patterns of industrial production, goods train mileage recovered steadily from 1915 onwards and in 1917 was 4% more than the pre-war peak in 1913. In terms of tonnage, merchandise and mineral traffic in 1917 was estimtated to be 9% greater than in 1913.

Despite the increase in the total volume of traffic and the change in the pattern and composition of the flows which had to be accommodated, very little relief was available from new construction. Once schemes already under way in 1914 had been completed, expenditure on capital account declined to negligible amounts: in 1918 the LNWR's gross capital expenditure on railway account was £147,719, reduced to a net £120,161 by offsetting credits. Income on capital account also fell: £1,479,000 of 1902 4% preference stock had been issued in 1914, at a discount which reflected hardening interest rates and stock-market uncertainty, and this more than balanced the capital expenditure in that year. In the following year the company raised more funds, but in a new form: a 4½% stock redeemable at par in 1925. Other railway companies had been driven to similar devices in the difficult financial circumstances of the Edwardian years: the fact that the LNWR had to adopt such procedures was a measure of the disruption of money markets caused by the war. Despite the terms of the issue, bank rate was at 5% for most of 1915, so it is not surprising that the new stock was also placed at a discount: its nominal value was £1,500,000 but only £1,437,846 was received. There were no further significant stock issues after 1915, but with large sums accruing in the balance sheet from items such as depreciation and the reserve fund there was no difficulty in covering the deficit on capital account.

The most extensive project still outstanding when war broke out was the suburban electrification scheme. The shortage of men and materials caused delays, but sufficient progress was made for tube trains to reach Queens Park on 11 February 1915 and to begin working through to Willesden on 10 May. The LNWR's power station at Stonebridge Park was completed on 24 February 1916 and this was followed on 1 October by the inauguration of electric services from Broad Street via the Hampstead Junction line to Richmond and Kew Bridge. On 16 August 1917 underground trains were extended to Watford and on the same day a peak hour LNWR electric service was introduced between Watford and Broad Street. However, although the Primrose Hill tunnels were completed the same year, the Ministry of Munitions ordered the suspension of work on the vital link between Primrose Hill and Chalk Farm, thus preventing the extension of electric working to Euston and Broad Street via Camden.

Delays also affected most of the other schemes which had been started or planned just before the war, despite the contribution that several of them could have made to easing the movement of vital wartime traffic. Widening between Abergele and Llandulas had begun in 1913; the new tracks were not ready for traffic until June 1916. Similarly, the doubling of a portion of the single-track Coventry–Leamington branch, started in 1914, was not completed until March 1916; at one stage the Ministry of Munitions diverted labour from this line on to other projects. A contract for a new goods station at Blackwood on the Sirhowy line had been let early in 1914; it was not opened for traffic until December 1918. Other peace-

time schemes which carried on into the war years were the alteration of passenger facilities at Euston, completed in 1915; the remodelling of Nuneaton station, finished in 1917; the provision of extra cattle accommodation at Holyhead; and the extension of goods facilities at Marsden, Ellesmere Port, and Mesty Croft near Wednesbury.

Some projects were undertaken as a direct result of wartime requirements, either on LNWR or government account. Two junctions were installed to create emergency alternative routes: in 1915 the GCR and LNWR lines were connected at Blaby, south of Leicester, and in 1916 the Hampstead Junction and Tottenham & Hampstead lines were linked at Gospel Oak. Extra sidings and loops were laid at many locations, while the particular concentration of munitions activities in the Coventry area involved the building of extensive sorting sidings as well as factory connections and passenger facilities for munitions workers. On the Chester & Holyhead line, similar provision had to be made for a munitions factory at Queensferry, and further west connections were installed from Foryd to the Kinmel Park army camp. Rail facilities were also required for other army depots at Hednesford, Milford & Brocton, and Prees Heath near Whitchurch.

With a general shortage of manpower and with government requirements and other priority projects absorbing the civil engineer's resources, it is not surprising that capital expenditure on new works and improvements on LNWR account fell sharply as the war progressed. Investment in rolling stock was also reduced as pre-war orders were completed, although the wartime demand for motive power ensured the continuing production of new locomotives. Crewe turned out ten 'King George V' 4-4-0s in 1915, followed by thirty 'Prince of Wales' 4-6-0s in two batches in 1915 and 1916, and forty 'Claughtons' spread over 1916 and 1917. More 4-6-2 and 0-8-2 tank locomotives were also built, while no less than fifty 'G1' 0-8-0s were added to the stock between the beginning of 1915 and the end of 1918. In addition, twenty 'Prince of Wales' locomotives were built by the North British Locomotive Company and delivered in 1915 and 1916. The need to place orders with an outside manufacturer reflected the heavy demands that by then were being made on the company's workshops to produce material for the war effort. In addition to their essential role in maintaining transport

within Britain, the railway companies made a major direct contribution to the supply of munitions and other military equipment and to keeping lines of communication open for the forces overseas.

Assistance was first sought early in September 1914, when the railways were asked to supply 12,250 stretchers for the army. The LNWR carriage works at Wolverton supplied 2,000 of this number at a rate of 300 per week. This was followed by a request for the manufacture of artillery wagons, which was shared out among twenty-two railway companies. The president of the Board of Trade then approached Calthrop and Bowen Cooke to establish what help the railways might be able to offer in producing munitions; Bowen Cooke obtained technical drawings of gun carriages from the Woolwich Arsenal and at a meeting on 20 October 1914 the chief mechanical engineers of a number of the larger companies agreed that their works could manufacture the required items. Further requests followed and at the end of October the Railway Executive Committee established a war manufactures sub-committee to act as a channel for such orders, which were undertaken at cost plus an allowance for supervision and overheads. With the setting up of the Ministry of Munitions in 1915 this aspect of the war effort was greatly expanded and

A 'Crewe tractor' with a train of shells on a narrow-gauge military line on the Western Front. *(LNWR Society collection, 2063)*

parts of the workshops at Crewe and Wolverton were given over entirely to military production. Besides producing items such as heavy forgings for guns, shells, fuses, and minesweeping paravanes, the LNWR turned out 138 'Crewe tractors' on Ford chassis adapted to run either on roads or 60 cm gauge military railways.

In addition, the company was called upon to assist with other rail transport requirements in both Britain and Europe. Ambulance trains were not only required for home use: in the autumn of 1914 Wolverton supplied vehicles for the first of these trains sent to France and by the end of the war the LNWR had provided seven ambulance trains for British army use overseas, together with four to US order. Wolverton also constructed a 14-vehicle advance headquarters train for Field Marshall Haig's use in France. Another special requirement was the production of armoured trains, which were used to patrol coastal lines in Scotland and eastern England. The first was ordered by the War Office in the autumn of 1914, when German invasion of Britain was thought to be immi-

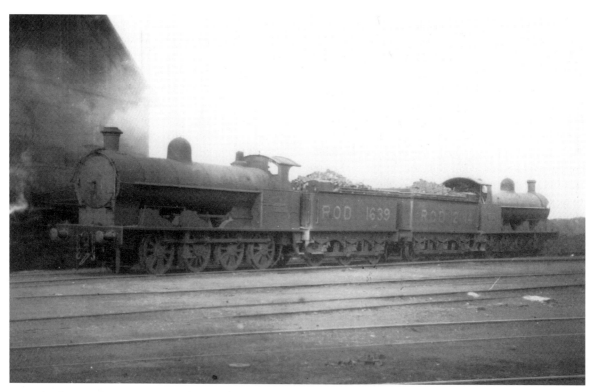

'G' class 0-8-0s nos 1639 and 2014 on war service at St Omer, France, 3 October 1918. *(LCGB Ken Nunn collection, 2095)*

nent, and Crewe undertook the task of adapting and armouring the vehicles and locomotives supplied by other companies for this purpose. A second train was ordered in December 1914. Other wartime tasks added to Crewe's workload included the repair of locomotives required for use overseas or on military lines at home and the supply of equipment and spare parts for locomotive running sheds abroad. In addition, with relaying on the LNWR's own system reduced from a pre-war average of about 140 track miles per annum to around 54 miles, some of the capacity of the Crewe rail mill was used to supply rails to other British companies. The equivalent of about 260 track miles was made available in this way and 56 further track miles were taken from stock for use overseas.

The diversion of existing railway resources to meet war requirements abroad was an important adjunct to the workshops' role in manufacturing or adapting items to military requirements. Besides supplying rails and other permanent way material the LNWR

civil engineer's department also made bridge girders available early in the war to repair damage to French railways. The railways also provided a ready source of reinforcements for the road transport capability of the army in the field: within the first two months of the war the LNWR supplied 489 horses to the War Office, 478 of which were already registered under the army horse reserve scheme. Some horse-drawn vehicles were also provided and motor vans and buses were quickly requisitioned for military purposes, resulting in the suspension of LNWR bus routes.

As the stalemate and attrition of the trenches went on, the transport situation behind the lines became more and more critical. During 1916 the Railway Executive Committee therefore came under increasing pressure from the War Office to release locomotives and wagons for use in France. The LNWR offered to supply seventy locomotives on the understanding that other companies would assist in making up the deficiency that this would leave; however, as the Ministry of Munitions refused to make materials available for further new construction or repairs, this condition could not be met. After renewed pressure Calthrop agreed in November 1916 to release seven engines, and to make a further thirteen available if other companies would help. These locomotives, all Webb 0–6–0s, were shipped before the end of the year; meanwhile intense negotiations between the War Office and the Railway Executive Committee, which included a visit by the latter to inspect transport conditions in France, led to an undertaking that the British railways would supply an additional 300 locomotives, together with 20,000 wagons. Further demands followed, including requirements for the Middle East campaign, and by the end of the war the LNWR had supplied 111 of the 516 locomotives sent from Britain for overseas use, 26 of them Webb '17" Goods' 0-6-0s, designed in 1873, and the remainder Whale 'G' class 0-8-0s. In addition the company provided 6,370 out of the 29,704 British goods wagons used abroad, together with 90 coaching stock vehicles.

War Office and Ministry of Munitions demands built up as the war progressed, but in the case of the company's shipping resources the impact of wartime requirements was immediate. The LNWR's fast and capacious North Wall and Kingstown passenger steamers were requisitioned as soon as war broke out and within ten days they had been converted at the company's Holyhead repair yard for Admiralty service. The *Cambria* and *Anglia* were subsequently adapted as hospital ships, and the *Anglia* brought King George V back to England from Boulogne on 1 November 1915 after he had been thrown from his horse and seriously injured while inspecting troops. Barely a fortnight later, on 17 November, she struck a mine in the English Channel and sank with the loss of ninety-seven lives. The *Anglia* was the LNWR's second naval casualty that month: on 5 November the *Hibernia*, renamed the *Tara* by the Admiralty, was torpedoed in the Mediterranean. Most of the LNWR crew survived and were eventually rescued from captivity in Libya by a British motorised column. Three of the North Wall cargo boats were also requisitioned for a short while for use as troop transports, but were returned to railway service.

The GWR's best Irish Sea vessels were likewise requisitioned and for a few days in August 1914 the LNWR's *Rathmore* was borrowed for the Rosslare route before being replaced at Fishguard by the *Duke of Connaught* from the L&Y and LNWR joint fleet. This allowed the *Rathmore* and *Greenore* to reinstate a night service between Holyhead and North Wall to supplement the daytime sailings on this route;

however, Greenore was left with reduced facilities. The *Galtee More* was retained as standby boat for the Holyhead services and for the Stranraer–Larne route, but also deputised for other companies' vessels, reaching the Channel Islands on occasions.

It was perhaps indicative of the then prevailing view that the war would not last long that the LNWR placed a further order with Denny's in November 1914 for four new cross-channel turbine steamers, to a specification which reflected the fact that the mail contract was due for renewal in 1915. These orders suffered the same fate as the *Curraghmore* and made little progress. The existing mail contract was extended on a year-to-year basis as the war went on, leaving the daytime Holyhead–Kingstown services to the City of Dublin company, which was not so badly affected by requisitioning. However, one of its vessels, the *Connaught*, was lost while on Admiralty service between Le Havre and Southampton on 3 March 1917, while her sister ship, the *Leinster*, was torpedoed off Kingstown on 10 October 1918 with very heavy loss of life. Because of the dangers from German submarines in the Irish Sea, a force of destroyers and armed launches was maintained at Holyhead and this was later augmented by American naval vessels. Unfortunately, this increased activity brought its own risks: the LNWR's *Slieve Bloom* was lost during the night of 30 March 1918 after colliding with an American destroyer. Earlier that month, on 14 March, the *Rathmore* was holed in a collision but was towed to Dublin and was later repaired. One of the Greenore steamers, the *Connemara*, was the victim of an earlier collision: she sank in a storm off the Irish coast on 3 November 1916 with the loss of all eighty-six passengers and crew after hitting an unlit collier. An L&Y vessel was then chartered for a while to maintain the Greenore service, but the schedule was subsequently reduced to three crossings each week and eventually, on 1 January 1918, to a twice-weekly cargo-only sailing.

The joint routes from Fleetwood and between Stranraer and Larne were also affected by wartime conditions, and the pressures on these services were increased by the suspension of the Midland's Heysham sailings in 1916. The Stranraer route's *Princess Victoria* was requisitioned in October 1914 and was placed in service with the South Eastern & Chatham Railway to assist in maintaining the vital cross-channel links from Dover; she also spent some time as a hospital ship. The *Princess Maud* was left to operate a daily return working between Stranraer and Larne, with the *Galtee More* deputising during refits. The nightly sailing in each direction between Fleetwood and Belfast was maintained, but one member of the L&Y and LNWR joint fleet, the *Duke of Albany*, was torpedoed in the North Sea on 25 August 1916 while under requisition

* * *

The material resources of the LNWR, together with those of other British railways, accordingly contributed directly to the war effort on land and at sea, and even in the air through Crewe's production of aircraft components. The company also provided a source of financial resources: dormant balances were invested in government securities and staff were encouraged and assisted to take up issues of war loan. Land and buildings also represented assets which could be used for national purposes: more than 7,000 extra allotments were created on LNWR land and warehouse space was made available for the storage of food reserves and military supplies. These efforts, however, were overshadowed by the very direct contribution the company's employees made to the war. When Sir Gilbert Claughton addressed the general meeting on 26 February 1915, 12,177 of the company's 93,000 staff had enlisted, of whom 1,002 were already casualties or missing. Four years later the annual report recorded that 31,742 LNWR employees had seen service, of whom 666 had been mentioned in despatches or decorated, including three awarded the Victoria Cross: Private Wilfred Wood, Private Ernest Sykes, and Lance-Corporal John Christie. Over 3,000 were killed in action or died of wounds, or were missing, presumed dead, and almost 9,000 were wounded.

More than 5,000 LNWR employees had been called up as reservists or territorials in the initial weeks of the war; in addition, over 4,000 volunteered during the same period. In view of the importance of railway work, steps had to be taken to ensure that there was some control over enlistment by railwaymen and a subcommittee of the Railway Executive was therefore formed to review ways in which railwaymen could be released for military service. One opportunity for staff saving had already arisen because of the control procedures: although the

financial arrangements generated their own accountancy and audit workload, the aggregation of revenue meant that it was no longer necessary to apportion traffic receipts between individual companies. This reduced clerical requirements in the Railway Clearing House and in the companies, allowing staff to be redeployed or made available for military service. Other manpower savings were made by reducing services such as porterage or by pooling collection and delivery arrangements, while efforts were made to substitute boys, women, and older men for those eligible for military service. The number of women employed on the LNWR increased to a maximum of 9,154, compared with 2,123 at the outbreak of war; clerical posts made up the largest single category, although women also took on a wide range of operating and workshop duties.

Despite these steps, the army's demands led to continual pressure for the release of railwaymen both for general service and to provide specialists for transport duties in the field. The attestation scheme introduced in the autumn of 1915 provided a means of allowing men to volunteer while at the same time giving the companies some control over their release for military service, but with the adoption of compulsory service in 1916 the tension between the needs of the companies and the demands of the military authorities began to grow. This was further exacerbated by the loss of workshop staff to better-paid work in munitions factories. Even after the formation of a Manpower Distribution Board to regulate competing demands, the railways were increasingly obliged to accept the substitution of unfit or older workers to allow the release of their men for the services. In addition, approximately 2,000 civilian platelayers were sent to France in 1917 to keep essential traffic moving, many of them released by deferring maintenance work at home. An LNWR divisional engineer undertook the direction of this force, and the first two of the eight volunteer companies to be formed were drawn from the LNWR, which also provided tools and supplies.

In addition to their service in the field or at sea, the company's staff supported the conduct of the war in other ways. The railways provided an important source of experienced managers and administrators for the new civilian and military departments that were created for key wartime tasks and the LNWR released a number of senior officers for such

purposes. Commander Holland, the marine superintendent, went to France with the expeditionary force
in 1914 as a temporary colonel in the Royal
Engineers, serving as deputy-director and then
director of inland waterways. He rose to the rank of
brigadier-general before his death whilst on leave on
26 June 1917. Holland's duties at Holyhead were
undertaken by the superintendent engineer, A T Orr,
who succeeded him on his death.

Among the first of the senior staff to be lent for
civilian duties with the government was Howard
Williams, son of the chief goods manager and himself
the company's mineral traffic manager. He was
released to establish the railway transport section of
the Ministry of Munitions in September 1915 and by
the time of Williams's return to the LNWR at the end
of 1917 he had become a deputy director-general in
the Ministry. Another secondee was H G Burgess, the
company's Irish traffic manager, who was appointed
director of transportation for cross-channel traffic in
June 1916. His responsibilities, exercised on behalf of
a number of government departments and agencies,
were to regulate Irish Sea shipping services and to
ensure the transport of essential commodities between
Britain and Ireland.

Further government demands arose from the
pressing need to maintain coal output and to ration-
alise its distribution. Early in 1917 the LNWR board
agreed to make their general manager's services
available to the Board of Trade so that he could take
up the newly-created post of controller of coal mines.
The directors also agreed to the release of Stanley H
Hunt, commercial assistant to the general manager, to
act as one of Calthrop's two assistants in his new
duties; Howard Williams was also lent for three
months at the end of 1918. The goods manager, I T
Williams, took over in February 1917 as acting
general manager and in the same month was also
appointed by the government to the new Canal
Control Committee. Sir Robert Turnbull, who had
continued to serve on the Railway Executive
Committee in a personal capacity, was again nominated to act as the LNWR's substantive representative
on the Committee in place of the general manager.
Calthrop himself was created a baronet in June 1918
in recognition of his work as controller of coal mines.

In coping with the demands of wartime traffic in
Britain, the LNWR, in common with other railways,
was therefore increasingly handicapped by the loss of

men and equipment as military requirements took
precedence. In addition, the diversion of coal and
essential raw materials to meet other priorities left the
railways facing shortages in their basic supplies. A
further irritant was the disruption caused by occasional air raids. Despite these problems, goods traffic
was kept moving, but a succession of measures
became necessary to enable the growing volume of
freight to be handled with the resources available.
These included more vigorous enforcement of demur-
rage regulations, the reduction of empty wagon movements through backloading and wagon pooling
arrangements, the use of Ministry of Munitions road
haulage for short movements, and, from September
1917 onwards, the regulation of coal traffic under the
regional distribution scheme introduced by Calthrop.
In the closing months of the war attempts were also
made to relieve the railways by encouraging greater
use of canals and coastal shipping.

With goods traffic so crucial to the war effort and
with troop trains also requiring priority, ordinary
passenger services had to bear the brunt of shortages
and capacity constraints. This became apparent in the
early days of the war: the movement of Admiralty coal
necessitated the diversion of north-and-west express
services from the Shrewsbury & Hereford line to the
GWR route via Birmingham and Market Drayton on
28 and 29 August 1914, while passenger services on
the North London and Oxford–Cambridge lines also
had to be suspended at times because of the volume of
troop movements. However, passenger services and
facilities were largely restored after the initial mobilisation was completed – by the end of August 1914 the
LNWR was once again advertising a wide programme
of excursion fares.

But more extensive curtailments soon became
necessary as wartime shortages began to take effect.
The Railway Executive Committee ordered the withdrawal of a number of 'competitive' services and
facilities from 22 February 1915, together with the
suspension of some excursion fares: among the
LNWR services withdrawn were the 'Sunny South
Specials' and the morning Wolverhampton–Broad
Street express. (The evening working from Broad
Street had been withdrawn just before the war). This
was followed by the complete cessation of excursion
fares from 29 March. In October 1915 the
Manchester–Bournemouth service was suspended
and measures put into effect in 1916 included the

withdrawal of tourist fares and all LNWR restaurant car services. Even with these restrictions, and despite government regulations which postponed or cancelled bank holidays, demand for travel remained high, so it became clear that more drastic steps were required if the resources required for passenger train operation were to be reduced.

In response to these pressures a package of additional restrictions was implemented from 1 January 1917. These included a 50% increase in ordinary fares, the withdrawal of weekend fares, severe reductions in passenger services, and the closure of some lines and stations. This enabled some 500 locomotives to be released and allowed significant savings in manpower and coal consumption: the eleven largest railways reduced their total fuel requirement by $11\frac{1}{2}\%$ in the first fortnight of 1917. The impact on the LNWR can be judged by the fact that only 20·5m passenger-train miles were operated in 1917, less than 65% of the peak level achieved in 1914, and about 7m fewer than in 1916. Part of the reduction was achieved by rationalising long-distance services, so that, for example, Euston's sole morning departure for Scotland was provided by the 9.30 am to Perth, which also carried a Liverpool portion; morning trains to Glasgow and Edinburgh were provided respectively from St Pancras and from Kings Cross. Interavailability of tickets, which had been applied briefly at the start of the war, was restored in partial compensation for the limitation of services on individual routes.

Local travellers also suffered: some passenger services had been withdrawn completely during the first two years of the war, including those on the Distington branch of the Whitehaven, Cleator & Egremont joint line, which closed to public passenger traffic as early as 1 September 1914; the Wigan–Leigh service, suspended on 22 February 1915; and the Wednesbury–Dudley Port service, withdrawn on 1 January 1916. However, no less than forty-four stations or halts were closed by the LNWR with effect from 1 January 1917, including some which had opened less than four years previously. Lines from which all passenger trains were withdrawn on 1 January 1917 included the Over & Wharton, Nantlle, Hammersmith & Chiswick, and Birstall branches, together with local services between Huddersfield and Stalybridge via the Friezland loop and between Birmingham New Street and Kidderminster. Further

station closures followed, while on 15 April 1917 passenger services were completely withdrawn from two further sections: the Garston Dock branch; and the northern tip of the GNR & LNWR joint line, between Bottesford south and north junctions, which until then had been used by Newark trains. The Medbourne branch of the joint line had closed to passengers a year earlier, with the withdrawal of the GNR Leicester–Peterborough service on 1 April 1916, and the final wartime withdrawal involved another joint railway: the suspension of the Nuneaton–Burton service on 1 April 1918 resulted in the loss of passenger trains over the Ashby & Nuneaton line between Moira south and west junctions.

Other measures were taken in 1917 and 1918 to economise on passenger train operation, including the withdrawal of some local services in the evenings and on Sundays and a general deceleration of express trains which resulted, for example, in a minimum schedule of 4 hours 40 minutes between London and Manchester, more than an hour longer than the pre-war best. Through carriages were curtailed to enable stock to be used more intensively and to cut down shunting requirements, while suburban stock was employed on some long-distance services to give higher capacity. Relief trains ceased to be provided and advance and through bookings were suspended at the holiday peaks in a further attempt to limit the demand for travel. Similarly, in an effort to limit the growth in season ticket journeys – which had been exempted from the 1917 fare increase – restrictions and increased charges were imposed at the beginning of 1918.

While the increasingly stringent constraints from 1917 onwards achieved their objective of squeezing resources out of passenger operations, they were ineffectual in actually limiting demand: exclusive of season ticket holders, the number of passengers carried on the LNWR in 1917 was around 101 million, compared with 92·5 million in 1913. Some of this extra traffic was, of course, a direct result of the war: servicemen travelling under warrants, or munitions workers commuting to and from their factories. Despite higher taxation and fares, leisure travel was stimulated by increased earnings from war work as well as by the pressures of working conditions: indeed, by giving travel vouchers and concessions to its workers the Ministry of Munitions partially undermined the Railway Executive Committee's attempts to damp down passenger traffic. The consequence of this combination of buoyant demand and restrictions on the railways' ability to serve it was, inevitably, a deterioration in travelling conditions: trains were fewer, slower, and overcrowded, fares were higher, and a wide range of facilities which the LNWR had developed to improve its service to passengers – such as connecting buses, luggage in advance, and on-train catering – had to be sacrificed to the overriding demands of the war. As was to happen a generation later, post-war attitudes to railways and to rail travel were coloured by experiences of wartime journeys and by the restrictions which the companies were compelled to impose on their passenger services in order to meet other national priorities.

CHAPTER NINE

The Final Years

The armistice of 11 November 1918 did not end the railways' military tasks: apart from the continuing needs of the occupying army in Germany and the contingents that were required elsewhere, repatriation and demobilisation of the main body of wartime forces was a major logistic undertaking which, like mobilisation in 1914, depended on careful preparation and close liaison between the railway and military authorities. Planning had started as early as 1917 and involved provision not only for British forces but also for the overseas troops that had been drawn into the war. It was envisaged that when full demobilisation started the railways would carry 40,000 men daily to dispersal camps in Britain, half from the channel ports and half from the home commands. Several of the camps were located on the LNWR, which was involved both in working troop trains to these centres and in making arrangements for the homeward transport of demobilised men. In the period up to the first week of July 1919 the LNWR ran 2,376 special trains, 1,587 of them to the Prees Heath camp near Whitchurch. The railways were also asked to undertake a number of additional duties arising from demobilisation, including the dispersal of army horses brought back from France for sale and making stations available as receiving centres for military greatcoats. This involved station staff in issuing a receipt and paying a gratuity of £1 on behalf of the War Office for each greatcoat returned, and then arranging the despatch of the coats to an army depot.

Such tasks were not the only reasons why the railways could not quickly be returned to a peacetime footing after the armistice. When it became apparent that the war was developing into more than a short-term emergency, it was accepted that the prolonged disruption of the railways' normal traffic and expenditure patterns would make a period of post-war re-adjustment necessary and that control would therefore have to continue into peacetime. In the autumn of 1916 the cabinet agreed that a two-year extension of

control and of the guaranteed income would be needed after the end of the war, and this decision was conveyed to Sir Gilbert Claughton in his capacity as chairman of the Railway Companies' Association.

It also quickly came to be appreciated that extending the period of government control would permit a breathing-space during which the political questions surrounding the future of the railways could be resolved. The Loreburn Commission, which had started taking evidence in 1914, had been abandoned because of the war, but the experience of working the railways as a unified organisation had strengthened the case against restoring the pre-war pattern of ownership and administration. A parliamentary select committee which reported in November 1918 concluded that the railways could not be allowed to return to their previous position; it went on to recommend that, while the wartime arrangements did not provide a suitable permanent basis for the future organisation of the industry, some form of unified control should be adopted, under either public or private ownership. Winston Churchill, who was then the minister of munitions, identified himself strongly with the case for nationalisation immediately before the general election of 14 December 1918 and it was generally assumed that Lloyd George's coalition was intent on bringing the railways into public ownership.

The Ministry of Ways & Communications Bill, introduced into the new Parliament on 26 February 1919 in breach of an earlier ministerial undertaking that there would be prior consultation with the Railway Companies' Association, contained a clause which would have permitted the state purchase of railways and other forms of transport. This particular proposal had been removed by the time the legislation emerged as the Ministry of Transport Act, but control of the railways was extended until 15 August 1921 to allow further time to formulate the details of future transport policy. The new minister of transport, Sir Eric Geddes, quickly set about the creation of an elaborate departmental structure which would have readily lent itself to the supervision of a state-owned railway network; he also set up machinery to administer the existing control arrangements and to exercise the extensive powers over railway charges and over railwaymen's wages which passed to the minister under the Act. The LNWR's Irish manager, H G Burgess, was among several senior railwaymen recruited to the new department; he was given charge of Irish transport matters, while W A Jepson, previously assistant to the general manager, was appointed as a member of the Rates Advisory Committee established under the new legislation. At the end of 1919 the Railway Executive Committee was replaced by a Railway Advisory Committee of twelve general managers and four union representatives, but this new committee's usefulness was in practice limited by its composition. Instead, a standing committee of general managers established by the Railway Companies' Association provided the effective continuation of the Railway Executive Committee and was the main interface between the companies and the Ministry of Transport on control arrangements.

It has been questioned whether the post-war government ever intended to meet the commitments which it had appeared to give about railway nationalisation. It is clear, however, that the deterioration of the national financial position after the war and the particular labour difficulties faced by the controlled railways introduced major new problems into the reorganisation of the industry. Despite the war bonus arrangements, industrial unrest was already growing before the armistice and had expressed itself in an unofficial strike on the GWR in September 1918 over the rejection of a demand for a 10s increase in the war wage. The strike spread to parts of the LNWR before the NUR secretary, J H Thomas, induced the men to return by threatening to resign.

Much to the dismay of the railway companies, ministers had given strong indications during 1917 that the unions' long-standing demand for an eight-hour day would be met after the war ended. This reduction in working hours was implemented from 1 February 1919, but the attempts by some companies to recover part of the concession by abolishing traditional breaks and allowances contributed to a further worsening of industrial relations. The unions had ended the wartime truce immediately after the armistice and their members' concerns about their earnings were quickly fuelled by the rapid inflation which followed the ending of price controls. The war bonus and the way in which it would be consolidated with standard wages therefore became a crucial element in negotiations. Although the locomen reached a satisfactory settlement in August 1919, other grades contended that the revised standard rates which they were being offered were too low. In the face of the government's refusal to compromise, a national railway strike was called from 27 September and achieved almost total support, although volunteers managed to operate a few trains. Ominously for the railways, some of the gaps left by the suspension of passenger and freight services were filled by road transport, which was strengthened by recalling army vehicles from the continent. The control arrangements created during the war provided a means of organising essential supplies, and emergency powers were used to enable lorries to be requisitioned to maintain the distribution of milk and food. Even the king turned to the roads, motoring from Balmoral to London to be on hand in the emergency.

These stop-gap measures were not, however, able to replace the railways in their basic task of keeping industry and commerce moving. While sufficient men returned to work during the course of the strike to enable the Railway Executive Committee to organise skeleton long-distance passenger services, there was mounting economic disruption. There were also warnings from other sectors of the labour movement that they would support the railwaymen, which fed fears that the socialist unrest on the continent might find a foothold in Britain. Lloyd George's cabinet accordingly capitulated and offered terms to the railway unions on 5 October which were sufficient for the strike to be ended immediately. Wages were stabilised at their existing level until September 1920 and a commitment was given to negotiate the subsequent arrangements by the end of 1919. In the ensuing settlement the railwaymen accepted a sliding scale to regulate the war bonus (which was increased by 5s to 38s), and a lump sum of £1 in lieu of backdating. New wages boards established under the Ministry of Transport Act came into operation early in 1920 and under these arrangements further improvements in basic rates and conditions were agreed that year. There were also adjustments under the sliding scale provisions.

The railways' labour costs grew rapidly because of

'George the Fifth' class 4-4-0 no 1623 'Nubian' piloting unnamed 'Claughton' no 2427, built in 1917, through Blisworth on the 11.05 am from Liverpool on 30 April 1921, during the coal strike. *(LNWR Society collection, 9421)*

these increases and the additional posts made necessary by the introduction of the eight-hour day: the LNWR general meeting in 1921 was told that the company's wage payments in 1920 stood at £20m, £14m more than in 1913. Over the same period the company's total operating expenditure increased from £11·3m to £34·1m; while higher commodity prices also had an effect, labour costs were clearly the largest single element in the aggregate increase, £15m of which had occurred after 1918. During a sample week in March 1921 the LNWR's staff complement was 101,483; at the outbreak of war it had been 93,106. Despite this growth in the aggregate workforce, the female employees recorded in the 1921 return, 3,534, were significantly fewer than the wartime peak of 9,154.

These increased costs fell directly on the exchequer, since the companies were still receiving their guaranteed pre-war net revenue, albeit in a depreciated currency. Until the end of 1917 the financial

terms had benefited the government because the ordinary revenue received by the controlled network was sufficient both to meet operating costs and pay the guaranteed revenue. Moreover, this was without any allowance for the value of traffic carried free for the government. From 1918 onwards, however, costs began to overtake revenue and in the financial year from 1 April 1919 to 31 March 1920 the government incurred a net deficit of more than £41m in meeting its obligations to the controlled companies. After consulting the Rates Advisory Committee the Ministry of Transport gave effect to increases in goods charges from 15 January 1920 which averaged approximately 55%. On 6 August 1920 ordinary passenger fares rose by 16·7%, making them 75% higher than in 1914; this was followed by substantial increases in workmen's fares and season ticket rates. Even after these measures a £49m deficit was forecast for the year ending 31 March 1921, so with effect from 1 September 1920 goods rates were raised to twice their pre-war level and flat-rate additions were made to reflect higher terminal costs.

Calculations of the revenue effects of these increases were however upset by the collapse of the post-war boom in the winter of 1920–1 and by disputes in the coal industry. A miners' strike in October 1920 was settled by government intervention, but the decontrol of the coal industry at the end of March 1921 was followed by a twelve-week strike which paralysed large sections of industry. Although attempts to involve the railway unions in sympathetic action through the 'triple alliance' did not succeed, the direct effects of the dispute were severe: passenger services were drastically reduced in an attempt to conserve coal and many freight trains were suspended for lack of traffic. In the changed economic conditions of 1921, with unemployment rising to almost 18%, many of the railwaymen's earlier gains were lost: the unions conceded the suspension of the guaranteed week and some of the other benefits for which they had fought in 1919, while as prices fell the operation of the sliding scale began to reverse earlier increases in wages.

In addition to having to deal with the deficit on current railway working, the government was also faced with the issue of retrospective adjustment to the compensation paid during the period of control. The railways contended that the amount of traffic which had been carried on government account and the problems caused by the backlog of maintenance – which they were having to make good at inflated post-war prices – justified further payment. Sir Eric Geddes opposed this case, arguing that the agreements had proved favourable to the companies, but in September 1920 he appointed a committee under Lord Colwyn to examine the question. While the companies themselves had formulated no specific financial claim, government-inspired press comment suggested that sums between £200m and £400m might be at stake. Despite this, the Colwyn Committee reported in February 1921 that the maximum that might be claimed was £150m, but its generally unsympathetic recommendations reflected the climate of hostility to the companies that the Ministry of Transport was apparently seeking to encourage, perhaps to deflect criticism of its own costs.

The compensation issue was eventually resolved by linking it with proposals for the reorganisation of the railway industry and during parliamentary debates in 1921 there was more than a hint that the offer of additional wartime compensation had been a means of obtaining the companies' agreement to the government's scheme. The shape of these proposals first began to emerge in June 1920, when Geddes indicated

that the government had discarded nationalisation as an option. This was followed by a white paper setting out more details, which included the amalgamation of railways into seven area groups, the setting of rates and charges to generate a net revenue equivalent to a pre-war standard, with government taking a share in any surplus to create a development fund, and worker participation in the boards of the new companies. The intended grouping structure was based on area monopolies: those who felt that the minister's proposals had been influenced by his time with the North Eastern Railway were strengthened in their view by the fact that the only change proposed in that company's status was the absorption of the one railway to challenge its monopoly, the Hull & Barnsley. So far as the LNWR was concerned, the intention was to merge it with the Midland, L&Y, North Staffordshire, and Furness to form a north western group. The independent Welsh companies were to be incorporated into the GWR: while the logic of territorial monopoly may have justified this overriding of the LNWR's close working links with the Rhymney Railway, the case for linking the Cambrian with the GWR in preference to the LNWR was perhaps less compelling. A separate Scottish group was planned, and the remaining entities would have comprised the southern companies, an amalgamation of the GCR, GNR, and GNR (thus reviving the pre-war 'three Greats' scheme), and a group encompassing the London underground companies.

These proposals provoked vigorous debate, both within and outwith the railway industry. External commentators concentrated on the implications for railway charges and on the perceived reduction in competition: to address the latter defect, various alternative proposals were made for an additional group based on the Midland Railway. Within the Railway Companies' Association, however, the main concerns were whether amalgamation would be voluntary or forced, the question of worker directors, and the proposal that the Ministry of Transport should retain extensive powers of intervention. Grouping as such was not seen as an issue, though in its detailed response on 8 December 1920 the Association, with only the North Eastern, Hull & Barnsley, and Barry railways dissenting, proposed an alternative structure of four main-line groups which foreshadowed the ultimate structure. The white paper proposal for London's railways was generally accepted.

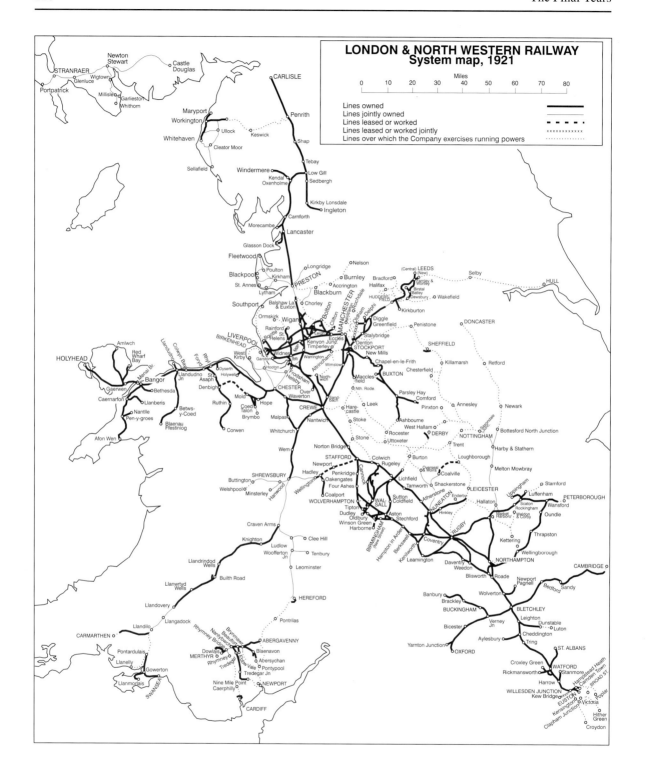

Figure 9.1 – LNWR system map, 1921.

Evidence that the government and the companies were moving towards an accommodation was provided by the dropping of direct worker representation in favour of reconstituted wages boards, a change which gained the support of the union leaders who saw the dangers of becoming too closely identified with the management of the railways. Discussion of the proposals and of the newly-published Colwyn Committee report at the LNWR general meeting on 25 February 1921 reflected the board's confidence that a satisfactory solution would be achieved. This confidence was well founded, for on 3 May, eight days before the publication of the Railways Bill, the Minister of Transport announced that there would be provision for the payment of £51m (£60m net of income tax) in settlement of the railways' various outstanding claims. Under the agreed arrangements the LNWR's share was £7,159,429, with interest of £10,230; small additional sums also accrued through various joint lines.

The Bill as introduced made provision for six groups which were a compromise between the white paper scheme and the Railway Companies' Association's alternative. The London proposals were abandoned to enable wider consideration to be given to the capital's transport needs, while the NER was to be grouped with its southern neighbours. Scotland, however, was to remain separate, although two groups were proposed instead of a single Scottish undertaking. The accompanying white paper strongly defended this arrangement, arguing that linking the Scottish railways with their English counterparts would create unwieldy organisations and would also require an increase in the Scottish companies' freight rates, which had traditionally been lower than those charged south of the border.

During the Bill's passage the government eventually deferred to strong pressure from the Scottish companies by agreeing to include the west and east Scottish groups with their English counterparts, although the amendment dealing with the west Scottish group was opposed in committee by Viscount Elveden and Major Hills, who were directors of the LNWR and Midland respectively. To satisfy another demand by the Scottish companies, and again despite the opposition of Elveden and Hills, who were joined by Sir Frederick Banbury, the GNR chairman, the financial basis for assessing amalgamation schemes was altered to take account of the prospective value of

a company within its new group and not simply its past earning power. With these and a number of other amendments the Railways Act received the Royal Assent on 19 August 1921, four days after the ending of government control. Under the Act's provisions a Railway Amalgamation Tribunal was established to determine grouping schemes, which were to come into effect no later than 1 July 1923. The Act also established a new statutory basis for railway charges and for industrial relations within the industry, and gave extensive powers to the Minister of Transport. Besides setting a limit to the independent life of the LNWR and the other companies covered by its provisions, the legislation accordingly marked the end of much of the existing framework within which the British railway system had been developed and regulated.

* * *

Despite this background of uncertainty and change, the task of putting the LNWR back on a peacetime footing was pursued vigorously. Many of the stations and halts closed in 1917 were reopened in 1919, including those on the Nantlle and Garston Dock branches, where passenger services resumed on 5 May. The Over & Wharton branch was reopened on 12 July 1920, while the reintroduction of Nuneaton–Burton trains on 1 May 1922 and a limited Wigan–Leigh service on 3 June 1922 restored two other sections of the passenger network. Continuing shortages and restrictions made the reinstatement of pre-war express service standards a slow process, but restaurant cars reappeared in March 1919, followed in 1920 by luggage in advance facilities and period excursion fares. In the summer of 1921 the best schedules between London and Liverpool or Manchester were reduced to 4 hours and through services between Lancashire and the Hampshire coast were reinstated. On 3 October that year 2-hour timings were reintroduced on the Euston–Birmingham service, while in December 1921 the Sussex coast 'Sunny South Specials' were reinstated; through services to Kent resumed the following June. The main suburban development was the completion of the long-delayed Chalk Farm–Queens Park section, which allowed electric services between Euston and Watford to commence on 10 July 1922, together with North London electric trains via Primrose Hill. The scheme

was finally completed on 30 October the same year when electric operation was extended to Croxley Green.

Development of the LNWR's maritime interests was also resumed with the ending of the war, though the decision of the Cunard line to operate the *Mauretania* from Southampton when she recommenced peacetime sailings on 6 March 1920 was a blow to hopes of rebuilding Liverpool's Atlantic traffic. At Holyhead, Captain W J C Nash OBE, who had risen in the company's own service, became marine superintendent in 1919 in succession to A T Orr, but the prospects for Irish channel shipping were clouded by the problems of achieving a settlement in Ireland and by the effects of partition. These also had a direct impact on Euston's Dundalk, Newry & Greenore outlier, which became a cross-border line as a consequence of the treaty of 6 December 1921 and suffered considerable damage during the Irish civil war. Despite the reintroduction of Holyhead–Greenore passenger sailings on 1 January 1920 there was therefore little opportunity to restore the previous status of this route.

The LNWR's principal thrust, however, was on the arterial crossing from Holyhead. After the temporary extension of the City of Dublin Steam Packet Company's Kingstown mail contract during the war, new tenders were sought in 1920 and the LNWR was at last successful in its bid. The long-delayed *Curraghmore* had been delivered in October 1919 and was initially put to work on the Dublin route; in 1920, following their release by the Admiralty and subsequent refitting, the two surviving express steamers also became available. Denny's had been able to resume work in 1918 on the LNWR's 1914 order for four larger and faster vessels, so to allow the new turbine steamers to perpetuate the names of their predecessors the veterans *Cambria* and *Scotia* returned to the fleet as the *Arvonia* and *Menevia* respectively. The first of the replacements, the *Anglia*,

achieved 24·7 knots during her trials and went into service on 11 May 1920. She and the *Curraghmore* took over the Post Office contract from the two remaining City of Dublin mail steamers on 28 November that year and the newly-delivered *Hibernia* entered service soon afterwards. The new *Cambria* and *Scotia* had been launched earlier in 1920, but their delivery was delayed by labour difficulties – the *Cambria* was eventually fitted out in Rouen – and they did not take up station until late in 1921. The new vessels were deeper-draughted than their predecessors and could not use the inner harbour at Holyhead without tidal restrictions; the LNWR therefore began work in 1921 to deepen and improve its berthage after obtaining an extension of its lease of the harbour. This work was not completed until 1923, so that during the time the mail service sailed under the LNWR flag it continued to operate from the Admiralty pier previously used by the CDSPC steamers.

A replacement cargo boat, the *Slieve Donard*, was also commissioned in 1921, giving the LNWR a complement of sixteen vessels on the Holyhead station, one more than in 1914. With the larger size of the new acquisitions, this gave a total capacity greatly in excess of that of the pre-war fleet. While the LNWR was also carrying the traffic previously handled by the Steam Packet company and re-employed some 260 of its men, the course of events in Ireland undermined the basis upon which this optimistic reinvestment in the railway fleet had been undertaken: indeed, after the new *Anglia* was damaged in a collision with the breakwater at Holyhead on 15 January 1922 she was taken out of regular service and used only at times of peak demand. In contrast with the Holyhead services, the joint routes were not re-equipped. The Fleetwood–Belfast service faced the renewal of competition from the Midland's Heysham route in May 1920 with only four of the pre-war *Dukes*, while although the return of the *Princess Victoria* from war service on 22 April 1920 restored a second steamer to the Stranraer–Larne fleet there was no attempt to reinstate the extra summer sailings that had been suspended in 1914.

Because of the modernisation of the Holyhead fleet, the capital invested in steamships at the end of 1921 stood at £2·63m, compared with £0·77m in 1918. While with hindsight this proved excessive, the bulk of the expenditure arose from earlier contracts

Opposite above: 'Precursor tank' 4-4-2T no 1985 at Northampton Castle with the Birmingham portion of the 'Sunny South Special' on 12 June 1922, the date when workings to and from the Kent coast were resumed. *(LNWR Society collection, 9407)*

Opposite below: An LNWR electric train at Carpenders Park on a Watford–Broad Street working in the early 1920s. *(National Railway Museum, NRM 1165/90)*

A commercial postcard showing one of the LNWR's post-war turbine steamers arriving at Carlisle Pier, Kingstown, with the funnels and masts of a sister ship visible behind the terminal shed.

which had increased in price because of the effects of the war. As a result the delivered cost of the *Curraghmore* and the four mail steamers was £1·82m, compared with the £738,500 approved in 1914. Although credits had been carried forward for wartime shipping losses, expenditure on new vessels represented the largest single item in the LNWR's post-war capital expenditure, which grew from £120,161 in 1918 to £1,703,276 in 1921. The latter figure was well in excess of the annual levels of investment immediately before the war, and more than half of the 1921 expenditure was attributable to steamships. However, as the cost of the new tonnage demonstrated, by 1921 the purchasing power of the pound was less than half of its 1914 level. Since only £1,877 was raised from 1918 onwards by the issue of stock, this post-war investment was financed almost entirely by an increase in the debit balance on capital account, which stood at almost £9·5m at the end of 1921.

Rolling stock and works forming part of the electrification scheme accounted for about £500,000 between 1918 and 1921 and a further £1m in 1922. Other post-war capital expenditure items included several station improvements, over 1,000 new wagons, investment at the company's workshops, and the replacement and expansion of the road motor fleet. This comprised 427 parcels or goods vehicles by the end of 1921, compared with 43 in 1913. In contrast, the number of horses used for cartage and shunting was 3,634, whereas there had been 6,187 in 1913. This increase in motorisation was not matched in the road passenger fleet, which numbered only five motor vehicles on 31 December 1921, compared with forty-one in 1913 and fifty-two in 1914. However, further diversification of the LNWR's passenger transport interests was provided by the acquisition of the Wolverton & Stony Stratford Tramway. This independent steam roadside tramway went into liquidation in 1919, and the LNWR purchased the undertaking for £6,504 at the end that year in order to ensure continued transport for its 700 Wolverton employees who used the service daily

Investment on capital account was supplemented by renewals and improvements out of revenue, which

were pushed ahead with the benefit of the accumu-
lated provision for deferred maintenance. Despite the
relief given by increased electric-train mileage, the
number of steam-hauled passenger vehicles increased
from 6,088 at the end of 1918 to 6,231 at the end of
1921. The freight fleet was also strengthened by
replacements and overhaul in addition to new provision on capital account: 1,556 wagons were renewed
in 1920, and 20,637 were given heavy repairs.
Nevertheless, the backlog of repairs and the build-up
of freight traffic were such that extra stock had to be
hired. At the end of 1920 the LNWR had 1,878
wagons on hire, including 700 mineral vehicles.

Similar pressures affected the locomotive fleet,
which expanded from 3,232 at the end of 1919 to
3,336 two years later. The average annual train
mileage per locomotive increased by 5·2% between
1919 and 1920: while it remained well below the 1913
figure of 16,522 miles, the war had resulted in a
significant increase in train loadings. One indication
of this was a 7% growth in assisting- and light-engine
mileage between 1913 and 1921. Almost 250 new
locomotives were put into service between the beginning of 1919 and the end of 1921, including
'Claughton' and 'Prince of Wales' 4-6-0s and the final
variant of the 0-8-0 heavy freight design, the 'G2'
class, of which twenty were built in 1921. In addition,
thirty-two 2-8-0s of GCR design were obtained from
government stock in 1919 and another twenty-two in
1921, though forty-two of the LNWR's 0-8-0s
remained overseas and were purchased by the government. The GCR 2-8-0s were not the only outside
acquisitions: ninety of the post-war 'Prince of Wales'
4-6-0s were built by Beardmore's, but the backlog at
Crewe remained so severe that new boilers were also
ordered from a variety of firms, while Armstrong
Whitworth was given a contract in 1919 for heavy
repairs to 240 locomotives. Some boiler repairs also
had to be sent outside. Despite these measures, at the
end of 1920 the LNWR had 460 locomotives awaiting
repair and 149 further 2-8-0s were then on hire from
the government to help to bridge the gap.

The effects of the post-war boom, which
contributed to this pressure on operating resources,
were reflected in the traffic figures which were
published once more from 1919 onwards, but of
course the continuation of control until 15 August
1921 insulated net revenue from fluctuations in costs
and earnings up till then. By reducing the contribution

to reserves the dividend was increased to 7½% in
1919 and 1920, and the same dividend was maintained for the following year despite the collapse of
the boom and the ending of control. However, no
addition was made to reserves in 1921, while the sum
of £400,000 received as the first instalment of the
additional wartime compensation contributed about
1% to the dividend. Costs were also cut by a 13%
reduction in train mileage, but even this drastic
response fell short of the drop of 27% in passenger
journeys and 32% in goods tonnage originating on the
LNWR in 1921 as a consequence of the coal strike and
the onset of depression. The outlook for decontrol
therefore hardly seemed promising.

* * *

The problems of post-war readjustment were
common to all British railways: indeed, while government control continued, company boards and
managements could have little direct influence over
the basic factors shaping the financial performance
and future of their undertakings. During this critical
period, however, the LNWR was placed at a particular
disadvantage by a series of losses which both undermined the company's internal continuity and deprived
it of key figures who might have been expected to play
a significant role in the wider course of events
affecting the future of the railways and the LNWR's
own part in that future.

The first of these losses was the death of Sir Guy
Calthrop on 23 February 1919, at the early age of 48.
The general manager had remained on secondment to
the Board of Trade as controller of coal mines and
most commentators agreed that overwork contributed
to his death from pneumonia following influenza. It
was already evident that the coal industry presented a
major and continuing task, but although Stanley Hunt
had returned to the LNWR from Calthrop's department on 1 January 1919 to take over from I T Williams
as chief goods manager, Williams's appointment as
general manager was not made substantive until after
Calthrop's death. This, together with the fact that
Williams was already 65, suggests that Calthrop had
been expected ultimately to return to his post with the
LNWR, while even in the interim his counsels as a
highly-placed and respected public servant would
have been important in the crucial post-war years.

After he succeeded Calthrop as general manager,

Williams was also nominated to the Railway Executive Committee; Sir Robert Turnbull once more stood down as the LNWR's representative but again was asked to continue in a personal capacity, which he did until his final resignation in September of the same year. The new general manager became Sir Thomas Williams in August 1919; a few weeks previously, at the end of June, his son Howard Williams had been moved from the post of minerals manager to become his assistant for staffing matters. Being related to a senior officer was never an obstacle to promotion in the LNWR, but, while Howard Williams had already served directly under his father in his previous post, the nature of the 1919 appointment was unique. Nevertheless, his personal abilities had been clearly shown during his service at the Ministry of Munitions, for which he received the CBE, while his standing in the industrial relations field was marked later in 1919 when he was appointed as one of the advisers to the British delegation to the Washington conference at which the International Labour Organisation was established.

Sir Thomas Williams's decision to retire at the end of 1920 came as no surprise in view of his age. Whether his son would have been a candidate to succeed him is an interesting unanswered question, for in June that year Howard Williams followed the path taken both by Calthrop and his own predecessor as minerals manager, J M Eddy, by emigrating to become the general manager of a British-owned railway in South America, in his case the Central Argentine Railway. While other senior officers might also have been regarded as potential successors to Sir Thomas, the publication of the grouping proposals at the end of June had made it clear that the LNWR's future as an independent company was likely to be limited. In keeping with the spirit of the government's proposals, therefore, negotiations were started with the Lancashire & Yorkshire Railway. When Williams's retiral was announced in December 1920 the board was able to state that Arthur Watson, the recently-appointed L&Y general manager, would also become general manager of the LNWR. Watson had shown considerable organisational ability during the war as chairman of the superintendents' conference and another factor in his favour was his comparative youth: he was 47 in 1920. Moreover, this was not the first time the LNWR had looked to Hunt's Bank when filling its most senior post, while Calthrop's appoint-

ment provided a precedent for the recruitment of an existing general manager. The difference in this case, however, was that Watson would retain his existing L&Y post – an aspect of the appointment which led to a parliamentary question – and it was clearly seen as a step towards amalgamation.

Before the succession to Sir Thomas Williams became an issue the LNWR suffered another unexpected loss, with the death of C J Bowen Cooke on 18 October 1920. Some reorganisation of the locomotive department had already taken place: F W Dingley had been appointed outdoor mechanical superintendent (locomotives and rail motors) from 1 July 1919, with responsibility for mechanical staff and repair work at running sheds. Following Bowen Cooke's death this remit was combined with the running function to make a separate department and Dingley was appointed on 1 November 1920 to the new post of chief superintendent of the locomotive running department. The previous deputy chief mechanical engineer, H P M Beames, was appointed on the same date as chief mechanical engineer for Crewe works, a designation which reflected his more limited responsibilities.

The LNWR therefore entered 1921, the year in which the government's proposals for the future of the railways would be put to the legislature, with a new management and organisational structure in one of its key departments and with a shared general manager whose background was with a different company. While there were obvious disadvantages in Watson's dual remit and separate reporting lines, the appointment nevertheless offered some potential benefits to both companies as a transitional arrangement. In particular, the L&Y board, whose previous chairman and former general manager, Sir John Aspinall, had resigned in 1919 to take up an appointment at the new Ministry of Transport, could have hoped to gain indirect access to the influence which Sir Gilbert Claughton carried in railway and political circles.

Unfortunately, this was not to be. The chairman had fallen ill in the month that Watson was appointed, and his place at the general meeting on 25 February 1921 was taken by the deputy chairman, the Hon Charles Napier Lawrence. In April it was reported that Sir Gilbert was making a good recovery, but at the beginning of June it was announced that he had retired as chairman for health reasons. Although he remained a director, his colleagues were not to have the benefit of their former chairman's guidance, for Claughton died on 27 June aged 65. As in the case of Calthrop, obituarists considered that the arduous demands of the war had contributed to his death.

Lawrence, who succeeded as chairman, was a son of Lord Lawrence of the Punjab; his younger brother, Sir Herbert Alexander Lawrence, had been Haig's chief of staff in France, and was a director of the Midland Railway. The new chairman was two years older than his predecessor and was also senior in terms of service on the LNWR board, to which he had been appointed in 1884. Lawrence had interests in insurance and in South American railways, including chairmanship of the Antofagasta & Bolivia Railway. He had been appointed as one of the two deputy-chairmen of the LNWR in 1903 and became the sole deputy in 1911. But despite Lawrence's long and senior standing on the LNWR board, the main respon-sibility for negotiating with government, with other company chairmen, and with labour leaders had been borne by Claughton during the decade of his chair-manship, and the importance of the latter's role, both directly and through the council of the Railway Companies' Association, had intensified as the

proposals for the post-war reconstruction of the industry had taken shape. While the war years and their immediate aftermath had taken their toll of a number of leading railway figures, the death of Claughton at such a crucial time, following as it did the earlier management losses, left the LNWR at a singular disadvantage among the major companies

While the passage of the 1921 Act signalled the start of the formal procedures for grouping, the close relationship which had already been established with the L&Y enabled the basis for an amalgamation of the two companies to be agreed as early as 25 March 1921, well before the publication of the Railways Bill. Once the procedures were on the statute book the agreement between the LNWR and L&Y was taken forward as a preliminary amalgamation scheme and implemented on 1 January 1922. From that date the two former companies were dissolved and a new London & North Western Railway came into exis-tence, with a directorate made up of six former L&Y directors and fourteen from the old LNWR board, chaired by Lawrence. An amalgamation often previ-ously considered thus finally came into effect, but the terms were a measure of the relative progress of the

Table 9.1 – LNWR STATISTICS, 1921 and 1922

	31 DEC 1921	31 DEC 1922
CAPITAL ACCOUNT:		
Total expenditure	£128,602,472	£197,905,294
Total receipts	£119,112,572	£184,118,432
ROUTE MILEAGE		
Owned	1,806·69	2,453·18
Joint (share)	207·13	200·55
Leased or worked	52·34	54·15
Total	**2,066·15**	**2,707·88**
SINGLE TRACK MILES (including sidings)	5,872·90	8,237·38
ROLLING STOCK:		
Locomotives	3,336	5,123
Rail motor vehicles	8	24
Electric stock	185	513
Coaching vehicles (hauled)	9,551	14,176
Freight vehicles	75,674	109,061

two constituents over the half-century since Parliament had rejected the previous proposal. Instead of the dividend enhancement offered in 1871, L&Y ordinary stock was exchanged for LNWR consols at 73% of par value in the 1921 scheme, reflecting the differential between the two companies' dividends and underlying valuations. Shares in both companies appreciated on the Stock Exchange once the terms of the amalgamation were announced, but a bigger percentage gain was shown by L&Y ordinary shares, suggesting that the markets felt the L&Y had struck a good bargain.

In addition to this amalgamation, two preliminary absorptions were agreed under the Railways Act provisions, bringing firstly the North London and Dearne Valley railways and secondly the Shropshire Union Railway & Canal company into the new LNWR. A year's notice had to be given to shareholders before an absorption could be ratified, so these two schemes were not finally approved until December 1922. However, as the companies concerned were already controlled by their larger partners, they effectively formed part of the new group from 1 January 1922 and were included in its accounts for that year. The effects of the amalgamation and these absorptions are shown in Table 9.1, which compares the financial and statistical position of the old and new LNWR companies.

In the last year before the grouping took effect the enlarged LNWR made good progress, aided by modest economic recovery and a fall in prices. As noted, the suburban electrification scheme was finally completed in 1922, while other service developments that year included the reinstatement of through carriages between Euston and Edinburgh. Net operating receipts for the railway and other businesses were 12% more than the combined 1921 totals of the constituent companies and the total net income of £10,187,299 was sufficient both to pay an $8^{1}/_{2}$% dividend – the highest since 1847 – and to bequeath a small balance to the company's successor. Capital expenditure of £840,244 was undertaken, £254,264 of which was attributable to new electric stock. A £575,000 loan inherited from the L&Y was paid off, leaving the final deficit on capital account at just under £14m.

For most directors and employees of the former LNWR, however, the main issues during 1922 were the reorganisation following the amalgamation with

the L&Y and the forthcoming grouping. The old LNWR board, already weakened by the death of Claughton, had lost another member in 1921: Ralph Brocklebank retired that November after thirty-eight years' service and died the following month. There were further changes in 1922: at the start of the year five of the remaining LNWR directors stood down as part of the amalgamation arrangements with the L&Y, among them Sir Robert Turnbull, and this was followed by the death on 2 February of Sir Edward Tootal Broadhurst, a board member since 1905. In addition, James Bishop, who had been the LNWR's secretary for almost eighteen years, retired at the end of 1921 and R C Irwin, his L&Y equivalent, took over as secretary of the combined company.

Irwin's redesignation was part of a widespread process of appointing L&Y officers to senior positions in the enlarged LNWR. This was a consequence of the amalgamation arrangements and to some extent reflected accidents of timing and seniority. But it was also clear that a further reduction in upper level management positions would be inevitable in the wider upheaval following the Railways Act, so in building the new LNWR's organisation it was important not only to have regard to seniority among existing L&Y and LNWR officers but also to have an eye to how they would stand when appointments were allocated in the larger amalgamation. In addition, however, an ex-L&Y general manager would almost inevitably tend towards the organisational structure which he had been instrumental in creating in his former company and to have closer affinities with Hunt's Bank and Horwich than with Euston and Crewe.

These two factors can be traced in the appointments and structure which took effect from 1 January 1922. Where seniority or incumbency gave a clear guide, as in the case of the secretary's post, this was followed. Thus Beames at Crewe was subordinated to George Hughes, chief mechanical engineer of the L&Y from 1904 (and himself an ex-Crewe man). On the civil engineering side, however, Ernest Trench, the LNWR's chief engineer since 1909, maintained his position. Other senior LNWR officers to remain in post were H C Burgess, principal assistant to the general manager since his return from the Ministry of Transport in October 1920, H L Thornhill, the solicitor, and Stanley Hunt, the chief goods manager.

The latter's responsibilities were however redrawn

in a way which effectively limited them to commercial functions. Control of goods handling passed to two divisional general superintendents, who also took over locomotive running responsibilities, together with the operating and passenger functions which had previously been exercised on the LNWR by the superintendent of the line. This model, which concentrated all operating functions in one department, was brought by Watson from the L&Y and in turn owed much to the Midland Railway's pre-war restructuring. The LNWR's superintendent of the line, Lancelot Horne, was appointed to the new southern divisional superintendency, which extended to Crewe; his curtailed geographical remit was balanced by wider functional responsibilities. The L&Y's general superintendent, Ashton Davies, added LNWR and joint lines north of Crewe to his previous portfolio. For engineering and locomotive running functions, however, the reconstruction was less radical: F W Dingley, redesignated superintendent of motive power (division A), was responsible to both divisional general superintendents for locomotive running on all ex-LNWR lines, whereas his ex-L&Y equivalent, F W Attock, was on Ashton Davies's staff and dealt only with former L&Y operations (division B) in the new northern division. The same 'A' divisional structure was maintained for a number of ex-LNWR all-line responsibilities, such as telegraphs and rolling stock running, and the chief engineer's department was similarly organised on an 'A' and 'B' basis to reflect the former ownership of way and works.

Within the chief mechanical & electrical engineer's department – Hughes brought his L&Y designation with him – there was a mixture of responsibilities. Beames was one of two divisional mechanical engineers, along with G N Shawcross at Horwich. The carriage and wagon functions, which had previously been departments in their own right on the LNWR, were brought within Hughes's purview. A R Trevithick, who had taken over from Earle at Wolverton in 1916, was redesignated divisional carriage superintendent; W W H Warneford, his successor both as works manager at Crewe and then as wagon superintendent, was likewise given the title of divisional wagon superintendent. Their ex-L&Y equivalent at Newton Heath, F E Gobey, became divisional carriage & wagon superintendent. The former L&Y electrical engineer, H E O'Brien, remained in the same position under Hughes; F A Cortez Leigh,

who had seen through the LNWR suburban electrification, had to be content with the post of divisional electrical engineer (division A).

Under this new regime locomotive building and repair at Crewe continued with little interference from Horwich, although Hughes encouraged exchanges of supervisory staff as a means of inculcating L&Y production standards and techniques at Crewe. In 1922 Crewe also adopted British Standard specifications for steel instead of producing to its own specification. The locomotives built at Crewe during 1922 were all 'G2' 0-8-0s, though work started on the only class designed under Beames, an 0-8-4 tank intended for the demanding conditions of the south Wales lines. In addition, further 'Prince of Wales' 4-6-0s were delivered from Beardmore's, while the North London fleet of locomotives was brought into LNWR stock. Naming of express passenger locomotives continued and was applied to a number of 'Prince of Wales' and 'Claughton' engines of earlier vintage, including three 1920 'Claughtons' which in February 1922 were named after the LNWR employees who had been awarded the Victoria Cross.

Another reminder of the war which also served to perpetuate something of the LNWR had been provided on 21 October 1921, when Field Marshall Earl Haig unveiled the company's memorial in Euston Square; a further fitting gesture was the visit by the Duke of York to Camden and Euston on 6 December 1922, three weeks before the company's operational existence ended. But in truth the LNWR heritage was already ebbing: the demoralisation at Crewe caused by the grouping process has been well chronicled, and the same trend was evident at Euston, as R Carrington Willis described in his account of his headquarters career, *My fifty-one years at Euston*. Events had moved quickly during the first quarter of 1922: after premature reports in February that the Midland and LNWR had reached agreement on amalgamation terms, a settlement was announced in March. This made provision for LNWR consols to be exchanged at par for the stock of the new company and for Midland stockholders to receive £62 10s of 4% preference stock for every £100 of 2½% preferred ordinary stock they held and £68 of ordinary stock for every £100 of deferred ordinary stock. There was a certain irony in the fact that Nathaniel Spens led the vote of thanks to the LNWR board at the special meeting to approve the amalgamation terms at the end of November 1922, for the two categories of Midland ordinary stock had been created in 1897 by a stock-splitting operation. Spens had unsuccessfully advocated similar measures at LNWR general meetings and some retrospective justification for his case was provided by the fact that on 22 March 1922 the combined stock-market price of £100 each of the preferred and deferred Midland stocks was £113, whereas £100 of LNWR consols stood at £89. The course of post-grouping dividends was to prove that the Midland's proprietors had obtained an even better deal than was then apparent, since prior charges quickly eroded the amounts available for distribution on ordinary shares, the largest proportion of which went to former LNWR shareholders. But this could not have been foreseen when the amalgamation terms were agreed, since they were drawn up on the assumption that the pre-war standard revenues could be maintained. Instead, advocates of the financial principles laid down by Moon could argue that the choice of LNWR consolidated stock as the datum for the amalgamated undertaking was an acknowledgement of the underlying soundness of the company and its capital structure.

Other elements of the amalgamation scheme were still to be resolved – the terms for the incorporation of the Caledonian Railway were not finally settled until 29 June 1923, and the North Staffordshire's inclusion was also delayed for statutory reasons – but the Midland and LNWR agreement was the crucial step in the process of the formation of the North Western, Midland & West Scottish group. The question of a more harmonious name exercised commentators from an early stage: Midland & North Western Railway or London, Midland & North Western Railway were being canvassed when the initial agreement was announced, while the adoption of the title of London & North Eastern Railway by the eastern group was seen as pre-empting, by its similarity, any hopes of retaining the LNWR's own name. It was also generally understood that the Midland directors were arguing strongly that their company's name must be included in the final choice. After suggestions that London, Midland & Northern Railway would be adopted, the variant London Midland & Scottish was eventually chosen. The amalgamation tribunal, which had a preference for short titles, took some persuading, but the name was finally approved as part of the preliminary amalgamation scheme dated 30 December 1922 which linked the London & North

Western, Midland, Furness, Glasgow & South Western, and Highland railways. At midnight the next day the LNWR lost its identity within the new LMS, although it was not until 23 February 1923 that the company's last meeting was held to adopt the 1922 accounts and confirm the final dividend.

In many ways the LNWR's experience during the larger grouping echoed what had already happened a year previously when it amalgamated with the L&Y. Superficially, little changed: the Hon Charles Napier Lawrence – shortly to become Lord Lawrence of Kingsgate – became the first chairman of the new company and Arthur Watson – soon to be honoured with a knighthood – was its first general manager, while many of the organisational arrangements introduced in January 1922 survived the transition to the LNWR's new existence as the western division of the LMS. A chief general superintendent, J H Follows of the Midland, was interposed, with headquarters at Derby; Lancelot Horne retired, dying prematurely in 1924, and Ashton Davies became general superintendent for the entire western division, based at Hunt's Bank. His assistants, C R Byrom at Euston and T W Royle at Manchester, effectively perpetuated the 1922 operating arrangements, though at a sub-divisional level within the new organisation. While Hughes remained chief mechanical & electrical engineer, rolling stock was removed from his responsibilities and placed under the former Midland carriage and wagon superintendent, R W Reid; the Wolverton and Earlestown officers retained their designations and reported to Derby instead of Horwich. On the locomotive side, mechanical engineers for the various constituent lines took their place alongside Beames and Shawcross, but the designation of Sir Henry Fowler, the Midland divisional mechanical engineer, as Hughes's deputy chief mechanical engineer was a further reduction in Crewe's status. Against this, however, both the chief engineer and the chief goods manager of the former LNWR became chief officers of the larger company.

On paper, therefore, the LNWR went into the new company with relatively minor adjustments to its 1922 structure. It also took the largest number of places on the board of the LMS, with twelve directors out of twenty-eight, compared with eight from the Midland. However, a third of the LNWR contingent represented the former L&Y, so ex-Midland directors balanced the pre-1922 LNWR element on the new board. The apparent ascendancy of the Midland interest was also reflected in other ways: Sir Guy Granet, its last chairman, reminded shareholders in November 1922 that the history of their company was founded upon amalgamations and went on to say that the grouping represented not the death warrant of the Midland but 'another step forward in its accustomed path'. The emphasis that many writers have placed on the subsequent elimination of the LNWR's locomotive and operating traditions may appear to substantiate this interpretation of the LMS's creation as a greater Midland Railway.

But a railway amounts to much more than the colour of its rolling stock, and it is possible to overstate the case. While Granet, at 55, was in a key position in the amalgamation and was an obvious deputy and successor to Lawrence, his background and outlook made him unlikely to take a narrow view based solely on Midland interests. Moreover, he must have been acutely aware that without his managerial and directorial experience, which was backed up by wider government and City connections, the Midland would also have gone into the amalgamation from a position of relative weakness. His successor as general manager, Frank Tatlow, was due to retire at the end of 1922, while he himself had rejoined the Midland as chairman because of the retiral of Charles Booth. Granet was very conscious of the management demands of the new company and made a direct approach to Sir Herbert Walker before the LMS was formed to invite him to become general manager of the amalgamated undertaking. Walker was widely regarded as the most experienced and able railway general manager of his day; that he was an ex-LNWR officer would have made its own contribution to the development of the LMS, but the fact that such an approach was made by the Midland chairman was itself significant both as a testimony to Granet's underlying motivation and as a footnote to the subsequent management history of the LMS.

Walker, though attracted by the offer, refused out of loyalty to the LSWR and the nascent Southern group; while it is interesting to speculate how the LMS might have developed had he accepted, this is just one of the many imponderables which mark these years. If Calthrop or Claughton had survived, if the LNWR board had looked elsewhere for a successor to Sir Thomas Williams, or if the government had adopted another approach in its post-war reorganisation of the railways, the course of events would have been significantly different. However, it is in terms of actual outcomes that the LNWR's final years have to be assessed: while it is clear that much of the company's unique heritage and standing was lost when the LMS was formed, it is also evident that the board had set the LNWR on this path when Arthur Watson was invited at the end of 1920 to take over the general manager's post. Consciously or not, by reading the government's intentions and anticipating the grouping by achieving a merger that had long been one of the LNWR's ambitions, the company's directors – who included Sir Thomas Williams from January 1921, as well as Sir Robert Turnbull, a former general manager and superintendent of the line – adopted a strategy which had already diluted the LNWR's distinct identity by the time the LMS was formed.

But by the standards of its time the Premier Line had served its customers, shareholders, and workforce well, and during the war years had demonstrated what its human and material resources could contribute to a greater national need. Although the LNWR's ending was muted and its final years and ultimate fate within the LMS have an element of anticlimax, its legacy was clear and substantial. As Lawrence told the shareholders at their final meeting, the company was handing over a line as well equipped as any in the country and was in a stronger financial position than it had ever been. No other eulogy was offered, nor indeed was needed, for those attainments were the summation of the guiding principles of the LNWR throughout its independent life.

TABLE A1

London & North Western Railway: capital, revenue, costs, and dividends, 1846–1922

Year	Total expenditure on Capital a/c	Working revenue Coaching	Freight	Total	Traffic expenses	Working ratio	Net revenue	Interest + other fixed charges	Dividends Total	Ord^y
	£	£	£	£	£	%	£	£	£	%
1845	*14,163,260*									
1846	18,042,004	1,422,646	650,320	2,095,056	790,469	37.7	1,497,702	133,756	1,260,388	10
1847	21,513,354	1,417,942	720,987	2,155,479	882,350	40.9	1,430,410	155,873	1,193,753	8$^1/_2$
1848	24,113,183	1,399,613	733,575	2,146,905	879,948	41.0	1,388,863	236,854	1,080,515	7
1849	28,192,031	1,366,970	795,575	2,185,717	878,649	40.2	1,420,088	321,678	1,010,148	6$^1/_4$
1850	29,040,671	1,403,767	913,703	2,345,734	900,466	38.4	1,584,685	445,225	988,168	5$^1/_4$
1851	29,511,303	1,665,411	932,713	2,626,111	1,068,821	40.7	1,798,233	496,926	1,118,832	5$^3/_4$
1852	29,662,085	1,435,360	1,010,717	2,474,665	1,083,057	43.8	1,662,393	489,548	1,080,060	5$^1/_4$
1853	30,762,512	1,467,823	1,160,514	2,660,007	1,196,023	45.0	1,663,922	498,731	1,079,160	5
1854	31,959,244	1,492,797	1,307,786	2,811,409	1,334,358	47.5	1,684,746	503,482	1,109,994	5
1855	32,360,307	1,489,635	1,402,798	2,877,474	1,331,109	46.3	1,724,904	548,523	1,127,869	5
1856	32,707,591	1,602,736	1,570,478	3,157,422	1,441,110	45.6	1,887,990	635,998	1,243,951	5$^1/_2$
1857	33,449,879	1,679,802	1,558,776	3,232,775	1,544,565	47.8	1,834,859	635,403	1,156,109	5
1858	34,486,609	1,497,072	1,464,790	2,959,621	1,506,165	50.9	1,635,498	656,336	955,965	4
1859	35,019,573	1,893,130	1,874,363	3,754,403	1,826,851	48.7	2,116,054	960,909	1,144,275	4$^3/_4$
1860	36,025,538	2,077,150	2,145,133	4,240,293	2,080,700	49.1	2,351,280	1,054,433	1,269,286	5$^1/_8$
1861	36,409,032	2,146,837	2,247,106	4,428,568	2,333,320	52.7	2,273,387	1,172,552	1,085,443	4$^1/_4$
1862	36,786,901	2,307,022	2,328,772	4,678,414	2,345,212	50.1	2,469,380	1,269,614	1,183,424	4$^5/_8$
1863	37,667,047	2,365,323	2,631,118	5,038,256	2,455,134	48.7	2,739,798	1,387,115	1,331,478	5$^1/_8$
1864	39,023,717	2,559,174	3,029,232	5,638,730	2,584,502	45.8	3,269,497	1,502,129	1,741,526	6$^3/_8$
1865	40,482,731	2,724,498	3,245,915	6,023,237	2,767,917	46.0	3,493,798	1,540,067	1,941,468	6$^5/_8$
1866	45,576,362	2,809,915	3,502,151	6,361,235	3,036,329	47.7	3,573,868	1,472,378	2,076,989	6$^3/_8$
1867	46,344,423	2,821,325	3,633,875	6,527,436	3,175,300	48.6	3,584,778	1,498,615	2,051,505	6
1868	51,023,219	2,849,190	3,634,373	6,558,081	3,183,202	48.5	3,629,197	1,448,417	2,154,775	6
1869	52,860,625	2,895,249	3,709,593	6,682,251	3,176,701	47.5	3,760,983	1,438,730	2,291,071	6$^1/_4$
1870	54,418,467	2,942,286	3,973,194	7,004,893	3,293,878	47.0	3,945,738	1,458,116	2,450,711	6$^5/_8$
1871	56,336,355	3,124,539	4,362,515	7,595,036	3,449,947	45.4	4,432,213	1,521,788	2,910,426	7$^3/_4$
1872	58,495,268	3,364,067	4,647,030	8,038,282	3,850,138	47.9	4,479,728	1,520,531	2,959,197	7$^3/_4$
1873	60,611,275	3,581,284	5,029,454	8,720,608	4,564,286	52.3	4,432,732	1,505,012	2,927,719	7$^1/_2$
1874	62,833,162	3,672,208	5,169,502	8,952,458	4,930,685	55.1	4,283,231	1,495,174	2,788,057	6$^7/_8$
1875	65,736,764	3,706,364	5,388,776	9,209,706	5,087,695	55.2	4,360,237	1,505,061	2,855,176	6$^3/_4$
1876	68,051,545	3,714,899	5,412,369	9,241,301	5,086,808	55.0	4,426,315	1,535,478	2,890,837	6$^5/_8$
1877	71,100,331	3,729,709	5,467,975	9,322,928	5,090,276	54.6	4,510,292	1,574,225	2,936,068	6$^5/_8$
1878	81,620,205	3,754,792	5,552,493	9,442,193	5,080,811	53.8	4,641,161	1,370,956	3,270,205	6$^1/_2$
1879	83,758,394	3,585,742	5,563,820	9,293,678	4,800,054	51.6	4,775,614	1,164,975	3,610,639	6$^1/_2$
1880	85,795,775	3,703,163	5,921,562	9,765,570	4,933,017	50.5	5,112,797	1,163,314	3,949,483	7$^3/_8$

Continued on p232; for notes see p234

TABLE A2

London & North Western Railway: mileage and traffic statistics, 1846–1922

Year	Route miles open	Train mileage		Total freight tonnage	Passengers					
		Passenger trains	Freight trains		Total (excl season tickets)	First class	Second class	Third class & parlia-mentary	Workmen's tickets	Season tickets (see note)
	miles	miles	miles	tons	no	no	no	no	no	no
1846	383.25									
1847	433.00									
1848	465.49									
1849	470.00			See note A						
1850	478.00									
1851	518.00									
1852	559.00									
1853	562.00									
1854	562.00									
1855	562.00									
1856	646.42	4,741,135	4,457,514	5,009,593	9,790,683	1,226,897	2,980,527	5,583,259		1,124
1857	656.53	5,082,624	4,655,671	5,460,971	10,095,746	1,295,750	3,135,356	5,664,640		1,225
1858	650.00									
1859	794.25	6,717,195	6,512,403	6,990,188	12,273,157					
1860	950.00	7,208,942	7,216,349	8,091,396	12,739,412	1,383,947	4,165,038	7,190,427		1,850
1861	1030.00	7,819,093	7,606,504	8,386,039	16,611,010	2,078,038	6,197,194	8,335,778		2,195
1862	1138.00	8,131,703	7,378,143	8,484,837	17,226,381	2,154,118	6,412,795	8,659,468		2,318
1863	1209.00	8,825,737	8,478,401	9,791,959	19,185,751	2,308,727	6,952,775	9,924,249		2,686
1864	1274.00	9,509,295	9,591,011	12,049,545	21,682,625	2,527,313	7,580,641	11,574,671		3,194
1865	1274.00	10,253,026	10,439,117	13,423,577	23,711,000	2,807,296	8,478,907	12,424,797		3,820
1866	1319.00	10,613,324	11,023,839	15,425,119	25,330,341	2,858,795	8,905,355	13,566,191		4,376
1867	1333.00	10,802,332	11,467,210	16,359,413	25,910,434	2,900,480	9,124,222	13,885,732		4,511
1868	1416.50	11,096,067	11,186,000	16,090,870	27,493,464	3,179,408	8,632,820	15,681,236		5,473
1869	1477.00	11,647,308	11,632,342	17,009,931	28,758,886	2,762,182	9,011,801	16,984,903		5,650
1870	1506.75	12,447,546	12,590,031	19,270,640	30,340,610	2,728,990	8,940,820	18,670,800		6,213
1871	1472.50	12,871,329	13,635,673	21,175,602	33,001,415	2,840,985	8,281,366	21,879,064		7,050
1872	1539.25	13,760,992	15,074,924	22,831,041	38,006,013	2,970,232	5,875,036	29,160,745		7,970
1873	1578.00	14,281,208	15,842,542	24,307,384	41,404,545	3,005,417	5,418,494	32,980,634		8,750
1874	1583.75	14,460,568	16,097,954	24,017,638	43,485,213	3,092,983	6,146,850	34,245,380		9,020
1875	1588.50	14,623,907	16,389,890	26,259,436	44,116,661	3,288,661	7,017,238	33,810,762		9,277
1876	1615.75	15,417,736	16,906,023	26,346,208	45,847,476	3,206,758	5,883,395	36,757,323		12,326
1877	1644.50	15,981,878	16,719,802	29,133,348	46,799,697	3,099,616	5,651,728	38,048,353		13,640
1878	1659.50	16,113,766	16,581,156	28,712,474	46,698,786	2,862,430	5,059,171	38,777,185		14,542
1879	1713.00	16,087,182	16,430,751	29,544,026	44,870,957	2,667,596	4,607,058	37,596,303		15,220
1880	1719.50	16,702,894	18,209,893	32,706,278	47,571,537	2,579,483	4,383,758	40,608,296		16,050

Continued on p233; for notes see p235

Year	Total expendi-ture on Capital a/c	Working revenue			Traffic expenses	Working ratio	Net revenue	Interest + other fixed charges	Dividends	
		Coaching	Freight	Total					Total	Ord^y
	£	£	£	£	£	%	£	£	£	%
1881	87,910,583	3,748,179	6,080,780	9,980,267	5,104,963	51.2	5,177,775	1,184,570	3,993,204	7$^1/_4$
1882	89,984,586	3,903,116	6,204,362	10,265,788	5,215,971	50.8	5,364,312	1,187,691	4,176,621	7$^1/_2$
1883	91,997,869	4,023,818	6,268,996	10,453,804	5,322,354	50.9	5,425,927	1,192,947	4,232,981	7$^1/_2$
1884	93,648,577	4,081,419	6,075,841	10,325,801	5,295,426	51.3	5,280,784	1,218,544	4,062,240	6$^3/_4$
1885	95,907,650	4,042,660	5,977,680	10,202,787	5,227,109	51.2	5,233,927	1,234,854	3,999,073	6$^1/_2$
1886	96,653,787	4,124,707	5,887,854	10,209,368	5,243,081	51.4	5,215,562	1,251,398	3,964,164	6$^1/_4$
1887	97,427,050	4,210,189	6,025,655	10,432,507	5,382,575	51.6	5,324,305	1,247,518	4,076,787	6$^1/_2$
1888	99,639,448	4,251,330	6,198,583	10,651,153	5,505,314	51.7	5,424,806	1,244,414	4,180,392	6$^3/_4$
1889	100,329,777	4,502,134	6,507,039	11,207,009	5,816,927	51.9	5,672,847	1,229,342	4,443,505	7$^3/_8$
1890	101,023,674	4,711,914	6,661,516	11,579,701	6,228,671	53.8	5,652,183	1,245,859	4,406,323	7$^1/_4$
1891	102,099,199	4,763,606	6,803,927	11,778,986	6,490,670	55.1	5,576,841	1,250,402	4,234,330	7
1892	103,238,060	4,799,947	6,721,393	11,725,010	6,547,347	55.8	5,447,505	1,281,310	4,085,524	6$^1/_2$
1893	104,247,688	4,778,732	6,251,831	11,223,499	6,467,868	57.6	5,002,217	1,289,073	3,671,004	5$^3/_8$
1894	105,181,130	4,830,228	6,572,048	11,610,456	6,429,977	55.4	5,396,839	1,300,679	4,042,701	6$^1/_4$
1895	105,828,840	4,971,530	6,583,437	11,775,815	6,499,336	55.2	5,503,431	1,317,606	4,118,617	6$^3/_8$
1896	106,452,209	5,225,515	6,872,061	12,319,376	6,753,554	54.8	5,816,199	1,289,026	4,427,394	7$^1/_8$
1897	107,357,382	5,384,431	7,061,005	12,678,909	7,156,583	56.4	5,810,091	1,288,592	4,431,963	7$^1/_8$
1898	108,503,775	5,558,347	7,347,626	13,140,984	7,572,030	57.6	5,846,365	1,291,033	4,467,827	7$^1/_8$
1899	109,772,578	5,770,321	7,590,713	13,603,579	7,990,023	58.7	5,894,539	1,284,647	4,520,001	7$^1/_8$
1900	111,426,253	5,993,476	7,631,869	13,883,530	8,575,250	61.8	5,588,718	1,318,132	4,190,551	6$^1/_4$
1901	112,940,163	6,054,646	7,590,143	13,901,296	8,829,263	63.5	5,327,848	1,367,323	3,885,173	5$^1/_2$
1902	114,300,795	6,166,429	7,881,649	14,307,839	8,959,230	62.6	5,606,712	1,365,596	4,138,247	6
1903	115,219,226	6,178,834	7,867,031	14,320,463	9,032,646	63.1	5,571,363	1,358,997	4,113,015	5$^7/_8$
1904	115,645,461	6,169,087	8,014,582	14,460,508	9,189,274	63.5	5,539,276	1,373,362	4,081,380	5$^3/_4$
1905	116,279,643	6,242,931	8,230,912	14,756,452	9,272,438	62.8	5,730,256	1,379,393	4,256,989	6$^1/_8$
1906	116,985,947	6,389,453	8,575,809	15,246,371	9,620,995	63.1	5,883,908	1,394,093	4,370,987	6$^3/_8$
1907	117,921,578	6,523,394	9,056,305	15,859,764	10,144,826	64.0	5,992,738	1,494,425	4,373,019	6$^3/_8$
1908	118,807,063	6,563,151	8,625,248	15,476,131	10,136,782	65.5	5,653,018	1,406,658	4,145,003	5$^3/_4$
1909	119,556,549	6,503,785	8,621,327	15,413,943	9,859,592	64.0	5,802,071	1,444,909	4,238,645	5$^7/_8$
1910	119,908,977	6,698,595	8,926,599	15,922,697	9,936,640	62.4	6,265,082	1,586,090	4,560,330	6$^5/_8$
1911	120,257,006	6,932,773	9,172,037	16,409,544	10,286,412	62.7	6,405,819	1,637,970	4,667,567	6$^7/_8$
1912	120,896,512	7,019,019	9,413,827	16,733,193	10,885,041	65.1	6,165,680	1,557,494	4,506,793	6$^1/_2$
1913		*7,871,674*	*9,191,550*							
1913	121,765,128	7,213,998	8,864,578	17,500,012	11,322,164	64.7	6,435,988	1,512,792	4,721,268	7
1914	122,998,379	n.a.	n.a.	17,610,699	11,745,141	66.7	6,103,714	1,543,312	4,351,400	6
1915	123,830,841	n.a.	n.a.	18,527,553	12,502,374	67.5	6,311,640	1,551,698	4,385,367	6
1916	124,351,013	n.a.	n.a.	19,719,478	13,655,960	69.3	6,456,473	1,598,665	4,419,701	6
1917	124,640,110	n.a.	n.a.	21,747,963	15,587,384	71.7	6,678,069	1,607,662	4,420,097	6
1918	124,760,271	n.a.	n.a.	25,310,604	19,074,358	75.4	6,836,932	1,623,270	4,849,318	7
1919	125,307,145	n.a.	n.a.	31,656,699	25,281,514	79.9	7,072,032	1,637,373	5,063,868	7$^1/_2$
1920	126,899,195	n.a.	n.a.	40,590,348	34,080,449	84.0	7,134,089	1,686,088	5,063,869	7$^1/_2$
1921	128,602,472	n.a.	n.a.	38,847,131	32,837,186	84.5	7,055,956	1,722,627	5,063,869	7$^1/_2$
1922	197,905,294	19,125,148	22,825,537	46,130,753	36,517,288	79.2	10,456,759	2,464,452	7,822,286	8$^1/_2$

For notes see p234

	Route miles open	Train mileage		Total freight tonnage	Passengers					
		Passenger trains	Freight trains		Total (excl season tickets)	First class	Second class	Third class & parlia-mentary	Workmen's tickets	Season tickets
1881	1749.25	17,366,522	18,821,956	33,736,790	48,787,854	2,516,381	4,115,904	42,153,688		16,756
1882	1758.00	17,987,805	18,792,679	35,082,756	52,027,867	2,452,504	4,053,737	45,521,626		18,309
1883	1777.25	18,765,729	19,331,049	35,447,660	54,171,819	2,432,139	4,055,853	47,683,827		18,419
1884	1794.75	19,576,553	18,372,312	33,606,510	54,936,033	2,320,332	3,985,590	48,630,111		19,539
1885	1810.75	19,642,321	18,331,906	32,794,701	53,875,286	2,136,168	3,668,257	48,070,861		21,117
1886	1834.00	19,537,777	18,087,551	32,934,212	55,568,578	2,066,297	3,506,354	49,653,208		22,630
1887	1840.75	19,696,709	18,390,475	34,953,499	56,730,707	2,012,399	3,421,636	51,296,672		24,024
1888	1876.75	19,875,824	18,765,181	35,922,619	56,778,905	1,915,851	3,331,935	51,531,119		25,656
1889	1876.25	20,772,337	19,771,553	37,487,175	59,333,417	1,928,402	3,280,254	54,124,761		27,315
1890	1876.50	21,611,099	20,287,911	37,358,724	62,890,079	1,915,100	3,326,066	57,648,913		28,825
1891	1890.25	21,833,524	20,660,865	37,685,007	64,566,889	1,894,553	3,294,303	59,378,033		30,526
1892	1887.50	22,322,238	20,914,461	37,498,235	67,165,420	1,994,861	3,317,228	61,853,331		33,135
1893	1891.00	21,822,937	19,309,051	33,365,981	67,394,176	1,885,405	2,927,902	62,580,869		34,677
1894	1891.25	21,467,625	19,999,222	37,231,466	69,907,478	1,891,921	2,928,939	65,086,618		36,628
1895	1912.00	21,961,481	19,694,484	37,051,969	71,372,502	1,879,988	2,811,982	66,680,532		38,040
1896	1912.50	22,995,666	20,307,502	39,215,491	75,927,941	1,979,980	2,939,920	71,008,041		41,399
1897	1912.25	24,276,761	21,210,013	40,942,688	79,110,585	1,977,342	3,274,976	73,858,267		44,162
1898	1910.25	25,483,452	22,065,200	41,898,395	82,069,384	1,976,723	4,239,454	75,853,207		47,435
1899	1928.00	26,285,278	22,515,697	44,229,850	85,488,175	1,978,264	4,735,493	78,774,418		49,312
1900	1940.75	26,624,498	22,598,619	44,465,277	86,929,191	1,959,587	5,086,901	79,882,703		50,586
1901	1940.75	26,657,263	21,285,217	42,723,084	86,703,430	1,912,328	5,368,882	79,422,220		52,215
1902	1941.50	27,034,937	20,604,853	45,148,432	86,647,130	1,896,367	5,831,676	78,919,087		55,527
1903	1946.75	27,225,732	18,176,481	45,442,795	85,961,954	1,862,787	5,950,973	78,148,194		65,209
1904	1946.50	27,642,003	17,887,713	46,785,626	84,682,391	1,754,815	5,765,478	77,162,098		70,623
1905	1947.00	28,319,859	18,351,765	48,846,750	84,017,920	1,729,641	5,385,134	76,903,145		73,690
1906	1947.00	29,296,499	19,195,784	51,582,307	85,835,498	1,631,929	5,023,996	79,179,573		77,211
1907	1947.25	30,063,319	20,303,045	54,990,296	84,894,907	1,480,116	4,702,300	78,712,491		80,074
1908	1953.75	29,964,219	18,768,425	51,964,172	82,933,250	1,374,357	4,412,859	77,146,034		80,771
1909	1965.50	29,769,899	17,342,128	52,139,454	80,937,375	1,315,085	4,206,190	75,416,100		82,938
1910	1966.00	30,255,210	17,237,324	53,894,503	81,896,273	1,302,542	4,064,950	76,528,781		85,296
1911	1966.00	30,705,230	17,467,424	54,720,400	83,114,817	1,245,075	3,390,605	78,479,137		92,494
1912	1968.75	29,294,317	17,164,407	54,517,214	79,005,445	1,418,116	324,589	77,262,740		92,164
1913				*57,656,257*	*92,540,230*	*1,538,818*	*281,301*	*69,975,603*	*20,744,508*	*58,016*
1913	2062.83	31,371,207	19,801,743	38,402,272	80,921,318	1,283,095	178,099	60,691,856	18,768,268	49,749
1914	2063.11	31,750,616	18,479,953	n.a.	n.a.	n.a.	n.a.	n.a.	n.a.	n.a.
1915	n.a.	n.a.		n.a.	n.a.	n.a.	n.a.	n.a.	n.a.	n.a.
1916	n.a.	n.a.		n.a.	n.a.	n.a.	n.a.	n.a.	n.a.	n.a.
1917	n.a.	n.a.	See note B		n.a.	n.a.	n.a.	n.a.	n.a.	n.a.
1918	n.a.	n.a.			n.a.	n.a.	n.a.	n.a.	n.a.	n.a.
1919	2066.08	23,071,112	17,565,041	32,347,898	101,816,838	2,150,321		58,905,799	40,760,718	76,407
1920	2066.14	24,840,289	18,300,701	33,730,516	113,873,294	2,000,998		64,007,144	47,865,152	87,159
1921	2066.15	23,734,072	13,751,327	22,922,509	83,458,800	1,158,034		53,339,774	28,960,992	78,693
1922	2707.88	43,357,035	22,589,154	45,637,880	168,254,983	2,715,480	40,518	107,649,157	57,849,828	152,473
1922				*69,904,888*	*176,497,771*	*2,912,289*	*48,301*	*114,872,047*	*58,665,134*	*169,177*

For notes see p235

ABBREVIATION   n.a.   not available

SOURCES
London & North Western Railway reports and accounts.
Bradshaw's *Railway manual, shareholders' guide, and official directory*, 1914 (for annual rates of dividend prior to 1913).

NOTES FOR TABLE A1

General

Until 1913, railway company accounts were prepared on a half-yearly basis, and the revenue and expenditure columns in the above table have been compiled by aggregating the appropriate six-monthly figures for the years 1846-1912 inclusive.

Changes within series

The working and traffic figures quoted above include subsidiary companies from the dates of their incorporation within the LNWR's main accounts.

There were a number of adjustments to the company's accounting practices during the period covered by the table. In order to ensure a degree of consistency, figures prior to 1869 have been reworked as far as possible to categorise income and expenditure on the basis prescribed in the Regulation of Railways Act, 1868. No amendments have been made to reflect subsequent changes, which until 1912 were generally minor.

The basis of railway financial and statistical returns was substantially altered with effect from 1913, so some post-1912 figures are not immediately consistent with earlier series. In particular, the new statutory accounts required separate returns for joint lines and for non-railway activities, whereas the LNWR had previously included these within the main body of its traffic revenue account. The principal coaching and freight entries for 1913 (and for 1922, when full reporting resumed) in Table A1 therefore relate solely to the company's direct earnings from railway traffic (including those from joint lines, such as the Shrewsbury & Hereford and Preston & Wyre, which were jointly vested in the owning companies). However, in order to provide some comparative information, the LNWR's proportion of coaching and freight receipts from its other joint interests – the Manchester South Junction & Altrincham; the Oldham, Ashton & Guide Bridge; and the Portpatrick & Wigtownshire – were extracted, together with income from steamship, road vehicle, canal, and dock activities. Adjusted figures for 1913 showing the total passenger and freight revenue attributable to the LNWR's railway and non-railway operations and its proportion of joint line receipts are shown in italics above the respective main entries for that year.

The outbreak of war in 1914 and the consequent government control of railways, which extended until 1921, resulted in a further interruption to most railway financial and statistical series, and only skeleton statements were issued during this period. The preliminary amalgamation between the LNWR and L&Y took place in 1922, the year when more extensive financial reporting was resumed, so the figures for that year reflect the inclusion of the L&Y, together with the North London and Dearne Valley undertakings. Because of this further break in continuity, no attempt has been made to disaggregate joint line and non-railway receipts for 1922, although earnings from these sources are included in the total column.

Notes on particular columns

Total expenditure on capital account

The figures in this column represent the LNWR's cumulative outlay on capital account at the end of each year, including the expenditure embodied in its own system and equipment and its investments in other undertakings. The totals include any adjustments to reflect the incorporation of the capital expenditure of subsidiary companies within the accounts during that particular year – for example, in 1878 over £10m was added because of the absorption of the Chester & Holyhead, Lancaster & Carlisle, and some other smaller lines – and are also net of any credits accruing in the year, such as those arising in 1862 when the LNWR disposed of its investment in the Caledonian Railway and part of its interest in certain other companies. For these reasons, the first differences between yearly totals do not necessarily equate to the actual capital expenditure during the period in question.

Working revenue

These columns summarise current operational income, and are the equivalent of the revenue totals in part 9 of the statutory form of accounts used from 1868 to 1912; they include elements of parts 8 and 10 of the revised statement which was required thereafter. As noted above, two adjusted figures have been added for 1913 to reflect minor revenue items which were excluded from the coaching and freight figures as part of the new arrangements, while, as explained below under net revenue, certain interest and dividend items which appeared in this section of the accounts from 1913 onwards have been transferred to their previous position.

Coaching revenue comprises income from passengers, mail, parcels, coaches, horses, and dogs (including, prior to 1913, steamer and passenger road vehicle traffic), while freight revenue comprises merchandise receipts net of the costs of collection and delivery, and income from mineral and livestock traffic. Dock and operational canal revenues, and the appropriate components of steamer and road vehicle traffic, were also classified under this heading until 1913. The total column includes the previous two columns, together with miscellaneous current income, such as rents and transfer fees, which typically amounted to less than 2% of total annual income. Totals for some early years are net of amounts paid to other companies under traffic agreements, while after 1912 earnings from non-railway activities and certain joint lines, which (as noted above) were previously also included within the coaching and freight entries, appeared in aggregate form only in this section of the accounts.

Total traffic expenses

This figure is the equivalent of the debit side of account no 9, and includes all current traffic and administrative costs, together with

Continued on p236

ABBREVIATION   n.a   Not available.

SOURCES
London & North Western Railway reports and accounts
Parliamentary papers: railway returns

NOTES FOR TABLE A2
General
The mileage and traffic statistics above are primarily intended to relate to the financial data summarised in Table A1, and accordingly are only given for those years where a direct correspondence can be established. Prior to the 1860s the LNWR's published accounts were supported by only limited statistical information, but in 1856 and 1857, and again from 1860 onwards, the financial details included in the parliamentary returns correspond with the company's accounts. For these years, therefore, the parliamentary statistics of mileage, passenger numbers, and tonnage have been incorporated in the table. As explained in the note below on passenger statistics, the figures in parliamentary returns prior to 1869 were used in preference to the equivalent passenger data in the LNWR's own accounts when this was appropriate.

Though parliamentary returns are available in varying detail for other years during the 1840s and 1850s, except for the years mentioned above these appear to have been compiled on a basis which differed from that of the LNWR's own contemporary accounts. These differences arose primarily in the treatment of subsidiary lines, with the result that the parliamentary and company statements were not directly comparable. As noted below (note A), the LNWR also compiled other statistical series on separate bases, and again these cannot be related immediately to the financial information shown in Table A1.

Changes within series
The figures quoted above include subsidiary companies from the dates of their incorporation in the LNWR's main accounts.

As indicated in the notes to Table A1, the basis of railway financial and statistical returns was altered with effect from 1913, so some post-1912 figures are not immediately comparable with earlier series. Figures from 1914 to 1921 were then affected by the war and government control, and for most of the wartime years only limited financial data were published.

1922 figures include the former Lancashire & Yorkshire, North London, and Dearne Valley undertakings.

Notes on particular columns
Route miles open
   1846-8; 1856-7; 1860-8: figures taken from parliamentary
      returns.
   1849-55; 1858-9: (italic figures) miles maintained, as stated in
      company accounts.
   1869-1912: miles constructed, from mileage statements in
      company accounts. [Includes leased and worked mileage and
      LNWR proportion of joint lines.]
   1913-22: mileage of lines open for traffic, from Table 1A of
      annual reports. [Includes leased and worked mileage and
      LNWR proportion of joint lines.]
[Some annual variations are attributable in part to reclassifica-
tions, particularly of joint mileage.]

Train mileage
From 1913 onwards the figures quoted, where available, are of train miles run by the company's engines on both LNWR and other lines, and include empty trains operated for traffic purposes on either the forward or return journey. Figures of total engine mileage, (including light, assisting, and shunting mileage) were also issued in some years. For comparison, these were as follows:

1913	1914	1919	1920	1921	1922
76,535,989	75,216,480	63,888,758	68,442,216	57,226,282	101,346,710

See also note B below.

Tons
From 1913 the available tonnage series are for goods originating on the LNWR system, and exclude traffic carried for the govern-ment between 1914 and 1920 [but see note B]. The 1913 and 1922 figures in italic type are of total tonnage carried over the company's network.

Passengers
The 1856-7 and 1860-8 figures are taken from parliamentary returns. [Prior to 1869 passenger statistics published in the LNWR's reports and accounts appear to reflect the number of tickets issued rather than journeys made – ie, a return ticket was counted as one journey rather than two. While the parliamentary returns were not entirely free of this defect, the LNWR passenger figures in the railway returns are higher than in the company accounts until 1869, when the series converged. The parliamen-tary statements of passenger numbers have therefore been preferred when the financial details derived from the two sources indicate that they were otherwise prepared on an identical basis in specific years before 1869.] See also note A below.

Series from 1913 onwards are for journeys originating on the LNWR system, excluding those made on government account. [See also note B.] As explained above, figures of total traffic conveyed over the company's network are available for 1913 and 1922 and have been added for comparison.

Season tickets
The treatment of season and periodical tickets was not consistent; though later parliamentary returns included a summary which aggregated these on a yearly equivalent basis this information is not available for the entire period. To avoid inflating the total number of season tickets the two figures for each half-year before 1913 have been averaged to give a yearly estimate.

Continued on p237

any operational expenditure relating to joint lines, canals, etc which was brought into the LNWR's revenue account.

From 1847 to 1864 the company operated a separate 'renewal of the road account', which was intended to provide for depreciation and betterment of the permanent way. For the purposes of this table any debits from the revenue account for this purpose have been reclassified as current expenditure and included within the total traffic expenses column. This accords with the LNWR's subsequent practice of charging all permanent way renewal costs to revenue in the year in which they were incurred.

Working ratio

This was a commonly-used yardstick of railway performance, derived by expressing traffic expenditure as a proportion of traffic income. A company's working ratio was an indication of how profitably it was handling its available traffic: the lower the ratio, the higher the margin on its traffic operations.

Net revenue

Figures in this column equate to the total of the credit side of account no 10 in the form prescribed in 1868, and of account no 9, 'Proposed appropriation of net income', in the post-1912 returns. Each year's total comprises the revenue balance brought forward from the previous year; the surplus of working income after deduction of traffic expenditure; bank and other interest; and dividends and other financial receipts from investments in other undertakings. In 1908 and 1909 transfers of £50,000 and £60,000 respectively from the general reserve were also credited to the net revenue account, but these have been omitted from the sums in the current table. [For further details of the general reserve account see below under interest and other fixed charges.] However, £400,000 received from the government in 1921 in respect of wartime arrears has been left within the total for that year.

The statutory accounts from 1913 onwards classified general interest and dividends from other companies as part of a railway's current receipts and expenditure. For the purposes of this table these items have been included within the net revenue account after 1912, as previously.

The revenue balance brought forward from the pre-amalga-

mation constituents was £166,106, as at 1 January 1846. The balance carried forward from that and subsequent years can be determined by deducting the two succeeding column entries for each year from the net revenue figure, with a further adjustment for the years 1906-20 inclusive to reflect the movements in the general reserve account detailed in the table below.

Interest and other fixed charges

This column totals the company's annual obligations in respect of chief rents, interest payments (including interest on debenture stock), and rentals and guarantees to other companies under lease and working arrangements (including, in the early years of the LNWR's existence, some traffic expenditure in respect of subsidiary undertakings which was not separately distinguished). It therefore represents the debit side of the company's net revenue account, apart from two items. As explained above, revenue contributions to the renewal of the road account during the years 1847-64 inclusive have been included under total traffic expenses, while transfers to the general reserve account have been removed from the main table because of their discretionary nature. The reserve account was established with effect from 1906, and net annual additions to this fund were as follows:

1906	£30,000	1911	£250,000	1916	£200,000
1907	£120,000	1912	£100,000	1917	£400,000
1908	-£50,000	1913	£100,000	1918	£100,000
1909	£50,000	1914	£100,000	1919	£100,000
1910	£200,000	1915	£200,000	1920	£100,000

No further additions were made after 1920, when the account totalled £2,000,000.

Dividends

The total column is the amount paid out annually as dividends on all classes of share: ordinary, preference, and guaranteed. The column headed ord^y is the annual rate of dividend paid to ordinary shareholders, and figures for years prior to 1913 are taken from the series in Bradshaw's *Railway manual…*, which annualised the half-yearly payments made by the major companies.

Workmen's tickets

From 1913 workmen's tickets were calculated separately on a single journey basis. Prior to that date the LNWR appears to have classed them with other season tickets in its own published statistics.

Further notes

Note A

As discussed above, the traffic statistics used in the body of the table are drawn from company or parliamentary sources which can be reconciled with the LNWR's financial results for each half-year. However, the company itself issued two additional series during the 1850s which, while not corresponding exactly with the mileage and financial figures adopted in the half-yearly accounts, provide a useful indication of trends.

The first appeared as an appendix to published reports during the early 1850s, and compared annual mileage and traffic figures with those for 1849. These differ from the principal LNWR accounts by including Buckinghamshire and a proportion of North Union traffic, which was not incorporated in the main revenue statement until 1856. The series is given in Table A3 below.

The other series consists of printed tables of passenger and goods traffic from 1849 to 1858, which were continued in manuscript until 1868 and have been preserved with the main set of LNWR reports and accounts in the Public Record Office [RAIL1110/269]. These are for annual periods ending on 30 June each year, and provide a detailed analysis of the earnings and costs of each category of traffic. Again, however, the figures, while extremely valuable, do not appear to be directly comparable with the main accounts. A summary is provided in Table A4.

Note B

No official series of train miles was issued during the war years. However, E A Pratt's *British railways and the great war* (1921), II, 983, quoted the following statistics of LNWR total goods-train mileage from 1913 to 1918 inclusive, which also appeared in the *Railway Gazette* of 9 January 1920.

1913	1914	1915	1916	1917	1918
20,029,834	18,721,612	19,381,544	19,705,875	20,816,336	20,412,774

The 1913 total cannot be reconciled exactly with any of the equivalent statutory figures, and the totals are also slightly higher than those shown in a graph of goods-train mileage from LNWR sources which appeared in G R S Darroch, *Deeds of a great railway* (1920), p 171. However, the relative movements are consistent with those plotted in the latter source, which also shows passenger-train miles graphically, with a decline to about 19.5m in 1918.

In addition, Pratt quoted a 1918 goods tonnage of 60,570,000 tons, inclusive of the estimated weight of free-hauled traffic, while the *Railway Gazette* of 24 May 1918 (p 611) cited a 1917 figure of 63.1m tons; the use of a 1913 comparator of 57,656,257 tons suggests that the 1917 statistic represented all goods and minerals carried over the LNWR system, rather than originating tonnage. The same *Railway Gazette* article gave approximate passenger numbers for 1917 as 101m, exclusive of season ticket holders (compared with 92,540,230 in 1913, which again was the total for all such traffic carried on the LNWR system). It also quoted a 1917 locomotive mileage of 65,494,664 miles, and compared this with the 1913 total of 76,535,989 miles, which was the figure for mileage run by the LNWR's engines on its and other companies' lines.

TABLE A3

London & North Western Railway: mileage, revenue, and traffic volumes, 1849 and 1852–4

Year	Miles open	Passengers		Merchandise		Coals		Cattle, parcels, mail ,etc £	Total revenue £
		Number booked	Revenue £	Tons moved	Revenue £	Tons moved	Revenue £		
1849	503½	6,103,657	1,213,249	1,312,021	699,577	758,866	71,852	239,929	2,224,607
1852	639	8,046,605	1,316,481	2,235,775	886,472	1,162,847	129,314	249,992	2,582,259
1853	639	9,808,057	1,329,381	2,660,892	995,902	1,398,274	153,458	263,579	2,742,320
1854	639	9,951,919	1,353,189	3,008,126	1,087,911	1,688,796	195,105	284,595	2,920,800

SOURCE:

London & North Western Railway reports and accounts

NOTES:

See Note A to Table A2 above

TABLE A4

London & North Western Railway: passenger and freight train mileage, revenue, costs, and profit, 1849–68

Year ending 30 June:	Miles open	Passenger and other coaching traffic				Goods, mineral, and livestock traffic			
		Train miles	Earnings	Total expenses	Net profit	Train miles	Earnings	Total expenses	Net profit
			£	£	£		£	£	£
1849	438	3,737,669	1,377,424	505,870	871,554	2,251,966	778,795	368,390	410,405
1850	476½	3,773,496	1,393,272	471,374	921,898	2,924,862	846,513	429,154	417,359
1851	525	3,934,605	1,453,408	498,992	954,416	3,191,852	931,461	466,580	464,881
1852	540	4,278,545	1,610,347	594,295	1,016,052	3,048,349	946,473	516,604	429,869
1853	554½	4,311,786	1,456,307	579,996	876,311	3,406,463	1,085,630	554,139	531,491
1854	554½	4,548,855	1,482,619	606,652	875,967	3,856,517	1,243,707	684,049	559,658
1855	555¼	4,528,316	1,468,931	619,988	848,943	4,090,868	1,352,456	756,883	595,573
1856	637	4,631,390	1,551,232	640,441	910,791	4,364,908	1,480,890	783,472	697,418
1857	637	4,738,442	1,630,003	679,990	950,013	4,690,256	1,609,105	855,806	753,299
1858	647	5,180,028	1,592,664	725,822	866,842	4,754,870	1,469,394	858,319	611,075
1859	735	5,667,572	1,627,421	768,737	858,684	5,245,392	1,617,727	956,510	661,217
1860	898	6,860,188	2,026,898	912,866	1,114,032	6,852,924	2,089,650	1,179,217	910,433
1861	968	7,638,722	2,118,697	1,024,157	1,094,540	7,549,448	2,179,243	1,347,720	831,523
1862	1039	7,770,994	2,177,791	1,079,790	1,098,001	7,243,863	2,247,952	1,366,022	881,930
1863	1152	8,597,097	2,353,460	1,153,418	1,200,042	7,954,696	2,483,392	1,404,823	1,078,569
1864	1217	9,069,238	2,463,455	1,137,256	1,326,199	8,990,404	2,822,208	1,538,669	1,283,539
1865	1267½	9,935,236	2,623,379	1,208,812	1,414,567	10,096,622	3,144,827	1,656,598	1,488,229
1866	1274	10,454,488	2,777,203	1,295,826	1,481,377	10,722,447	3,362,426	1,833,107	1,529,319
1867	1314	10,718,576	2,805,820	1,389,185	1,416,635	11,316,770	3,547,176	2,024,526	1,522,650
1868	1338	10,951,016	2,850,578	1,446,756	1,403,822	11,221,690	3,622,958	2,044,106	1,578,852

SOURCE

London & North Western Railway, *Annual results of the working of the goods, mineral , and cattle traffic...*; *Annual results of the working of the passenger traffic...* [in Public Record Office, RAIL1110/269].

NOTES

See Note A to Table A2 above.

Expenditure columns include an allowance for capital.

Sources and Bibliography

LNWR RECORDS

The main primary source drawn upon during the preparation of this volume was the collection of LNWR archival material which is now located at the Public Record Office in Kew. Most of the principal series are contained in the RAIL410 sequence, although some important LNWR papers – such as the run of the company's reports and accounts – are found in general RAIL classes. The surviving records of constituent and absorbed undertakings, and of the various joint committees in which the LNWR participated, are also classified separately. Full finding aids are available at Kew, but a published listing of the main LNWR sequences is available in Volume 172 of the series issued by the List & Index Society: *British Transport Historical Records, London & North Western Railway Company and Midland Railway Company* (1980). The London & North Western Railway Society has also compiled a useful guide which is available to its members.

The records upon which I chiefly relied were the reports and accounts and main board minutes of the LNWR and of its principal constituents, supplemented by reference to relevant committee and subcommittee volumes for particular periods or issues. These included minutes of the LNWR's special, traffic, and locomotive & general stores committees, together with various supporting reports. I also made extensive use of the minutes of the officers' and goods conferences, which are a particularly helpful source for confirming opening dates and service details, and in addition contain valuable material on operational and commercial matters. The bound series of general manager's and secretary's circulars are another useful source. A manuscript index of LNWR minute entries containing opening dates can be found at RAIL1005/289.

OTHER COLLECTIONS

Parliamentary deposited plans and their supporting reference material provide the main source of detailed information about intended routes, and I made considerable use of the comprehensive collection of these documents at the House of Lords Record Office when researching individual lines. Railway companies were also required to deposit copies of such plans locally, and in most instances these have survived in the appropriate county record offices. For convenience, I consulted county deposits in several instances, including plans held at the Cumbria, Lancashire, Gwynedd, Staffordshire and Warwickshire record offices. I also drew on other holdings at some of these offices during the course of my research, including siding diagrams and other documents at the Cumbria record office in Carlisle which relate to the Whitehaven, Cleator & Egremont Railway, the Sutherland papers at the Staffordshire record office, and the Gwynedd record office's photographic archive. In addition to

depending heavily upon the Scottish Record Office's series of railway reports and accounts, I referred to its holdings of Caledonian Railway, Portpatrick & Wigtownshire Joint Committee, Carlisle Citadel Joint Committee, and Railway Executive Committee records and to papers in the Dalhousie collection.

CONTEMPORARY PUBLISHED SOURCES

Besides the records of the companies themselves and the documents created as part of the authorisation procedures, published parliamentary and governmental material provides a rich source for the study of British railway history. In preparing this book I drew information from the Acts of Parliament relating to the LNWR and its constituents; from the reports of the various select and departmental committees and royal commissions mentioned in the text, together with the evidence presented to them; and from various *ad hoc* or annual reports and returns. The yearly statements of railway capital, mileage, rolling stock, traffic, income, and expenditure, usually referred to as the *Railway returns*, are among the most important of these, and the summary reports and commentaries on these figures prepared by the Railway Department of the Board of Trade are an extremely valuable overview of trends within the railway industry. In addition, the *Parliamentary papers* for particular years contain information on subjects such as railway staff numbers and wages, numbers of shareholders, mail contracts, and express train arrivals. They also provide sequences of returns relating to interlocking and to railway accidents, while individual accident reports contain much useful material on layouts and operating procedures.

These official papers are supplemented by several other serial publications which also constitute an invaluable source for the historian. One of the most helpful is Bradshaw's *Railway manual, shareholders' guide, and official directory*, which appeared annually from 1848 to 1923, although the final form of its title dates from 1863. I used this publication extensively for its summaries of legislative and financial information relating to the LNWR and other companies. The *Railway year book*, which began publication in 1898, provides useful historical and operational information which fell outwith the scope of Bradshaw's *Manual*, while Mihill Slaughter's *Railway intelligence*, which appeared annually from 1853, devoted even more detail than Bradshaw to financial matters.

Contemporary railway journals are also a crucial record: although much of their emphasis during the early years of the system's development was on financial and parliamentary matters, the leading weekly papers are a unique source of contemporary comment on railway issues, and provide information about the activities of some smaller companies which has not been preserved elsewhere. I relied principally on the *Railway Times,* but also consulted various volumes of Herapath's *Railway & Commercial Journal* and the *Railway News.* These titles were all eventually merged into the *Railway Gazette,* which I used for the later years of the LNWR's history; I also drew upon the *Railway Engineer*'s coverage of some technical and operational developments. In addition, the *London & North Western Railway Gazette,* which first appeared in 1912 as the magazine of the staff athletic association under the somewhat unpromising title of the *Premier Railway Athletic Gazette,* quickly developed into a comprehensive monthly staff publication whose coverage included biographical notes and a wide range of useful background information about the company.

For train service particulars I relied where possible on the LNWR's own *Public Time Tables,* supported by reference to *Bradshaw's Railway Guides* and to surviving working timetables, which were issued on a divisional basis. As noted, the minutes of the officers' conference also contain useful information about service changes.

The various editions of the Railway Clearing House sectional maps provide a record of the physical development of the network in each area, and I supplemented my use of these by referring also to the RCH *Junction diagrams* and to contemporary Ordnance Survey sheets for areas such as Lancashire, south Wales and the midlands. Some historical Ordnance Survey material has now been commercially reprinted and is thus more easily accessible. Similarly, the modern reprints of the editions of the *Junction diagrams* for 1914 and 1915 are a useful addition to the resources available to the railway historian and can be conveniently used together with the *Pre-grouping atlas and gazetteer* or one of the other compilations of historical maps of Britain's railways to expand the detail in the system maps included in the present volume.

OTHER PUBLISHED MATERIAL

The succeeding list of publications is intended to serve two purposes: to indicate some of the secondary sources used in the preparation of this book, and to provide an introductory bibliography for readers wishing to explore particular aspects of the LNWR's history in more detail. It does not purport to be complete in either respect: any attempt at this would be superfluous in view of the availability of George Ottley's exhaustive *Bibliography of British railway history* (2nd edn, 1983), and its *Supplement* (1988). Much of the coverage in the following sections is therefore devoted to more recent books and pamphlets which are not included in Ottley. Similarly, although articles and notes in railway periodicals provide a valuable source of information on particular lines, I have not duplicated the detailed catalogue of such material in the Branch Line Society's *Branch line index* (3rd edn, 1991), compiled by G C Lewthwaite. Instead I have only cited articles which are not listed there and which were drawn upon substantially during the preparation of this book.

References in the various sections and subsections below are arranged alphabetically by author under their respective subject headings. The abbreviation [nd] indicates that no date of publication is shown, while a year appearing in square brackets represents a publication date that has been inferred or supplied from another source.

1: BRITISH RAILWAY HISTORY (GENERAL, AND ECONOMIC AND POLITICAL ASPECTS)

Alderman, G, *The railway interest* (1973).
Bagwell, P, *The Railway Clearing House in the British economy* (1968).
Gourvish, T R, *Railways and the British economy, 1830-1914* (1980).
Lewin, H G, *Early British railways* (1925).
ditto, *The railway mania and its aftermath* (1936).
Parris, H, *Government and the railways in nineteenth-century Britain* (1965).
Railway News, *The jubilee of the Railway News 1864-1914* (1914).
Simmons, J, *The Victorian railway* (1991).
Simnett, W E, *Railway amalgamation in Great Britain* (1923).

2: LONDON & NORTH WESTERN RAILWAY AND ITS PREDECESSORS
including other works of particular relevance
a: General
Hendry, R P & Hendry, R P, *The North Western at work* (1990).
Neele, G P, *Railway reminiscences* (1904).
Railway Gazette, *LMS centenary of the opening of the first main-line railway* (1938).
Railway News, *The diamond jubilee of the London & North Western Railway Co* (1906).
Smith, G R, *Old Euston* (1938).
Steel, W L, *The history of the London & North Western Railway* (1914).
The Times, *London Midland & Scottish Railway centenary* (1938).
Whishaw, F, *The railways of Great Britain and Ireland* (2nd edn, 1842, repr 1969).

b: Reference and chronologies
See section 4 for area chronologies.
Butt, R V J, *The directory of railway stations* (1995)
Clinker, C R, *London & North Western Railway: a chronology 1900-1960* (1961).
ditto, *Register of closed passenger stations and goods depots* (new edn, 1988).
Greville, M D & Spence E, *Closed passenger lines of Great Britain, 1827-1947* (revised edn, 1974).

c: Organisation and management
Acworth, W M, *The railways of England* (5th edn, 1900).
Findlay, G, *The working and management of an English railway* (6th edn, 1899).
Gourvish, T R, *Mark Huish and the London & North Western Railway* (1972).
Paish, G, *The British railway position* (1902).

Robbins, R M, 'From R B Dockray's diary', *Journal of Transport History,* vii (1965-6), 1-13; 109-19; 149-59.

Turnbull, G L, 'The railway revolution and carriers' response: Messrs Pickford & Company 1830-50', *Transport History,* ii (1969), 48-71.

d: Industrial relations

Bagwell, P S, *The railwaymen: the history of the National Union of Railwaymen* (1963).

Blaxland, G, *J H Thomas: a life for unity* (1964).

Grigg, A E, *In railway service: the history of the Bletchley branch of the National Union of Railwaymen* [nd].

See also Hendry & Hendry *under (a) above.*

e: Locomotives and locomotive running, etc

Baxter, B (ed Baxter, D), *British locomotive catalogue 1825-1923,* Vols 2A-B (1978-9).

Cooke, C J Bowen, *British locomotives* (2nd edn, 1894).

ditto, *Some recent developments in locomotive practice* (1902).

Dunn, J M, *Reflections on a railway career* (1966).

Hawkins, C & Reeve, G, *LMS engine sheds,* Vol 1 (1981).

Nock, O S, *LNWR locomotives of C J Bowen Cooke* (1977).

ditto, *Premier Line: the story of London & North Western locomotives* (1952).

Reed, B, *Loco Profile No 15: the Crewe Type* (1971).

Talbot, E, *An illustrated history of LNWR engines* (1985).

ditto (as editor), *The LNWR recalled* (1987).

Tuplin, W A, *North Western steam* (1963).

Williams, C, *A register of all the locomotives now in use on the London & North Western Railway* (1922).

f: Coaching stock

Casserley, R M & Millard, P A, *A register of West Coast Joint Stock* (1980).

Ellis, C H, *Railway carriages in the British Isles from 1830 to 1914* (1965).

Gillham, J C, *The age of the electric train* (1988).

Jenkinson, D *An illustrated history of LNWR coaches* (1978).

g: Signalling

Foster, R D, *A pictorial record of LNWR signalling* (1982).

h: Architecture, liveries, etc

See also sections 1e-1g above.

Nelson, J, *LNWR portrayed* (1975).

Talbot, E; Dow, G; Millard, P; & Davis, P, *LNWR liveries* (1985).

i: LNWR works and works towns

Chaloner, W H, *The social and economic development of Crewe 1780-1923* (1950).

Reed, B, *Crewe locomotive works and its men* (1982).

West, Bill, *The trainmakers: the story of Wolverton works* (1982).

j: Irish services (including joint shipping routes and connecting railways).

Barrie, D S M, *The Dundalk, Newry & Greenore Railway and the Holyhead-Greenore steamship service* (1957).

Duckworth, C L D & Langmuir, G E, *Railway and other steamers* (1968).

Hughes, D L & Williams, D M, *Holyhead: the story of a port* (1967).

MacHaffie, F G *The short sea route* (1975).

McNeill, D B, *Irish passenger steamship services* ,Vol 1 (1969).

Murray, K A, 'The Dublin railways', *Journal of the Irish Railway Record Society,* viii (1968), 156-65.

Pearsall, A W H & Davies, H H, *The Holyhead steamers of the LNWR* [nd].

Thorne, H D, *Rails to Portpatrick* (1976).

k: Wartime arrangements

Darroch, G R S, *Deeds of a great railway* (1920).

Pratt, E A, *British railways and the great war* (1921).

Railway News, *Records of railway interests in the war* (4 parts, 1915-17).

l: Biographies and autobiographies

Booth, H, *Henry Booth* (1980).

Bulleid, H A V, *The Aspinall era* (1967).

Hill, G, *The Worsdells: a Quaker engineering dynasty* (1991).

Klapper, C F, *Sir Herbert Walker's Southern Railway* (1973).

MacInnes, A G, *Recollections of the life of Miles MacInnes* (1911).

Stevenson, D, *Fifty years on the London & North Western Railway* (1891).

Webster, N W, *Joseph Locke: railway revolutionary* (1970).

Willis, R C, *My fifty-one years at Euston* (1939).

See also Neele, *(a) above,* Gourvish *(c),* Dunn *(e), and* Reed *(i). In addition to the obituaries and details of senior appointments appearing in the general railway press, the* London & North Western Railway Gazette *and its successor, the* London Midland & Scottish Railway Gazette *(later* Magazine*), included numerous biographical notes on LNWR officers and directors, while particulars of some directors and a few leading officials can also be found in standard biographical reference works.*

3: OTHER COMPANIES

For absorbed companies, and smaller regional undertakings in England & Wales, see Section 4.

Barnes, E G, *The rise of the Midland Railway* (1966).

ditto, *The Midland main line* (1969).

Butt, J, & Ward, J T, 'The promotion of the Caledonian Railway company', *Transport History,* iii (1970), 164-192; 225-57.

Channon, G, 'A nineteenth-century investment decision: the Midland Railway's London extension', *Economic*

History Review, 2nd series, xxv (1972), 448-70

Dow, G, *Great Central* (3 vols, 1959-65).

Gough, J V, *The Midland Railway – a chronology* (2nd edn, 1989).

Grinling, C H, *The history of the Great Northern Railway* (new edn, 1966).

Irving, R J, *The North Eastern Railway company 1870-1914* (1976).

MacDermot, E T (revised C R Clinker), *History of the Great Western Railway* (2 vols, 1964).

Marshall, J, *The Lancashire & Yorkshire Railway* (3 vols, 1969-72).

Stephenson Locomotive Society, *Caledonian Railway Centenary, 1847-1947* (1947).

Tomlinson, W W, *The North Eastern Railway: its rise and development* (new edn, 1967).

Wrottesley, J, *The Great Northern Railway* (3 vols, 1979-81).

4: RAILWAY DEVELOPMENT IN PARTICULAR AREAS

The relevant volumes of the Regional History of Railways *provide definitive modern accounts of the development of the LNWR's and other companies' routes in particular areas. The reader is referred to this series for more comprehensive local coverage of the various regions served by the LNWR, and for details of related developments in Ireland and Scotland. As noted in the general introduction to this bibliography, journal articles included in the* Branch Line Index *are not listed individually here, and reference should be made to that source for details of available material in the periodical literature.*

a: Cheshire, Lancashire, north Derbyshire, Yorkshire, Westmorland and Cumberland

Bairstow, M, *The Leeds, Huddersfield & Manchester Railway* (1984).

Bardsley, J R, *The railways of Bolton* [1960].

Basnett, L, *The first public railway in Lancashire: the history of the Bolton & Leigh Railway* (1963).

Baughan, P, *North of Leeds* (1966).

Biddle, G, *The railways around Preston* (1989).

Bowtell, H D, *Rails through Lakeland* (1989).

Carlson, R E, *The Liverpool & Manchester Railway project 1821-1831* (1969).

Cumbrian Railways Association, *Carlisle: 150 years of railways* (1986).

Dixon, F, *The Manchester South Junction & Altrincham Railway* (2nd edn, 1994).

Donaghy, T J, *Liverpool & Manchester Railway operations 1831-1845* (1972).

Goode, C T, *The Ashbourne to Buxton Railway* (1990).

Gradon, W McG, *Furness Railway: its rise and development* [1946].

ditto, *A history of the Cockermouth, Keswick & Penrith Railway* [1948].

ditto, *The track of the ironmasters* (1952).

Greville, M D, *Chronology of the railways of Lancashire and Cheshire* (1981).

Greville, M D & Holt, G O, *The Lancaster & Preston Junction Railway* (1961).

Griffiths, R P, *The Cheshire Lines Railway* (1947).

Jeuda, B, *Railways of the Macclesfield district* (1984).

Joy, D, *Cumbrian coast railways* (1968).

ditto, *Railways of the lake counties* (1973).

ditto, *Main line over Shap* (1967).

McLoughlin, B, *Railways of the Fylde* (1992).

Marshall, J, *The Cromford & High Peak Railway* (1982).

Mountfield, S, *Western gateway: a history of the Mersey Docks & Harbour Board* (1965).

Norton, P A, *Railways and waterways to Warrington* (2nd edn, 1984).

Parker, N, *The Preston & Longridge Railway* (1972).

Parkin, G W, *The Mersey Railway* [nd].

Reed, B, *Crewe to Carlisle* (1969).

Reed, C, *Gateway to the west: a history of Riverside station, Liverpool* (1992).

Rimmer, *The Cromford & High Peak Railway* (1962).

Robinson, P W, *Rail centres: Carlisle* (1986).

Rush, R W & Price, M R C, *The Garstang & Knott End Railway* (1964).

Simmons, J, *The Maryport & Carlisle Railway* (1947).

Simpson, Bill, *Railways in and around Bolton* [nd].

Stocks, W B, *Pennine journey* (1958).

Thomas, R H G, *The Liverpool & Manchester Railway* (1980).

Tolson, J M, *The St Helens Railway* (1983).

Townley, C H A; Appleton, C A; Smith, F D; & Peden, J A, *The industrial railways of Bolton, Bury and the Manchester coalfield* (2 vols, 1994-5).

Townley, C H A; Smith, F D; & Peden, J A, *The industrial railways of the Wigan coalfield* (2 vols, 1991-2).

Waring, R, *The Leeds new line* (1989).

Western, R G, *The Lowgill branch* (1971).

b: Wales and the marches

Anderson, V R & Fox, G K, *An historical survey of Chester to Holyhead railway track layouts and illustrations* (1984).

Barrie, D S, *The Brecon & Merthyr Railway* (1957).

Baughan, P, *The Chester & Holyhead Railway* Vol 1 (1972).

Boyd, J I C, *Narrow gauge railways in north Caernarvonshire* (3 vols, 1981-86).

ditto, *The Wrexham, Mold & Connah's Quay Railway* (1991).

Christiansen R & Miller, R W, *The Cambrian Railways* (2 vols, 1967).

Cook, R A & Clinker, C R *Early railways between Abergavenny and Hereford* (1984).

Goodall S P, *The Prestatyn & Dyserth branch line* (1986).

ditto, *The Vale of Clwyd Railway* (1992).

Halsall, D A, 'A Welsh railway accident', *Newsletter of the Transport History Group,* i (1977), 8-21.

Morris, R K, *Rail centres: Shrewsbury* (1986).

ditto, *Railways of Shropshire: a brief history* (1983).

Page, J, *Rails in the valleys* (1989).

Rear, W G, *Anglesey branch lines* [nd].

ditto, *The Denbigh & Mold line* [nd].

ditto, *LMS branch lines in north Wales* Vol 1 (1986).

ditto, *Railways along the Clwyd valley: Corwen to Rhyl* [nd].

Robbins, M, 'The first water troughs', in *Points and signals* (1967), pp 114-20.

Smith, D J, *Shrewsbury to Swansea* (1971).

Smith, M, *Portrait of the Central Wales line* (1995).

Tasker, W W, *The Merthyr, Tredegar & Abergavenny Railway and branches* (1986).

ditto, *Railways in the Sirhowy valley* (2nd edn, 1992).

See also relevant sections of R A Cooke, Track layout diagrams of the Great Western Railway and BR Western Region, *for layout details of former LNWR and joint lines which were transferred to Western Region administration.*

c: South of Crewe: the midlands and south of England

Atkinson, J B, *The West London joint railways* (1984).

Barker, T C & Robbins, M, *A history of London Transport,* Vol 1 (1963).

Borley, H V, *Chronology of London railways* (1982).

ditto, *The West London Railway and the West London Extension Railway* [nd].

Clinker, C R, *The Birmingham and Derby Junction Railway* (1956).

ditto, *The railways of Northamptonshire* (1960).

ditto, *Railways of the west midlands: a chronology, 1808-1954* [1954].

ditto, 'The southern division of the LNWR in the 1870s', *Railway Magazine,* 106 (1960), 13-19; 26; 126-32.

Ellaway, K J, *The great British railway station: Euston* (1994).

Elliott, P H, *Rugby's railway heritage* (1985).

Fink, D P J, *Walsall stations* (1981).

Foster, R, *Birmingham New Street: the story of a great station,* Vols 1 & 2 (1990).

Foster, R D & Instone, M R L, *Track diagrams of the London & North Western Railway and its successors: section 5 – Northamptonshire* (1988).

Franks, D L, *The Ashby & Nuneaton Joint Railway* (1975).

ditto, *Great Northern and London & North Western Joint Railway* (1974).

Gadsden, E J S, *The Aylesbury Railway* (1962).

Goudie, F W & Stuckey, D, *West of Watford* (1990).

Gough, J V, *The Northampton & Harborough line* (1984).

Gould, D, *The London & Birmingham Railway 150 years on* (1987).

Grigg, A E, *Town of trains: Bletchley and the Oxbridge line* (1980).

Hurst, G, *LNWR branch lines of west Leicestershire and east Warwickshire* (1993).

Jackson, A, *London's termini* (2nd edn, 1985).

Lee, P, *The Trent Valley Railway* (1988).

Long, P J & Awdry, W V, *The Birmingham & Gloucester Railway* (1987).

'Manifold', *The North Staffordshire Railway* (1952).

Rhodes, John, *The Uppingham to Seaton railway* (1990).

Robbins, M, *The North London Railway* (1937).

Simmons, J, *Rugby junction* (1969).

Simpson, Bill, *The Aylesbury Railway* (1989).

ditto, *The Banbury to Verney Junction branch* (revised edn, 1994).

ditto, *Oxford to Cambridge railway* (2 vols, 1983).

ditto, *The Wolverton to Newport Pagnell branch* (1995).

Smith, D J, *New Street remembered* (1984).

INDEX

Italic main entries are ship's names; italicised page numbers denote illustrations